The Pact

STEVEN
M. GILLON

The Pact

*Bill Clinton, Newt Gingrich,
and the Rivalry That
Defined a Generation*

OXFORD
UNIVERSITY PRESS

2008

OXFORD
UNIVERSITY PRESS

Oxford University Press, Inc., publishes works that further
Oxford University's objective of excellence
in research, scholarship, and education.

Oxford   New York
Auckland   Cape Town   Dar es Salaam   Hong Kong   Karachi
Kuala Lumpur   Madrid   Melbourne   Mexico City   Nairobi
New Delhi   Shanghai   Taipei   Toronto

With offices in
Argentina   Austria   Brazil   Chile   Czech Republic   France   Greece
Guatemala   Hungary   Italy   Japan   Poland   Portugal   Singapore
South Korea   Switzerland   Thailand   Turkey   Ukraine   Vietnam

Copyright © 2008 by Oxford University Press, Inc.

Published by Oxford University Press, Inc.
198 Madison Avenue, New York, New York 10016

www.oup.com

Library of Congress Cataloging-in-Publication Data
Gillon, Steven M.
The pact: Bill Clinton, Newt Gingrich, and the rivalry
that defined a generation / Steven M. Gillon.
    p.   cm.
Includes bibliographical references and index.
ISBN 978-0-19-532278-1
1. United States—Politics and government—1993–2001.
2. Clinton, Bill, 1946– 3. Gingrich, Newt.   I. Title.
E885.G55 2008
973.929—dc22   2007038722

9 8 7 6 5 4 3 2 1

Printed in the United States of America
on acid-free paper

This book is dedicated to Dr. Lawrence P. Buck

CONTENTS

ACKNOWLEDGMENTS

I COULD NOT HAVE WRITTEN this book without the support of the University of Oklahoma, the insight of many colleagues and scholars, and the encouragement of friends. I am indebted to David Boren, president of the University of Oklahoma; Provost Nancy Mergler; and Dean Robert Con Davis-Undiano for giving me the freedom to work on this project. Special thanks to Carolyn Morgan, Robert Griswold, and Mindy Jones for all of their help and support over the years. Research assistants George Milne, Paul McKenzie-Jones, and Chris Davis provided a steady stream of material. Nick Davatzes, Gary Ginsberg, and Julian Zelizer read the entire manuscript and offered many helpful suggestions. James T. Patterson, who is one of America's most eminent historians and also a good friend and mentor, read an early version of the manuscript. He scribbled detailed notes on nearly every page. His comments, always penetrating and always constructive, sent me back to the library for another six months, but they also made this a much better book. At Oxford University Press, Susan Ferber guided the project from beginning to end, making numerous helpful suggestions along the way.

Of course, it would have been impossible to write this book without the cooperation of the two people profiled: President Bill Clinton and Speaker Newt Gingrich. I had the opportunity to interview the president at the very beginning of this project. Although he never formally responded to written follow-up questions, the president did give many of the people around him permission to speak with me. I am especially indebted to Speaker Gingrich, who not only made himself available for interviews, but also opened up his private papers and encouraged all of his close associates and aides to cooperate. For the critical years 1996–98, I depended heavily on the recollections of Erskine Bowles, who served as President Clinton's chief of staff, and Arne Christenson, who served the Speaker in the same role. Both men gave generously of their time, provided valuable insight into the private relationship between Clinton and Gingrich, and offered details that allowed me to unearth the buried promise of Social Security reform in 1997. A special word of thanks also goes to Rick Tyler, the Speaker's spokesman and press secretary, for being so responsive and helpful.

As always, I'm grateful to all my friends at The History Channel: Abbe Raven, Charlie Maday, Susan Werbe, Nancy Dubuc, Tim Nolan, Mike Mohamad, and Libby O'Connell. For most of the time I was researching and writing this book, I was also launching a new show, *Our Generation,* on the History Channel. My thanks to all the staff—researchers, producers, associate producers, and editors—who put the show together. John Verhoff and Aaron Goldman put together a fine team and they insulated me from much of the day-to-day detail so I could continue working on this project. The series never would have launched without the generous support of the American Association of Retired Persons (AARP). Perhaps no organization in America has done more to help us understand the evolving needs and desires of the generation represented by Bill Clinton and Newt Gingrich than the AARP. I'm grateful to the organization, and especially Emilio Pardo and Hugh Delehanty, for all of their encouragement, wisdom, and support.

This book is dedicated to Professor Lawrence Buck of Widener University. It was Dr. Buck who inspired me to become a historian. Until I walked into his medieval history class in the spring of 1976 as a college sophomore, I had been a mediocre student who dreamed of someday being a professional baseball pitcher. By the time the class ended, I had for the first time discovered the value of learning, reading, and debating, and dreamed of using my mind, not my arm, to make a living. (It was a wise decision, especially given that I was never going to make much of a living off my 65 mph fastball.) Nearly everyone has a story about a teacher who changed his or her life. Dr. Buck changed mine, and for that I will always be grateful.

PREFACE

SHORTLY AFTER 7:00 PM on Monday, October 28, 1997, House Speaker Newt Gingrich, accompanied by his chief of staff, Arne Christenson, made the brief trip from his Capitol Hill office to the White House. The purpose of the visit was to hammer out the final details of the 1998 budget with the president. But as his car moved down Pennsylvania Avenue past the monuments that symbolize the nation's past, the historian in Gingrich could not help thinking that he too was making history on this warm fall evening. For the past few months, his closest aides had been holding secret meetings with senior White House officials. In private sessions and late-night phone calls they discussed the parameters of a proposed deal between President Clinton and the Speaker that would rock the Washington establishment. Now it was time for the two men to meet face to face to finalize the arrangement. "This wasn't just another meeting," reflected White House Chief-of-Staff Erskine Bowles. "We all knew we were making history."[1]

Both sides went to great lengths to maintain secrecy. The president did not tell his vice president, the Democratic leadership in the House, or even his wife, about the meeting. He knew that many members of his administration and Democrats in Congress would erupt if they learned that he was dealing with Gingrich. After all, Gingrich had climbed to power, becoming Speaker in 1995, by attacking leading Democrats, including a former Speaker of the House, Jim Wright of Texas. Democratic antipathy for Gingrich was surpassed only by conservative hatred of Clinton. Some conservatives had already tried to remove Gingrich as Speaker a few months earlier because they felt he had gone soft on the president. Knowing that he could not survive another revolt, Gingrich did not tell other members of his senior staff about the meeting, fearing that it would leak to hardline members of his caucus.

To avoid being spotted by reporters, Gingrich approached by the South Lawn and came in the diplomatic entrance. Once inside the White House, the Speaker and his aide were quickly ushered into the elevator and taken to the Treaty Room on the second floor of the residence. Waiting to greet him were Bowles, legislative director John Hilley, and the president.

The five men took their seats around a small coffee table as a photographer circled around recording the moment for the history books. The president settled into a crimson wing chair decorated with gold Napoleonic wreaths. Gingrich sat to his left on a royal blue late-eighteenth-century Chippendale sofa, the oldest piece of furniture in the White House. It was appropriate that George P. A. Healy's portrait *The Peacemakers* (1868), depicting Abraham Lincoln conferring with his military advisors at the conclusion of the Civil War, looked down on them. Over the past few years, the two adversaries had waged their own civil war that included a budget showdown that twice forced the federal government to close its doors. The political battles had left deep scars. "Trust was not a part of the relationship," recalled Bowles, who played the key role in brokering the meeting. Clinton, who often referred to

A White House photographer snapped this picture of the secret meeting in the Treaty Room between President Clinton and Speaker Gingrich. This photograph was declassified in November 2007 in response to the author's freedom of information request. (William J. Clinton Presidential Library.)

Gingrich as "a hater," could not forgive the Speaker for allowing the ongoing investigations into Whitewater, along with the drumbeat of attacks against his wife and other members of his administration. Gingrich, who once told the president that he was "a lying son of a bitch," was still smarting from the budget battles and the barrage of negative campaign ads Clinton ran against him in 1996.

Through it all, however, the two men had managed to maintain some grudging respect for each other, as well as a mysterious personal chemistry that baffled those around them. The 1996 election, which returned both men to power, convinced them they needed to work together in order to secure their place in the history books. "They both knew that their legacies were tied to each other," Bowles later reflected.[2]

The atmosphere in the room was collegial, intimate, and friendly. "It was a poker game," recalled Bowles. "Nobody showed all their cards, but they showed more than they had ever shown before."[3] Each man was feeling out the other, trying to figure out what he could accomplish, but also what was feasible to expect of the other. It had to be a "win-win" situation to work. "Clinton and Gingrich were combustible," recalled Christenson. "They were both, as the preeminent political leaders of their parties, calculating whether there was an opportunity for something big that would be in their interests, but also enough in the other person's interest, that they could make a deal."[4]

Clinton started the conversation by talking about his recent trip to South America, but the conversation soon strayed to the challenges of governing— a favorite theme for both men.[5] Leading a divided nation was difficult, they agreed, and politics had become ugly and partisan. At one point, Bowles suggested that after leaving office Gingrich and Clinton devote themselves to purging politics of "the ugliness that has infected it." While concurring that modern times were difficult, they also agreed that most Americans held a romantic view of the past. Nearly everyone celebrated the spirit of cooperation that existed during World War II when, in reality, Franklin Roosevelt and Army Chief-of-Staff George Marshall had spent a lot of time trying to build support on Capitol Hill. Clinton added that the House passed the extension of the selective service bill in 1941 by only one vote.

Gingrich was first to raise directly the issue of cooperation, suggesting that he and the president use their work on the North American Free Trade Agreement (NAFTA) and the historic balanced budget bill passed in August 1997 as models for the future. Before Clinton could respond, Gingrich was breaking down the possible areas of agreement into conceptual boxes. One box contained the issues over which they would continue to fight. "My favorables may never recover from what you did to me," he said, referring to the thousands of negative ads the White House ran against him in the 1996 elections. "But I'm not complaining," he added. "We'll still fight in some areas." A second included tactical questions such as appropriations on which they could cooperate. The third box was reserved for "a few big-ticket items" they could work on together. Clinton nodded in agreement with each point before interrupting. "This is a great opportunity," he said, "and we need to be prepared to take risks to do something that could be very significant." Gingrich talked about how Reagan's farewell address was such an emotional experience for many conservatives because it reminded them of why they had worked and fought so hard. "When you give your farewell address in three years you need to know why it was worth all the pain," he told the president. "You need to have some big ideas and then make them operational." Clinton nodded. "I agree," he said.

They both knew what was in that "third box"—an unprecedented effort to reform Social Security and Medicare. "We had solved the short-term problem of the deficit," recalled Bowles. "Now it was time to address the long-term structural problems facing Social Security and Medicare."[6] Both men were ready to take on the political risk of tackling the infamous "third rail" of American politics. Clinton was looking for a bold initiative in his final years that would define his presidency, answer critics who claimed he had failed to make a lasting imprint on the office, and encourage historians to rank him among the nation's "great" presidents. For his part, Gingrich was also thinking about how history would remember him. His idol was Henry Clay, the nineteenth-century Whig Speaker of the House who used his influence to expand American power abroad and preserve the Union at home. Gingrich wanted to be remembered as a great statesman, not just as a conservative firebrand rebel and mastermind of the 1994 Republican takeover of Congress.

The actuarial steps needed to shore up Social Security and Medicare were straightforward and, with government coffers beginning at last to overflow with revenue, easier to achieve than at any time in the recent past. "We always knew that finding common ground on Social Security wasn't terribly difficult from a policy standpoint," reflected Bruce Reed, the president's chief domestic policy advisor. "The policy differences were always the easiest to bridge." There was a growing consensus on both sides of the aisle in favor of having Social Security tap into the stock market to increase the rate of return on retirement funds. However, difficult questions remained unanswered: Who would manage the money: individuals or the government? Would private accounts replace checks guaranteed by the government, or would they simply be an add-on to the existing system? Politics, not economics, presented the biggest obstacle. Any long-term solution to solving Social Security required increasing the age of eligibility and changing the formula used to calculate the annual cost of living adjustment (COLA)—two steps guaranteed to arouse powerful opposition from across the political spectrum. In addition, neither party had an incentive to tackle such a politically charged issue. Democrats did not want to alienate organized labor or senior citizens—two groups they needed if they ever planned to win back control of Congress. Conservative Republicans were determined to use the budget surplus to cut taxes, not fund social programs. Besides, Congress had become so polarized that it was nearly impossible to propose bipartisan solutions to major problems. House liberals would reject any reform effort that would allow their nemesis Newt Gingrich to claim credit; conservative Republicans did not want to hand Bill Clinton a legislative victory. "They had given up trying to work with the White House," recalled Reed.[7]

Despite the odds, both men signaled their willingness to build a bipartisan coalition and to challenge the orthodoxy of their own parties. In private conversations with Gingrich and with Texas Republican Bill Archer, powerful head of the House Ways and Means Committee, the president promised to "provide political cover" for Democrats and Republicans by announcing his support for raising the minimum age required for Social Security and for changing the COLA formula. The president was willing to oppose the leadership of his own party and support the Republican demand for private accounts. Although most Republicans planned to use the surplus for a massive tax cut, Gingrich privately accepted the administration's position that the surplus should be used first to save Social Security "for all time," with any remaining amount used for a tax break.

Ironically, Clinton's hopes for the future rested on an alliance with the man most responsible for frustrating his previous legislative efforts. Bowles suggested that the president and Speaker were now "partners." Gingrich demurred. "I would prefer to say we are a coalition, not partners," he said. It was an important distinction for Gingrich. "Partners are on the same team," he reflected. "We were never going to be on the same team." The two men were not looking to create a third party, but instead to forge a new center of gravity that would pull together moderates in both parties. "I understood that I would have to fight some of my old guard," Gingrich recalled. "He understood that he would have to fight his hard left. Together we could shape about a 60 to 65 percent majority. I was happy for him to be a successful president. He was comfortable with us being a successful Republican Congress."[8]

The goal, they agreed, was to develop a clear strategy before the president's January State of the Union address. The central question they needed to resolve was, "How do we launch this, build an echo chamber, and bring our allies into it?" Both sides were confident. "We had the world going with us," recalled Bowles, reflecting White House optimism.[9] "We saw how the pieces would fit together pretty quickly," said Christenson, expressing the view from the Republican side.[10]

Before the meeting ended, the two former adversaries had decided to put the past behind them and create a new center/right political coalition of moderate Republicans and conservative Democrats to push their ambitious overhaul of Social Security and Medicare through Congress. Not since 1944, when Franklin Roosevelt had reached out to former Republican presidential candidate Wendell Willkie, had two leading political opponents plotted such a dramatic political alliance. Both men were confident that their new "coalition" would rival the New Deal and the Great Society in terms of the significance of legislation enacted. "There is no question in my mind in October of 1997, that we were looking forward to a period where we would cooperate on a broad range of really big issues," Gingrich recalled.[11]

That brief moment of possibility ended, however, with public revelations four months later of Clinton's affair with Monica Lewinsky—an affair that started during the dark days of the first budget shutdown in 1995. "Monica changed everything," Bowles reflected with a tone of both resignation and anger. "There were real opportunity costs—we had so much planned for 1998."[12]

On an emotional level, the Lewinsky scandal exposed the cultural fault line in America over the legacies of the 1960s. Politically, it forced Clinton to seek refuge in the liberal wing of his party, the same group he had agreed to abandon a few months earlier. "All opportunities for accomplishment were killed once the story came out," reflected a senior White House official. "If we cut a deal with the Republicans on Social Security there was every possibility that the Democrats, who were the only people defending him in the Congress against these charges, could easily get angry and abandon him." With conservatives in an uproar, Gingrich lost his political wiggle room and was forced to appease his right-wing base. If Gingrich did not "feed the conservative beast," recalled a colleague, he would have been removed from his job as Speaker.

Neither man has ever spoken publicly about their proposed coalition, or acknowledged that the secret meeting took place—until now. Over the past few years, Gingrich had hinted in public speeches about how the Lewinsky affair derailed the possibilities of major reform, but he never detailed the nature of his evolving relationship with Clinton or the specifics of their agreement on Social Security. When I started working on this book my plan was to use Clinton and Gingrich as metaphors for the intense partisan divisions that shaped the politics of the 1990s. In the course of my research, which included unprecedented access to the Speaker's private papers and interviews with key players, I came across the notes of their secret meeting. The typed, four-page summary shed new light on the relationship between the two men and exposed a previously unknown dimension of American politics in the 1990s. The role that Clinton and Gingrich played in intensifying partisanship is well known. But the story of how they attempted and failed to heal partisan divisions in 1997 has yet to be told.

His memory jogged by the notes, Gingrich elaborated on his dealings with Clinton, his high hopes for forging a new centrist coalition, and his frustration over how the president's recklessness derailed such a promising historical moment. In January 2006, I called Bowles at his Charlotte office and explained how Gingrich viewed the meeting and its significance, fully expecting him to offer an alternative "White House interpretation" that downplayed its importance and minimized the role that the Lewinsky scandal played in preventing Social Security and Medicare reform. Instead, I discovered why Bowles had earned the reputation for being a straight-shooter. He asked to see the notes of the meeting and offered to share them with the president. He made clear that he never spoke with writers without the president's permission, which he received. When I called him back a few days later, there was no spin—just frustration, a touch of sadness, and, after a long silence, emphatic agreement. "That's absolutely 100 percent right," he said. In that discussion, and a later meeting at his office, Bowles talked about his shuttle diplomacy between the White House and Capitol Hill, the careful planning that went on behind the scenes to broker the meeting, and his disappointment with the president and his actions in the Lewinsky affair. The small number of White House aides involved in the negotiations supported his version of events and added valuable insight and detail on the Clinton–Gingrich relationship.[13]

In retrospect, it seems clear that the Clinton years were a period of missed opportunities. A brief ten-year window separated the end of the Cold War and the dawn of the new age of global terror. During that unique period of peace and prosperity, the nation had an unprecedented chance to tackle important domestic issues. By the fall of 1997 a number of forces had come together to create a rare moment of bipartisanship—a moment that both Bill Clinton and Newt Gingrich hoped to grasp. Yet, less than a year later both men were fighting for their political lives as the nation engaged in a prolonged, partisan, and often personal debate over impeachment of the president.

Nearly every major domestic political success, potential breakthrough, and setback of the mid- and late 1990s was a byproduct of the complicated personal relationship between the two dominant political figures of the decade. Despite their obvious differences, they possessed a unique personal chemistry, which traced back to their childhoods. Both men were "abandoned" by their biological fathers and raised by distant and, in Clinton's case, abusive stepfathers. At the same time, they were surrounded by doting, overprotective women. "Strong and doting mothers, broken homes, tenuous roots—how do these traits play out in men who finally realize their largest ambitions for power?" asked the journalist Frank Rich.[14]

The most common answer was that they were looking for father figures, trying to win the affection and respect they never received from either their biological or adopted fathers. "They were the two neediest people in Washington," reflected a senior Republican who worked closely with both men. While pop psychology provided limited insight into their characters, their childhood experiences had a direct impact on the way they dealt with each other. Each man felt he had special insight into the emotional and intellectual makeup of the other. Both were convinced they "understood" the other in ways that many of their aides, who grew up under very different circumstances, never could. That bond allowed them to take political risks, making a major breakthrough on Social Security possible, but it also led to many of their most serious political blunders.

It is also impossible to understand the relationship between Clinton and Gingrich without examining how they were shaped by the tumultuous events of the 1960s. They spent most of their public lives fighting over a host of new questions and issues that emerged from that contentious era. Surprisingly, they led similar lives during the 1960s. Both spent most of the decade on college campuses, avoided the draft, experimented with drugs, and empathized with the youthful rebellion sweeping the nation. Over time, however, they would emerge as leaders of competing cultural armies battling over the legacy of the decade. In many ways, they embodied the best and worst qualities of their generation. Like many young people who came of age in the 1960s, Clinton and Gingrich embraced the equalitarian ethos of the time. They shared an impatience for change, an eagerness to challenge authority, and a determination to make a difference. Yet they could also be immature and self-indulgent, unable to forgo immediate gratification even when it threatened their noblest goals. Their lives help tell the larger story of a generation, its great possibilities, and its unrealized potential.

The Pact

CHAPTER ONE | Growing Up

IT IS REMARKABLE that two men who would become metaphors for partisan division in the 1990s started out in life under such similar circumstances. Erskine Bowles remembers sitting at the breakfast table in early 1995 reading a lengthy *New York Times* profile of Newt Gingrich shortly after he won election as Speaker of the House. After finishing the piece he turned to his wife and said, "You could substitute the name Clinton for Gingrich and have written nearly the same article."[1]

Born three years apart, both men grew up in dysfunctional families, raised by overprotective mothers and emotionally distant, often abusive, stepfathers. Newt's mother, Kathleen, or "Kit," Daugherty was 16 when she married Newton McPherson on September 12, 1942. A strapping six feet three inches tall, "Big Newt" liked to get drunk and pick fights at the local pub. Three days after they were married, Newton, hung over from a long night at the local pool hall, slugged his wife after she tried waking him for work in the morning. She packed her bags, moved in with her mother, and filed for divorce. "We were married on a Saturday, and I left him on a Tuesday," she said. "I got Newtie in those three days."[2]

On June 17, 1943, nine months to the day after they were married, she gave birth to a baby whom she named Newton Leroy McPherson after her estranged husband. By the time he was born, Newt's father had joined the merchant marines and played no role in raising him. That responsibility fell to Robert Gingrich, a career soldier whom Kit married in 1946 when Newt was three years old. "Big Newt," looking for a way to get out of paying child support, allowed Gingrich to adopt his son. Although young Newt would change his name, he and his adoptive father always had a strained relationship. Aloof and demanding, Robert Gingrich preferred doing cross-word puzzles to talking with his children. "His father seemed like a cold, austere kind of person," recalled a former campaign worker.[3] Newt's mother, who went on to have three daughters with Gingrich, summed up the differences between the two men in a 1994 interview with the New York Times: "Newtie is a talker," she said. "Bob is not."[4]

Three months before Bill Clinton was born on August 19, 1946, his father, William Jefferson Blythe, was killed in a car crash near the town of Sikeston in southern Missouri. A gregarious salesman, Blythe was traveling from Chicago to Hope, Arkansas, to visit his pregnant wife when his Buick blew a tire and skidded off the road. Facing the prospect of raising her son alone, Virginia decided to leave young Bill with her parents while she trained as a nurse anesthetist in New Orleans. She graduated and returned home full time in 1948 and married Roger Clinton, a "handsome, hell-raising, twice divorced man," Bill Clinton reflected. Roger was also an alcoholic and, over time, his behavior became more erratic and violent. Young Bill had a vivid memory of one occasion when his mother tried to go to the hospital to visit a dying relative. "Daddy said she couldn't go," and to underscore the point, "Daddy pulled a gun from behind his back and fired in Mother's direction," Bill wrote in the police report. "The bullet went into the wall between where she and I were standing."[5]

While it is difficult to speculate about the long-term impact their troubled childhoods had on their personalities and temperament, the short-term consequences are fairly clear. Growing up in dysfunctional families, in worlds that lacked stability, Clinton and Gingrich learned to impose order on their chaotic lives. Friends describe both men as precocious, but physically awkward: bigger than most kids their age, overweight, and lacking in athletic ability. They possessed a driving, nearly all-consuming ambition. Even as a child, Gingrich talked about becoming an important historical figure and, according to some accounts, announced as early as high school that he wanted to become Speaker of the House of Representatives. Clinton was just as driven, but he was able to disguise his ambition behind a veil of warmth and charm. Clinton coped with living in an alcoholic family by becoming a model of good citizenship, social grace, and academic achievement. Admired by his classmates and teachers, he excelled in and out of the classroom. A childhood friend observed that within a few days of his enrollment in grade school, "most kids knew who he was and wanted to be around him."[6] At Hope High School he was the best musician in the band, the math whiz, winner of the Elks Club leadership award, a National Merit Scholarship semifinalist, and junior class president.

Newt, focusing all of his energy on intellectual pursuits, immersed himself in studying animals and collecting fossils. In 1955, when he was 12, he told his mother he was going to the library and instead rode a bus almost 20 miles to Harrisburg to try to convince local officials to "dedicate a piece of land where a zoo might be established, with moat." The local newspaper picked up the story, describing him as "an earnest young man." After listening to Newt provide a detailed cost analysis of the project, including the price of every animal, the reporter noted: "A few minutes conversation with Newton leaves an awed adult with a flying start toward an inferiority complex."[7] As a sophomore at Baker High School in Columbus, Georgia, Newt handed in a 200-page, single-spaced paper on the balance of naval power between Russia, Great Britain, and the United States. "Newt was better read in history, politics, and government than I was," said his high school English teacher. "He had a keen mind, a very good analytical mind." When he graduated from high school his classmates voted him "most intellectual."[8]

There were, however, subtle but important differences in the influences that would shape them as adults. Bill Clinton experienced the contradictions of growing up in the 1950s. Although born in bucolic Hope, Clinton spent most of his childhood in Hot Springs, where gambling saloons existed side by side with Baptist churches. Clinton loved and respected his stepfather even though he was an alcoholic who abused his mother. Two of the most important influences in his life were his mother, Virginia, who smoked, gambled, and drank liquor, and his high school principal, Johnnie Mae Mackey, who preached the values of church, family, and patriotism. He grew up in a tolerant family in the racially intolerant South. His grandfather's local store, which sat on the edge of Hope's local black community, served blacks and whites at a time when law and custom required that blacks drink at separate water fountains, worship at segregated churches, and sit in the back of the bus. "I am a living paradox," young Clinton wrote in a high school autobiographical essay, "deeply religious, yet not as convinced of my exact beliefs as I ought to be; wanting responsibility yet shirking it; loving the truth but often times giving way to falsity."[9]

There was little ambiguity in Newt Gingrich's childhood. Fear of communism and the rigid style of his stepfather shaped young Newt's view of the world. Where Clinton was forced to reconcile the paradox of good and evil, Gingrich's world was framed in moral absolutes. Clinton was introspective, full of doubt and uncertainty; Gingrich never questioned his convictions. The most memorable experience of Newt's childhood took place in 1958 when the family, living in France while his father was stationed there, took a tour of the World War I battlefield of Verdun during Easter weekend.

"That last day was probably the most stunning event of my life. It was a sense of coming face to face with an unavoidable reality," he told biographer Mel Steely.[10] That "unavoidable reality," he concluded at the age of 15, was "that civilizations die." The experience, he claimed, changed his life. "It is the driving force which pushed me into history and politics and molded my life," he wrote in his 1984 book, *Window of Opportunity*.[11] Later that year, while working as a gardener in his housing complex, he realized "that our civilization was facing a mortal threat from the Soviet empire." That summer he decided that he would "dedicate my life to understanding what it takes for a free people to survive and to helping my country and the cause of freedom."[12]

At an age when most young men are focused on playing sports and meeting girls, Newt was fantasizing about saving the world. He created a grand, heroic narrative where the forces of good and evil clashed, and where great men did battle. He never doubted that he would be at the center of that heroic struggle. Even as a teenager, he thought of himself as a "transformational figure" who would save America from its enemies. As early as 1958, long before assassinations, war, and Watergate, he feared that western civilization was in decline and in need of a hero to save it. "If you decide in your freshman year in high school that your job is to spend your lifetime trying to change the future of your people, you're probably fairly weird. I think I was pretty weird as a kid."[13]

Bill Clinton's view of the world and his role in it reflected the youthful ambition of an idealistic boy growing up in 1950s America. Hoping to make a difference in the world, he received constant encouragement from people around him that he possessed remarkable talents. His mother turned their house into a shrine, decorating it with his awards and trophies. But his ideas and his ambition remained unformed. He embraced the signs of change that were rippling through American culture in the 1950s. His idol growing up was Elvis Presley, the hip-swinging renegade who became a symbol of youthful protest against his parents' generation's definition of reality. Gingrich, on the other hand, worshiped John Wayne, the symbol of an older, simpler America where standards of right and wrong were clear and unambiguous. "I had imprinted John Wayne in his mid-40s as my model of behavior," he recalled.[14]

Growing up in an alcoholic family, Clinton learned to navigate conflict by playing the role of peacemaker. "I think my desire to accommodate is probably due in part to the sense that I had from my childhood, that I was the person who had to hold things together in my home, to keep peace," Clinton reflected.[15] Living in an adult world with an emotionally distant stepfather, Gingrich found that defiance was often the surest way to gain attention. "Newtie would do anything to get Bob's attention," his mother recalled.

When he was 15 and living in Orleans, France, Newt went into town after his father explicitly told him to stay home. His father confronted him when he returned, picked him up off the ground, and held him against the wall while his feet dangled above the floor. "It is hard to be belligerent when your feet aren't touching the ground," his stepfather said, reflecting on the moment.[16] In high school, Newt secretly started dating his geometry teacher, whom he would eventually marry. His father was so opposed to the relationship that he refused to attend the wedding. Later, the *Washington Post* speculated that Gingrich "spent his life—particularly his political life—plotting to overthrow every authority figure who stood between him and his agenda."[17]

If their paths had ever crossed in their early years, it is likely that Bill Clinton would have sought out the socially awkward, perpetually serious, shy kid with the thick glasses who seemed always burdened with a stack of heavy books and preoccupied with questions that were too weighty for someone his age. Clinton enjoyed the company of friends, and often was both the brightest and the most popular kid in school. Although nearly everyone liked him, young Bill never felt comfortable with the "cool kids." He enjoyed talking to everyone, but had a special affinity for reaching out to people who were different, or somehow out of the mainstream. He allowed no one to escape his charm. He would have had a hard time, however, charming a young Newt who, having spent much of his childhood following his father from one army base to another—from Fort Riley, Kansas; to Orleans, France; to Stuttgart, Germany; and, finally, to Fort Benning, Georgia—always seemed more comfortable with adults than with his peers. Newt was formal and old-fashioned, and always seemed older than his age. "I think it's fair to say I lived a long period of my life autonomously," Gingrich confessed to Gail Sheehy in 1995. "I was never alone, but I was lonely."[18] "I grew up in a world of strangers," he told me.[19]

Despite their temperaments and personalities, both men were fascinated by politics from an early age. "My uncle taught me to smile at Eisenhower on the television and to turn Adlai Stevenson off," Gingrich reflected.[20] In the 1960 election, Gingrich supported Richard Nixon; Clinton's idol was John F. Kennedy. On election night both teenage boys waited anxiously for the results. It was not until the following morning that Kennedy was declared the winner. "One of the longest nights of my life was sitting by the radio listening to Nixon lose in November 1960," said Gingrich.[21] Kennedy's election signaled the beginning of the tumultuous '60s—a decade that would change the lives of Newt Gingrich and Bill Clinton and alter the course of American history.

CHAPTER TWO | It's the '60s, Stupid"

T HE 1960S MARKED a critical breaking point, a cultural divide that would shape American politics and culture for the rest of the century and beyond. Many young protestors took to the streets to demonstrate their frustration with the slow pace of civil rights reform, the growing fear of nuclear war, and the widening commitment to Vietnam. The clashes between protestors and police in the streets of Berkeley, Chicago, and Detroit were far less violent than the bloody battles between Union and Confederate armies that took in place at Bull Run, Antietam, and Gettysburg. Both civil wars, however, produced a generation that was scarred by the memory of the struggle, deeply divided over its meaning, and determined to win a long-term fight for the hearts and minds of the American people.

The standard narrative of the 1960s tells the story of a monolithic generation of young people rising up to stamp out racism, end the Vietnam War, and expand opportunities for women. It is true that many in the generation who came of age in the prosperous postwar years rejected the moderation and conformity of their parents' world, focused their attention on a new set of social and cultural questions, and shared a sense of impatience. Unprecedented prosperity served as the midwife of cultural revolution. The generation coming of age in the 1960s was the first in history where a large percentage of its members were able to focus their energies on enjoying the benefits of abundance. According to the pollster Daniel Yankelovich, the '60s generation replaced an ethic of "self-denial," forged during the Great Depression, with an ethic of "self-fulfillment." Instead of asking, "Will I be able to make a living?" they wanted to know, "How can I find self-fulfillment?"[1]

But it was also a generation that was at war with itself, deeply divided over how to address questions of racial injustice, the proper role of government in American life, and the nation's place in the world. Television, which highlighted the angriest confrontations between students and police and focused on the most colorful cheerleaders of the counterculture, created the false impression that the nation's young people were monolithically left of center. They were not. In 1968, right-wing presidential candidate George Wallace scored best among people under 30.[2] Some young people chose to protest injustice—to burn draft cards, demonstrate against the war, and participate in sit-ins—while many others chose to drop out of the system, experiment with drugs, and find cultural outlets for their rebellion. While some joined the New Left, others found a home in the emerging New Right. The vast majority of younger people, however, never participated in a protest march or a civil rights demonstration, and they were just as divided over the Vietnam War as older Americans.

These deep generational fissures forged during the 1960s never healed. They were obscured during the 1970s by stagflation, and during the 1980s by the elevated fear of Soviet expansionism. The Cold War ended, however, just as some in the '60s generation were ready to assume positions of power. Some who had demonstrated in the streets during the 1960s now clashed in the halls of Congress, where they employed many of the same weapons—the same sense of self-righteousness, ideological fervor, and impatience—that had characterized their earlier contests.

The struggles between Newt Gingrich and Bill Clinton, the first representative of the '60s generation to occupy the White House, were a continuation of the bitter generational battles left over from the 1960s. "If you want to understand the differences between me and Newt, you have to go back to the '60s," Clinton told me. "If you think the '60s were generally good, chances are you are a liberal. If you think the '60s were bad, chances are you're a conservative."[3] With the exception of the civil rights movement, which he supported, Gingrich had no quarrel with Clinton's framework. As the president saw it, "Newt said that America had been a great country until the '60s, when Democrats took over and replaced absolute notions of right and wrong with more relativist values. He pledged to take us back to the morality of the 1950s, in order to 'renew American civilization.'" Clinton viewed the decade differently, believing it represented a healthy challenge to the oppressive orthodoxy of the 1950s.

By the 1990s, the ideological battle over the meaning of the 1960s would boil down to a debate over a culture of "choice." The battles over Vietnam, racial rioting, and student protesting had faded into memory, but they had left a lasting impression on the nation. Taken together, the social movements of the decade expanded the range of individual choices people had about the way they lived their lives. The civil rights movement dramatically expanded options for African Americans. Along the way, it spearheaded other empowerment movements, especially for women and homosexuals. The range of choices expanded beyond political rights into the world of culture. A generation of young people came of age in the 1960s questioning all forms of authority, loosening the rules of behavior that had guided their parent's generation. The cultural revolution initiated by the 1960s had a ripple effect that touched nearly every institution in society.

The dramatic changes prompted a backlash among traditionalists, who complained that "counterculture" values had seeped into every institution of American society, breeding permissiveness and eroding the moral glue that held society together. "The central line of cleavage in the '60s generation," reflected Clinton friend and former secretary of labor Robert Reich, "was over the question of authority in society."[4] Neoconservative thinkers focused on the public policy consequences of a culture that valued liberation over responsibility. They claimed that the abandonment of older values such as family, hard work, and discipline produced an epidemic of single motherhood, homelessness, and legal abortion. "I know of nothing positive coming from that period; it was an unmitigated disaster," observed Allan Bloom, author of the best-selling book *The Closing of the American Mind* (1987).[5] While neoconservative intellectuals critiqued the secular consequences of the 1960s, religious fundamentalists probed the moral and religious results, claiming that the culture of individualism led to moral decay. Evangelist Pat Robertson claimed that "the excesses of the '60s" produced a host of social ills, including "family breakdown . . . illegitimate births . . . drug addiction . . . [and] crime."[6]

Over time, Newt Gingrich would help mold both the secular and religious arguments into a powerful ideological weapon. During the 1990s, he would spearhead a conservative effort to redefine the meaning of the decade, transforming it into a metaphor for a constellation of issues that resonated with millions of Americans who feared the erosion of traditional values and authority in society. Mention of the '60s was like a tap just beneath the knee, designed to produce the appropriate reflex: images of privileged students burning the American flag, radical feminists assaulting the family, militant minorities rioting in the streets, activist judges forcing parents to bus their children across town, arrogant intellectuals mocking cherished values and blurring the distinction between right and wrong, and faceless government bureaucrats wasting hard-earned tax dollars while people on welfare did not have to work. Gingrich assumed for himself the noble task to "save western civilization" from its own excesses by rooting out the countercultural influences in contemporary life and re-establishing clear standards of right and wrong.

Along the way, he and other conservatives transformed Bill Clinton into a metaphor for '60s excess and a harbinger of cultural change—the antiwar activist who supported civil rights for blacks and equal rights for women. Clinton viewed himself as a political moderate trying to push his party back into the mainstream. Yet, stylistically, everything about him reminded conservative voters of the things about the 1960s they most disliked. "Bill Clinton and Hillary Rodham may have been moderates on individual policies," reflected Reich, "but they looked and they acted and seemed in every respect like people who had been on the 'other side' of the upheavals of the 1960s." According to Reich, Clinton became "emblematic of what the conservatives saw" as the promiscuous '60s. "He grew up in an overly permissive home, smoked dope, had sex outside marriage, had no real self-discipline, and didn't understand the importance of discipline in society."[7] Over time, Clinton would trim his sideburns, cut his unruly hair, and adopt all the conventions of middle-class respectability, but he could never escape the cultural baggage of the 1960s. As one local Arkansas voter put it: Bill Clinton became a representative of the "libertine generation—what's happened to us, screwing around and smokin' dope and doin' all those kinda things—lying, cheatin,' and not going to church and prayin.'"[8]

———

Both men were part of a massive wave of young people that flooded college campuses during the decade. In 1965, 41 percent of all Americans were under the age of twenty. College enrollments soared from 3.6 million in 1960 to almost 8 million in 1970. The college campus was home for Newt Gingrich from 1961, when he entered Emory University as a freshman, until 1978, when he won election to Congress. After graduating from Emory in 1965, Newt moved to New Orleans, where he entered a graduate program in history at Tulane University. In 1970, after finishing his Ph.D. degree, he accepted a teaching position at West Georgia College. Bill Clinton started his freshman year at Georgetown in 1964 and ended the decade as a Rhodes Scholar at Oxford, before returning to the United States to earn a law degree at Yale in 1973. In 1976, he left his teaching job at the University of Arkansas Law School to make a successful bid for state attorney general.

Although he would later be stereotyped by conservatives as the epitome of youthful excess during the 1960s, Clinton was decidedly conventional in a decade that valued the unconventional. Many young people on both the Left and Right were assaulting the citadel of consensus liberalism at the same time that Clinton was embracing it. Clinton was entranced by John F. Kennedy and the spirit of change and reform that his election in 1960 represented. He had been captivated by the president's stirring inaugural address, which called for "a struggle against the common enemies of man: tyranny, poverty, and war," and promised a "New Frontier" of opportunity and challenge. Kennedy tapped into Clinton's innocence and his idealism: his belief that heroic men could accomplish great things, guarantee a growing economy, and maintain peace abroad and social harmony at home. Like the youthful president, Bill Clinton believed that prosperity had rendered obsolete ideological conflict and social struggle. "Politics," Kennedy told the graduating class at Yale in 1962, was to "avoid basic clashes of philosophy and ideology" and to embrace "ways and means of reaching common goals."

In July 1963, an excited Bill Clinton traveled to Washington D.C., as part of a Boys Nation retreat where they were scheduled to attend a White House ceremony with the president. Although he was only sixteen, Clinton, at six foot three and two hundred pounds, towered over the other kids and easily maneuvered himself to the front of a reception line in the Rose Garden. On a warm summer afternoon, a photographer captured the moment when Bill Clinton shook hands with his childhood idol, President John F. Kennedy. "When he came back from Washington, holding this picture of himself with Jack Kennedy, and the expression on his face," his mother Virginia recalled, "I knew right then that politics was the answer for him."[9]

By the time of the fateful meeting between a current and a future president, Kennedy was already under assault from activists on the Left, for his slow response to the civil rights struggle and his confrontational Cold War rhetoric, and from the Right, for his efforts to expand federal power and willingness to negotiate with the Soviets. The previous year, young leftists had created the Students for Democratic Society (SDS) and issued the *Port Huron Statement,* calling for a "New Left" to address the feelings of "helplessness and indifference" that plagued the nation. A liberal consensus was already showing signs of unraveling, but Clinton embraced Kennedy and the politics that he espoused.

By the middle of the decade, the cultural battle lines that would define the worlds of Bill Clinton and Newt Gingrich had taken shape. On one side stood the defenders of traditional values, who stressed the need for clear standards of right and wrong and placed a premium on authority and order in society. On the other side was a growing but still amorphous challenge to all forms of authority that emphasized the importance of individual expression and saw self-fulfillment as its highest ideal. Young people were at the forefront of the challenge to authority, but the emerging culture wars did not break down along neat generational lines. Class and geography also influenced which side of the divide people stood. Young people in rural areas, or from working-class backgrounds, were just as likely as their parents to embrace the older standards, while highly educated older Americans living in cities often found themselves swept up in the momentum for change.

While their generation was forcing the nation to choose sides in the culture wars, both Bill Clinton and Newt Gingrich were struggling to survive in the rapidly disappearing middle ground. Unlike many people his age, Clinton did not want to attack the establishment; he wanted to join it. Not even the assassination of President Kennedy, just four months after their meeting in the Rose Garden, could dampen his idealism. He took up the challenge that Kennedy had set for him and for other young people. That spring, he told his high school graduation class "that our generation will remove complacency, poverty and prejudice from the hearts of free man."[10] That same year, in another commencement address, President Lyndon Johnson was announcing his vision of a Great Society, "where men are more concerned with the quality of their goals than the quantity of their goods." Not surprisingly, Clinton decided to travel to Washington D.C. for college so he could be near the action. It was a time of tremendous optimism. "Johnson was a Southerner, and at that moment the whole country had very high hopes for him, and I did, too," he reflected.[11]

By 1967, protests were becoming common on many college campuses, but they were rare at Georgetown. It remained decidedly mainstream and conservative, with a rigorous Jesuit curriculum and strict dress code that required men to wear dress shirt, jacket, and tie to class. On weeknights, students were required to be in their rooms. University officials did their best to keep the sexual revolution at bay, establishing a strict curfew on weekends and prohibiting "guests of the opposite sex, alcoholic beverages, pets, or firearms" in dorm rooms.[12] Clinton watched the protests taking place all around him—the racial riots that were ripping apart American cities, anti-war demonstrators burning draft cards, disaffected youth losing themselves in drugs and alcohol. As a young man, Clinton sympathized with the desire for change and the frustration with mainstream politics, but he was personally and culturally too deeply attached to the ideals of conventional politics to seriously consider "tuning in and dropping out," and he was too closely wedded to the establishment to consider bringing it down. "Though I was sympathetic to the zeitgeist, I didn't embrace the lifestyle or the radical rhetoric. My hair was short, I didn't even drink, and some of the music was too loud and harsh for my taste."[13]

A friend later described Clinton and his friends in 1967 as "boringly respectable."[14] Classmates remember an affable Clinton with a soft Southern drawl who within days of his arrival in Washington knew the name of every member of the freshman class, and won election as class president. Emmett Tyrell, a contemporary at Georgetown and later conservative pundit, referred to Clinton as "a student government goody-goody."[15] At the end of his junior year, Clinton campaigned for president of the student council under the banner "A Realistic Approach to Student Government," only to be beaten by a wide margin by a candidate who tied him to the status quo. According to biographer Robert Levin, "by the standards of the counter-culture of 1968," Clinton "remained a pro-establishment moderate."[16]

Like many members of his generation, Bill Clinton enjoyed an extended adolescence that allowed him to experiment with new ideas and new living arrangements well into his twenties. He led a cosmopolitan life during the late 1960s, traveling around the world, attending world-class universities. His curiosity, both intellectual and personal, drove him to experience first-hand as much of the ferment of the decade as possible. He surrounded himself with a diverse group of people antiwar protestors, civil rights leaders, future gay rights leaders, and feminists. He could recite the poetry of Dylan Thomas, the words of Martin Luther King's famous "I Have a Dream" speech, and the lyrics to "Abraham, Martin, and John." He would name his daughter after a Joni Mitchell song, "Chelsea Morning."

Newt Gingrich shared little in common with his student peers. Like many had done in the 1950s, Newt Gingrich married young and started a family. In 1962, as a nineteen-year-old college freshman at Emory, Newt married Jackie Battley, his twenty-six-year-old former high school geometry teacher. Nine months later they had their first daughter, Kathy. Their second daughter, Jackie Sue, followed in 1966. While he was busy earning a degree, his wife supported the family by working as a teacher in a nearby school. Since he was busy both earning a degree and helping to raise a small family, Gingrich was removed from the rhythm of college life. He had moved well beyond adolescence. Having grown up in the company of adults, Gingrich learned to act like one from a young age.

No one would ever have called Newt a hippie. He is easy to pick out in photographs from the time. In a room full of bearded, long-haired, casually dressed young men, Newt is often the only one with the short-cropped hair, sport coat, and tie. His distinctive, thick, dark-rimmed glasses added to his old-fashioned, bookish image. "You've got to realize what a relic of the 1950s Newt was," said his friend David Kramer. "Newt was 50 when he was 25. He was a very socially conservative guy with wife even more socially conservative than he was. He wore a suit and a tie to class." He had little interest in the music of the time. "I once took him to a Jefferson Airplane concert and tried to convince him that it was interesting music," Kramer said. "I don't think I was too successful. . . . I would tell him wild tales of California [counterculture] and he was interested, as with everything, to know if this had any political value."[17] He experimented with pot, but did not like it. In 1995, he told a reporter that smoking marijuana in the 1960s "was a sign we were alive and in graduate school in that era."[18]

"He looked at everything through the prism of politics, especially Republican politics," said Chip Kahn, a close friend who would later manage Gingrich's first political campaign.[19] He loved talking politics and he enjoyed the mechanics of campaigns. While an undergraduate he founded Emory's "Young Republican" club and he worked in an unsuccessful Republican campaign for Congress. "Newt was the only person I knew who had multiple phone lines coming into his apartment [in college] when he was essentially just a kid," said friend Linda Tilton. "He'd frequently be talking politics with [two] people at once, running from one phone to the other to tell each person what the other one was saying."[20]

Despite his 1950s "organization man" appearance, Gingrich ultimately absorbed the rebellious spirit of the time and embraced many aspects of the revolt against authority. In October 1964, students at the University of California at Berkeley organized a sit-in to demonstrate against a decision by the administration to enforce campus regulations prohibiting political demonstrations at the entrance of campus, giving birth to the free speech movement on campus. The movement spread to other campuses and broadened and championed many causes, from opposing dress codes to fighting tenure decisions. In March 1968, the Tulane administration refused to allow the school newspaper to publish two "obscene" pictures. Gingrich became a leader of a new organization, MORTS (Mobilization of Responsible Tulane Students), created to protest the decision. The group organized marches to the president's home, "occupied" the university center, and even orchestrated a boycott of several local businesses owned by board members. Gingrich was part of the MORTS delegation that met with the college president and, eventually, resolved the issue peacefully.[21]

MORTS leaders described their organization as "a mood rather than a machine," claiming their "ideology has caught the imagination" of a large number of students. Instead of becoming a party and running candidates in the student elections, it issued a "platform," written, in part, by Gingrich. It called for an expansion of student rights and privileges, and demanded a "free press on campus" and creation of a system that would allow students to have input in all areas of academic life, including the hiring and firing of faculty. They also opposed compulsory attendance of classes.[22]

The following year, Gingrich and his friend David Kramer organized another group, called H.E.R.E. (Honesty Efficiency and Responsibility in Education), which urged the university to hire an outside consulting group to "thoroughly examine every facet of non-academic University operations." Believing that the administration was inefficient and wasteful, it wanted the school to make public the results of a review by the management consulting firm of Booz, Allen and Hamilton from 1966–67. The administration claimed that it had dismissed the firm before the study was completed. Gingrich was not satisfied. "It is absurd for the administration to talk of crisis in private American universities on one hand and then refuse to face up to that crisis," he said.[23]

Years later, his critics would point to his involvement with student protests as evidence of hypocrisy, denigrating the leader of the New Right assault on the 1960s for himself being a student protestor. In 1984, the Democratic Congressional Campaign Committee hired an investigator to travel to Tulane to uncover information about Gingrich during his student days. After combing through old newspapers and interviewing friends, they concluded that the "Newt Gingrich of today is certainly different from the Newt Gingrich of his college and early political career." It named Gingrich as "undoubtedly one of perhaps eight to ten main campus activists during his years at Tulane." He was "an activist and certainly liberal," but "he probably could not have been characterized as a radical leftist," the report concluded.[24]

The critics were only partially right. Gingrich shared with the Left a distemper, an impatience for change, a willingness to challenge the status quo, and a belief that liberalism was failing the nation. He was asking many of the same questions as those on the Left, but he was moving toward different answers. He was more contrarian than conservative, more libertarian than liberal. He was a Republican more out of instinct than ideology. Culturally, he felt more at home in the party. Republicans looked and sounded more like him. Gingrich would move sharply to the right in later years, but there is a common thread that tied the old student-activist Gingrich to the new conservative one. It was during these Tulane years, his friend David Kramer reflected, that "I heard Newt for the first time say that a corrupt elite was falsifying the popular will." Gingrich, he said, "threw rocks at authority at every opportunity" during the 1960s.[25]

In the 1960s, Gingrich embraced the critique of young people who were leading the charge against the university establishment. During the 1970s and 1980s, as the Right mobilized to attack the remnants of the old liberal order, Gingrich refashioned himself as a conservative. Whether organizing protests on campus or in the halls of Congress, he was always the disgruntled outsider. What makes him complicated, however, is that he often desperately wanted to join the very establishment he was trying to destroy. In 1970, he accepted a position as a professor of history at West Georgia College. As a junior professor, he issued scathing denunciations of the state of higher education, even as he applied for the position as president of the university. Years later, he would try to destroy the reputation of Congress so that he could some day become its Speaker.

On one of the most contentious issues of the decade, civil rights, Gingrich was much closer to the liberal wing of the Democratic Party than he was to the Republicans. He supported the Republican calls for cutting back on the size of government and for boosting military spending, but he was uncomfortable with the party's opposition to civil rights and its willingness to use race as an issue to peel off white voters in the South. Having grown up on desegregated military bases, he was shocked when he moved back to Georgia to see black and white water fountains. In the South, it was the Democratic Party that helped create and sustain the world of Jim Crow, and he believed the Republican Party should return to its Lincolnian roots and renew its call for emancipation. According to friends, he practiced what he preached, sending one of his daughters to a mostly black Head Start program. In 1968, after Martin Luther King was murdered in Memphis, he volunteered to work as Louisiana co-coordinator for the presidential campaign of Nelson Rockefeller, a liberal Republican governor of New York with a strong civil rights record.

He gave a glimpse of how he planned to influence politics during his stint on the Rockefeller campaign. Gingrich worked with local African American leaders to challenge the way the state party selected delegates for the national Republican Convention in Miami. In Louisiana, Republicans selected two delegates from each congressional district, then held a state convention to select an additional ten at-large delegates, for a total of twenty-six. The sixteen delegates selected in local congressional districts supported either Richard Nixon or California Governor Ronald Reagan. All the delegates were white. A group calling itself Concerned Louisiana Negro Republicans (CLNR), complaining that blacks were excluded from the delegate selection process, planned a protest at the state convention to force the party to select at least five African American delegates. The idea was similar to the bold challenge of the Mississippi Freedom Democratic Party (MFDP) to the lily-white delegation at the 1964 Democratic convention. An outgrowth of the Student NonViolent Coordinating Committee (SNCC), whose membership included radicals like Stokeley Carmichael, the MFDP eventually was forced to settle for two at-large seats at the convention, but the effort later led the party to rewrite the rules to guarantee equal representation in state delegations.

Newt Gingrich was no Stokeley Carmichael, but he saw the CLNR challenge as a way to make a statement about both civil rights and Republican politics. The Republican Party in Louisiana, and throughout the South, was made up of segregationists hoping to reap political benefit from the defection of white voters from the Democratic Party who were disgruntled by their party's growing support for civil rights. Gingrich wanted to see the Republican Party move in the opposite direction, supporting civil rights and trying to appeal to blacks. He favored a convention rule requiring proportional representation of African Americans from states with large black populations. There was also a political motive behind his support. Most CLNR leaders were Rockefeller supporters, and Gingrich saw the challenge as a way to get more Rockefeller delegates selected to the national convention. Critics complained that they were "using the race issue to try to get Rockefeller in by the back door." In the end, the Reagan and Nixon forces beat back the challenge and retained tight control over the carefully scripted Republican Convention.[26]

––––––

For Clinton, as for most members of his generation, the Vietnam War was the central issue of the time. In 1965, Lyndon Johnson made his fateful decision to send American combat troops to Vietnam. "Vietnam," observed Michael Herr in *Dispatches,* "was what we had instead of happy childhoods."[27] The so-called "greatest generation" had set a trap for its children. They had fought in a war that unified the nation, highlighted the nobility of American ideals, and underscored the benefits of American power. Those who fought in World War II then sent their children off to a war that would leave them fractured and divided, but longing for the grand dreams and noble pursuits of their parents. "As an inheritance from the previous generation, Vietnam was a poisoned chalice," observed Clinton biographer Nigel Hamilton, "a criminal legacy that turned a whole generation of Americans from sixties idealists into liars."[28]

President Johnson's decision to escalate the conflict in Vietnam fanned the flames of student discontent. On March 24, 1965, students at the University of Michigan organized the first anti-Vietnam teach-in. Organizers planned lectures and discussions about the war in the hopes of "educating" students about the dangers of American involvement in Vietnam. The restrained and respectable form of protest spread quickly to other college campuses. By late 1965, students were planning mass demonstrations, burning draft cards, and chanting "Hey, Hey, LBJ, how many kids did you kill today?" Student anger reached a new level when, in January 1966, Johnson ended automatic draft deferments for college students. The threat of the draft pushed many young people to protest the war. The demonstrations swelled in size and intensity as protestors burned draft cards and an occasional American flag.

By 1967, SDS leaders called for a strategy of "common struggle with the liberation movements of the world" by means of "the disruption, dislocation and destruction of the military's access to the manpower, intelligence, or resources of our universities."[29] Radicalized by the escalation of the war, many members of the New Left openly supported the North Vietnamese, even carrying Viet Cong flags during protests. The militant message angered many Americans, but it resonated with frustrated college students. By the end of 1967, SDS membership had swelled to over 30,000.[30]

The pain of Vietnam was personal for Clinton. He supported Johnson and only slowly, painfully turned against the war. He confessed that as late as the summer of 1966 he had not developed a clear position on Vietnam, but he instinctively supported the president. That year he took a job working for J. William Fulbright, his home state senator who was chair of the Senate Foreign Relations Committee and an outspoken critic of the administration's policy. Reading everything he could, Clinton realized "that our country was being misled about our progress, or lack of it, in the war."[31] But he was uncomfortable with the tactics and strategy of the antiwar protestors. He grew up in a town steeped in tradition and unquestioned patriotism, yet lived in a rarified world surrounded by critics of American involvement in Vietnam. "Everyone he respected and cared for was dedicating his life to opposing the war, but every value of his community and his family was pulling on the other side," recalled David Mixner, an antiwar activist.[32]

Unlike many young people on the Left, Clinton did not see Vietnam as the reflection of a deep sickness in American society. It was instead a tragic mistake. He was deeply skeptical of the "self-righteous sanctimony on the right or the left."[33] He resented the arrogance and self-righteousness of privileged middle-class students and their shrill attacks on the establishment that he wanted so eagerly to join. By 1966 he identified with the National Student Association (NSA), a mainstream alternative to the more radical SDS. The organization, he recalled, "was full of people like me, who were uncomfortable with the more militant SDS but still wanted to be counted in the ranks of those working to end the war."[34]

The way the two men dealt with the draft reveals a great deal about their relationship to the larger events of the decade. In 1948, Congress enacted a peacetime conscription law that allowed for a number of exemptions. Since draft quotas were low, the selective service classified all registrants as available for immediate induction (I-A), then controlled the size of the I-A pool by liberalizing the rules for exemptions and deferments. Young men could avoid the draft by attending college or graduate school. The most important new development was the expansion of hardship and dependency deferments to include fatherhood. By 1966, hardship, fatherhood, and marriage deferments outnumbered student deferments by almost two to one.

As a result of the patchwork of deferments, young men coming of age in the 1960s faced what Todd Gitlin called "the war dilemma." Whether they joined the military, stayed home, or fled to Canada, they were forced to make painful choices: to be a conscientious objector, to change career or family plans and become eligible for an exception, to join the national guard, to enlist, or to become eligible for the draft. Some went to Vietnam. The majority, however, found some way to avoid the war, either by fleeing the country or, more commonly, by staying in school or making career decisions that would allow them to be eligible for a deferment. Over the course of the war, almost 16 million of the 26.8 million draft-age men avoided military service.

Clinton's dealings with the draft, and his often devious ways of explaining his actions, would haunt him for the rest of his career. He skirted the law in his effort to avoid service even as he professed a desire to serve. While a Rhodes Scholar in England, he received his draft notice on April 30, 1969, and was scheduled to be inducted that summer. He returned home at the end of June and tried getting in the National Guard, but there were no available spots. His eyesight was not good enough for the Air Force, so he decided to enroll in law school at the University of Arkansas and join the Army Reserve Officers' Training Corps (ROTC). He signed a letter of intent, which was enough to get the draft board to waive his induction date. Since it was too late to attend the required ROTC summer camp, Colonel Eugene Holmes agreed to let him return to Oxford for a second year. On December 1, the United States instituted a lottery system. The new system did away with most deferments, and assigned each day of the year with a number for all men born on that day. The lower the number was, the greater the chances of getting drafted. Clinton's birthday, August 19, was assigned number 311, making it unlikely he would be drafted.

Two days later, on December 3, Clinton wrote a long letter to Colonel Holmes thanking him for keeping him out of the draft. The letter provided a window into the tortured mind of a bright and thoughtful young man struggling with the war. He said that he came to despise the war "with a depth of feeling I had reserved solely for racism in America." He said that he had come to the belief that the draft was "illegitimate. No government really rooted in limited, parliamentary democracy should have the power to make its citizens fight and kill and die in a war they may oppose." The draft was necessary in World War II, he argued, "because the life of the people collectively was at stake." That was not the situation in Vietnam, however. He went on to say that the decisions he made about the draft were "the most difficult of my life." He chose the path he did—manipulating, not resisting, the draft—to "maintain my political viability within the system."[35]

His effort to avoid the war was not uncommon for his generation, but Clinton went to great lengths to cover his trail. The details of the story would change over time, but for years Clinton refused to admit that he had ever been drafted, or that he had received a deferment. Not until 1992, during his campaign for president, was he forced to tell the truth. Still, the war remained a source of political and personal pain long after it ended. In his memoirs, he said he had "searched his heart, trying to determine whether my aversion to going was rooted in conviction or cowardice. Given the way it played out," he concluded, "I'm not sure I ever answered the question for myself."[36]

The draft was inciting many in his generation to protest, but Gingrich remained remarkably detached from the war and from the movement to end it. Since he was eligible for an exemption deferment for a 3-A (married-with-children exemption), Gingrich never agonized over the morality of the war or his responsibility to serve in it. According to friends, Gingrich supported the decision to send troops to Vietnam. Over time, as casualties mounted and support at home eroded, he complained about the way the war was being fought, but never wavered in his belief that the war was just. Because the Johnson administration "refused to explain with authority why the war was legitimate," he said, the government "ceded the entire moral debate to those who did not understand why we were doing it." If Johnson had properly explained to the American people why it was necessary to fight in Vietnam, he would have reasserted America's moral authority and waged a war using all the instruments of military power. "We would have won in 18 months," he reflected.[37]

For Gingrich, the war remained largely an abstraction: he read books about it and engaged in discussions and debates about it, but it never directly touched him or influenced decisions he made about his future. The difference between the experiences of the two men could be found in letters they wrote just three months apart. Clinton wrote his famous letter to Colonel Holmes in December 1969 while studying in England. A few hundred miles away, in Belgium, Gingrich was finishing the research for his dissertation. In September, Gingrich wrote a letter to his friend Chip Kahn saying that he was "seriously trying to figure out a way to get more education in management and technology." He hoped that another graduate degree in either business administration or information sciences would "greatly increase my long term market value." He wondered if his desire to get an additional degree was "a conditioned reflex from a graduate student faced with leaving the womb of higher education or if it makes sense in terms of long run income and promotability."[38]

Most members of his generation needed to factor Vietnam into the equation about their "long-term market value," or, in the case of Bill Clinton, in considering their "political viability." For Clinton and millions of others, Vietnam was a burden they would have to carry with them, whether they fought or not. Although the methods he used to avoid service were devious, Clinton opposed the war on moral grounds and struggled with his decision. Gingrich, who supported the war and considered himself a foreign policy hawk, never considered going to war as an option. Gingrich experienced the war largely as an abstraction. For Clinton, who invested an enormous amount of emotional energy into avoiding the draft, the experience became a part of the fabric of his identity. Their experiences with the draft mirrored their relationship with the decade itself: Clinton felt a deep personal connection to the events of the decade and he would spend much of his life trying to heal the divisions forged over race and the war. Because Gingrich never developed a deep emotional attachment, his impressions and views were more malleable, more open to revision later in life.

The nation, however, could not escape the reality of the war. Vietnam became a looking glass in which the nation saw itself. It was not an appealing sight. By the beginning of 1968, the American troop commitment had reached nearly 500,000. American planes had dropped more than a million and a half tons of bombs. But the war remained deadlocked. More than 16,000 U.S. soldiers had lost their lives, with more than 10,000 killed in the previous twelve months. Johnson's credibility received a crowning blow on January 31, 1968, when communist troops launched an offensive during Tet, the lunar New Year. The Vietcong invaded the U.S. embassy compound in Saigon and waged bloody battles in the capitals of most of South Vietnam's provinces. The U.S. forces scored a decisive military victory in the field, but the television images seemed to contradict the administration's optimistic statements that the war was coming to an end. After Tet, polls for the first time showed that a majority of Americans opposed the war. It provided fuel for the long-shot candidacy of Senator Eugene McCarthy, who challenged President Johnson in the Democratic primaries.

The traumatic events that followed—the assassinations of Martin Luther King and Robert Kennedy, the violence that engulfed the Democratic Convention, and, finally, the election of Richard Nixon in November—left liberals angry and demoralized. A dispirited Bill Clinton watched the 1968 Democratic Convention on television from a hotel room in Shreveport, Louisiana. The man with an instinctive feel for the center watched as the middle ground disappeared and forces pulled the nation, and his party, in opposite directions. "I understood how both sides felt," he wrote later. "I was against the war and the police brutality, but growing up in Arkansas had given me an appreciation for the struggles of ordinary people who do their duty every day, and a deep skepticism about self-righteous sanctimony on the right or the left."[39] He understood the significance of the events of that year, referring to 1968 as "the year that broke open the nation and shattered the Democratic party; the year that conservative populism replaced progressive populism as the dominant political force in our nation; the year that law and order and strength became the province of Republicans, and Democrats became associated with chaos, weakness, and out-of-touch, self-indulgent elites. . . ."[40]

The events of the 1960s affected Clinton and Gingrich in different ways, but they left both men, and many members of the '60s generation, with a greater willingness to question authority. "I was more skeptical of authority" after the 1960s, Gingrich reflected, "because I had seen it fail." He also learned a valuable lesson from observing from the sidelines how the Left shaped the political debate. The 1960s, he said, "made me aware of the importance of cultural politics and aware of the importance of authority rather than power."[41] The realization that the "wise men" whom he admired and hoped to emulate could be so disastrously wrong on an issue as important as Vietnam also disabused Bill Clinton of much of his youthful innocence. He learned that well-intentioned people could produce bad policy, and that there were limits to the public's willingness to embrace change and reform. It was a painful lesson he would learn many times in the years ahead.

―――

By the early 1970s the cultural battle lines in America began to harden. The 1960s had shaken the political foundation, raised a new set of issues, and exposed old fissures. Most important, the decade gave birth to a new language of cultural populism that would transform the political universe, adding to the polarization of American politics. The populist tradition possessed an innate faith in the wisdom of the "common man" and a simplistic belief that elites and selfish interests were often responsible for thwarting the "will of the people." Since the days of the New Deal, Democrats had used the language of economic populism to cement the loyalties of the white middle class. As late as the 1960s, they were still running against the memory of Herbert Hoover and the Great Depression, reminding voters that the Republicans were the party of "Hoover boom and Hoover bust," while the Democratic party, the home of Franklin Roosevelt and Harry Truman, was responsible for lifting millions of Americans out of poverty and into the ranks of the middle class.

Social unrest in the 1960s provided Republicans with a powerful alternative lexicon that depicted the Democrats as the party of cultural elites who were out of touch with the mainstream values of average Americans. Richard Nixon managed to sustain support for the war by tapping into the deep class resentments that shaped attitudes toward the war, and toward antiwar protestors. By 1969 many Americans—even those who opposed the war—were convinced that a willful minority of violent youth, militant blacks, and arrogant intellectuals had seized control of the public debate, showing contempt for mainstream values and threatening social stability. *Newsweek* noted in a special October 1969 issue, entitled "The Troubled American," that "the average American is more deeply troubled" about the direction the nation was headed "than at any time since the Great Depression." Nixon appealed to his treasured "silent majority" by playing on public fear of urban violence and social disorder. The party of FDR, he told wavering Democrats, had been hijacked by antiwar protestors and New Left radicals. "The time has come," Nixon declared in a campaign speech, "to draw the line, . . . for the Great Silent Majority . . . to stand up and be counted against the appeasement of the rock-throwers and the obscenity shouters in America."

By 1969, Nixon had exploited with brilliant efficiency the growing cultural divisions in America. Although Gingrich would use the same politics of polarization to help Republicans gain control of Congress, in the early 1970s he was still searching for a way to heal the divisions and forge common ground. In his application for a professorship at West Georgia College in 1970, he described himself as "a critical progressive seeking reform rather than a new leftist advocating radical change."[42] He was an innovative and popular teacher who set up a special interdisciplinary program in environmental studies. It was also during these years that he immersed himself in the works of futurist Alvin Toffler and management guru Peter Drucker, who convinced him that America was in the midst of a transformation to a new information age. Old political arrangements were becoming obsolete. Neither traditional liberal nor conservative approaches would suffice: political leaders needed to develop new strategies and new answers. Gingrich's fascination with new-age thinkers underscored just one of the many dimensions of his complicated, sometimes contradictory thinking. He was a historian who was interested in the future, not the past; a scholar who wanted to be a politician; a progressive who considered himself a Republican; the rebel who wanted to be accepted by the establishment.

In a series of campus talks he gave at Tulane and West Georgia College in 1969 and 1970, Gingrich spelled out his philosophy. Because students were his audience, he often appealed to their sentiments and seemed sympathetic to their critiques. In later years he would describe the student revolt in harsh terms, but at the time he suggested that protestors posed legitimate questions that needed to be addressed. The student rebellion, he argued, exposed the soft underbelly of American colleges and universities. Colleges, he wrote, "taught students to question all authority—political, parental, ecclesiastical—but demands child-like reverence for itself." Universities were incapable of providing answers "to the most fundamental questions students are asking," because the issues they raised threatened the "comfort of an educational bureaucracy far more irresponsible, inefficient, and arbitrary than the most incompetent government agency." He disagreed that protests were simply "a political tool to win concessions." Instead, they were "often desperate, sometimes misdirected, attempts to find meaning in an increasingly irrelevant university system." They were "symptoms of a deeper malaise."[43]

Nixon had turned the "silent majority" against the young, but Gingrich still sided with the youthful challenge to authority and placed much of the blame for the public distemper on outdated institutions that had failed to respond to their legitimate concerns. The nation, he said in words that Jimmy Carter would echo later, was experiencing "a crisis of confidence in American institutions." He called for a "new morality" that required the nation to "heed the cries of that 11% of our population which is Black," at the same time that it does not ignore "that 13% of our population which is White and voted for [George] Wallace." "We must coexist with totalitarian government in the name of human survival. But in the name of human dignity we must object to totalitarianism and seek its decline. We must love this country as the greatest in history, the one which has given man more dignity, more freedom, and more opportunity than any other. Yet our love must be so great that we admit our flaws and seek to meet the future as successfully as we have met the past."[44]

There was nothing in his message that Bill Clinton would have disagreed with. By the end of the decade, frustration with the war pushed Bill Clinton closer to the Left at just the time that the Left was falling apart, but he remained comfortably cloistered in the mainstream of American politics. After writing his letter to Colonel Holmes, Clinton spent his Christmas vacation traveling through Europe on a five-week train tour that included extended stops in Oslo, Helsinki, Moscow, Prague, and Munich. His trip was his farewell to Europe, because that spring he packed his bags and returned to the United States to enroll at the Yale Law School. While traveling in Helsinki, Clinton contacted a former classmate from Georgetown, who had not seen him since graduation. "He had a beard and curly long hair," his friend observed. "He looked quite different from Mr. Cleancut America."[45] By the time he returned home in the summer of 1970, Clinton was an antiwar activist. He spent that summer in Washington, mobilizing support for a congressional resolution to bring about an end to the war.

While enrolled at Yale, Clinton spent much of his time working for the antiwar Senate candidacy of Joseph Duffy. It was during his work on this campaign, and later as a Texas organizer for presidential candidate George McGovern, that Clinton came face to face with the cultural divide that would shape his life in politics. He watched as conservatives turned Joseph Duffy, "a coal miner's son," into "a weak, ultra-liberal elitist," and George McGovern, "a genuine war hero," into "a spineless, wild-eyed leftist." Construction workers would greet Duffy on the campaign trail with signs reading "SDS, Pot and Duffy Go Together" and "A Vote for Duffy is a Vote for Khrushchev." Watching the white working class flood out of the party made him appreciate that "the Democratic party was headed for minority status" if it did not find a way to get these people back into the fold. The experience taught Clinton a lesson—one that he would be forced to learn over and over again. "Our society," he discovered, "can absorb only so much change at a time," and those who advocate reform must reaffirm core values of "opportunity and responsibility, work and family, strength and compassion."[46]

The divisions in America were growing wider and hardening, but as late as 1974, as Clinton and Gingrich launched their political careers, there were more similarities than differences in their lives and worldviews. They stood on opposite sides of the Vietnam debate, but they both managed to maintain a healthy distance from the war itself. One was a Republican, the other a Democrat, but neither was entirely comfortable with the direction in which their parties were moving. They both positioned themselves as alternatives to radicalism, and believed in achieving change from within the system. They resented the arrogance of the Left and the stale conformity of the Right.

They saw politics as a clash of ideas, not just a battle over turf. While they may have staked out different positions on many issues, they shared an optimistic, forward-looking temperament that emphasized the need for change. At heart, they viewed themselves as reformers. Their paths never crossed, but if they had, it is likely they would have agreed on more than they disagreed on, and, by all accounts, they would have spent endless hours discussing both. Over time, however, they would emerge as leaders of cultural armies fighting over the legacy of the decade.

CHAPTER THREE | Paths to Power

EARLY ON A cold Monday morning in January 1974, Bill Clinton stood in front of a small crowd of family and friends at the Avanelle Motor Lodge in Hot Springs, Arkansas, and announced his candidacy for Congress. Ignoring his potential primary challengers, Clinton launched into an assault on the incumbent Republican opponent, tying him to the misdeeds of the Nixon White House and the developing Watergate scandal. "Of all the men in Congress, he is one of those who has allowed the President to go as far as he has," Clinton told the appreciative crowd. A few months later, in April, Newt Gingrich gathered a dedicated group of supporters on a rainy Georgia night at his Watson Street headquarters in Carrollton, Georgia, to announce that he was also running for Congress. Calling himself a "common sense conservative," he attacked the "political hacks" who did not "understand what is happening to the people they supposedly represent."[1]

It is revealing that Bill Clinton and Newt Gingrich ran for elective office for the first time in 1974. It was the year that Watergate shook the political establishment, when public distrust of Washington, along with anger with the rising price of gasoline, was running high. With the public growing increasingly cynical of politicians, they presented themselves as outsiders fighting against entrenched special interests. Both men were products of the new social and demographic realities of post-1960 politics. They hailed from the South, reflecting how both wealth and power had shifted from the rust belt to the sunbelt. They earned reputations early on as brilliant political strategists who were fascinated by ideas and willing to challenge the conventional wisdom. "We were both overgrown graduate students," Gingrich admitted.[2] They employed a media-savvy style of politics to lead a generational assault against the entrenched leadership of their respective parties. In Arkansas, the press described the young men and women who participated in Clinton's assault on the old liberal order as the "diaper brigade." In Georgia, reporters wrote about the "young turks" who joined Gingrich's challenge to the Republican establishment.

In their initial campaigns for office in the 1970s, Clinton and Gingrich spoke a common language of populist discontent. In fact, reading their speeches, it is hard to tell them apart. Both focused their attacks on entrenched bureaucracy and greedy special interests while appealing to the economic frustration of the struggling middle class. The "only difference between Democrats and Republicans," Gingrich told audiences, was that "Republican presidents favor big business while Democratic presidents favor big labor." "The American middle class is under siege," he said at numerous campaign stops. "Every year the Congress passes more and more legislation that discriminates against the middle class."[3] Clinton sounded similar populist themes, attacking the "huge, unmanageable bureaucracies" of big business that are "making a killing on this inflation." If Congress and the president did not act quickly and decisively, he warned, "our private economy as well as our government will be dominated soon by large and distant bureaucracy."[4]

A unique set of historic circumstances forged a temporary truce in the emerging culture war over the legacy of the 1960s. Anger over the Watergate affair focused public wrath at the White House, allowing politicians of both parties to campaign as antiestablishment candidates determined to uproot corruption in Washington. In 1974, Richard Nixon replaced hippies and student protestors as the target of populist discontent. The Vietnam War, a driving force in feeding the cultural resentments, was winding down and the nation was not emotionally ready for the debate over who "lost Vietnam." Most importantly, polls showed that economic issues were once again at the forefront of the public's mind, temporarily muting cultural anxieties. Inflation, which never exceeded 5 percent between 1955 and 1972, and was often as low as 2 or 3 percent, suddenly exploded to nearly 10 percent by the end of 1973. In 1974 retail prices increased by 11 percent and wholesale prices by 18 percent. "During the 1960s, we fought the pigs," declared former Students for Democratic Society (SDS) founder Tom Hayden. "Now we fight the high price of bacon."

Despite their similar messages in 1974, clear differences in style and substance would soon emerge. As a Republican running for office in the overwhelmingly Democratic state of Georgia, Gingrich believed he needed to polarize voters to shake up traditional loyalties and gain media attention. Gingrich believed that the Democratic Party had created a great opportunity for Republicans to exploit by nominating Hubert Humphrey in 1968 and George McGovern in 1972. The key to Republican success lay in tapping into voter anxiety that the Democratic Party had lost touch with the values of middle-class voters. Gingrich needed to revitalize and redefine the language of cultural populism that worked so well for Nixon on the national level. The situation was complicated in Georgia, where whites were increasingly alienated from a party they believed had moved to the left on most issues, notably race, and had expressed their discontent by voting Republican in presidential elections. They remained loyal to Democrats on the local and state level, however. He needed to find a message and a strategy that would break through, challenge entrenched political loyalties, and create a new image for the Republican Party. As a first step, however, he had to even the playing field by undermining the moral authority and political credibility of his opponent.

In 1974 and 1976, Gingrich ran against Jack Flynt, an old-school segregationist and a product of the Georgia Democratic establishment. He had signed the Southern Manifesto in protest of the Supreme Court's *Brown v. Board* decision, and he had opposed both the Civil Rights Act of 1964 and the Voting Rights Act of 1965. At the time, there were no Republicans in Congress from Georgia, and most observers felt that Flynt's seat was safe. Polls showed that Democrats made up half of voters. Only 10 percent were registered Republican, with the remainder calling themselves independent.[5] "The idea that a guy named Gingrich, with a high voice, with no personal money, who wasn't even a southerner, could take down such a powerful figure and get elected to Congress was unthinkable to most people," reflected Chip Kahn, who managed the campaign.[6] After interviewing "Dr. Gingrich," a staff member at the Republican National Committee recommended that the party not provide the novice candidate with financial support. "I was very much impressed with him as an individual; however, as a candidate I would rate him as fair at this time," he wrote. "It appeared to me that he was not as aggressive or forceful as he should be to make a good candidate. He spoke in a very low voice, barely audible, perhaps he would need some training for political speaking."[7]

Gingrich, however, was looking ahead and understood how the political terrain in the South was shifting away from the Democrats. Since he was running against a conservative, Gingrich attacked from the Left. "He was the progressive, forward-thinking reformer running against an old style conservative Democrat," recalled Ann Woolner, a local reporter for the *Atlanta Constitution,* which endorsed Gingrich in his effort to unseat Flynt.[8] In 1974, a campaign staff member reported that many Republicans were reluctant to support Gingrich because "they prefer a known conservative Democrat to a possible liberal unknown Republican."[9] Throughout the South, Republicans discovered that the easiest way to peel disaffected whites away from Democrats was to play the "race card." Gingrich moved in the opposite direction: he wanted to win over blacks who were dissatisfied with Flynt. Instead of the race card, he played the "ethics card" in his effort to reach suburban white voters. He dismissed Flynt as an "absentee landowner who comes home to check the vineyards every two years, at election time."[10] He criticized Flynt for leasing land that he owned to Ford Motor Company, claiming that the cozy business arrangement influenced Flynt's decision to support looser government regulations on automobile emissions.[11] He avoided referring to himself as a Republican, and often claimed he was a "common sense conservative" concerned about overspending in Washington, while railing against "stupidity," "incompetency," and "indifference" in Washington. "The politicians have had their chance," he declared, "and now it is time the people had theirs."[12]

Despite the poor impression he made in his interview with the Republican Campaign Committee, Gingrich emerged during the campaign as a powerful speaker who impressed audiences with his ability to recite specific facts at the same time that he talked about the grand sweep of history. "I was always amazed by his ability to get up in front of any group and just have them enthralled," Kahn said.[13] One observer said of Gingrich's performance in the only televised debate that he was the perfect media candidate: "His hair and dress were immaculate. His debating style was Kennedyesque—the jabbing fingers, the use of statistics, the quickness at parry and thrust."[14] Flynt was late in realizing the threat Gingrich posed, but in the final weeks stepped up his attacks on the "liberal college professor."[15]

Even with Watergate dragging down Republican candidates across the country in 1974, Gingrich managed to secure more than 48 percent of the vote in what had been considered a secure Democratic district. What was most surprising to him was that black voters supported a segregationist Democrat over a pro–civil rights Republican. The experience taught Gingrich a clear lesson: he could win election in the solid Democratic South only if he developed a "scorched earth" style that would shake up traditional—and now largely obsolete—alliances between Georgia voters and the Democratic Party. Democrats crossed over in presidential elections because they saw a clear ideological difference between the parties. Local elections were still about personality, patronage, and potholes. Gingrich, who claimed to have shaken 60,000 hands and made 139 speeches, felt he lost because of traditional Democratic loyalties. "If it had not been for the voters [*sic*] ability to vote straight tickets, I would have beaten him by 40 percent. In a sense the voters were voting for the Democratic nominee, not John Flynt." On election night, Gingrich conceded defeat and announced that he would be running again in 1976. "I am not inclined to run out of ambition," he said.[16]

In 1975, as the campaign prepared for a rematch with Flynt, staff members took inventory of the candidate's strengths and weaknesses. His major liability, they concluded, was that he was a Republican who was viewed by many as a "liberal" college professor with a "Yankee name and accent." On the positive side, he had gathered around him a "band of intelligent, committed" leaders, and had gained "pretty good name recognition" and respectable "media support." Perhaps most valuable was that his "personal philosophy" was "close to the reform-populist-conservative mood of the vast majority of the district."[17] Not surprisingly, he hit hard on the populist theme. "Those of us who work for a living are being discriminated against," he said in announcing his candidacy. "The tax laws favor the rich. The welfare laws favor the poor. The courts favor the criminal over the victim. Bureaucrats order us around while we foot the bill." He realized that populism alone was not going to break up the Democratic establishment in Georgia. "He wasn't just arguing for change," recalled Kahn, "He wanted to make Flynt into a corrupt figure."[18]

His strategy was not just to win elections on debating points, but to destroy his opponent's credibility. He followed the advice of strategist Lee Atwater. "Republicans in the South could not win elections by talking about issues," he said. "You had to make the case that the other candidate was a bad guy." He once again raised the issue of the land Flynt leased to the Ford Motor Company, charging that the financial relationship influenced the congressman's decision to oppose the Clean Air Act. He also attacked him as a "do-nothing" chairman of the House Ethics Committee. "There are criminals in Congress, and Jack Flynt's committee has been protecting them for the two years he has been chairman," he said. "The record of scandal and coverup cannot be defended." Although he placed most of the blame on Democrats in Congress, he charged that Republicans lacked "the courage, the intelligence, and the charisma to lead us out of the wilderness of misgovernment."[19]

In 1976, Gingrich was running for office just one year after U.S. helicopters lifted from the roof of the American embassy in Saigon, marking the chaotic withdrawal from a tragic war. Hawks stressed that the war could have

Newt Gingrich is pictured here during his unsuccessful 1974 campaign for Congress. (Chip Kahn.)

been won if the politicians had been courageous enough to stand up to the peace movement and bold enough to give the military the resources it needed for victory. Although Gingrich would later claim to share that view, he carried a different message on the campaign trail, where he told audiences that the war had been a mistake and the United States needed to recognize the limits of its military power. "We cannot be the world's policeman," he said. "Neither can we be its nurse." Instead, the nation "should revert to the American Revolutionary war flag which showed a snake and the title 'don't tread on me.' Our policy should be one of not attacking others and being strong enough to ensure that they wouldn't dare attack us."[20] The press responded to his energy, his intelligence, and his calls for reform. Newt was, recalled Steely, "something of a darling of the press." The *Atlanta Journal* described Gingrich as "middle of the road, young and candid."[21]

But fate was against him in that race. A peanut farmer from Plains, Georgia, named Jimmy Carter, was heading the Democratic ticket that year, attracting local Democrats to the polls. The Carter tide helped carry Flynt

THIS IS
NEWT GINGRICH...

Newt Gingrich is 31 years old and lives in a small home in Carrollton with his wife Jackie and their two daughters, Kathy and Jackie Sue. The family are all active members of the First Baptist Church in Carrollton where Newt is a Deacon. Newt is also a member of the Carrollton Kiwanis Club. The son of a career officer in the United States Army, Newt lived in several states and in Europe before settling in Columbus, Georgia. He attended Columbus College, Emory University, Georgia State University, and Tulane University where he received his Doctorate in Modern European History. He has been active in political affairs for 15 years, as a volunteer worker, campaign organizer, and party official. He has taken leave from his job as a history teacher at West Georgia College to run this important congressional race. On announcing his candidacy, he said: "As a father I am fearful for my children's future and of the problems they will face if this country continues to decay. As a citizen, I am fearful for this country as it enters a rapidly changing world with leaders who do not understand the nature of those changes. I am undertaking what promises to be an uphill fight because I can no longer sit idly by while my future . . . and the future of this country . . . are endangered by political hacks who are betraying us through their incompetence and their indifference."

Newt Gingrich is a family man with a home in Carrollton and a basic interest in the needs and the future of the 6th District.

In all of his campaigns, Newt Gingrich went out of his way to reassure conservative voters that he was a good family man, as can be seen in this flier from one of his early campaigns. (Chip Kahn.)

over the victory line on election day with 51.7 percent of the vote to Newt's 48.3 percent. Ironically, it was black voters who represented Flynt's margin of victory. The *Atlanta Constitution*'s headline read: "Blacks Gave Flynt Victory," observing that it was "ironic because he had opposed voting rights legislation throughout his career."[22] Turnout in the heavily black areas was 68 percent over 1974, and 86 percent of them voted for the segregationist Democrat. Gingrich scored his strongest support from suburban areas, which made up 66.9 percent of his overall vote, while his lowest totals came from rural districts.[23] Fortunately for him, the suburban areas were the ones experiencing the largest increase in population.[24]

Flynt, who suffered a mild heart attack in the final days of the 1976 campaign, was not prepared for another arduous campaign against Gingrich in 1978. He announced his retirement, giving Gingrich the opportunity to compete for the open seat in 1978 against Virginia Shapard, a liberal state senator with textile money. Gingrich continued preaching a message of economic populism. "The central theme of the Newt Gingrich campaign is protecting your paycheck and my paycheck," he said in his announcement speech. "I ask you the voters, to give me a chance to fight for you and your children. We need a fighter in Washington. We need someone who understands the pain of inflation and the threat of unemployment."[25]

There was, however, a significant shift in Gingrich's tone and message in 1978. In his past two unsuccessful campaigns for office, Gingrich had avoided labeling himself as a Republican. He used his support for civil rights and the environment, along with his crusade for ethics reform, to win over traditionally liberal voters clustered around West Georgia College, while utilizing his populist message to attract conservative support. Since he was trying to appeal across the political spectrum, Gingrich would send his campaign manager, Chip Kahn, to secure the endorsement of both liberal and conservative groups. "I was talking out both sides of my mouth," recalled Kahn.[26] In 1978, Gingrich reluctantly realized that as a Republican he had no chance of winning liberal support in a race against Shapard, so he moved sharply to the right. His attacks became sharper, more personal. He charged Shapard, "a former welfare worker," with sidetracking a welfare reform bill to stop "cheaters." "If you like welfare cheaters, you'll love Virginia Shapard," one ad declared. Gingrich caught the attention of the White House, which viewed the seat as vulnerable. A campaign consultant warned cryptically: "Repubs have a good cand.—could easily pick up seat."[27]

The *Atlanta Constitution,* which had endorsed Gingrich in his first two losing campaigns for Congress, endorsed his opponent in 1978, claiming that his campaign had "gone beyond vigor and into demagoguery and plain lying." The editors said they had supported him in the past, because "we believed he would bring a needed freshness and imagination to the job. His imagination, however, seems to be running away with him in this election year."[28] His staff had similar worries, fearing that his angry attacks would undermine his candidacy. "The biggest problem with the candidate is his arrogance and his mouth," they noted at a steering committee. "He *must* convey to the voters the idea that he is their servant and not someone who is better and smarter than they are and thus is God-ordained to be their congressman."[29] They tried to compensate, by surrounding him with his loving and supportive family, using soft background music to lighten the tone. "We worked the opposite way right from the beginning," said Mel Steely. "The [radio spots] we used had nice little guitar music in the background— soothing, soft, quiet stuff." They told him not to attack, "although Newt's natural style *is* to attack."[30]

Gingrich went out of his way to present himself as a reassuring symbol of traditional values. His campaign fliers always pictured him with his family. "America needs a return to moral values," they proclaimed. He suggested that his opponent was a bad parent because she planned, if elected, to commute between Washington and her family. In campaign literature, he featured a smiling picture of his wife, Jackie, and their two daughters. "Newt's family is like your family," one flier declared.[31] "He had two pretty young girls and he and Jackie held hands everywhere they went and that was impressive to people in a community like Carrollton even in the 1970s," said a local minister.[32] The reality was much different, however. During his first campaign for office in 1974, Gingrich had an affair with a young staffer. "The 1974 campaign had placed a tremendous strain on his marriage," noted Steely.[33] The marriage never fully recovered. There were rumors of other affairs as well, but Gingrich understood the value of presenting a pleasing image of traditional values.

In addition to the stylistic changes, Gingrich added a new ideological weapon to his arsenal—support for the Kemp-Roth Tax Bill. The 1970s witnessed the emergence of a powerful antitax groundswell. "You are the people," declared Howard Jarvis, the seventy-five-year-old leader of the crusade for California's antitax Proposition 13 in 1978, "and you will have to take control of the government again or else it is going to control you." Between 1960 and 1980, federal, state, and local taxes increased from less than 24 percent to more than 30 percent of the gross national product. The burden often fell heaviest on traditional Democratic constituencies— working-class families and elderly people on fixed incomes. While taxes kept rising, Americans were losing faith in government and the way it spent tax dollars. Many Democrats registered their discontent at the polls. Proposition 13, a referendum that voters approved by a 2–1 margin, reduced assessments, limited property taxes to 1 percent of full value, and prevented the easy passage of new taxes. "This isn't just a tax revolt," insisted President Carter's pollster, Pat Caddell. "It's a revolution against government." The success in California emboldened tax reformers in other parts of the country. A dozen states followed California's lead, though most chose more moderate measures. Only two states—Idaho and Nevada—passed Prop 13 look-alikes.

Sponsored by New York Congressman Jack Kemp and Delaware Senator William Roth, the legislation called for a slashing of federal income taxes by one-third. The idea was the brainchild of economist Arthur Laffer, who argued that hefty cuts in corporate and personal tax rates would stimulate investment and encourage production and consumption. By lowering taxes on the wealthiest Americans, the government would provide an incentive for them to reinvest, creating new business and more jobs. According to a staff member, "the Kemp-Roth issue changed the dynamics of the campaign in 1978." Gingrich bragged that it "exceeds anything I have seen in 18 years of politics and 5 years campaigning in its potential to create a conservative majority in this country." Support for tax cuts would become the central pillar of Gingrich's approach to government and a major ideological weapon against the Democrats. Not only did it make his populist message more potent by allowing him to offer an alternative, but it also allowed him to have the best of both worlds. He could campaign as a tax-cutting reformer while also promising to protect popular government entitlements such as social security. Tax cuts carried a double-barreled populist message: it underscored that individuals could decide for themselves how to spend their own money, and it was a way to punish the Washington bureaucracy by denying it the money it craved. There was another advantage: it allowed Gingrich to present a clear, if simplified, picture of the future. It sharpened his ideological edge at the same time that it softened his image. "He made Kemp-Roth the answer to welfare, farm problems, tax loopholes, and high unemployment," recalled an aide.[34]

His tough tactics and solidly conservative message alienated liberals and many in the media, but they earned him a victory on election night. After falling short in his first two attempts, Gingrich won the election by 50,000 votes. Nationally, Republicans scored well campaigning on a platform of lower taxes and less spending. The GOP made modest inroads into the Democratic majorities swollen by Watergate, gaining three Senate and twelve House seats. More Republican freshmen were elected to the House in 1978 than in 1974 and 1976 combined. There was a growing sense that

Republicans had turned the corner on Watergate and were now prepared to seize the offensive in Washington. The young college professor from Georgia planned to lead the attack.

_____

While Gingrich was trying to tear apart the Democratic coalition in Georgia, Clinton was struggling to mend it in Arkansas. Instead of polarizing voters, Clinton used his youth and personal charm to romance them. One Arkansas newspaper called him "a living monument to the god 'Charisma.'"[35] "He became everybody's darling," observed John Starr, editor of the *Arkansas Democrat*. Like many southern Democrats in the 1970s, Clinton emphasized the healing power of economic growth and avoided divisive questions of race. "If the symbol of the old Arkansas was a 'whites only' sign, the symbol of the new Arkansas is a dollar sign," observed the *New York Times*.[36]

The key in Arkansas, still an overwhelmingly Democratic state, was to win over disaffected suburban whites while retaining the support of traditional Democrats, especially African Americans and organized labor. In 1974 Clinton took a leave of absence from his law school job and announced he was running for Arkansas's third congressional district seat, which was then occupied by a popular Republican, John Paul Hammerschmidt, who had not faced a serious Democratic opponent since 1966. It was the only hotly contested race in an overwhelmingly Democratic state. Clinton, noted the *Northwest Arkansas Times,* "is an attractive young man with the populist leanings of the 'new' Democratic Party in the South." It also pointed out that his degrees from Georgetown and Yale "aren't necessarily assets when it comes to winning voters in several of Northern Arkansas' least sophisticated counties."[37]

Before he could challenge the incumbent, he needed to win the May Democratic primary against two other candidates, and later a runoff against state Senator Gene Rainwater. Clinton started with 12 percent name recognition and almost no money, but he won both contests. Within a matter of months, he was considered the frontrunner, if, as the *Northwest Arkansas Times* observed, "being the focus of criticism of foes is a valid measurement."[38] His opponents complained that he was too young and inexperienced, and that as a former McGovern campaign worker, he was also too liberal for the conservative district. The charges did little to slow down Clinton's momentum. He worked harder and overtook them using his knowledge, empathy, and skill. The state American Federation of Labor and Congress of Industrial Organizations (AFL-CIO) had been prepared to endorse one of his opponents, but after an inspiring meeting with Clinton, switched sides. "Bill's knowledge and facility with words made our people fall in love with him," said one labor leader.[39]

Clinton's knowledge of the issues and his ability to connect with voters even impressed conservatives who were initially put off by his youthful demeanor. In March, Clinton, wearing a brown tweed jacket and his characteristic bushy hair and sideburns, was campaigning in a drug store in rural Arkansas when he was introduced to a car dealer and former legislator named Hugh Hackler, who told Clinton he was already committed to another candidate. After fifteen minutes, Clinton got him to switch his vote. "That's the kind of effect a hippie-looking, freshman-looking guy had on a 65-year-old-businessman," recalled a campaign worker who witnessed the exchange. "That's how effective he is at talking to people. I've always felt that if he could talk to every voter for 15 or 20 minutes, then two-thirds of them would vote for him."[40]

With the nation mesmerized by the unfolding Watergate scandal, Clinton attacked his Republican opponent by tying him to the unpopular Nixon. He denounced Hammerschmidt as "one of the strongest supporters of, and apologists for, the abuse of presidential power and policies that have wrecked the economy."[41] Nixon's resignation on August 8, and the elevation of the amiable Gerald Ford to the presidency, took some of the steam out of Clinton's campaign. "My campaign had been gaining momentum," he wrote in his memoirs, "but with the albatross of Nixon lifted from Hammerschmidt's shoulders, you could feel the air go out of it."[42] On September 8, Ford revived the Watergate issue when he issued Nixon "a full, free, and absolute pardon . . . for all his offenses against the United States." Clinton attacked the pardon, claiming it weakened "the people's faith in the fair operation of our legal system." But it also gave him some political traction. "We were back in business," he reflected.[43] By early October, a poll showed Clinton trailing his opponent by a narrow margin, 43.3 to 38.1 percent, with 18.6 percent undecided.

Initially, Hammerschmidt had ignored the young, inexperienced challenger, but with polls showing the race tightening, he responded with blistering attacks on Clinton's "radical, left-wing philosophy." He claimed that Clinton was a captive to liberal special interests, especially organized labor, and that he was far to the left of most voters in the district, using Clinton's work on the 1972 McGovern campaign as evidence. In addition to having to deal with public anger over Watergate and Ford's pardon of Nixon, Hammerschmidt confronted a deteriorating economy and a strong anti-incumbent backlash. In October, the government reported that prices had increased 12.1 percent over the previous year, the steepest increase since 1947. President Ford rejected Democratic calls for wage and price controls and instead announced a voluntary campaign to "whip inflation now" (WIN),

In the 1980s, Bill Clinton would lead a centrist revolt against the liberal wing of the Democratic Party. For many conservative voters, however, he could never shed his image as a child of the 1960s. Here he is pictured with long hair and a beard at Yale with Hillary Rodham. (William J. Clinton Presidential Library.)

which failed to slow the pace of rising prices or stop the unemployment rate from creeping upward.

The struggling economy provided Clinton with the opportunity to escalate his populist attacks in the final days of the campaign. The central theme of his campaign, he said, was "the failure of Congress as a whole to solve the economic problems of this country and especially the inability to change federal government policies which are hurting the people of this

In 1972 Clinton campaigned for antiwar candidate George McGovern. (Photo by David P. Garland. William J. Clinton Presidential Library.)

district—the small farmer, the small business people, retired people and wage earners." He claimed that his opponent "is one of those most responsible for the fact that we have inflation and recession in this country."[44] Hammerschmidt, he declared, "seems to be following the old administration policy of WIN buttons for the average citizen and windfalls for the oil companies, shipbuilders, and international grain dealers."[45] While he spent much of the campaign attacking his opponent's record and tapping into the anti-incumbent sentiment, Clinton also put forth a few positive proposals. He called for a more progressive tax structure, a national health insurance program, incentives for energy conservation and solar power, and more funding for education.

On election day, Clinton lost by 6,000 of the 172,000 votes cast, 52 to 48 percent. Clinton actually won more counties, but his opponent carried the more populated Fort Smith area. Clinton did better than any previous opponent. "I felt lucky to survive," Hammerschmidt later said.[46] Clinton's strong showing boosted his recognition in the state and made him "the darling of the Democratic party." Ernest Dumas, an editorial writer for the *Arkansas Gazette,* described Clinton as "the boy wonder that year," who almost beat an unbeatable candidate. "That's what we all wrote about—Bill

Clinton, here's the man to watch, the rising star."[47] Clinton believed that he had won by losing. "We accomplished a miracle out here," he told his staff. "We started with no name recognition and look what we accomplished. We scared the pants off that guy."[48] His first experience running for elective office also taught him a lesson that would be reinforced over the years. He "saw firsthand, in thousands of encounters, that middle-class voters would support government activism to solve their problems, and those of the poor, but only if the effort was made with due care for their tax dollars, and if efforts to increase opportunity were coupled with an insistence on responsibility."[49]

Realizing that he could not beat Hammerschmidt in a rerun, Clinton declared his candidacy in 1976 for state attorney general. "The office of attorney general would allow you to work on consumer affairs, white collar crime, energy matters and other issues of interest," a campaign aide wrote him. "It would also provide a proving ground for the future by giving you the experience in government that some people in 1974 said you lacked."[50] Clinton took an unpaid leave from his job at the law school to campaign full time. He ran on a populist platform that called for consumer protection and a tough stance on law and order. He promised to work for mandatory sentences for certain crimes, legislation to compensate the victims of crime, and increased support for police and other law enforcement agencies.[51] To underscore that he would be tough on crime, he stressed his support for the death penalty when it was "fairly applied." "I don't think the death penalty is categorically unconstitutional," he told a local audience in West Memphis, Arkansas.[52]

In a surprising move, he refused to sign a petition sponsored by the local AFL-CIO that called for the abolition of the state's right-to-work laws, which prevented unions from making membership a condition of employment. Although he lost labor's endorsement, he overwhelmed his opponents by his sheer desire and organization. He visited every courthouse in the state and he had legions of former law students working around the state. He easily won the primary by a thirty-point margin. Since there was no Republican opposition, which was not uncommon in still heavily Democratic Arkansas, he was assured of victory in the fall election. With his election guaranteed, Clinton spent most of the fall working on the successful presidential campaign of another southerner, Jimmy Carter. The close public connection he forged with Carter would later come back to haunt him.

Clinton never considered the attorney general office anything more than a brief stop on the road. "It was accepted that Clinton, when he arrived in Little Rock, was the governor-in-waiting," observed biographer David Maraniss.[53]

In March 1978, he announced his candidacy for governor from the front lawn of the old state house, promising voters better jobs, incomes, and schools. The *Arkansas Gazette* called him "the only truly distinguished figure" in the race. He finished first in a five-man primary, garnering 59.6 percent of the vote and avoiding a runoff. His underfinanced and unknown Republican opponent, Lynn Lowe, never had a chance. Clinton won the election in 1978 by a wide margin, winning 65 percent of the votes cast. At the age of thirty-two, he was the youngest governor in the United States in four decades.

There were, however, clear warning signs. His message was mainstream and reassuring, but Clinton seemed threatening to many conservative voters. One Democratic official who showed Clinton around the state in 1974 described him as "bushy-headed and side-burned," adding "Yoked with Ivy League and Oxford pedigrees, Clinton's appearance was apt to provoke not only mistrust, but also dislike." Initially, Clinton made little effort to make himself more acceptable to voters. He traveled around the state in his 1970 American Motors Gremlin, the first American subcompact with a distinctive style that often appealed to younger drivers, with a bumper sticker proclaiming: "Don't Blame Me. I Voted for McGovern."[54] He was both appealing and attractive because of his intelligence and charm, but also threatening because he seemed culturally so alien, so clearly a product of the 1960s. Conservatives found him dangerous because he seemed like a harbinger of cultural change. To accept Bill Clinton was to acknowledge that America itself had changed and had, at some level, embraced the liberalizing influences of the 1960s.

Ironically, although Gingrich was a more partisan figure, Clinton inspired more passion. "It was amazing to me," recalled a 1978 campaign worker. "There was something in his personality and style that engendered that kind of passion on the part of people who wanted to keep him from being elected."[55] In his first race for office, conservative preachers called him a homosexual and a drug dealer. Years later, Clinton remembered his encounter with a man playing dominos at a diner in rural Arkansas. ""You're a long-haired hippie professor from the university," the man told him. "For all we know, you're a Communist."[56] Republicans circulated a false story that Clinton had participated in a student protest by climbing up a tree and holding a banner during President Nixon's 1969 appearance at an Arkansas football game. The rumors were demonstrably false, but they lingered. In 1979, he asked an assembly of high school students if they had heard the rumor, and "half the students and three-quarters of the teachers raised their hands."[57]

The most frequent rumors were about his womanizing. During his 1974 campaign for Congress, Clinton was dating Hillary Rodham, a fellow Yale law student living in Washington. It was, however, a well-known secret that he had developed a serious relationship with a young volunteer in his Fayetteville headquarters, and had women in several towns in the district. "He was careless," recalled aide Betsey Wright.[58] He had hoped that his marriage to Hillary in 1975 would stem the rumors before the next election. He also needed a strong partner, someone who could tame his excesses, impose discipline, and force him to make tough decisions. Rodham was ideal for the role. Raised in a comfortable middle-class community in Park Ridge, Illinois, she entered Wellesley in 1965 as a Goldwater Republican and left four years later as an experienced student activist and a self-avowed liberal. As the first student at Wellesley ever asked to give a commencement address, she spoke about how her generation was driven to protest by the "gap between expectation and realities" and about how so many members of her generation, raised in sheltered environments, were now learning to question authority. Protest, she argued, was "an attempt to forge an identity in this particular age" and a way of "coming to terms with our humanness." The speech, along with a photo of Rodham, was later featured in *Life* magazine.

Believing the law offered an effective tool for changing society, Rodham enrolled in Yale Law School in 1969. The following fall she spotted Bill Clinton. He was "hard to miss," she reflected, saying he looked "more like a Viking than a Rhodes Scholar."[59] The first time she heard him speak, he was bragging about the size of the watermelons in Arkansas. Eventually they dated, and then shared a small apartment off campus. She was scheduled to graduate a year before him, but chose to stay in New Haven for an additional year of study so they could be together.

After graduation in 1973, Clinton returned to Arkansas and Rodham went to Washington, where she worked as one of the forty staff attorneys for the House Judiciary Committee impeachment inquiry into Richard Nixon. After Nixon resigned in August, she traveled to Arkansas to help out on the campaign and teach at the law school. Initially, Clinton refused to give up his other his girlfriend. Over the next year Rodham debated whether to marry him. Could she really find happiness in Arkansas, far away from the centers of power in New York and Washington, with a man who seemed incapable of fidelity? But they shared a special bond and, like her, he was fiercely ambitious and interested in many of the same causes. When they married in 1975, David Maraniss wrote, "She understood his talents and his flaws. He might not be faithful, but together they could be faithful to their larger mission in life."[60]

Instead of ending the rumors, marriage to Hillary would just help produce new ones. In the past, Clinton was accused of womanizing; now he was charged with infidelity. Hillary also became the target of rumors. "The whispering campaign took a more scurrilous tack," recalled reporter Meredith Oakley. Word spread that Hillary was a lesbian and was having an affair with another "ardent feminist" on Clinton's staff."[61] In other ways, too, she compounded his image problem. Being married to a Chicago feminist with coke-bottled glasses did little to make him appear less threatening to conservative Arkansas voters.

Hillary made few concessions to her new environment. She was among the first generation of liberated women coming of age in the 1960s who refused to acquiesce to the familiar stereotypes about women's proper place in society, and to many she came across as aggressive and demanding. At the law school, many men resented her style and her intelligence. "Some of the guys were not used to being taught and led by a strong woman," a student told Maraniss. She "looked out of place. She dressed like a throwback to the sixties."[62] Hillary refused to wear makeup, which drove Clinton's makeup-loving mother crazy. "I would grind my teeth and wish I could sit Hillary on the edge of my tub and give her some makeup lessons," she complained.[63] Her refusal to take her husband's last name seemed confirmation that she was too "hippie-ish" for Arkansas voters. "It almost became a symbol of how Bill and Hillary were different than us," said Betsey Wright, Clinton's chief of staff from 1983 to 1990. "Bill went off to that fancy college, married a girl from Illinois who wouldn't take his name."

Hillary was perplexed by the hostility that she and her husband engendered among some voters. On election night in 1974, as they were leaving the campaign headquarters, the phone rang. Hillary picked it up thinking it was a friend or a well-wisher. Instead someone shouted: "I'm so glad that nigger-loving Commie fag Bill Clinton lost." Hillary hung up the phone, asking: "What could inspire such bile?' It was, she reflected, "a question I would ask many times in the years ahead."[64]

It was also becoming obvious to Clinton that he would need to deal with a new set of social issues that threatened the fragile Democratic coalition. By the mid-1970s, the moral fervor of the civil rights movement spread to other marginalized groups, who now demanded political recognition and equal rights. A riot at the Stonewall bar in New York City in June 1969 had ignited a nationwide grassroots "liberation" movement among gay men and women. Gays were not the only group challenging gender stereotypes. In 1972 Congress passed Title IX of the Higher Education Act, which banned discrimination "on the basis of sex" in "any education program or activity receiving federal financial assistance." That same year, Congress passed and sent to the states the Equal Rights Amendment (ERA), which proposed barring discrimination on the basis of sex. The most dramatic change came in the area of reproductive rights. On January 22, 1973, the Supreme Court declared in the landmark case, *Roe v. Wade*, that a woman had a constitutional right to an abortion. Writing for the majority, Justice Lewis Blackmun asserted that the fourteenth amendment, which prohibited states from denying "liberty" to anyone without "due process," established a "right of privacy" that was "broad enough to encompass a woman's decision whether or not to terminate the pregnancy."

These challenges to established gender roles widened the cultural divisions in America and precipitated a political backlash among traditionalists. As much as possible, Clinton tried to deflect attention away from cultural concerns and to focus on economics. On the campaign trail in 1978, he sometimes encountered hecklers who interrupted his speech asking him for his position on the ERA or gay rights. Clinton always tried to steer the conversation back to safer, more familiar issues. "Okay. I'll talk about it," he shouted to a persistent critic who demanded to know his position on the ERA. "I'm for it. You're against it. But it won't do as much harm as you think it will or as much good as those of us who support it wish it would. Now let's get back to schools and jobs."[65]

Potentially the most explosive, and dangerous, issue for Clinton concerned his actions in avoiding the draft. In the final days of his successful 1978 campaign, Billy G. Green, a retired Air Force lieutenant colonel, called a press conference to announce that Clinton was a draft dodger who had protested against American involvement in Vietnam. Green claimed to have seen the Army Reserve Officers' Training Corps (ROTC) file containing the agreement between Clinton and Colonel Holmes. He contended that Clinton had reneged on a promise he made to enter the ROTC in exchange for a one-year deferment to return to Oxford to finish his studies. Clinton refuted the charges, saying that he had canceled his agreement with the ROTC and had re-entered the draft. For now, his response quieted critics, but it was only the beginning of his struggle to explain his actions during the 1960s.

| Newt Gingrich: Wedges and Magnets

NEWT GINGRICH ENTERED the House in 1979, a key moment in the evolution of the Republican Party. Just five years earlier the Watergate scandal had engulfed the Nixon White House, damaged the party, and demoralized its leadership in Congress. By 1979, however, the mood had shifted. Jimmy Carter was fighting a losing battle against stagflation at home while struggling to establish his credibility as a strong leader abroad. Gingrich, and the other thirty-five Republican freshmen elected that year, brought a new set of attitudes and ideas to Congress. A confidential internal report commissioned by the Republican congressional leadership observed: "Freshmen had not been exposed to the demoralizing impact of Watergate, the Agnew and Nixon resignations, the Ford defeat, and maneuvering in a Congress dominated by two-to-one Democrats. Where older members saw persistence and shrewdness, the freshman saw timidity and indecision." The report noted that among younger members "there is widespread support for more vigorous, determined, and strategically managed leadership." It concluded: "The circled wagons era of staving off the Democratic assault and surviving Watergate has ended." The Republicans wanted "to play the role of attacking Indians, while the Democrats circle their wagons for awhile."[1]

Perhaps no one was more eager to play the role of "attacking Indians" than Newt Gingrich who, a week after he was sworn in as a new member of Congress, placed a statement in the *Congressional Record* complaining about corruption in the House. "The people are demanding we clean up our own House," Gingrich wrote. "On a personal basis, I am sure each of us would be upset if our vote on an important item of legislation was canceled by the vote of a convicted felon. And how could we explain to the people if a measure was decided by one vote—and that one vote came from a convicted felon?" Although he did not mention him by name, Gingrich was referring to Democrat Charles Diggs of Michigan, who had been convicted the year before on kickback charges. It would take three years for the ethics committee to recommend censure, and Diggs eventually resigned his seat in 1980. Gingrich had fired the first shot in the new ethics wars that would become central to destabilizing the House, upsetting Democrats and inspiring Republicans.[2]

Ironically, Watergate, which Gingrich claimed cost him election in 1974, created a new political environment that was perfectly suited to his guerilla tactics. Congress had responded to the abuse of presidential power by expanding its own power. Congress enlarged the personal staffs of individual senators and House members, augmented committee staffs in both houses, and increased the research service of the Library of Congress. Congressional staffs, for example, increased by 41 percent between 1972 and 1978. Congressional leaders also agreed to structural changes that greatly diffused authority in the House of Representatives. In 1974, House Democrats adopted "the subcommittee bill of rights," which parceled out the power of the original 22 committees to subcommittees. The number of House subcommittees increased from 119 to 148 between 1971 and 1979. While reformers celebrated the changes, many legislators complained that the redistribution of power made it difficult to build coalitions that could pass legislation. "We created a new order but not a new command," complained one reformer. The breakdown of authority and the fragmentation of power provided ample opportunity for political entrepreneurs to make their mark quickly and effectively. The days when a new member of Congress was expected to be seen but not heard had passed.

Television played a key role in the process. The same year that Gingrich entered Congress the House began gavel-to-gavel coverage of floor proceedings through C-SPAN. Speaker O'Neill reluctantly agreed with one qualification: the camera only show close-ups of the person speaking and not reveal what was going on in the chamber itself. Before the advent of TV, congressmen earned their reputations in committee rooms, often behind closed doors. Now they had the ability to communicate directly with voters and opinion makers without having to negotiate their message or defer to senior members of their own party. "C-Span does work best for the minority party," reflected Republican Congressman Robert Walker. "The majority controls the process—and looks like it's closing things down."[3] Walker found that when he challenged Democrats in front of the cameras, and an often empty chamber, "the phones in my office would light up." By 1984, C-SPAN was connected to 16 million homes and had developed a small but devoted following. "Newt immediately understood this was a great opportunity," Walker reflected.[4]

In the 1980 election Republicans proved that their message was resonating with the public by seizing control of both the White House and the Senate. For many conservatives, the 1980 election represented the inevitable triumph of Richard Nixon's Republican majority. "Like a great soaking wet shaggy dog, the Silent Majority—banished from the house during the Watergate storms—romped back into the nation's parlor this week and shook itself vigorously," observed the columnist William Safire.[5] Reagan's appeal, however, transcended Nixon's "silent majority," which was a coalition of anger and resentment. In the past conservatives had warned of the pain and sacrifice that would be necessary to maintain fiscal responsibility. The new theory of supplyside economics, however, allowed Reagan to forecast that his administration could promise deep tax cuts, dramatic increases in military spending, and only modest cuts in domestic programs, while still balancing the budget. Reagan gave conservatism a new fighting faith, a sunny demeanor, and an optimistic worldview. Newt Gingrich was watching and learning. Over the next decade, he would adopt much of Reagan's rhetoric and policies, but he never learned how to project his warmth and optimism.

Despite Reagan's victory, the House remained a Democratic stronghold. Gingrich believed that Republicans were winning the war of ideas, but in the House, Democrats used the advantage of incumbency to insulate themselves from public pressure. He planned to smoke them out by widening the ideological differences between the parties and forcing Democrats to choose sides. President Ronald Reagan pursued that strategy brilliantly during his first year in office, pushing through the major components of his economic plan—a 30 percent reduction in both personal and corporate income taxes, large cuts in government spending for social programs, and tight monetary policy to squeeze inflation out of the economy.

By 1982, however, some 10 million Americans were out of work, and the unemployment rate—9.5 percent—stood at its highest rate since 1941. "Main Street U.S.A. is in trouble," said a Senate Democrat looking forward to the 1982 midterm elections, "and they're going to turn to us." Gingrich not only worried that Democrats would make gains in the election, but he also feared that Reagan would start compromising with Democrats. What may have been the best strategy for the White House was not necessarily the best approach for congressional Republicans. Reagan needed to blur ideological distinctions to make himself more acceptable to moderate voters; House Republicans needed to accentuate ideological differences to distinguish themselves from Democrats. In 1982, Reagan, following the advice of moderates in the Senate, such as Robert Dole of Kansas, agreed to a $98 billion tax increase over three years. Gingrich felt the strategy was counterproductive and lashed out at Dole, calling him the "tax collector for the welfare state."[6] Gingrich joined eighty-nine other Republicans in opposing the measure, which passed both houses with bipartisan support.

In the November midterm elections, Democrats used the recession to blunt the Reagan revolution. Although Republicans retained control of the Senate, Democrats won twenty-six House seats, seven governorships, and six more state legislatures. Gingrich was disappointed in his own election results. He won with a 55.3 percent showing, far short of the 60 percent he had wanted. "I am in trouble," he concluded. "Our friends were not frightened enough, trained enough and committed enough to work and give as effectively and enthusiastically as we needed." He was aware that many of his supporters felt that he had "grown out of touch" and many voters were "confused by my space and computer ideas." Gingrich also felt that he had not been tough enough in his attacks on his opponent, Jim Wood. "We failed to thoroughly discredit Jim Wood as an alternative to the point where people would feel they *had* to split their ticket," he observed in a postelection memorandum.[7]

Internal memos reveal that Gingrich, and many of his aides, believed that both he and the conservative movement were floundering early in the 1980s. Gingrich was especially frustrated with his own inability to emerge from the pack of young Republican congressmen. He was at the forefront of no national issues. Friends complained that he was notoriously disorganized and unfocused, jumping from one grand scheme to the next with little or no follow-up. His staff worried that his fascination with space, computers, and the future led the Atlanta media to call him "Newt Skywalker," more interested in outer space than in his own constituents.[8] Staff members reported that they were "intellectually and professionally confused by you and your most recent behavior," Mel Steely reported in a summary. "They don't know where you are heading and have the feeling that you don't either."[9]

"Newt tends to be bold but careless, imaginative but undisciplined, and creative but sloppy," concluded administrative assistant Frank Gregorsky.[10] Newt, he observed, spent "three-and-a-half years dibbling and dabbling. He will launch one project in a big way, get tired of it, then go on to another. He always has priorities, but they change so much." That was why, he observed, "Newt and his works are a strange blend of strengths and weaknesses, of stunning intellectual breakthroughs followed by slipshod follow-thru." It was also the reason "why so many new people are attracted to him, while so many veterans decide not to reenlist."[11] Gregorsky feared that by 1986 "voters will largely have stopped believing that a man can be in the House for 7-plus years, never pass a bill, never take charge of a tough issue, and still be a national leader."[12] He found it "astonishing" that Gingrich "has been a congressman for almost five years and is still avoiding responsibility for everything."[13]

Gregorsky's assessment was harsh, but it reflected many staff members' opinions that Gingrich was languishing, lacking the discipline and focus to realize his real potential as a congressman and a national leader. Gingrich was also feeling restless and unfocused, worried that the Reagan Revolution had finished act I, but failed to prepare the nation for act II. Shortly after the 1982 election, Gingrich traveled to New York to meet with Richard Nixon in search of guidance. The disgraced former president suggested that Gingrich put together a group of "young turks" to challenge the moderate leadership of his party and start articulating an alternative message. Gingrich took the advice to heart, returned to Washington, and started recruiting young conservatives to spearhead a revolution within the Republican Party. "What are you planning to do next year—and maybe the next ten years?" he asked Minnesota Congressman Vin Weber. The result of his efforts was the creation in 1983 of the Conservative Opportunity Society (COS)—a key moment in Gingrich's rise to power and the evolution of the modern conservative movement. It was through his efforts in the COS that Gingrich reached out for the first time to the grassroots conservative establishment—the informal web of organizations and lobbying groups in Washington devoted to right-wing causes.

Gingrich would rise to power by tapping into the anger and resentment of an emerging conservative movement, and the interest groups that provided its political muscle. The veteran Washington journalists Dan Balz and Ronald Brownstein referred to the constellation of groups that gathered under the GOP umbrella as the "antigovernment coalition." A powerful "New Right" movement infused the cause with money, passion, and votes. Like traditional conservatives, the religious right believed in small government, low taxes, and free enterprise. Unlike the Old Right, however, they viewed politics through the prism of morality. America, they preached, confronted a crisis of the spirit, brought on by the pervasive influence of "secular humanism," which stressed material well-being and personal gratification over religious conviction and devotion to traditional Christian values.

Paul Weyrich, a conservative political strategist and a Gingrich mentor, described the battle between the conservative profamily forces and liberals as "the most significant battle of the age-old conflict between good and evil, between the forces of God and the forces against God, that we have seen in our country."[14] In 1979, the New Right emerged as a powerful political force with the formation of the Moral Majority. Abandoning traditional fundamentalist disdain for mainstream politics, founder Jerry Falwell combined old-time religion with sophisticated computer technology, targeting potential contributors and lobbying for political candidates who shared his conservative views. "Get them saved, baptized, and registered," Falwell advised his ministerial colleagues.

While they supported different agendas, from lowering taxes to supporting school prayer and opposing gun control, the new conservative coalition spoke a common language of disdain for Washington. Although inspired by the success of Ronald Reagan, they believed that the "great communicator" had been too timid in pushing his reform agenda. They were determined to go beyond Reaganism by not simply trying to slow down the growth of the federal government, but by turning it back. As Reagan faded from the national scene, Gingrich established himself as the spokesman for this new, militant conservatism. "Gingrich is Reaganism at warp speed," observed conservative activist Grover Norquist. Gingrich, noted conservative journalist David Brock, was the man who would "tether the culture war to the political war." "We saw him as the natural successor to Reagan—a younger Reagan with a handle on the future, a leader both smarter and tougher."[15] Yet there were always lingering doubts about Gingrich. "Though he was known as a man of ideas, no one really knew what Newt stood for. Some feared that in his heart of hearts he was an opportunist, a nihilist even, using conservatism as a vehicle to win power."[16]

In the past, Gingrich had shied away from controversial social issues. His natural instinct was to focus on topics that could be used to build majorities. His chief of staff wrote a memo in 1983 complaining that his boss handled the social questions "with platitudes, concessions to whatever crowd or person wants a statement, and hopes they'll go away." On abortion, he complained to Gingrich, you "lean toward whatever side yelled at you last."[17] Gingrich seemed intellectually reluctant to frame issues in moral terms. "I would never vote against my conscience," Gingrich told his staff. "On the other hand, I also make it a habit to have relatively few things I feel bitterly moral about."[18] After 1983, however, he spoke out strongly against abortion and gay rights and in favor of prayer in public schools. There would be no more middle ground on social issues.

It was also in the mid-1980s that Gingrich started using the 1960s as an ideological wedge. Although he had initially been sympathetic to student protestors, he now reinterpreted the decade as part of a radical assault on traditional American values. He adopted the standard neoconservative critique, which argued that a new cultural elite had institutionalized "counterculture values"—self-gratification, opposition to authority, and a moral relativism that blurred clear distinctions between right and wrong. But he added his own rhetorical flair and provided a hint of historical respectability, placing the critique of a handful of intellectuals into a sweeping framework of American history to suggest that the nation was living through a radical new phase. "From the arrival of English-speaking colonists in 1607 until 1965, there was one continuous civilization built around a set of commonly accepted legal and cultural principles," he wrote. "Since 1965, however, there has been a calculated effort by cultural elites to discredit this civilization and replace it with a culture of irresponsibility that is incompatible with American freedoms as we have known them."[19]

The claim that 1965 marked an abrupt and radical departure in American history, more significant in its impact than the American Revolution, the Civil War, or the industrial revolution, is impossible to support. As the journalist John Taylor observed, Gingrich "offers up a history of American values in a scheme so hysterically partisan, so transparently dishonest, so willfully stupid, that it's impossible to believe even Newt himself would expect anyone to take it seriously."[20] But Gingrich was not making a historical argument; he was using history to make a political point. His message was simplistic and inaccurate, but also clear and compelling: the problems facing contemporary American society could be traced back to student protestors, hippies, yippies, militant blacks, and angry feminists.

Gingrich had found his mission: he would be the pied piper of the new conservatism, merging the moralistic rhetoric of the New Right and the mystical conservative faith in tax cuts into a powerful ideological message. Relying less on his congressional staff and more on the interrelated web of conservative interest groups in Washington for information, expertise, and political support, he made it his mission to build a bridge between the grassroots conservative movement and the Republican Party leadership. To unite the fractious conservative coalition of big business, social conservatives, tax-cuts advocates, and libertarians behind his leadership, Gingrich created a shared enemy—the "corrupt liberal welfare state." The differences between the parties were moral, not political, he declared. His style appealed to many angry, young conservatives. "I can't speak for others, but to me," observed Brock, "Newt's appeal was based less on political philosophy or ideology than on raw emotion. I instinctively identified with his fanatical hatred of the left." Unlike the cool detached style of Reagan, Gingrich "had the style of the angry campus revolutionary."[21]

His angry polemics against the inefficiency of the welfare state, his disdain for liberal elites, and his talent for grabbing his opponents by the political jugular won Gingrich the support of conservatives. His thinking, however, was always more sophisticated than his rhetoric, and his attitude toward government more complicated than his partisan diatribes would suggest. In 1984, he published *Window of Opportunity*, which pulled together speeches and lectures he had given over the past decade. The tone is relentlessly optimistic, emphasizing the benefits that enhanced technology would have on American life, from breakthroughs in medicine to the possibility of living in space camps. Technology, he argued, would transform nearly every institution in American society and change the way we work, play, and learn. He attacked the perverse incentives of the liberal welfare state, but also pointed out the limitations of a "laissez-faire policy toward adaption and change."[22] The challenges facing the nation, he argued, transcended traditional political boundaries and required imaginative and creative solutions.

In his early years in Congress he also took positions that ran counter to the conservative trend. In 1979, his first entry in the *Congressional Record* was in support of Martin Luther King's birthday. During the 1980s, he supported sanctions against South Africa's apartheid regime.[23] In his first term, he supported the Alaska Lands Act, which prevented oil exploration of a large tract of land. In 1983, he was one of the first Republicans to join with environmental groups to call for the resignation of controversial Interior Secretary James Watt. In many of his early speeches and writings, he stressed how the nation needed to adjust to the rapid pace of technological change. He often referred to himself as a "Teddy Roosevelt" Republican, stressing the need for limited but strong federal government.

Over time, Gingrich discovered that his followers were not interested in his ideas about how technology would transform health care in America; they wanted to hear him eviscerate liberals for protecting waste and inefficiency in government. Conservatives relished stories about how liberals were living in the past, but ignored his warnings about how they needed to abandon their outdated belief that all government was evil. Gingrich gave conservatives what they wanted, hoping that once he gained power and destroyed the old liberal order, he would have garnered enough trust and support to convince the Right to rethink many of its assumptions about government. After 1984, Gingrich's rhetoric became more strident, his tone angrier and more partisan, his reasoning more simplistic. A decade after *Window of Opportunity,* he published *To Renew America,* which was little more than a scathing polemic against the failures of the "liberal welfare state." Talk of computers that could restore vision to the blind and of daily flights into space was replaced with ominous warnings of social decay. Anger displaced optimism. "Either we will pull ourselves together for the effort or we will continue to decay," he wrote. "There is virtually no middle ground."[24]

It is likely that the need to raise large sums of money influenced the militant partisanship that came to define Gingrich's rhetoric. He came out of the 1982 campaign season more than $30,000 in debt—a large sum for a congressional campaign at the time. Gingrich instructed his staff to develop a more aggressive direct mail campaign, to organize "get acquainted" break-fast meetings, and to reach out to political action committees.[25] Conservatives had discovered that subtlety was not an effective fundraising strategy. Richard Viguerie, a conservative activist who discovered how to use computers to target potential supporters and the direct mail to reach them, said the advantage of the new technique was that it "allows a lot of conservatives to by-pass the liberal media, and go directly into the homes of the conservatives in this country." The purpose of direct mail, declared a New Right leader, was "to organize discontent."[26] The easiest way of getting people to contribute was to oversimplify issues, turn debates over public policy into a clash of good versus evil, and demonize the opposition. In fundraising letters Gingrich warned that "for nearly two decades, this country has been decaying steadily." Why? "It's because of the liberal welfare state views that have governed the United States for the last half century. And it's because of the liberals in Congress who've blocked the changes we've needed to avoid this decay."[27]

Over the next few years Gingrich developed the blueprint of his political message—the message that he would eventually fine tune into the 1994 "Contract with America." It combined a militant rhetorical style that attacked the moral underpinnings of the Democratic Party with a positive Republican ideological message that revolved around tax cuts and family values. The key to the strategy was to nationalize local congressional elections by polarizing issues and exaggerating the differences between the two parties. Using the successful Democratic campaigns of 1948 and 1964 as models, Gingrich concluded that Republicans "must emphasize a wedge of issues that drive our opponents away from the American people, while having a secondary theme of magnet issues that attract the American people to us." He predicted that it would "take three to five elections to become a majority." Republicans would only be successful if they recognized that "We are waging a peaceful civil war to take power from our opponents...."[28] Finally, the Republicans needed to depict their opponents, and the Democratic Party in general, as corrupt. "The U.S. House of Representatives is dominated by an increasingly corrupt, illegitimate left-wing machine whose values have been defeated in every Presidential election since 1964," he wrote.

Before he could take on the Democrats, he had to win over the leadership of his own party, which was no easy task. "We believed we had a chance to be a majority and only two things stood in our way," Weber said. "The first thing was the Democrats. The second thing was the Republicans."[29] The Republican leadership paid little attention to Gingrich. "The mainstream Republican establishment in the House viewed Gingrich as this 'acid-throwing, bomb-throwing nut,'" said Congressman James Rogan.[30] Since he believed that Democrats used brute power and corrupt practices to hold on to their majority, Gingrich said the Republicans needed to abandon their strategy of accommodation and adopt an aggressive, confrontational approach. "If we behave the way we have always behaved, we will remain in the minority," he wrote. "We need large-scale, radical change."[31] The vast majority of Americans supported Republicans on the issues, but "ruthless" Democrats used the power of incumbency and their allies in the media to blur differences. "Less aggressive and less ruthless Republican politicians begin with less power, fewer resources, and scattered allies who form a majority but are not knit together as a community." He anointed himself as the man to forge that community.[32]

Believing that he had developed a language and strategy for uniting social and economic conservatives, Gingrich began his frantic effort to unite the party behind his leadership. He joined the network of interest groups and think tanks, and their corporate sponsors, who promoted conservative ideas. He gained control over the National Republican Congressional Committee (NRCC), and pushed it to coordinate legislative and campaign strategies. In the past, the NRCC had focused its resources on winning individual races. Gingrich emphasized the importance of nationalizing local elections, and developing common themes and tactics to articulate a unified Republican message. In 1986, former Delaware governor Pete DuPont handed over GOPAC, a political action committee he had founded to help recruit and train Republican candidates. Gingrich used the funds to travel around the country recruiting training and campaigning for candidates. He hired marketing professionals to identify issues, "65 percenters," that would resonate with a majority of the public. Instead of sending candidates checks, he sent them videotapes and cassettes. "It was like subscribing to a motivational course," noted two reporters, "with Gingrich a cross between Norman Vincent Peale and a Marine drill sergeant."[33] The tapes were designed to develop a vocabulary of positive words to use to describe Republican initiatives—liberty, freedom, truth, opportunity—while using "bad" words to label the Democrats—decay, corrupt, permissive, and pathetic. GOPAC distributed thousands of cassettes and videotapes to potential GOP candidates, teaching them to speak "Gingrich." He used GOPAC to recruit and train a generation of candidates who would talk and think like him. "We are on the way to becoming the Bell Labs of politics," he declared.[34]

There emerged during these years the tension in Gingrich's approach to politics that would plague him for the rest of his career. On substantive issues of policy, Gingrich was often creative, thoughtful, and intellectually independent, capable of challenging the conventional wisdom of his own party—a quality that made him suspect to many conservatives. At the same time, however, he could be ruthlessly partisan. He had spent his entire public life battling against what he regarded as an entrenched, arrogant, and often corrupt Democratic Party. He developed an instinct for the political jugular in the rough and tumble of a one-party state, and fine tuned his skills in the trenches of a Democratically controlled Congress. Gingrich made a distinction between politics—the sometimes inflammatory words you have to say to win elections—and governance—the responsible steps that elected officials need to take to solve problems. "The media make a great mistake in describing Newt as an ideologue," observed Republican Congressman Mickey Edwards. "He has been successful primarily because he is not strongly ideological. He is a good organizer who listened to the frustrations of the Republicans in Congress and figured out the strategy and tactics to help them become a majority."[35] Throughout his career, the visionary, thoughtful policy maker competed with the ruthless, take-no-prisoners, political strategist. He could arouse the Republican faithful by framing issues as choices between good and evil. Yet, Gingrich never fully believed his own rhetoric. Intellectually, he understood that policies are often negotiated in the gray area between ideological extremes. Unfortunately for him, an entire generation of Republicans would come to power adopting his strategy and his message, but failing to appreciate the distinction between means and ends.

In 1984, while much of the nation was focused on Reagan's landslide victory over Walter Mondale, Gingrich was leading a grassroots revolution within the Republican Party in the House. In May 1984, conservatives used the empty House floor to condemn Democrats, including Majority Leader Jim

Wright, as appeasers. Several days later an angry Speaker Tip O'Neill took the House floor, shaking his finger at Gingrich, shouting "you deliberately stood in the well before an empty House and challenged these people and you challenged their Americanism! It's un-American! It's the lowest thing I've ever heard in my 32 years here!" Personal insults are not permitted on the House floor. Mississippi's Trent Lott leaped to his feet demanding that the Speaker's words be stricken from the record. Gingrich got the reaction he wanted. In an unprecedented rebuff of a Speaker, the House voted to reprimand O'Neill and his comments were stricken from the *Congressional Record*— the first Speaker since 1795 to have his words taken down by the House. House Republicans rewarded Gingrich with a standing ovation. "Gingrich . . . really is a shrill and shameless little demagogue," Wright noted in his diary that night.[36] Gingrich loved the attention. "I am now a famous person," he crowed.[37] The incident was covered by all three network news broadcasts that evening and the front page of the *Washington Post.* O'Neill later grumbled that he helped transform Gingrich and his crowd from "backbencher-rabble rousers" into serious partisan contenders.[38]

Later that year Gingrich used a disputed congressional election in Indiana to highlight how power had corrupted the Democratic Party. On election day, embattled incumbent Democrat Frank McCloskey seemed to have won by a razor-thin seventy-two-vote margin over his Republican opponent, Richard McIntyre. A few days later, however, officials discovered an accounting error and gave McIntyre a thirty-four-vote edge. He was then certified the winner by Indiana's secretary of state, a Republican. When Congress convened in January 1985, House Democrats refused to seat McIntyre and instead created a special task force, made up of two Democrats and one Republican, to decide the winner. Eventually the task force voted to seat McCloskey. On May 1, 1985, McCloskey took his seat in the House after a full House vote that broke down on party lines.

The incident tapped a raw nerve for Republicans trapped in minority status in the House. Olympia Snowe, a moderate from Maine, claimed the election "symbolizes frustrations that have been building up for years." It outraged conservatives and even many moderates who believed the Democrats used brute power to steal the election. "The action validated Newt's thesis," Weber recalled. "The Democrats are corrupt, they are making us look like fools, and we are idiots to cooperate with them."[39] Initially, Gingrich called for Republicans to shut down the House by engaging in civil disobedience. Most Republicans were unwilling to go that far, and many were troubled by Gingrich's heated rhetoric in the days leading up to the opening of the new Congress. But they did agree to participate in a symbolic demonstration. When McCloskey took his seat, Gingrich led the entire House Republican delegation out of the chamber and down the steps of the Capitol. But a few minutes later their leader, Bob Michel, shook McCloskey's hand. In Gingrich's eyes, it was a sign of appeasement. "The Indiana incident legitimized Newt's claim to leadership," said Republican strategist Rich Galen. "It gave him the moral standing that he otherwise never would have had. It may have taken him another decade to become leader."[40]

Gingrich scored his biggest victory in 1987 when he helped bring down Jim Wright, who succeeded Tip O'Neill as House Speaker. He focused his attacks on a book deal Wright had negotiated that guaranteed an unusual 55 percent royalty. His goal, however, was to make Wright a metaphor for a corrupt Democratic Party. In September, while leading the crusade against Wright, Gingrich asked a group of fellow conservatives whether he should pursue a "scorched earth fight" on ethics. A colleague responded with advice that provided the rationale for Gingrich to step up his attacks. "If the Democrats can be made to be illegitimate ethically," he said, "they may be perceived as illegitimate politically."[41] Gingrich was no longer interested in guerilla warfare; he wanted to wage total war, destroying the credibility and character of his opponents as a first step toward undermining them politically. He would be relentless and ruthless in the pursuit of that goal.

When the House Ethics Committee refused to act, Gingrich turned to the media, contacting newspaper editors, calling television news producers, lobbying public interest groups, and telling supporters to call radio stations and keep the issue on the agenda. "The number-one fact about the news media is that they love fights," Gingrich once said. "When you give them confrontations, you get attention." Wright, he said, was "the most corrupt speaker in the 20th century," a man "so consumed by his own power that he's like Mussolini."[42] Gingrich's strategy paid off. "We worked on the assumption that if enough newspapers said there should be an investigation, Common Cause would have to say it. Then members would have to say it. It would happen," he told reporters. The House launched a probe of Wright in the summer of 1988. The following year, following an ethics committee report saying he had violated sixty-nine house rules, Wright was forced to resign as Speaker.[43]

His success in bringing down Jim Wright revealed how Gingrich skillfully manipulated the mainstream media to serve his partisan agenda. While most conservatives distrusted the "liberal" media, Gingrich sought them out, knowing that battles were won or lost in the media. He understood that his strategy of polarization played into the rules of conventional journalism. He needed to simplify issues in black and white; television reporters needed information presented in fifteen-second sound bites. "He understands that to communicate something to the mass public requires more emotional symbolism than to communicate something to the elite of the country, which is what most of us spend our time doing," COS colleague Vin Weber said.[44] Journalists needed "balance," and Gingrich's penchant for colorful quotes guaranteed that he would provide the conservative balance to any story. "Gingrich courts the press, believing that political battles are won and lost in newspapers and on television," author Nicholas Lemann wrote. "He promotes himself especially to reporters who are inclined to dislike him, because in the course of portraying him as an ogre they do him the great service of making him a star."[45]

The Democratic leadership, under siege from Reagan, and feeling pressure from its younger members, responded to Gingrich's actions by clamping down on rules, limiting debate. The weaker the Democrats became, the more they were forced to resort to using brute force to maintain their majority. Democrats hogged committee staff positions, averaging 5.3 staffers compared with 2.6 for each Republican. The Democrats limited the Republicans' ability to offer amendments and raise points of order from the floor. In committee rooms, chairmen prevented Republican bills from ever making it to the floor. The attitude among Democrats, recalled Massachusetts Representative Joe Moakley, was: "Hey, we've got the votes. Let's vote. Screw you."[46] Gingrich set in motion a chain reaction: the more he embarrassed the Democrats, the more they cracked down, and the more moderate Republicans were convinced the Democratic leadership of the House was arrogant and corrupt.

Even in the Senate, with its traditions of mutual respect, the partisan differences were flaring. In 1987, Democrats tossed out the rules of civility in attacking Robert Bork, a Reagan appointee to the Supreme Court. Democrats employed all the tools typically reserved for political campaigns to defeat the nomination. Liberal interest groups mobilized and coordinated the message in an effort to define Bork for the public. "Robert Bork's America is a land in which women would be forced into back-alley abortions, blacks would sit at segregated lunch counters, rogue police could break down citizens' doors in midnight raids, schoolchildren could not be taught about evolution, writers and artists would be censored at the whim of the government and the doors of the federal courts would be shut on the fingers of millions of citizens," Massachusetts Senator Edward Kennedy thundered.[47] On October 23, 1987, the Senate rejected Bork's confirmation, with forty-two supporting votes and fifty-eight opposing votes. According to the *New York Times*, the verb "to Bork" might be defined as "to destroy a judicial nominee through a concerted attack on his character, background and philosophy."[48]

While Gingrich played an important role in the growing partisanship in Congress, larger historical and institutional forces were driving the process. In 1968, third-party candidate George Wallace famously declared "there ain't a dime's worth of difference" between Democrats and Republicans. Wallace had a point. The nation was engaged in a heated debate over civil rights and Vietnam, but the two parties remained remarkably close to the center. The conservative South kept a brake on the liberal leanings of the Democratic Party, while a sizeable coalition of northeastern liberals and moderates nudged the Republicans to the left. By the 1980s, however, the two parties were becoming ideologically more coherent and less diverse— conservatives were flocking to the Republicans, liberals to the Democrats.

The debate over the "culture of choice" that emerged in the 1960s polarized many voters into liberal and conservative camps on issues ranging from abortion to gay rights. With the nomination of Ronald Reagan in 1980, Republicans staked out their claim as the conservative party, passing a platform that strengthened their position against abortion while dropping its support for the Equal Rights Amendment (ERA) and promoting school prayer and tuition tax credits. At the same time, the Democratic Party called for passage of the ERA, supported abortion rights, and added "sexual orientation" to its antidiscrimination plank. Reagan appealed directly to the religious right, appearing before twenty thousand evangelicals in August, asking for their support. Christian Coalition leader Ralph Reed called the gathering "the wedding ceremony of evangelicals and the Republican Party."[49] Over the next few years, the Republican Party benefited from a dramatic influx of white, conservative evangelicals. In 1976, Jimmy Carter won 56 percent of the born-again vote. By 1984, evangelicals voted for Ronald Reagan by a lopsided 81 to 19 percent.

The movement of the once solidly Democratic South into securely Republicans hands represented the most significant change in American politics in the last half of the twentieth century. After 1964, many southern whites fled the Democratic Party after Lyndon Johnson announced his support for federal civil rights legislation. On the night that Congress passed the Civil Rights Act of 1964, a somber Johnson told an aide: "I think we've just handed the South over to the Republican Party for the rest of our lives." His prediction turned out to be painfully true. While southern white voters switched to the Republican Party, newly enfranchised African Americans flooded into the Democratic Party. The percentage of blacks registered to vote in the eleven states of the old Confederacy rose from 29 percent in

1960 to 62 percent in 1970. The movement of conservative whites into the Republican Party accentuated its rightward tilt at the same time that the growing influence of more liberal blacks pushed the Democratic Party to the left.

The media played a major role in the growing political divisions as well. The rise of cable television, and the advent of the twenty-four-hour news cycle, made the business of news more competitive, and its tone more adversarial. Television often preferred drama over discourse; conflict over consensus. A generation of post-Watergate journalists, inherently skeptical of government and the claims of its leaders, were more willing to abandon the rules of objective journalism, which stressed neutrality and balance, and interject opinions and analysis. More important, the proliferation of news sources—television, radio, and, increasingly, the Internet—allowed people to hear opinions and viewpoints that reinforced their own beliefs. In the past, the three major networks needed to reach the broadest possible viewership and appeal across the political spectrum. Increasingly, news followed the consumer trend toward niche marketing, reaching smaller audiences of like-minded viewers. While still in its infancy, the Internet would reinforce the trend by introducing software allowing people to customize the information they received, resulting in what a journalist called "The Daily Me"—a customized view of the world filtered to allow exposure to individuals who share identical interests and ideas.

At the same time, a series of reforms designed to make the major political parties more democratic limited their ability to forge consensus at the same time that they enhanced the power of well-organized special interest groups. The proliferation of primaries after 1968 reduced the influence of traditional party brokers, who had exercised a moderating force, and gave birth to a new style of politics requiring candidates to raise large sums of money and to develop messages that resonated with their most ideological followers. Campaign finance laws, intended to curtail the corrupting influence of money in politics, led to a proliferation of political action committees, which expected loyalty for their largess. In 1974, the first year Bill Clinton and Newt Gingrich ran for elective office, there were only 608 political action committees. By 1987 the number had soared to over 4,000. In an effort to turn out their base, candidates frequently used emotionally charged, negative television ads designed to arouse passion and indignation. Powerful new computers allowed campaigns to design more effective direct mail and fundraising appeals. The negative tone and simplistic appeals alienated many middle-of-the road voters, who either declared themselves independents or dropped out of the system altogether. In the South, voter turnout declined from 73 percent in 1960 to 54 percent in 1988. The defection of the moderates only increased the power of the ideological fringe in each party.

The same sophisticated technology that allowed candidates to identify potential supporters also permitted state legislators to perfect the art of gerrymandering. Ever since 1811, when Massachusetts Governor Elbridge Gerry approved a long, salamander-like district to help sustain the Federalist Party, legislators had been using the redistricting process for political purposes. By the 1980s, however, sophisticated software that merged polling and census data increased the possibilities for mischief, allowing parties to manufacture hundreds of "safe" congressional districts. The result was that Democrats and Republicans nominated and elected representatives who were frequently either to the left or the right of the general public. Instead of building coalitions in the center, they won elections by playing to their base.

In a clear sign that they were looking for more partisanship leadership, House Republicans elected Gingrich to the position of party whip in 1989. Although Gingrich won by only two votes (87–85) over the conciliatory Edward Madigan of Illinois, the election was the culmination of years of frustration and represented a turning point in the evolution of the modern Republican Party. The election broke down along generational lines, with many of the younger members, including some moderates, rejecting the party's traditional policy of accommodating the majority and gambling that Gingrich's strident, accusatory style would shake things up in the House. "I think people felt we accommodated ourselves for a number of years and we've ended up with fewer seats," said Illinois Representative Lynn Martin. "Let's try something else." "Even a bunny rabbit, when cornered, will fight back," said Henry Hyde. Or as Congressman Dick Armey told reporters: "I've long since thought that we need a little more emphasis on the word 'opposition' and a little less emphasis on the word 'loyal.' "[50]

Republicans got what they asked for, and then some. Over the next few years, Gingrich transformed the dispirited, disorganized Republican caucus into a disciplined army that relentlessly attacked the hapless Democrats. But it created problems with the leadership of his own party. While Gingrich was rising within the House Republican ranks, Ronald Reagan had passed on the White House to his Vice President George H.W. Bush. The president's team had opposed Gingrich's election as minority whip. When he won, "there was unhappiness at the high levels of the White House," an anonymous administration official told the *Washington Post*. "They never regarded him as a trustworthy player."[51] They had reason to question his loyalty. Gingrich planned to use his position as minority whip to continue building toward a Republican majority, which meant motivating conservatives, recruiting strong candidates, and winning competitive races by highlighting the ideological differences between the parties. He would work with the White House when it aided the cause, but he had no intention of blindly supporting the president's agenda.

While the White House wanted to demonstrate leadership by forging a bipartisan solution to the growing budget deficit, Gingrich needed to unify Republicans and undermine Democratic strength in Congress by polarizing issues. That conflict came to a head in 1990 when the president renounced his famous "Read My Lips: No New Taxes" pledge at the 1988 Republican convention, and agreed to a budget compromise with Congressional Democrats that included $133 billion in new taxes. Gingrich not only refused to support the deal, but he also led 105 House Republicans in a stunning defeat of the plan. "I was astonished that they didn't understand we were the party of no taxes," he said. "I do think the actual fight was one of the saddest things I've ever been involved in." The president eventually got a tax hike passed, but the internal fighting made him look weak. Senate Republican Leader Bob Dole criticized Gingrich. "You pay a penalty for leadership," Dole complained in a speech on the Senate floor. "If you don't want to pay the penalty, maybe you ought to find some other line of work."[52] Gingrich, however, felt liberated by his break with the administration, believing it established his independence from the White House, energized conservatives, and reinforced the public perception that the Republicans were the party of low taxes.

Gingrich won control of the House by eroding public faith in the institutions of government. What was not clear at the time was that he believed that he could reassemble the shattered pieces of public trust once the Republicans had taken control. He convinced voters that the Democratically controlled House was corrupt, and incapable of governing. In his swift rise to prominence and power, Gingrich made allies and enemies, but very few friends. Most of his colleagues found him cold, distant, and impersonal. "I spend a lot of time in the Republican cloakroom, and Newt is the least friendly or gregarious of all the Republican Members," a colleague warned Gingrich's chief of staff in 1983. "He comes in and either goes to the phone or to the Member he wants to talk to. He never sits around and trade [sic] stories or tells jokes."[53] He formed few close friendships. "Newt doesn't do friendships," said Joe Gaylord, one of his closest associates.[54] Privately, many staff members complained about his "intellectual arrogance." In advice that was remarkably prophetic, Gregorsky noted: "Being self-confident and a good salesman is fine, but intellectual ruthlessness and personal invalidation can ruin a politician."[55]

Conservatives and moderate Republicans were attracted to him not because they liked him or even agreed with his methods, but because his tactics worked. They were convinced, as moderate Nancy Johnson told her colleagues, that Gingrich possessed "the vision to build a majority party and the strength and charisma to do it."[56] Behind the scenes, Gingrich built alliances with moderate members of his party. Many were surprised by the contrast between his reasonable, open-minded, and compromising private style and his bombastic public persona. In the mid-1980s, Republican moderates formed the "92 Group" to rival the COS. Over the years, Gingrich made numerous efforts to reach out to them, often attending meetings and talking with them individually to find common ground. Many members found him open to a wide range of ideas and always willing to focus on areas of agreement.

Oddly enough, although he was spearheading a conservative revival in the House, movement conservatives never fully trusted him. "He's not one of us," said Paul Weyrich, a leader of the New Right. "But he will do business differently. He is an opportunity to break out-of-the-box we've been in."[57] Movement conservatives were attracted to leaders like Ronald Reagan, who possessed a handful of deeply held, unquestioned beliefs about the way the world worked. Gingrich was too intellectual, too willing to challenge conventional thinking, to win over many conservatives. "When I hear about an issue, or when I'm considering a policy, the first question I ask is, 'Does this conform to the Judeo-Christian teachings on whatever subject it is we're talking about?'" explained Weyrich. "He does not start at that point. He starts at a different point. Is this good for the country? Is this good for the Republicans? Is this going to strengthen his majority?" Politics, not conviction, drove Gingrich to embrace much of the New Right agenda.[58]

Details of his sometimes sordid private life made many social conservatives uncomfortable with getting too close to Gingrich, or having their fortunes tied too closely to his. There were the ongoing rumors in Washington and at home that he was having affairs with members of his staff. In the early 1980s, the *Atlanta Journal-Constitution* decided to investigate the rumors. "I felt like a *National Enquirer* reporter," recalled Ann Woolner, a former *Atlanta Journal-Constitution* reporter. "I told my editors that I was hearing these rumors about Newt's behavior and we were trying to figure out what to do. They said 'check them out and see where it goes.'" The argument for probing into his personal life was that he made ethics such an important issue and there seemed to be a contradiction between his public standards and his private behavior. They were, however, difficult stories to document, but after some initial investigation, Woolner was convinced the stories were true. "There was a decision by the editors not to go with the story."[59]

The editors of *Mother Jones* magazine had no such qualms about reporting the unsubstantiated, but widely circulated, stories. The author, David Osborne, planned to write a piece about Gingrich as a "New Ideas Republican," but quickly switched gears after spending time in his home district. The story reported on various affairs, but much of it focused on the tawdry details of his divorce. In 1978, shortly after he won election to Congress, Jackie was diagnosed with uterine cancer. She suffered a recurrence in 1980 after he had filed for divorce. According to press accounts, he went to her hospital room where she was recovering, pulled out a legal pad, and started discussing the details of their divorce. She threw him out of the room. Later, she filed court papers claiming that he was providing only $700 a month for her and his two girls, ages 17 and 14. Unable to pay for basic necessities, she faced having her utilities cut off. Her situation was so dire at one point that her local church took up a collection. "The devil has taken him," she told the congregation.[60]

Osborne saw Gingrich's behavior as "political hypocrisy." While campaigning as a family values candidate, he was cheating on his wife. "He was unfaithful to his wife and his aides were betting on election night how long before he was going to dump her," he observed. Gingrich called the article "probably the most disgusting thing that's happened to me in politics."[61] Despite the explosive nature of the charges, the national media failed to give it wide circulation. Local Atlanta newspapers never picked it up. When he filed for divorce, less than two years after promising to keep his family together, the *Atlanta Journal-Constitution* ran a six-paragraph item.

Most conservatives were willing to overlook his indiscretions as long as he was advancing their cause. As David Brock later pointed out, many conservative leaders were plagued by a discrepancy between their private behavior and their public rhetoric. Gingrich was no different. "He struck me as another member of the decadent and hypocritical conservative elite, using whatever rhetorical flourishes he thought necessary to inflame cultural animosities in the right-wing base of the party," observed Brock. "What I underestimated was Newt's capacity for hypocrisy: his ability to live his personal life as he wished . . . while leading a scorched-earth crusade to have the government enforce right-wing political and social values—the very opposite of the ideals of liberty and limited government he claimed to espouse."[62]

Gingrich's antics had the desired effect of outraging most Democrats. "Gingrich is the man who is principally responsible for destroying civility in the House of Representatives," reflected Wisconsin Democrat David Obey. "He recruited and trained an entire generation of Republican leaders to divide the public and attack Democrats."[63] One Democrat complained that Gingrich tried to take over the House not at the ballot box, "but with hand grenades."[64] After Wright's resignation, fellow Texas Democrat Jack Brooks warned: "There's an evil wind blowing in the halls of Congress today that's reminiscent of the Spanish Inquisition. We've replaced comity and compassion with hatred and malice."[65] His political adversaries viewed him the same way as did many of his friends: as an opportunist. "I had seen him use the ethics issue from the day he arrived," recalled California Congressman Victor Fazio, "not because he cared about ethics but because of his ongoing effort to expose the Democratic Congress as corrupt and out of touch."[66]

While he had made himself a force to be reckoned with in Washington, he had paid little attention to his district. He was often bored and indifferent to the day-to-day problems that occupy the time of most congressmen. He delegated constituent work to his staff, so he could focus on grand strategy. According to Gregorsky, and other staff members, Gingrich saw himself as a crusader on a mission to save western society. He believed that treating people with dignity and respect were incidental when you were charged with such a noble calling. "Personalities," Gingrich told his staff, "are irrelevant when you're trying to save the West." In Washington he thought of himself as a "master surgeon" who was removing liberal cancer from the body politic; in his district he played the role of the "family physician" who offered guidance and remedies for life's small problems.[67]

Many constituents, even conservatives, found him distant and arrogant, out of touch with their local needs. In 1990, his opponent, David Worley, a thirty-two-year-old lawyer, tapped into unease with Gingrich by depicting him as a hypocrite, more interested in promoting himself than serving the needs of his district. Worley said Gingrich seemed more interested in appearing on *Good Morning America* (nine times) than before the farmers in Haralson County (three times). "Our basic theme was Newt Gingrich has forgotten you," Worley said. The national Democratic Party ignored the race, believing that Worley did not have a chance of winning, but the message struck a responsive chord with voters, even with traditionally Republican voters. On election day, Gingrich won by only 983 votes of the nearly 156,000 cast, a small enough margin to require an automatic recount. He lost six of the twelve counties in the district. The election results suggested that Gingrich was building an ambitious national agenda on the back of a fragile coalition at home. Gingrich got the message. The voters, he said, had sent him a message: "I ought to come home and pay attention."[68]

| Bill Clinton:
The "New Democrat"

ACCORDING TO HIS BIOGRAPHER, Clinton's 1978 inauguration as governor of Arkansas "had the aura of a generational rite." His friends from around the country traveled to Little Rock to watch one of their own, "the first in their class," reach political prominence, and at such a young age. The shaggy-haired governor brought with him the idealism and the expectations of his generation. "Bill started his two-year term with the energy of a racehorse exploding from the gate," recalled Hillary. "He had made dozens of campaign promises, and he started fulfilling them in his first days in office."[1]

When he took office, Arkansas ranked last in the nation in state per capita spending on education. Believing that the state could no longer depend on agriculture for its survival, Clinton proposed a massive overhaul of the education system, including large increases in teacher pay and a mandatory testing program. He expanded the role of the Department of Economic Development in an effort to recruit new business to the state and keep those that were already there. He tackled a host of other problems as well. In an effort to improve Arkansas roads and highways, he increased taxes on registration fees on cars and pickups. He attacked fraud in the welfare system, reformed the food stamp program, and developed aggressive energy conservation measures.

By all accounts, the governor tried to accomplish too much, too fast. "I was always in a hurry to get things done," Clinton later admitted, "and this time my reach often exceeded my grasp."[2] In his first two years he managed to offend just about every important group in the state. The hike in automobile registration fees turned out to be the most costly mistake. He had planned to levy the highest fees on heavy trucks that did the most damage to the roads, but the legislature shifted the burden to cars. Clinton signed the bill anyway—a decision he later described as one of the "dumbest mistakes" he ever made. The tax hit rural residents and the elderly the hardest and eroded much of the goodwill he had built up in his initial campaigns for office. "I had shot myself in the foot," he reflected, "blowing five years of hard work among rural Arkansas—and a lot of blue-collar city people, too—with the stroke of a pen."[3]

Clinton found himself sailing against stiff political headwinds. The national economy was suffering from the twin problems of inflation and high unemployment. The downturn lowered state revenue, preventing him from giving teachers the raises he had promised. Adding to his difficulties was a decision President Carter made in 1980 to send several hundred Cuban refugees to Fort Chaffee in northwest Arkansas. Initially, Clinton welcomed the refugees, pointing out that they "came to this country in flight from a Communist dictatorship." Within weeks, however, more than 19,000 refugees flooded into the camp. At one point, over 300 refugees stormed the gates and escaped the camp. When federal troops refused to intervene, Clinton called in the National Guard and pleaded with the White House not to send any more refugees. In June, Carter agreed, but two months later he broke that promise and announced that he was sending 10,000 more refugees to Arkansas.

Compounding his political problems was a continuing sense by many voters that Clinton, despite his deep roots in the state, was culturally alien. "Bill Clinton was one of the most charming, polite people you'd ever want to meet," observed a local official, "but the public perception of his whole administration was of a bunch of thirty-year-old bearded liberals who were going to tell these dumb Arkies how to do things."[4] Many of his staff members were young, wore casual clothes, and sported beards and long hair. Even a celebrated event, like the birth of his daughter Chelsea in January 1980, provoked controversy. Papers speculated whether Chelsea would be a Clinton or a Rodham. "That really ran against the grain of the conservative element of Arkansas, the traditional families, if you would," his Republican opponent Frank White recalled. "In some parts of the world, New York, perhaps California, for a wife not to have her husband's name, that was fine, but boy! The South was not ready for that!"[5]

Hillary had a difficult time adjusting to the spotlight and to the traditionally minded Arkansas establishment. "The pressures on me to conform had increased dramatically when Bill was elected Governor in 1978," she reflected. Thrown into "an unblinking spotlight," she discovered for the first time how her "personal choices could impact my husband's political future."[6] She was an independent, professional woman, among the leading edge of feminists who took for granted that men and women should be treated equally and afforded the same opportunities. Living in Arkansas, she was constantly reminded of the persistence of older attitudes and assumptions. Some judges would casually make condescending comments in open court, such as "How pretty you look today," or "Come up here so I can get a good look at you." Once, when she was seven months pregnant, chatting with the judge in court, she mentioned that she and her husband were attending "birthing" classes on Saturday mornings. "What?" she recalled the judge saying. "I've always supported your husband, but I don't believe a husband has any business being there when the baby is born!"[7]

Politically, the bigger problem was the way many people in Arkansas viewed her. "People in Arkansas reacted to me much as my mother-in-law had when she first met me: I was an oddity because of my dress, my Northern ways and the use of my maiden name."[8] At one point a friend joked about staging an elaborate ceremony on the steps of the capitol. "Bill would put his foot on my throat, yank me by my hair and say something like, 'Woman, you're going to take my last name and that's that!'" at which point "flags would wave, hymns would be sung and the name would change."[9]

In 1980, voters took out their frustrations with Clinton in the voting booth. A seventy-eight-year-old retired turkey farmer, Monroe Schwarzlose, challenged the governor in the Democratic primary, attacking him for being "out of touch" with Arkansas and for increasing car registration fees. He won a surprising one-third of the vote. In the general election, Frank White, a born-again Christian with strong support among conservatives, picked up on the themes. He accused Clinton of hiring outsiders, including many married couples. In an obvious dig at Hillary Rodham for continuing to use her maiden name, he said it was impossible to know how many married couples Clinton had hired "because they don't have the same last names."[10] White, a veteran, could not pass up the opportunity to raise the issue of Clinton's lack of service in the military, reminding voters that Clinton "chose not to join the armed services, so he has no compassion for military people." White tapped into a feeling among some Arkansas voters, especially conservative whites, that the former Rhodes Scholar and Ivy Leaguer in the governor's mansion was arrogant, aloof, inaccessible, and egotistical. According to the *Arkansas Gazette,* White preyed on the feeling that Clinton was overly ambitious and "more interested in his political future than in them."[11]

In the final weeks of the campaign, White unveiled a devastating television ad showing rioting Cubans at Fort Chaffee. The ad claimed that Clinton cared more about his relationship with Jimmy Carter than he did about the people of Arkansas, declaring that Clinton "sold out the state of Arkansas for national political gain."[12] White hammered away at the issue on the campaign trail, telling audiences that the president's decision to "dump" the refugees in Arkansas was made "purely because he knew his good friend Clinton would work with him."[13] He dismissed Clinton as a "self-serving politician who won't and never will stand up to the federal government."[14]

Clinton, who believed that he had responded forcefully and effectively to the riots, dismissed the charges. It soon became evident, however, that they were eroding his support. Less than three weeks before the election, Clinton held a 2–1 lead over White, including a twenty-five-point lead among independents. By October, that lead had been cut to six points.[15] Hillary had also dismissed the attacks because "everyone in Arkansas knew what a good job Bill had done containing the violence." Then she started getting hostile questions at school assemblies and civil meetings, such as, "Why did the Governor let the Cubans riot? Why didn't the Governor care about us more than about President Carter?"[16]

On election day, Clinton became the youngest ex-governor in America. He received 48 percent of the vote, a steep decline from his 63 percent in 1978. It was a shocking upset, especially since Clinton had been considered a wunderkind in Arkansas, a man already touted as presidential timber. The pro-Clinton *Arkansas Gazette* claimed that a number of factors explained the loss, including a bad economic climate and tactical mistakes by the Clinton campaign. But chief among the reasons for White's victory was the success of "conservative causes, such as the so-called Moral Majority," in registering new voters and getting them to the polls.[17] These first-time voters were unlikely "to vote for a continuation of the status quo," and their participation was especially noticeable in the northwest part of the state "where White was a big winner."[18]

Clinton was swept out of office by a Republican tide that roared across the country. By the end of the 1970s, the cultural divide forged during the 1960s had become a wide chasm. Jimmy Carter had used the momentum from Watergate to squeeze out a narrow victory in 1976, but he ran into a host of problems, at home and abroad, that reinforced the perception that the Democratic Party was both incompetent and out of touch with mainstream voters. Stagflation—rising inflation and high unemployment—sapped the economy of strength and made it a difficult year for incumbents. Abroad, the Soviet army had invaded Afghanistan, raising fears that it would strike at valuable Middle East oil supplies. Iranian militants overran the American embassy in Tehran, holding seventy American hostages for 444 days. Republicans tapped into the public disenchantment with the Carter administration, winning control of the White House and the Senate. Over time, the shattering of the New Deal coalition and the rise of conservatism in the 1970s would provide Bill Clinton with the opportunity to refine the liberal message and rise quickly to the top of a dispirited party. For now, however, Clinton needed to find a way to get back into the political game.

———

Within days of his 1980 defeat, Bill Clinton was planning his comeback. He traveled the state, meeting with editorial writers, local rotary clubs, and just about anybody who would talk with him. Hillary noted that "Bill had now lost two elections—one for Congress, and one as an incumbent Governor—and many wondered whether this defeat would break him."[19] He asked everyone he could why he lost. A friend gave him the most direct answer: "Bill, the people thought you were an asshole!"[20] He was determined to recapture the governorship. "There was absolutely no doubt that I would run again. The very moment I was conceding defeat, my mind was spinning with ideas about what I had to do to stay active and get back."[21]

He hired Dick Morris as a campaign consultant and asked him to gage voter sentiment. Morris recalled seeing Clinton shortly after the election, now working in a small Arkansas law firm, seemingly in a "state of confusion." "He seemed so out of place," he recalled, "a big man cramped into a little office in a local law firm, walking out to the corridor to see whether he could borrow a secretary to do his typing for him."[22] What Morris found in his polls surprised Clinton. It turned out that voters still liked him, but they felt that he had grown too arrogant, too distant. They voted against him not to end his career, but to teach him a lesson in humility. Clinton could make a comeback, Morris said, but first he needed to apologize for past mistakes. Reluctantly, Clinton agreed and taped a thirty-second ad that started running in February 1982. When I was growing up, he said, "my daddy never had to whip me twice for the same thing."[23]

It was an unprecedented and risky strategy. In 1980, candidates did not make heavy use of television commercials, and when they did, it was often in the final weeks of a campaign. Here Clinton was using television as the main vehicle for reintroducing himself to the public, bypassing the editorial pages of local newspapers and appealing directly to voters in the comfort of their living rooms, and doing it nearly a year before the general election. Initially, the ads caused a drop in Clinton's rating since they reminded voters why they did not like him, but over time they insulated him from attacks on his first term as governor. The success of the ads taught Clinton a valuable lesson about the power of television, the importance of defining issues early in the campaign, and the need to use polls to chart public opinion. "He learned a lesson that few of us could ever survive," said close aide Betsey Wright.[24] He took polls to help measure public attitudes and he used paid advertising to educate the public and make them more receptive to his initiatives.

Before he could have a rematch with Governor White, Clinton needed to win a competitive Democratic primary against a bitter rival, Jim Guy Tucker, and a lesser known candidate, Joe Purcell. Both men moved to the right in an effort to court more conservative voters. One of the painful lessons Clinton had learned from the 1980 race was the power of negative advertising and the importance of responding quickly to criticism. "When someone is beating you over the head with a hammer, don't sit there and take it," he said. "Take out a meat cleaver and cut off their hand."[25] He was determined, he said, "never to practice unilateral disarmament again."[26] Tucker attacked Clinton for commuting the sentences of dozens of convicted murderers in the final weeks of his term as governor. Clinton returned the fire, labeling Tucker a "liberal" who opposed welfare reform and supported expanding the food stamp program. The *Arkansas Gazette,* pointing out that Clinton's charges on the food stamp program were false, ran an editorial titled: "Bill Clinton on the Low Road."[27]

The Morris strategy was paying off: while Tucker's negative ads had little impact, Clinton's attacks appeared to drive his opponent's ratings down fifteen points. "The polls showed a tremendous backlash of sympathy for Clinton because he had already apologized," Morris said. On May 25, Clinton won the primary with 42 percent of the vote, but he failed to win a majority. Much of Tucker's support migrated to Purcell, who made it into the runoff with Clinton, scheduled for two weeks later. Although Purcell led in many polls, he lacked a strong organization that could turn out the vote on election day. Frank White inadvertently aided Clinton by running ads in the final weekend attacking him. Clinton responded with radio spots pointing out that White, who was detested by activist Democratic primary voters, was supporting Purcell. On the June 8 runoff, Clinton won with 54 percent of the vote. At Clinton headquarters that night, jubilant aids cheered, "We Want Frank! We Want Frank!"

This time Frank White had a record for him to run against and the economic slowdown was hurting him. His big initiative was to require public schools to teach the biblical version of creation alongside evolution. The move, while popular with religious conservatives, was ridiculed by the press. The *Arkansas Gazette* pictured White as a monkey eating a banana. In his campaign speeches, Clinton carefully sidestepped the controversy of evolution, emphasizing the same populist economic themes that had won him election in 1978. He accused White of being the tool of the moneyed interests, telling a Democratic Women's Club audience, "He's got half a million dollars because the people who wanted decisions from the Governor's office paid for them." Clinton ran a tough ad attacking White for allowing large increases in utility rates while cutting back on Medicaid: "Frank White—Soft on utilities. Tough on the elderly."[28] Diane Blair, an Arkansas political scientist, later wrote that Clinton's ads "portrayed White as an untrustworthy, interest-dominated plutocrat who might run with the good-old-boy hounds by day but slept with the utility foxes at night, while Clinton was just a caring and concerned, down-home Baptist family man who wanted nothing more than another chance to fight the fat cats on behalf of the little guys."[29]

White returned to the themes that had worked for him in 1980, attacking Clinton for his unpopular increase of vehicle registration fees and his well-known desire to seek national political office. He also mounted a new attack, painting Clinton as weak on crime because, during his term as governor, he commuted the sentences of many offenders and set only one execution date. All of this, according to White, demonstrated that Clinton was "a 'tax and spend' politician who is soft on crime and lets his ambitions overshadow the state's best interests."[30] In the final days of the campaign, White, who had received the endorsement of the National Rifle Association, also launched an aggressive television campaign accusing Clinton of supporting gun control. Clinton called White's resort to the gun issue a "desperate" tactic designed to shift attention away from "the gut economic issues" on the minds of the voters. "When the going gets rough at the end of the campaign," Clinton argued, "the fellow that's behind says the other one is for gun control." Asserting that he had never supported gun control, Clinton told 400 people at a fish fry in West Memphis, "Any person who is sucker enough to fall for that gun control bit is shooting himself in the foot." In Clinton's opinion, White's use of the crime and gun control issues, like his negative campaigning in general, represented an intentional diversion from more substantive issues. "He knows if you vote for yourself, on jobs, utility rates, education," Clinton quipped, "he's a goner."[31]

At the end of a campaign that brought over 72 percent of the state's registered voters to the polls, Clinton won by a surprisingly comfortable ten-point margin, carrying fifty-six of seventy-five counties. It was, the *Arkansas Gazette* said, "an almost exact reversal" of the previous election's result. The two candidates spent close to $3 million—much of it on the radio and television advertising responsible for setting the campaign's negative tone—making the race the most expensive in state history. With this victory, Clinton became Arkansas' first governor to reclaim the office after having surrendered it in a previous election.[32]

Clinton returned to office a different politician from the idealistic reformer who won election in 1978. He learned to temper his idealistic rhetoric with realistic results: Americans, he realized, liked the rhetoric of grand reform but preferred the reality of incremental change. "What I've learned is that people will accept change if it is based on common sense values, [and] if you don't force them to reject things that give form and meaning to their own lives," Clinton said.[33] By 1982, Clinton had forged the broad outline of the political philosophy and strategy that would guide the rest of his career. Clinton tried to answer the question that Robert F. Kennedy posed in the final days of his 1968 presidential campaign: "How do we seek to change a society that yields so painfully to change?" An assassin's bullet ended Kennedy's quest for an answer. Now Clinton planned to finish the journey.

Although he would be accused throughout his political career of lacking firm principles, there was a guiding theme to Clinton's political message. As a governor and later as president, Clinton was constantly searching for a way to restore public faith in progressive government. He would develop different answers at different times; sometimes his responses were contradictory, and often his efforts to square the political circle left the impression that he believed in nothing at all. The reality, however, was much different. Clinton never abandoned his faith in the idealism of John F. Kennedy, or his belief in the noble intentions of Lyndon Johnson's "Great Society." But he had also witnessed how many of the programs launched in the 1960s failed to live up to expectations, produced unintended consequences, and gave birth to a powerful conservative backlash. Until 1980, these were largely abstract questions that he debated during late-night bull sessions with friends. After his 1980 defeat, the gap between liberal ideals and political realities directly impacted his future in politics. "It was a near-death experience," he observed, "forcing me to be more sensitive to the political problems inherent in progressive politics: the system can absorb only so much change at once; no one can best all the entrenched interests at the same time; and if people think you've stopped listening, you're sunk."[34]

Clinton searched for the ideological "seams" that connected liberals and conservatives. Was there a way for government to provide for the general welfare without violating deeply held American values of individualism, self-help, and limited government? Was it possible to maintain the loyalty of the party's traditional constituencies—labor, blacks, city dwellers, the poor—while luring back into the fold the rapidly growing white, largely suburban, middle class? Could a Democrat articulate a broad, nationalistic message that appealed to Americans, without appearing to be pleading to "special interests"? One of the reasons why Clinton inspired so much passion, especially among his conservative enemies, was because he was asking the central questions that needed to be answered to revitalize liberalism as a fighting faith. He was threatening because he seemed to possess all the talent, both intellectual and political, to update the liberal tradition and bring it back from the political wilderness.

Clinton would develop answers to many of those questions over time, but for now he championed a new, tempered liberalism that focused on two issues: unemployment and education. "I tried never to let the spotlight stray too far from schools and jobs," he wrote.[35] He told the state legislature that he wanted to dedicate "more of our limited resources to paying teachers better; expanding educational opportunities in poor and small school districts; improving and diversifying vocational and high technology programs; and perhaps most important, strengthening basic education."[36] Having learned from his first term that he needed to lay the groundwork before launching bold initiatives, Clinton appointed Hillary the unsalaried chairperson of the Arkansas Education Standards Committee. She traveled around the state, holding hearings in all seventy-five Arkansas counties on ways to improve the failing school system. The hearings were designed to keep the issue before the public and prepare them for his recommendations. What she heard from the estimated 10,000 people who voiced their opinions was that teacher salaries should be raised, but incompetent teachers should be fired. The plan Clinton eventually sent to the legislature called for a small tax increase, but tied the salary raise to a testing program for teachers. "No test, no tax," he declared. The move alienated the powerful teachers union, but won widespread public support. The state's largest union, the Arkansas Education Association, condemned Clinton for supporting the test and rallied other traditional Democratic groups to oppose it. But with polls showing 60 to 65 percent of the public behind the idea, Clinton stood his ground. The program that eventually passed the legislature, and which Clinton signed into law, fell short of his goals, but still represented a major legislative and political achievement.[37]

The fight over education reform in Arkansas called into question the conventional wisdom that Clinton lacked the stomach for tough fights. After his stunning defeat in 1980, Clinton simply learned to pick his fights more carefully. "I learned that if you do a lot of things, and you talk about a lot of different things while you're doing it, the perception may be that you haven't done anything," he recalled.[38] Realizing that an elected official has limited political capital, he learned to focus his energy and priorities. On the vast majority of issues he was willing to find reasonable compromises, but on high-priority items such as education he was willing to pull out all the stops and use his considerable political and intellectual skills to push the agenda forward, even against tough political opposition. He made minor accommodations to political realities, but he fought tenaciously to protect the core of his reform agenda. Oddly enough, Clinton would forget the lesson he learned from his 1980 defeat after he became president. Fortunately for him, Gingrich, like many of his opponents, would misread his record as governor, seeing only the more visible soft side of Clinton and missing his tough, tenacious streak.

In addition to the political adjustments, both Bill and Hillary made stylistic changes as well. On the day that her husband announced his comeback, Hillary changed her surname to Clinton. Although she developed a reputation for being a tough-minded commercial litigator and one of the top lawyers in the state, when in the governor's mansion, Hillary played a more traditional role, attending social functions and giving interviews about her favorite foods (coconut meringue pie from Sue's Pie Shop in downtown Little Rock) and how much she spent on flowers each year for official state occasions ($2,853 in 1990). "She was wearing nice suits, her hair was styled, and she was wearing makeup. She even acted perky, as if she'd been away at cheerleader camp for two years."[39] The governor tamed his curls, cut his sideburns, and traded the blue jeans and out-of-state advisors that had dominated his previous administration for a suit and tie and a staff with close ties to the Arkansas Democratic machine.[40]

The national political scene had changed dramatically in the few years that Clinton had been out of public life. With Reagan at the helm, conservatives set the political agenda in the 1980s, taking their fight to the Democrats, landing a series of punishing ideological and electoral body blows. Oddly enough, by undermining support for the established Democratic leadership, the conservative resurgence created an ideal opportunity for a challenge from an outsider like Bill Clinton. President Kennedy may have been Clinton's hero, but in many ways Ronald Reagan was his mentor. By transferring power from Washington to the state capitals, the "Reagan Revolution" forced the states to once again become the "laboratories of democracy." During the progressive era, the states championed measures that eventually became models for federal legislation. In the 1980s, governors were forced to develop new, pragmatic solutions to expanding economic growth, protecting the environment, and providing for the poor. "The big umbrella under which his evolution began and continues," said former aide Betsey Wright, "is the legacy of the Reagan era's shift of responsibility for policies and budgets to the states and the governors." The need to find innovative ways to address issues such as education, health care, and welfare reinforced Clinton's desire to question liberal orthodoxy. He joined a handful of other governors, both Democrats and Republicans, who embraced the notion of "entrepreneurial government," which favored introducing competition to break down the large, inefficient bureaucracies that held monopolies over crucial government services.[41]

The 1980s were a fertile political and intellectual period for both Newt Gingrich and Bill Clinton. Ironically, Gingrich turned to powerful Washington interest groups to create a new conservative credo and a powerful antigovernment message. Clinton used the state to develop new ideas for revitalizing liberalism and restoring faith in the federal government. Gingrich absorbed and synthesized different strands of conservative thought, which he wove together to create a tougher, more focused message for the Right. At the same time, Clinton was pulling together an eclectic mix of messages and strategies designed to revive the Left. As early as 1985, Clinton was moving toward a form of centrism, recognizing "that the established dogmas of both national political parties are inadequate to the needs of the present."[42]

While experimenting with new governing strategies that used conservative means to achieve liberal goals, Clinton embraced the vocabulary of the communitarian movement, which was a reaction against both the Reagan-era celebration of rugged individualism and the liberal fascination with rights. Many critics charged that Democrats needed to articulate a broader vision that was greater than the sum of its various interest groups. They believed that Americans were longing for a sense of togetherness, a desire to build social bridges, and a new public philosophy that emphasized the responsibilities of citizens as well as their rights. Clinton wove the message into his standard stump speech. Instead of preaching about fairness and justice, Clinton talked about "opportunity and responsibility." Clinton spoke a language of reconciliation, emphasizing the need to build a "constructive partnership" between business and government, to share "responsibilities and opportunities," and to foster a sense of "mutual obligations."

Where Gingrich saw his mission as developing a tougher, more partisan style of conservatism, Clinton believed his challenge was to defend the Democratic majority by co-opting the most appealing aspects of conservatism without sacrificing liberal ideals. Gingrich's goal was to sharpen differences with Democrats; Clinton's plan was to blur distinctions. Clinton responded to the Republican social agenda by weaving appeals to values and individual responsibility into his traditionally populist message. In speech after speech, he affirmed his support for "the moral and cultural values that most Americans share." He was a Democrat who often sounded like a Republican. He championed welfare reform but argued that government needed to spend more on education and training before it cut benefits. He called for using the tax code to reward businesses that expanded jobs. Clinton also understood the value of symbolism—of using small acts to convey that he understood the value of discipline and hard work. As governor he supported and signed a law that denied driver's licenses to teenagers who dropped out of school. He required that fathers be listed on birth certificates to make it easier to track them down for child support. He launched programs that fined parents who failed to attend parent–teacher meetings. He incurred the wrath of the teacher unions by imposing teacher testing, but he also raised taxes to increase salaries and reduce class size.

The results of his success were evident in the election booth. In 1984, the same year that Reagan scored a landslide victory, Clinton won by a massive 63 to 37 percent margin. In 1986, he won by another landslide—63.9 percent to 36.1 percent. What made Clinton especially attractive was his ability to build biracial coalitions, to appeal to traditional Democrats while also attracting more suburban, white voters who usually voted Republican. In 1986, he ran up his largest margins in largely black districts of Desha County (76 percent), Lee County (74 percent), and Mississippi County (68 percent). But he also scored well in Republican counties in northwestern Arkansas. In 1982, White outscored him in Republican Sebastian County by a 64 to 35 percent margin. In 1986, Clinton won 49.4 percent of the vote.[43]

The "Great Communicator" taught Clinton that politics in the media age was as much about public performance as about policy prescriptions. He admired Reagan's mastery of television, his ability to use language to hit emotional chords and provoke a response from his followers. Clinton, who grew up listening to the speeches of John F. Kennedy and Martin Luther King, understood the power of words and rhetoric in building a bond with an audience. "To watch Clinton campaign is to see a natural politician in his habitat," observed the Boston Globe's Curtis Wilkie. "He speaks extemporaneously with the fervor of an evangelical minister. In crowds, he moves gracefully, shaking every hand extended to him. Stopping to talk to individuals, he fixes his eyes on their faces. Listening to their plaints, he clutches their arms as if it were part of a healing process."[44]

His talent cut both ways. Clinton was such a gifted natural politician that he raised the expectations of his followers and the irrational fears of his opponents. Some of his supporters believed that Clinton possessed the political will to achieve just about anything he wanted. When he failed, or compromised, they assumed it was because of a lack of conviction, not a lack of political support. Throughout his career, Clinton was nagged by persistent questions about his character, integrity, and backbone. Critics complained that his defeat in 1980 reinforced his need to please, and made him less willing to endorse controversial ideas and more likely to support the status quo. "He backed off anything controversial," said John Brummett, a columnist for the *Arkansas Times*. "He gave every possible factor in his defeat equal and total weight and decided never to try any of that again."[45] The nickname "Slick Willie," made popular by the Arkansas columnist Paul Greenberg, became a shorthand for the perception that Clinton lacked convictions. In Arkansas, many liberals were let down when he refused to leverage his political capital to fight for a civil rights bill or to challenge the state's right-to-work status. "Liberals are kind of piously disappointed in Clinton because they want to refurbish Arkansas in their image and he hasn't done that," a Clinton aide told the *Boston Globe*'s Wilkie. "They are chasing the ideal, while we're trying to get the whole kit and caboodle moved toward that ideal—not in one term or one decade. Arkansas is slow to move. In Arkansas, we are reluctant to take risky moves or to change our past, because we love it so."[46]

———

By the mid-1980s, Clinton's success on the state level attracted the attention of the national Democratic Party, desperately searching for a new face and an updated message. Walter Mondale's crushing defeat in 1984 forced many Democrats to reconsider their party's direction. At no time in the twentieth century had a major party suffered the electoral landslides experienced by the Democrats between 1968 and 1984. That year, Reagan carried as many states (forty-nine) as the Democratic nominee for president won in the five straight presidential contests after 1968. In losing four of five presidential contests, Democrats won only 43 percent of the popular vote and 113 electoral votes. During the Roosevelt years, Democrats had retained the allegiance of the South and West while pulling heavily from ethnic and blue-collar voters in the Northeast and Midwest. But in 1984, Mondale won only 28 percent of the white southern vote, and his 44 percent showing among Catholics was the lowest of any Democratic presidential candidate since 1924.[47]

Mondale's defeat inspired a group of conservative, mostly southern Democrats to challenge the leftward drift of the national party by creating the

Democratic Leadership Council (DLC). Its founder, Al From, a veteran congressional aide and political strategist, believed that the Democratic Party was too wedded to liberal assumptions about the power of the federal government to solve all social problems, and so closely tied to a handful of special interests that it failed to articulate a broader vision of the national good. The organization he created was focused on exorcizing the ghosts of the Great Society by updating the Democratic agenda, refocusing its priorities, and changing its rhetoric. If it were to survive, the party needed to develop a message and policies that would win back middle-class voters who decided elections, and who increasingly felt comfortable pulling the Republican lever. The "New Democrats" also complained that the party had been traumatized by Vietnam, unwilling to use force to project power and protect American interests. They called for a muscular foreign policy more like JFK's than Jimmy Carter's.

The DLC referred to themselves as a "new generation of Democrats" offering a "new choice to Americans." The group's politics and philosophy appealed to Clinton, who had been articulating many of the same ideas. Always a skilled counter-puncher, Clinton was most comfortable in the ideological seams, picking and choosing ideas and employing language that defied categorization. Many traditional Democrats criticized the growing DLC influence within the party. Jesse Jackson dismissed the group as "Democrats for the Leisure Class." Liberals claimed that "New Democrats" were abandoning the party's historic mission to help outcasts and had failed to learn the "lessons of Vietnam."[48] The DLC, however, provided an ideological home and a political launching pad for Bill Clinton. It was ironic that a man who emerged on the national political scene by criticizing the public policy legacy of the 1960s and by trying to pull the party back to the middle would later emerge as a metaphor for the cultural excess of the decade.

Despite the doubts of his liberal supporters and the fears of his conservative opponents, Clinton emerged as a leading light in the Democratic Party. In 1987 he started testing the waters for a presidential run. In the first six months of the year he made thirty-four trips to twenty states, and he dispatched aides to key primary states to gauge the political temperature. He gave every indication that he was going to throw his hat into the ring. In May, however, the *Miami Herald* forced frontrunner Gary Hart, who had challenged Walter Mondale in 1984, out of the race by exposing his affair with Donna Rice. The Hart exposé changed the rules by which the way the press covered politicians. Hart was not the first presidential candidate to have an affair, but he was the first to be followed and exposed by the press. Clinton had the misfortune to come to national prominence just as the rules of the game were changing. "After the Hart affair," he wrote in his memoirs, "those of us who had not led perfect lives had no way of knowing what the press's standards of disclosure were."[49] Clinton had already earned a reputation among journalists as a womanizer, and the rumors intensified in the weeks following Hart's withdrawal. How would the Hart incident impinge on his candidacy, and how would the press address the issue? "Governor, you're gonna make Gary Hart look like a damned saint," a state trooper reportedly told him. "Yeah," Clinton responded. "I do, don't I?"[50]

While momentum for him to run was building, Clinton was concerned about how the infidelity story would play with the public, and how it would reflect on his marriage. According to Morris, whom Clinton consulted, the issue "loomed large in his consideration. It loomed very large."[51] A few days before the planned announcement, Betsey Wright decided to confront Clinton about the rumors. They sat together in her living room while she asked him to name every woman with whom he had an affair. In the end, Clinton decided it was not his time to run. He apologized to the friends who had gathered in Little Rock for the announcement. Later in the day, he released a statement to the press saying, "I need some family time; I need some personal time."[52]

Massachusetts governor Michael Dukakis moved in to fill the vacuum, using his superior organization to secure the Democratic nomination after a spirited challenge from civil rights leader Jesse Jackson. Dukakis gave Clinton the greatest opportunity yet: the chance to give the nominating address before a prime-time audience at the Democratic Convention. Much of the speech was written by Dukakis aides, using words, rhythms, and styles unfamiliar to Clinton. As he was about to begin, Clinton recalled later, he realized that the house lights were still on and there was no signal to the delegates that they should shut up and listen. The convention whips were working against him, encouraging the disconcerting buzz on the Omni arena floor rather than trying to quell it. For a moment, Clinton considered scrapping the text and winging it. But he decided to plunge ahead, ignoring signs from convention managers to cut it short. He droned on for thirty-three minutes. When he said "and in conclusion," the hall erupted in cheers. He later called his speech "thirty-two minutes of total disaster."[53] Johnny Carson was even harsher, joking that the speech "went over about as well as the Velcro condom."[54] The experience, however, did little to dampen his ambitions or the expectations of party leaders for his eventual run for the presidency.

The Bush campaign turned the fall election into a battle over the legacy of the 1960s, trying to convince the public that Dukakis was soft on crime, unpatriotic, weak on defense, and an enemy of family values. Bush's most effective advertisement told voters about Willie Horton, an African American who had raped a white woman while on leave from a Massachusetts prison while Dukakis was governor. "If I can make Willie Horton a household name," said Bush's campaign manager Lee Atwater, "we'll win the election."[55] Clinton was shocked that Dukakis never understood the ideological potency of the charges or offered a rebuttal. Instead, the nominee traveled the country offering detailed proposals for student aid, health care, and a jobs program. Clinton went to Boston to offer his assistance to the campaign. "I pleaded with the people in the campaign to hit back," he observed. "But they never did it enough to suit me."[56]

On election day, Bush became the first sitting vice president since Martin Van Buren in 1836 to be elected directly to the presidency. He won 53.2 percent of the popular vote and carried forty states with 426 electoral votes. Dukakis won only ten states and the District of Columbia for a total of 112 electoral votes and 46 percent of the popular vote.

The 1988 election had just ended, but Lee Atwater, the tough-minded chairman of the Republican National Committee and architect of President's Bush's successful campaign against Dukakis, was already looking ahead to 1992. He understood that Clinton could be a formidable opponent. "I ain't worried about Mario Cuomo," Atwater said. "Bill Clinton does worry me."[57] Fearing that a moderate southern governor would pose a real threat, Atwater recruited a local congressman, Tommy Robinson, to challenge Clinton in the 1990 race for governor. "Bill Clinton's a good politician. I'd just as soon head him off right now instead of the president having to face him in 1992, or whoever in 1996."[58] Even if Robinson could not beat Clinton, he could "tar him up and down" and make him less threatening in 1992. "We're going to throw everything we can at Clinton—drugs, women, whatever works," he was reported as saying. "We may win or not, but we'll bust him up so bad he won't be able to run again for years."[59] The plan fell apart when Robinson lost the Republican primary to Sheffield Nelson, a wealthy businessman.

Although he was from a small state, and was best known nationally for his long-winded speech at the 1988 Democratic Convention, Clinton emerged as a dark-horse candidate for president in 1992. The national party viewed him as an up-and-coming star and Clinton did nothing to discourage speculation that he had national ambitions. He charmed the press and just about everyone else with whom he came in contact. He also turned his chief disadvantage, being the governor of a small southern state, into an asset. A decade of work with the National Governors' Association provided him with political contacts. He also had the chance to think seriously about domestic issues and develop new policy ideas. He was a progressive who also favored the death penalty. He was an outsider who could distance himself from the failures of the Carter administration. As a governor he had also managed to avoid many of the post-Vietnam foreign policy issues that made Democrats look weak. He never had to cast a vote on whether the United States should give back the Panama Canal, support arms limitations with the Soviets, or provide money for the Contra rebels fighting to overthrow a communist government in Nicaragua.

In April 1989, DLC Director Al From flew to Little Rock to meet with Governor Clinton. He believed that the Arkansas governor was the most promising of a batch of young talent that could redefine the party's message and win the 1992 election. "Have I got a deal for you," he said. "If you take the DLC chairmanship, we will give you a national platform, and I think you will be president of the United States." From promised to provide Clinton with staff, access to fundraising, and a platform. Clinton accepted the position and used the DLC platform to hone his message, raise money, and travel the nation.[60]

Over the next few years, Clinton became a regular at DLC meetings and dinners. The organization, and its think tank, the Progressive Policy Institute, provided him with a steady diet of new ideas. Many Gingrich aides were a part of the same discussions, and Gingrich, according to the journalist Joe Klein, "never missed a meal." It represented a point of intellectual intersection between the "New Democrats" and the "New Republicans." Although their partisan differences would widen over time, they shared a recognition that the old industrial-age solutions, consisting of centralized bureaucracies and assembly line production, were giving way to a new, decentralized, high-technology economy. Government needed to evolve with the changing economy and the new demands of its citizens. In the years before they were to assume the leadership of their respective parties, both men were part of a fluid conversation about problems and potential solutions that ran against the grain of standard partisan debates. Intellectually, Gingrich recognized that Republicans needed to abandon their deep-seated aversion to all forms of government regulation; Clinton realized that liberals needed to rethink their instinctive desire to create a new government program for every problem.

When the DLC met in the spring of 1991 for what the *New York Times* called "the first cattle show of the 1992 campaign," other potential candidates were still clearing their throats, but Clinton was in full campaign roar.[61] Using only a single sheet of paper with twenty-one word cues, Clinton outlined the domestic problems facing the country, from economic decline to chronic poverty to the crisis in health care. But he argued that the

Democratic Party would never get a chance to address those problems unless it regained the confidence of the middle class. Instead of engaging in a familiar debate between the Left and Right, Clinton redefined the choices and changed the political battle lines, emphasizing the themes of opportunity, responsibility, and community. "Our burden is to give the people a new choice rooted in old values. A new choice that is simple, that offers opportunity, demands responsibility, gives citizens more say, provides them responsive government, all because we recognize that we are community. We're all in this together, and we're going up or down together." The speech in Cleveland produced, in the words of one organizer, "an inexorable movement to a Clinton presidential run."[62]

In what would be a common theme in Clinton's career, his most destructive behavior often followed his most promising performances. Two days after his speech in Cleveland, Clinton was back in Little Rock attending the Governor's Quality Conference when he spotted twenty-four-year-old Paula Corbin Jones handing out name tags at the reception desk. According to her later court testimony, which Clinton denied, a state trooper approached her, saying, "The governor said you make his knees knock."[63] The trooper later escorted her to the governor's hotel room, where Clinton proceeded to try and kiss her before dropping his trousers and underwear and asking her to perform oral sex.

Even while allegedly maintaining an active social life, Clinton wanted to stifle media speculation about his private life. Adopting the same strategy he used in his re-election effort in 1982, he decided to tackle the infidelity question up front, hoping to inoculate himself against future questions. He and Hillary appeared at a Washington press breakfast. His aides encouraged reporters to ask him about his private life. "We have been together for almost 20 years and we are committed to each other. It has not been perfect or free from problems, but we are committed to each other and that ought to be enough."[64] He hoped that would be the end of it.

On October 3, 1991, Bill Clinton gave the speech he had been rehearsing for much of his adult life: "Today I proudly announce my candidacy for president of the United States," he told a gathering of supporters in a flag-draped ceremony in Little Rock. At forty-five years of age, Clinton was young enough to project the same youthfulness and vitality of his childhood idol, JFK, but he also projected a newfound sense of middle-aged respectability. He stood at six foot two inches, and carried well his 230 pounds. His unwieldy brownish-red mane and long sideburns had been replaced by a well-manicured and distinguished-looking grey. His intense blue eyes and square jaw made him look like a president from central casting.

As he emerged on the national scene and started his run for the presidency, Clinton was a bundle of contradictions. George Stephanopoulos, a young, idealistic liberal who had previously worked on Capitol Hill for Richard Gephardt, was impressed by Clinton's intellect and his grasp of issues. "He seemed to know something about everything—from the party rules for picking superdelegates to turnout in black precincts on Super Tuesday, from how the credit crunch was bankrupting small businesses in New Hampshire to how microenterprise loans could help farmers in the Mississippi Delta," he recalled. Watching him give a powerful sermon before an all-black audience at the Church of God in Christ convention in Memphis, Stephanopoulos realized that he could be the next RFK, the leader who could bring blacks and whites together. But there were still lingering doubts and questions. "Was there any danger that he would pull a Gary Hart and sabotage his own campaign?" he asked. "Impossible," he concluded. "I was certain that Clinton was too smart and too ambitious to be so self-destructive."[65]

| The Critical Year: 1992

T
HE 2,210 PARTY faithful who gathered for the Republican Convention in the air-conditioned Houston Astrodome in August 1992 were
looking for inspiration. The mood was sour. Just a year earlier, President
George H.W. Bush had waged a brilliant military offensive that expelled
Saddam Hussein from Kuwait and pushed his popularity to unprecedented
heights. But with the Cold War over, and with no clear foreign threat to
distract them, Americans were beginning to focus more attention on problems at home, where a soaring deficit and rising unemployment eroded
support for the administration. "The United States has never been less
threatened by foreign forces than it is today," observed the *New York Times,*
"but the unfortunate corollary is that never since the Great Depression has
the threat to domestic well-being been greater."[1]

Conservatives had always been suspicious of the aristocratic Bush, believing that he lacked Ronald Reagan's deeply embedded faith in conservative principles, his gift for political theater, and his ability to articulate
grand visions that touched a resonant chord with Americans. The president
confirmed those suspicions in 1990 when, over strong conservative objections, Gingrich's included, he signed a bill that attempted to address the
budget deficit by combining modest cuts with moderate tax increases. The
move led to a revolt in the party and produced a spirited primary challenge
from conservative commentator and speechwriter Patrick Buchanan. Bush
managed to crush the revolt, but his party was deeply divided, looking for a
message that would unite it.

For months, Newt Gingrich had been firing off memorandums to the
president and his staff imploring him to adopt a more aggressively ideological

message. As early as February, Gingrich complained that the president's campaign strategy was "unacceptable and must be improved *dramatically*." He even took the liberty of outlining a "vision statement" for the president. "We are engaged in a struggle to govern based on the values, hopes, dreams and fears of the vast majority of Americans. Since the welfare state power structure is opposed to those values we are inevitably in conflict with the Democratic Congressional leadership, much of the bureaucracy, much of the elite news media, most trial lawyers, most of the union leadership (especially the big city employee unions) and most big city machines."[2] The president's advisors ignored the advice, but the memos kept coming. "I am close to despair about the self-destructive patterns and habits of this administration," Gingrich wrote the president in April. "We are inconsistent, uncertain and unreliable."[3]

By August, however, with the president trailing Clinton by nearly twenty points in the polls, the White House switched gears. On opening night of the convention, vanquished primary opponent Patrick Buchanan set the tone for the gathering by claiming that America was in the midst of a "cultural war." "There is a religious war going on in this country for the soul of America," Buchanan shouted. "It is a cultural war, as critical to the kind of nation we shall be as the Cold War itself. And in this struggle for the soul of America, Clinton and Clinton are on the other side and George Bush is on our side." Many of the speakers that followed over the next couple of days echoed the theme of cultural conflict, attempting to paint Clinton as a symbol of the radical 1960s. "The gap between us and our opponents is a cultural divide," Dan Quayle told the convention. "It is a difference between fighting for what is right and refusing to see what is wrong." Marilyn Quayle told the nation, "Not everyone demonstrated, dropped out, took drugs, joined the sexual revolution or dodged the draft."[4] At the same time, delegates adopted a rigidly conservative platform that opposed abortions and denounced gay rights.

Now, finally, the party seemed to be listening to Gingrich's advice. Throughout the convention week, he added his powerful voice to the chorus of attacks, calling the Democratic platform's section on families "the Woody Allen plank," referring to the filmmaker who had admitted to having an affair with his twenty-one-year-old adopted daughter. "Woody Allen having non-incest with a non-daughter to whom he was a non-father because they were a non-family fits the Democratic platform perfectly," Gingrich said. The Democratic Party, he said, "despises the values of the American people." Republicans uphold Judeo-Christian tradition, while Democrats are committed to "multicultural nihilistic hedonism."[5]

The Republican Party declared war on the 1960s at their convention, a war that made Bill and Hillary Rodham Clinton into metaphors for all the social and cultural changes that were transforming American society. One reporter, listening to the verbal attacks, noted, "To hear the Republicans tell it, Bill Clinton is a gay-loving, tax-raising, draft-dodging, water-polluting, pot-smoking adulterer with a radical feminist wife."[6] For the past four decades, fear of Soviet aggression had united the ideologically fractious Republican coalition of libertarians, fiscal conservatives, and social moralists. Now with the Cold War over, Republicans found a new enemy: the 1960s. In the process, noted conservative journalist David Brock, they made Bill and Hillary Clinton "the first two-career, baby-boomer couple who had come of age in the 1960s to vie seriously for the White House" into "accidental culture warriors."[7]

———

Ironically, President Bush's brilliant military victory in the Persian Gulf provided candidate Clinton with an opening by boosting his ratings to unprecedented levels and scaring off many "big name" Democrats. One after another the party's leading contenders—New York Governor Mario Cuomo, House Majority Leader Richard Gephardt, Tennessee Senator Al Gore—announced they would not run. Instead, a handful of new faces dominated the Democratic field. Dubbed the "six pack," they included two sitting governors: Clinton and Virginia's L. Douglas Wilder, the first African American to govern a state. Jerry Brown, the eccentric former governor of California, also threw his hat in the ring. From the Senate came Vietnam War hero and Nebraska Senator Robert Kerrey and Iowa liberal Tom Harkin. Former senator Paul Tsongas of Massachusetts, who had spent the past seven years battling cancer, planned to return to public life by running for president.

In the weeks leading up to the first primary in New Hampshire, Clinton emerged as the Democratic challenger with the most compelling new message. Even before the primary, Clinton's face graced the cover of *Time* magazine, and the *Washington Post* labeled him the "front-runner."[8] It was Clinton's private life, not his public positions, that aroused the greatest controversy. The 1960s came back to haunt him, with questions about sex, drugs, and Vietnam nearly destroying his presidential campaign. A few weeks before the New Hampshire primary, Gennifer Flowers, a Little Rock nightclub singer, announced that she had been Clinton's mistress for years—and produced taped phone conversations to prove it. The affair dominated the news for days until Clinton went on national television with his wife at his side to acknowledge problems in their marriage but deny Flowers's charges, claiming that he had a "friendly but limited" relationship with her. (Years later he admitted to having sex with her.)

No sooner had he dodged that bullet when the *Wall Street Journal* fired another one. Less than two weeks before the primary, the *Journal* challenged Clinton's story about how he managed to avoid the draft during the Vietnam War, suggesting that manipulation, not luck, had saved him from serving in the military.[9] Clinton claimed that he had voluntarily placed himself in the draft while he was a Rhodes Scholar at Oxford University, but that his number was never called. Shortly afterward, ABC News acquired a copy of the letter twenty-three-year-old Clinton had written to Colonel Holmes in 1969 thanking him for "saving me from the draft." "From an era of love beads, bell-bottoms and a tie-dyed T-shirt saying 'Make Love, Not War,' the war in Vietnam has returned to haunt the Democratic Party," observed the *Boston Globe*'s Martin Nolan.[10]

Ironically, for all the moderate positions he would take on issues of policy, Bill Clinton came to represent the cultural challenge of the 1960s. Most Americans learned who Bill Clinton was from the cover of a supermarket tabloid. Before they knew about his "Third Way" or ever heard the phrase "New Democrat," they would know him as an accused adulterer and draft dodger. He made his national television debut on *60 Minutes,* defending himself against the charges while confessing that his marriage had been less than perfect. Clinton had spent his public life polishing his image as a political moderate and policy innovator, and as a spokesman, if not always a model, for mainstream values. Now, in the most important race of his life, as he was trying to define himself for a national audience, he found himself labeled as cultural rebel. As the journalist Joe Klein observed, the two stories combined Clinton's "most commonly assumed depravities: a surplus of libido and a deficit of integrity."[11] A few months later, he added to doubts about his character when he was asked if he had ever smoked pot. His claim that he "did not inhale" provoked nationwide derision, but it was his evasiveness that angered most reporters. When asked previously whether he had ever used drugs, he had responded, "I never broke the laws of my country."[12] It was only when asked whether he had broken the laws of some other country that he admitted to trying marijuana. "That's the first time the question was asked the right way," he said later.

Clinton could not understand why the media and the public were so fascinated by his past and by his sex life. It was true that the media had never before probed so deeply into a candidate's affairs, both real and rumored, but Clinton carried the burden of being the "first" in a number of categories: the first major presidential contender born after World War II, the first representative of the '60s generation to run for president, and the first to be declared the Democratic frontrunner since the Gary Hart affair in 1987. Clinton wished the media would focus on his policy prescriptions for an ailing economy, but they were more interested in his biography, the public and private. "He wanted to be talking about economic recovery, educational improvement and tax cuts for the middle class in the days leading up to Tuesday's primary," observed the *New York Times*. "Instead, he was forced to talk about the choices he made in one of the most divisive periods in American history.[13]

Despite his innate desire to build consensus, Clinton emerged during the 1992 campaign as a threatening cultural figure. Clinton's biography reminded many Americans of the cultural divisions of the 1960s. "It is his genius, and lament, to embody every division of our era," observed the *Washington Post*'s Michael Powell. "The Boy from Hope who is really from Hot Springs. The Bubba become Oxford scholar. The anti-war marcher who joined ROTC and eluded the draft. The family man who can't stop straying."[14] He had believed that his greatest challenge would come from an ingrained and embittered Left. But his candidacy aroused the passion of the Right. Since the days of Richard Nixon's "silent majority," conservatives had demonized the indulgences of the 1960s. The charges had usually been abstract. Now, with Bill Clinton, they found a flesh-and-bones representative of their critique.

Even with the stories of womanizing and draft dodging swirling, Clinton was not easy to cast as a radical. He was the moderate governor of a conservative southern state with a mainstream appeal and a reassuring message. Clinton was even more threatening to conservatives because he represented a new value structure even as he reaffirmed an older one. His talent for blurring ideological distinctions clashed with the conservative view that there existed clearly defined rules of right and wrong. The Right viewed him as a Trojan Horse of the cultural revolution—a reassuring and attractive figure who carried within him the seeds of an alternative culture. As fellow Rhodes Scholar and future Secretary of Labor Robert Reich observed: "The right hated the Clintons because they believed they embodied the values of the 1960s, at the same time they were a portrait of conventional success. He never paid a price, and the right could not tolerate that."[15]

In the short run, the combination of the sex and draft stories took their toll. The candidate's often evasive answers to the draft reinforced the perception of Clinton as "Slick Willie." With public trust eroding, Clinton's political career appeared over. In the forty-eight hours following the draft story, Clinton dropped 17 percent in the polls. I fell "like a turd in a well,"

Clinton later joked. Clinton responded to the crisis by engaging in a burst of campaign activity. Promising to fight "till the last dog dies," the governor campaigned eighteen hours a day, appearing on television shows, standing for long hours at shopping malls and street corners, shaking every hand he could reach, and talking to every ear that would listen. "This was all about Clinton," Stephanopoulos reflected, "his pride, ambition, and anger, his need to be loved and his drive to do good."[16] When he finished second to former Massachusetts senator Paul Tsongas by a 33–25 percent margin, Clinton labeled himself the "comeback kid," and prepared to battle Tsongas in his native South. Unable to connect with voters or to raise the funds needed to continue, the other candidates—Kerrey, Harkin, and Wilder—dropped out of the contest.

Although he had justified his candidacy as a challenge to the party's liberal orthodoxy, Clinton attacked Tsongas from the left, attempting to rally the party's traditional constituency groups—minorities, senior citizens, organized labor—to his candidacy. Abandoning his "New Democrat" theme, he criticized his opponent for suggesting that entitlement programs needed to be cut, for supporting an energy tax to encourage conservation, and for proposing a capital-gains cut at the same time that he advocated cuts in cost-of-living increases for senior citizens. "Isn't it time we closed the book on the '80s?" Clinton asked in a campaign commercial. The Massachusetts senator responded by calling Clinton a "pander bear," who would say anything to please voters. On March 10, Clinton overwhelmed Tsongas, carrying eight states in the South, while his opponent had to settle for victories in Massachusetts, Rhode Island, and Delaware. On March 17, Clinton racked up victories in two major industrial states, Illinois and Michigan. Two days later Tsongas suspended his candidacy. Former California governor Jerry Brown jumped in to take his place as the "anti-Clinton" candidate, but was quickly overwhelmed by Clinton in the crucial New York primary.[17]

By the end of the primary season the public expressed disenchantment with both the Democratic and Republican nominees. Bush managed to vanquish his primary opponent, but he failed to inspire public confidence in his presidency. Bush's approval ratings had sunk to lows not seen since the days of Jimmy Carter's malaise. At the same time, nearly 25 percent of registered voters said they were unlikely to vote for Clinton "because of questions about his character." By the time he won the California primary in June, Clinton was running third in the polls behind President Bush and maverick billionaire Ross Perot, campaigning as a third-party candidate. "I don't think you can minimize how horrible I feel," Clinton told his staff that spring, "having worked all my life to stand for things, having busted my butt for seven months, and the American people don't know crap about it after I have poured $10 million worth of information into their heads."[18]

For six weeks leading up to the Democratic Convention in New York, Clinton worked without distraction painting a positive picture of himself. Instead of resisting reporters' probing questions about his past, Clinton would construct his own biography. If he was going to have any chance of winning in November, Clinton would have to refine his message, sharpen his image, and prove that he was a candidate whom people could trust. He developed an effective new slogan: "Putting people first." To demonstrate that he could stand up to traditional Democratic interest groups, he went to Jesse Jackson's National Rainbow Coalition Convention and attacked the black rap artist Sister Souljah for making racially antagonistic statements. Two days later, Clinton told the United Auto Workers that he supported the North American Free Trade Agreement. Taking advantage of unconventional media outlets, he revealed to MTV viewers what type of underwear he wore. Later he went on a late-night talk show, put on dark Ray-Ban sunglasses, and played a few verses of "Heartbreak Hotel" on the saxophone.

In July, the Democrats assembled at New York's Madison Square Garden in a hopeful mood. During the first few days of the convention, Clinton managed to transform himself in the eyes of many Americans from a pot-smoking adulterer who dodged the draft into the middle-class son of a single mother who had devoted his life to public service. "Slick Willie" had been transformed into the "man from Hope." Perhaps the boldest move was his selection of a running mate. Four days before the opening of the convention he abandoned the unwritten law that a vice-presidential candidate should provide geographical and ideological balance when he chose fellow southerner Al Gore, a senator from Tennessee. "My life is a testament to the fact that the American dream works," he told audiences. "I got to live by the rules that work in America and I wound up here today running for President of the United States of America." The party managed to avoid its usual fights over controversial social issues and to adopt a platform that underscored Clinton's "New Democrat" message. Even the conservative *Wall Street Journal* seemed impressed, observing that instead of dividing the economic pie, the platform "focuses on making the pie grow."[19]

Hours before ascending the podium to give the most important speech of his life, Clinton received a boost from an unlikely source—Ross Perot. The unpredictable Perot announced that he was withdrawing from the race, claiming that "the Democratic party has revitalized itself." The timing could not have been better for Clinton. Perot cut loose his army of independent voters on the same day that Clinton would command the nation's media with his acceptance address. Clinton took full advantage of the opportunity. He told the convention that he accepted the nomination "in the name of all those who do the work and pay the taxes, raise the kids and play by the rules, in the name of the hardworking Americans who make up our forgotten middle class." In a direct appeal to Perot voters, Clinton announced a "New Covenant" with the American people. "We offer opportunity," he declared. "We demand responsibility."[20]

Clinton's speech underscored his attempt to portray his candidacy as a fundamental break with the party's past. The press and the public responded favorably. The *San Francisco Chronicle* declared that Clinton's nomination represented "a historic and dramatic shift for the party."[21] Polls revealed a massive shift to Clinton—more than the expected increase from the intense media coverage. Clinton's favorable rating shot up from 41 percent to 59 percent, and he jumped from five points behind into a twenty-three-point lead over Bush. The increase eclipsed the boost Dukakis received from his nomination four years earlier. After the convention, Perot supporters, by a 2–1 margin, preferred Clinton to Bush.

———

Bill Clinton was not the only candidate dealing with a "character" issue in 1992. In Georgia, Democrats still controlled the legislature and they were determined to get rid of Newt Gingrich. After the 1990 census, they redrew the boundaries of his original district, making it more Democratic. Gingrich had a choice: he could run in his old, more liberal district, or he could find a new area that was more Republican. Instead of trying to hold on to his old seat, Gingrich decided to move to the newly created, heavily Republican sixth district. A reporter for the *Atlanta Journal-Constitution* described it as "endless ribbons of asphalt that lead to mazes of office parks occupied by workers who come from a vast sea of swim-tennis subdivisions."[22] The *Washington Post* called the new gerrymandered district "a Republican pollster's dream, a sprawl of affluent suburbs as far as the eye can see, a Lexus in every driveway and a Lean Cuisine in every microwave."[23] Nearly 60 percent of the residents had college degrees. More than 60 percent had incomes greater than $50,000, compared to 38 percent nationally.

It was still a risky move. Gingrich had to adjust to a new suburban district where he had no roots and no organization. If he was going to be successful, he needed to communicate with suburban voters, especially educated women, who had never been strong supporters of his partisan tactics. His opponent in the primary was a seasoned Republican with deep roots in the district. He also knew that if he could prevail in that race, it would virtually guarantee him a seat in Congress, giving him a solid base to launch his conservative revolution in the 1990s. He embarked on a new kind of campaign—a listening tour of the district to convince voters that he did not have all the answers, and that he wanted to learn from them.

His primary opponent, former state representative Herman Clark, turned Gingrich into a symbol of Washington arrogance, pointing out that while campaigning as a reformer, Gingrich supported a $35,000 congressional pay raise. In his efforts to undermine the credibility of the House Democratic leadership, Gingrich had unintentionally provided his opponent with a potent weapon to use against him. In 1991, Gingrich turned an internal audit that found that many congressmen had overdrawn from the House-managed bank into a national story. The problem was that Gingrich and a handful of Republicans were among the congressmen who wrote bad checks. Members of his own party pleaded with him not to make a big issue out of the incident, but Gingrich could not walk away from such a tempting opportunity to attack the "corrupt" Democratic leadership, even if it meant hurting individual Republicans. "This is about systemic, institutional corruption, not personality," he said. "To ask the Democratic leadership to clean things up would be like asking the old Soviet bureaucracy under Brezhnev to reform itself. It ain't going to happen."[24]

Back at home, Gingrich was feeling the heat. At nearly every campaign stop, his primary opponent pointed out that Gingrich wrote twenty-two bad checks from the House bank, including a $9,463 check to the IRS, and that he rode around Washington in a chauffeured limousine at taxpayers' expense. "The man was elected in 1978, and since that time he has become just another Congressman, part of the inside-the-Beltway gang up there," charged Clark. Clark drove the point home with clever radio and television ads sung to the tune of "Old MacDonald."

> With a bounced check here
> and a pay raise there,
> Here a check, there a check,
> everywhere a bounced check.
> Newt Gingrich wrote a rubber check,
> to the I.R.S.[25]

This attack resonated even with voters in a heavily Republican district, raising questions about whether Gingrich was a real reformer or just an opportunist. "Newt Gingrich is going to go down in history as the most hypocritical politician ever," said Matthew Glavin, the head of a conservative research organization.[26] "As a conservative, Newt has been out there talking the conservative rhetoric, but when it comes down to action, he's got his hand in your pocket just like every other politician."[27] The *Atlanta Journal-Constitution* editorialized, "You can't preach about the evils of the entrenched political elite from the back seat of a chauffeured Lincoln."[28]

The attacks forced Gingrich to go on the defensive. The man who turned assailing Washington into an art form, complaining about wasteful spending and corruption, campaigned by promising voters that he could use his insider status to their benefit. "If you had the choice between the No. 2 ranking Republican in the House or you can have a freshman who doesn't have any idea who the cabinet members are, has never met any of them and has never worked with the president, which one do you think can do more for Cobb County?" he asked.[29] Still, as he marched in a traditional July 4th parade, shaking hands and greeting bystanders, people shouted out: "Where's your limo?" and "How 'bout them checks?"[30]

Democrats, who realized their best chance of defeating Gingrich would come in the Republican primary and not the general election, poured money and resources into the Clark campaign. The Democratic Congressional Campaign Committee aired anti-Gingrich spots during the primary, and a number of liberal groups, including the Sierra Club, Ralph Nader's Public Citizen, and the powerful Association of Trial Lawyers, provided money. Gingrich viewed Clark's challenge as part of the larger Democratic effort to defeat him. "It all started when I began the investigation of Jim Wright. From that day on there has been a core group in the Democratic party that would do anything to beat me, and if they can use Herman Clark to beat me, they will."[31]

In what would prove to be one of the most consequential primary campaigns in recent memory, Gingrich held on to his seat in Congress by only 980 votes out of the more than 70,000 cast. He finished with 35,699 votes, or 51 percent, to Clark's 34,719 votes, or 49 percent. Gingrich outspent his opponent eight to one, investing as much money in the final week on television ads—$100,000—as Clark did during the entire campaign.[32] "It cost us $35 a vote the way I figured it," said Gingrich spokesman Tony Blankley.[33] Despite his enormous resources and national name recognition, Gingrich had now won two elections by the narrowest of margins, revealing that even those who knew him best, and who benefitted most from his power, were deeply ambivalent about the man and his message.

———

Gingrich had dodged another electoral bullet in one of the most Republican congressional districts in the nation, but it did little to diminish his desire to play a major role on the national stage. He continued to offer the president political advice. Over Labor Day, Gingrich warned Republicans not to underestimate Clinton. "Bill Clinton is one of the greatest campaigners I've seen," he said. "Don't take him for granted."[34] The situation grew even more complicated after Perot decided to get back into the race. Gingrich believed Perot posed a special threat because he could siphon off enough voters to prevent Bush from winning. He did not believe that Clinton could win a majority, but he feared that together with Perot, they could prevent a Republican victory. "A forty-five percent Perot, thirty percent Bush, twenty-five percent Clinton race was very plausible," he observed in a memo.[35]

The fall campaign turned into a referendum on George Bush's domestic leadership. The president's greatest asset, his handling of the Persian Gulf War, barely showed up on the public's radar screen. "Foreign policy has never had less salience," said Democratic pollster Mark Mellman. In 1984, the last time an incumbent ran for re-election, Reagan had used the image of a bear wandering in the woods to underscore the need to elect someone who would stand up to the Soviet threat. Eight years later, said Mellman, "The bear has committed suicide." Instead voters directed their anger at the administration for the sluggish economy. By October, Bush's job approval rating had sunk to 25 percent, and nearly half of all voters said they would not vote for him under any circumstances.

Clinton entered the fall campaign with a double-digit lead in national polls and comfortable margins in the key battleground states of Pennsylvania, New Jersey, Ohio, and Illinois. Clinton aides were determined to avoid the mistake of the Dukakis campaign, which had failed to respond quickly to Bush's relentless attacks. James Carville, the governor's colorful and pugnacious campaign consultant, established a "war room" on the fourth floor of the Clinton headquarters in Little Rock. From here Carville and his team monitored Bush's every move, tracked news reports, and prepared instant responses to Republican attack ads. The purpose of the war room, Stephanopoulos recalled, "was to make us appear relentless, to intimidate, to make anyone who was paying attention think of us as aggressive, different, and a little unpredictable—pretty tough for Democrats." The campaign themes were summed up on a handwritten note Carville posted in the middle of the room: "Change vs. More of the Same"; "The economy, stupid"; and "Don't forget health care."[36]

On the campaign trail, Clinton fused two different strains of populism into a potent political message for change. He told independent suburban white voters of his support for law and order, capital punishment, and individual responsibility. Clearly distinguishing himself from the party's more liberal past, he described welfare as "a second chance, not a way of life," and promised "to end welfare as we know it." Before the party faithful Clinton promised to provide "basic health care to all Americans," to protect social security, and to tax the rich.[37] A charismatic personality and compelling speaker, Clinton called for using the power of the federal government to promote economic growth through education and job training. Most important of all, Clinton developed a style of politics that made him credible as a messenger of change. He understood the impact of television, was comfortable performing for the cameras, and understood the new participatory style of campaigning, where issues were discussed on evening talk shows and in town-hall forums. Clinton viewed foreign policy as an extension of his domestic agenda. "If we're not strong at home, we can't lead the world we've done so much to make," Clinton told an audience at Georgetown University. Not wanting to appear weak, Clinton emphasized his willingness to use American force overseas when needed. "We can never forget this essential fact: Power is the basis for successful diplomacy. And military power has always been fundamental in international relationships."[38]

Bush employed many of the "wedge issues" that Republicans had used so effectively against Democrats in the past. Clinton, Bush said, was an "elitist," an "Oxford-educated . . . social engineer" who preferred European-style socialism to the rugged individualism Bush learned from the Texas oil fields. He questioned Clinton's character and Vietnam draft status, and charged that Clinton was a traditional "tax-and-spend" Democrat who was soft on crime.[39] At the same time, Vice President Dan Quayle barnstormed the nation questioning Clinton's patriotism and trustworthiness. "The American people want their president to be faithful to their country," he told audiences. "They want a president to be faithful to their principles. They want a president who is faithful to their family."[40] Bush picked up the theme, claiming that Clinton's participation in protests against the Vietnam War was unpatriotic. His campaign issued a press release suggesting that the KGB had arranged a Clinton trip to the Soviet Union in 1969.

The end of the Cold War made Republican attacks on Clinton's patriotism appear shrill, and the public backlash forced the Bush campaign to retreat. The response underscored a key difference between 1988 and 1992: cultural "wedge issues" had lost their bite. "Wedge issues don't work on Clinton because he's taken positions that inoculate him," observed a centrist Democrat. The Democratic nominee routinely mentioned his work-oriented welfare views, posed with police officers and their widows at law-and-order events, and emphasized his support for the death penalty. Bush persisted in his attacks on values, despite overwhelming poll evidence showing that voters were more interested in economic issues. "Every time Bush used some of these issues," a frustrated Republican observed, "it would reaffirm with some voters that he was out of touch with the most important issue."

The polls froze as the candidates prepared for a series of three debates over a nine-day period beginning on October 11. The debates were the first to include an independent candidate along with the two major party nominees. Bush probably wished Perot had stayed away from the first debate in St. Louis. The independent poked fun at Clinton's claim that his experience in Arkansas made him qualified to be president, comparing Arkansas to a "corner grocery store." He reserved his best shots, however, for Bush, accusing him of mismanaging the economy. When Bush touted his experience in the Oval Office, Perot responded, "I don't have any experience in running up a $4 trillion debt."[41]

The informal format of the second debate in Richmond, Virginia, which allowed candidates to take questions from a studio audience with a moderator directing follow-up questions, played to Clinton's strengths. The debate began with the moderator blunting Bush's assault on Clinton by asking the candidates to refrain from personal attacks. The defining moment came when a woman in the audience asked the candidates how the national debt had impacted them. She meant to say recession, but only Clinton was quick enough on his feet to appreciate the confusion. Perot said that the deficit impacted him because he was willing to "disrupt my private life" to run for president. Bush's response seemed to confirm doubts about his candidacy. "I'm not sure I get it," he said. Clinton launched into a "I feel your pain response," walking up to the woman, looking her in the eye, and saying that as the governor of a small state he knew people who were out of work and wondering how they would pay their bills.[42]

Bush, who trailed by wide margins in most opinion polls, seemed to come alive in the final debate, finally making pointed jabs at Clinton. He made Clinton the issue, challenging his record in Arkansas, his "waffling" on the issues, and his record as a tax-and-spend liberal. He warned taxpayers they would have to "lock your wallet" if Clinton and "a spendthrift Democratic Congress" brought back the days of Jimmy Carter.[43] He called on Clinton "to level with the American people" about his draft record, saying he was unfit to be president. "The bottom line is we simply cannot take the risk on Governor Clinton," he told supporters.[44]

Despite his strong final performance, the debates did little to lift Bush's standing in the polls. As the election moved into the final weeks, Gingrich's frustration with the Bush campaign peaked. He felt that Clinton had successfully turned the election into a referendum on personality, not values. In

October, with only days left, Gingrich prepared a memo called "The 8 Steps to Defeating the Democratic Ticket in 1992." "We must define our own values and principles and contrast clearly the very great difference between us and the values and principles of the Democratic ticket. This is not a race between two personalities and tickets sharing the same values. This is a race between two very different systems of values, principles and goals." He believed that the Republican antitax, antigovernment message resonated with more than 60 percent of the public. They needed to exploit the "moral authority gap." "The campaign must be the equivalent of a trial with the voters as a jury." In another handwritten memo he said, "Anger against Congress is so great that it is easier than it has ever been to assert that Congressional Democratic proposals are destructive and must be stopped. In this climate opposing Congress is better than cooperating with it."[45]

Bush got the hint. He sharpened his "T&T" (trust and taxes) attacks. In the frantic final weeks, Bush referred to Clinton and Gore as "two bozos." Calling the governor "Slick Willie," Bush said, "He is bobbing and weaving, and you cannot do that as president." On another occasion in Wisconsin, he referred to the Democratic ticket as "Governor taxes and Ozone man." The president's closing attack ad of the campaign showed a picture of Arkansas as a barren wasteland while the narrator recited Clinton's tax-and-spend record as governor. In the Little Rock war room, Clinton aides watched as their candidate's lead dropped from double digits to less than five points in the final week. "How scared are you?" George Stephanopoulos asked James Carville. "How scared?" Carville repeated. "I'm this scared: if we lose, I won't commit suicide, but I'll seriously contemplate it."[46]

At home, Gingrich confronted a feisty Democratic opponent who picked up where his primary opponent left off in June. A local lawyer and a political novice, Tony Center, hammered away at Gingrich on the "character" issue. In October, polls were showing that the race was tighter than expected, forcing Gingrich to spend more time than he wanted in the district and less time traveling around the country. In September a poll showed that only 28 percent of residents gave Gingrich a positive rating. Nearly 70 percent described him as a "typical politician."[47] "Under normal circumstances, the district would elect a Republican congressman without a fight," said a local Republican pollster. "But because Newt has moved here and because he is Newt, there is a fight."[48]

Center continued to attack Gingrich for his limousine use and bank overdrafts. "Newt most emphatically describes what's wrong with Congress," Center told audiences. "He's a mouthpiece for an idea, but he does not live that idea." To underscore his point, Center used the ugly details of Gingrich's divorce from his first wife, Jackie, to hit the "character" nerve. Center ran a television ad claiming that Gingrich "delivered divorce papers to his wife the day after her cancer operation." The ad went on to charge that "the same Newt Gingrich who used taxpayer money for his limo, had to be ordered by the court to pay for his kids' heat and electricity. No more perks. No more lies. No more Newt." The directness of the attacks shocked local observers and attracted the attention of the national news media, which saw a potential upset. Gingrich, who made ethics the centerpiece of past campaigns and accusation and innuendo a part of his political style, expected that his integrity and private life would never come into question. "This filth is so sickening," he said. "If survival in public life means this level of degradation, I don't want to be part of it."[49] Yet he never acknowledged or accepted his role in creating the culture of ethical inquisition that would eventually destroy him.

———

Voters rewarded Clinton on election night, giving him 43 percent of the popular vote, compared to 38 percent for Bush. Clinton's margin in the Electoral College was far more decisive. He won 31 states and 357 electoral votes. The ticket ran ahead of the Republicans in every age group, but scored especially well with young voters. Clinton also won a larger percentage of white voters than any Democratic nominee since Jimmy Carter in 1976 and helped the Democrats retain control of both houses of Congress. Perot won a bigger share of the vote—19 percent—than any third-party candidate had since Teddy Roosevelt in 1912. "That Bill Clinton survived, won his party's nomination and then defeated a sitting president who'd once enjoyed record levels of public support must rank as one of the most extraordinary political stories in American history," observed Joe Klein.[50]

In a victory speech to a joyous crowd in Little Rock, Clinton described the election as a "clarion call" to deal with a host of ignored domestic problems and to "bring our nation together." The same evening, Newt Gingrich was in his home district celebrating victory. After a bruising campaign, he scored a decisive victory against his Democratic opponent, winning by a comfortable 58 to 42 percent margin. Although Clinton carried Georgia for the Democrats, he garnered only 29 percent of the vote in Gingrich's Republican district. In a clear sign of the sea change taking place in southern politics, Gingrich, who had been the sole Georgia Republican in Congress for most of his tenure, was now joined by three others. It was the first time since Reconstruction that Georgia had sent so many Republicans to Congress.[51]

Clinton and Gingrich were two men moving in opposite directions headed for an inevitable confrontation in the 1990s. While Gingrich was riding a rising tide of conservative activism, Clinton was struggling to energize a demoralized Democratic coalition. Gingrich had to fight his way to the top, challenging the ingrained Democratic establishment and the leadership of his own party; Clinton charmed his way to the top of a leaderless party desperate for a fresh face and new ideas. As an emerging leader in the minority party, Gingrich used polarization to enhance his power and strengthen his party's competitive position. As a rising star of a beleaguered but still dominant party, Clinton worked hard to blur differences and reforge some common ground. Each filled his party's need: Gingrich the firebrand rebel who had an instinct for the juggler; Clinton the charismatic leader who could bring people together. As an executive, Clinton always needed to force compromise in order to move his agenda forward and so was accustomed to building bipartisan coalitions. As the leader of a party that was in decline, he recognized the necessity of reaching out to Republicans. It was also his nature to be accommodating. Gingrich, on the other hand, was by nature combative and had risen to power by attacking Democrats, not by building coalitions with them.

For Gingrich, issues were always defined in terms of right and left. For Clinton, distinctions of left and right were meaningless. He operated in the grey area between ideological extremes. Clinton was a disciplined and measured politician. Although long winded, he was always careful and precise in his use of language. Gingrich was often bombastic and emotional. As governor, Clinton exercised the art of practical politics, always tempering his idealism with the possibility of success, weighing the political consequences of every action and every word. As only one voice in a minority party in Congress that lacked votes to pass legislation, Gingrich did not have to worry about taking political responsibility for his words or deeds. Clinton was forced to build a broad coalition that included blacks and whites, conservative Democrats and moderate Republicans. Hailing from a predominantly white, middle-class district, Gingrich was never forced to broaden his message or his appeal.

They connected with their audiences in different ways. Clinton created the illusion of intimacy; Gingrich made no effort to create that illusion. Clinton was tender and empathetic; Gingrich cold and standoffish. Gingrich impressed people with his intellect and his ability to articulate a grand vision and break down problems into smaller components. He framed issues in a way that gave conservatives reason to fight. Clinton possessed similar intellectual gifts, but he seduced his audience with his warmth. "Newt's power comes from his brilliance," said former Gingrich campaign manager Chip Kahn. "Clinton is brilliant, but his power comes from his human touch."[52]

Clinton consciously toned down his intellect, emphasizing his southern drawl and a casual informality that belies his Yale and Oxford education. Gingrich recited ancient philosophers and obscure theories to impress audiences with his wisdom. Clinton was a natural storyteller where the larger lessons were often hidden in homespun tales; nearly every Gingrich point had a four-step plan. Clinton touched people, placing his hand on their shoulders as his eyes scanned them, trying to read body language, searching for some clue about how they were responding to his message. Gingrich was often so wrapped up in his own thoughts that he barely knew there were other people in the room. While both men loved to talk politics, Clinton had a much wider cultural vocabulary and enjoyed chatting about everything from sports to movies. Their styles and personalities were different but equally persuasive. Part preacher and part professor, they were always on message and certain of their convictions.

As they moved onto the national stage they were men with very different image problems. Gingrich, who had earned a well-deserved reputation as a pugnacious and partisan brawler, needed to soften his image; Clinton, who often came across as too accommodating, wanted to project toughness. Although Clinton's easy-going manner and warm personality made him appear soft, it disguised a hard inner core. Gingrich's tough exterior disguised an often soft and vulnerable interior.

Both men challenged the traditional politics of their parties and called for a "third way"—a new approach to thinking about problems that questioned conventional liberal and conservative notions. Both men pushed their parties to think about the future, realizing that the party that responded to these new challenges would likely dominate the political scene. "You had these two figures who were trying to move these tectonic plates," said Gingrich advisor Joe Gaylord.[53] Gingrich was frustrated with Republican politics in Congress and pushed his party to adopt new ideas and a more confrontational style. Clinton was eager to distance himself from the liberal excesses of his party's recent past while keeping alive the tradition of activist government.

| First-Term Blues

ALTHOUGH THEY WERE CLEARLY rising stars in their respective parties, Bill Clinton and Newt Gingrich had little direct contact before 1992. They met casually at public events in the 1980s when Clinton was in Washington lobbying on behalf of the nation's governors, but for the most part they observed each other from a distance. "We had a distant awareness of each other," recalled Gingrich, who remembered a brief encounter with Clinton during a national governor's convention in 1988.[1] The first official meeting between the two men took place on January 26, 1993, shortly after Clinton assumed office, when Gingrich attended a congressional leadership meeting at the White House.

The Clinton presidency was already off to a rough start. The press praised Clinton for his touching and uncharacteristically brief (fourteen minute) inaugural address. "Let us give this capital back to the people to whom it belongs," Clinton said, reinforcing the populist theme of the campaign. Within days of taking the oath of office, however, the president found his new administration engulfed in controversy. Clinton had promised during the campaign to focus "like a laser beam" on the economy, but he created a political firestorm during his first week in office by proposing to lift the longstanding ban on homosexuals in the military. He also blurred his "New Democrat" message with a fruitless search for a cabinet that "looked like America." According to two observers, his efforts to find a female attorney general looked like "an auction between left-wing interest groups," and produced a public relations fiasco when he was forced to withdraw his first choice, Zoe Baird, after it was revealed that she had hired an illegal immigrant to work as a nanny.[2] Congressional Democrats were publicly fretting about

Clinton's slow start. His indecisiveness and inability to stay on message renewed doubts about whether he possessed the strength of character to be an effective leader.

In order to help get back on track, Clinton gathered bipartisan leaders from the House and Senate in the cabinet room to coordinate strategy and plead for bipartisanship. Gingrich watched as the president worked his way around the room, shaking hands, always making some personal comment designed to create a false sense of intimacy. "He was compelled to have one transactional moment with everyone in the room."[3] When he got to Gingrich, the president commented on how much he liked his tie. After the initial pleasantries, they took their seats around the large, oval mahogany conference table. The president sat in the tallest chair, strategically located in the center of the room.

As minority whip, Gingrich sat across the table from the president and to his right, listening as Clinton opened the meeting. "Want your cooperation hear from where you're coming," Republican Leader Robert Michel noted in cryptic shorthand, observing that the president spoke with "no notes or crib cards." Vice President Gore picked up on the theme of cooperation. "We have a patriotic duty to end grid lock," he insisted. While members of the Republican leadership offered suggestions and observations, Gingrich scribbled a note on White House stationery to his friend and future biographer Mel Steely. "I am in a personal meeting with the new President. He is very smart," he wrote. "We will see if he is equally wise." Gingrich managed to have the last word at the meeting. According to Michel, he was "very complimentary" of the president personally but "admonished" him for lifting the gay ban. He also sent a clear warning signal as the president and his team were developing its economic package. "Government sacrifice first," he said, "not families."[4] Shortly after the meeting, Gingrich told his staff: "I thought I had met FDR without polio."[5] Although he admired Clinton's political skills and his intellect, Gingrich also believed that he was superficial and lacking both discipline and backbone. Privately, he dismissed him as "a frat boy who reads books." He was determined to challenge the new president's mettle.

The Democrats in the room presented a more immediate concern for Clinton. The president was flanked on one side by the majority leader in the Senate, George Mitchell, a former federal judge known for his modest manner and tenacious style. On the president's right sat the Democratic Speaker of the House, Thomas Foley, who first won election to Congress in 1964, the same year Bill Clinton graduated high school. After twelve years of Republican rule, many members had never served under a Democratic president before and were unaccustomed to responding to the will of a president of their own party. "Democrats didn't defer to presidents," observed speechwriter Michael Waldman, "they investigated them."[6] The presence of these two men, along with Missouri Congressman Richard Gephardt, who harbored presidential ambitions of his own, and Michigan's David Bonior, a staunch ally of organized labor, underscored that the congressional leadership was more liberal than the president, and either indifferent or hostile to his New Democrat agenda. Most House Democrats felt little loyalty to the president. He won with only 43 percent of the popular vote and ran behind most House members in their home districts.

Since he had slim majorities in both houses, Clinton needed all the Democratic votes he could muster to get his agenda through Congress. Clinton took office with 259 House Democrats and 58 Senate Democrats—considerably fewer than the number on hand when Jimmy Carter took office in 1977. Clinton was determined to avoid the mistakes that Carter made in his first few months in office when he had surrounded himself with a Georgia "mafia" with few ties to Capitol Hill; alienated many powerful leaders of the Hill, including Speaker Tip O'Neill; and appeared indifferent to the needs of congressional Democrats. "There was a terrific fear in the first year that he would become like Carter," said Paul Begala.[7] To avoid these problems, Clinton surrounded himself with a staff that had close ties to Capitol Hill: George Stephanopoulos had worked for Richard Gephardt; Leon Panetta, first budget director and later chief of staff, had served many years in Congress. "At almost every turn, these advisors urged cooperation, not confrontation, with Congress as the way to steer clear of Carter's difficulties," observed journalists Dan Balz and Ronald Brownstein.[8]

As a result, Clinton acceded to the wishes of congressional Democrats. "Instead of setting out to command a broad bipartisan majority across the country, we settled for a narrow, shrinking majority of our own Democratic ranks," recalled domestic policy advisor Bruce Reed. Mitchell and Foley talked him out of pushing welfare reform until after he passed heath care reform. They warned him against pursuing both campaign-finance reform and lobbying reform. "Members will think you're out to take away their current livelihoods and their future livelihoods in one fell swoop," they said. At one point, Clinton complained that he felt tied to Congress "like Ahab to Moby Dick, with the same results." Clinton, recalled Reed, "was looking for the center of the Democratic caucus that he needed to pass legislation; not the center of public opinion he needed to claim a mandate."[9]

A slim majority and divided party were not the only serious obstacles the new president faced. In the past, the president's power derived from his ability to use the "bully pulpit," defining issues and shaping public debate. By 1992, however, the media had become fragmented and the president's voice was often drowned out by talking heads. As the first president elected after the Cold War, he was forced to govern without a unifying cause or threat that enhanced presidential power. In the past, Democratic and Republican presidents tapped into deep-seated fears of Soviet aggression to forge a sense of national unity. With the potential threat of imminent nuclear annihilation removed, politics became more personal. The president assumed a new celebrity status, and while Clinton played the role well, he often blurred the line separating public and private—a distinction that he would later cling to in order to save his presidency.

He also confronted a GOP right wing in full revolt, unwilling to accept him as president. "Clinton stirred up feelings of hatred" among conservatives not seen "since the McCarthy era," reported the authors of *The Right Nation*. The right wing, noted David Brock, "with its portrayal of the Clintons as the apotheosis of the 1960s, was able to set the terms of engagement against the new administration."[10] Conservatives believed they were engaged in a war for the soul of America, and they viewed the election in 1992 of a draft-dodging, pot-smoking womanizer as an indication that they were losing the war. The editorial pages of the *Wall Street Journal* savaged him daily, while the *American Spectator* published a series of articles, mostly untrue, about the president's promiscuous sex life and shady business practices. Moral Majority founder Jerry Falwell sold 150,000 copies of a tape that accused the president of murdering witnesses to cover up his involvement in a cocaine-smuggling ring.[11] Republican officials learned that the best way to raise money was to demonize Clinton. The message of Republican fundraising appeals was "red meat.... one hundred percent anti-Clinton," said a Republican National Committee official.[12] In one letter, Republicans attacked Clinton for supporting "far-out social concepts of diversity, multi-culturalism and political correctness." The appeals worked. By 1993, 93 percent of Republicans believed the federal government "no longer represents the intent of the Founding fathers."[13]

Clinton's difficult transition only confirmed Gingrich's suspicions that he was a weak and ineffectual, albeit charming and smart, president. In the months after Clinton won election, Gingrich had been reaching out to Republicans in Arkansas to learn more about the new president from the people who knew him best. Most of what he heard repeated the familiar, but inaccurate, notion that Clinton lacked backbone. "If you push he will bend," he was told.[14] "They said he worked hardest to bridge differences with his enemies, and he was toughest on his friends," said Arne Christenson.[15] As a leader of the minority party, Gingrich was primarily looking for vulnerabilities to exploit. His strategy leading up to the 1994 elections was, as it had been for the previous decade, to polarize the debate between Democrats and Republicans. He planned to target those districts that had elected Democratic congressmen but had also voted for Bush over Clinton. By defining the issues and polarizing the choices, he would force voters to choose either the Clinton program or the Republican alternative.

In addition, he planned to continue his efforts to make the Democrats, both in Congress and now in the White House, appear incompetent and out of touch. The key was to arouse public disdain for a Democratically controlled federal government and to reinforce the perception that Clinton was a weak and ineffectual leader. It was a two-pronged approach: on issues where they agreed, Gingrich would provide the votes, but he would muddy the waters, making the process appear chaotic and creating the impression that Clinton was incapable of governing. On key items of the president's agenda that he opposed, Gingrich would twist the arms of fellow Republicans, even many moderates, to get them to withhold their support. Without Republican votes, the president would be forced into the arms of his more liberal Democratic allies on Capitol Hill, which would further blur the centrist message of his campaign. Clinton may not have been a 1960s liberal, but Gingrich was going to make him look like one. Although he had always managed to avoid ideological labels in the past, Clinton fell into the trap set by both his allies and enemies.

The president realized that Gingrich had little interest in hearing his pleas for bipartisanship. "Clinton viewed Gingrich as a smart guy and a very formidable adversary and a very able political strategist," observed Paul Begala. "He saw Gingrich's vision and tactics as divisive and nihilistic."[16] He had watched as Gingrich "skewered" President Bush for his 1990 compromise budget deal with the Democrats because it included a modest tax increase. If he was willing to undermine a sitting president of his own party, "I could only imagine what he intended to do to me," Clinton thought.[17] He was the leader of a conservative clique in Washington that viewed the presidential administration as "usurpers." Gingrich and the New Right, he reflected, "thought they had found a formula to describe us in a way that would basically move us out of consideration with the American people" by tapping into "the receding memory of the 60s."[18] Their primary goal, he believed, was the acquisition of power.

The first big test would be over the budget. Clinton wanted to propose a budget that included many of his campaign promises: a middle-class tax cut along with "investments" in social programs. However, economic and political realities conspired against him. In 1993, with the federal deficit swelling to nearly $300 million, Clinton reluctantly agreed it was more important to convince the Federal Reserve Bank and the capital markets that he was serious about cutting the deficit. "You mean to tell me that the success of my program and my re-election hinges on the Federal Reserve and a bunch of fucking bond traders?" he shouted at his staff in frustration. While the decision to attack the deficit appealed to disaffected Perot voters, the president ran into opposition from liberal congressional Democrats when he tried cutting social problems. "The discussion was, 'The chairman won't like this, the sub-committee chairman won't like that,'" recalled Begala.[19] In the end, since he was unable to make significant cuts in existing programs, the president was forced to abandon his tax cut pledge. The legislation he sent to Congress contained only one ambitious new social program—a national service corps by which college students could pay off federal education loans through community work. It also called for increasing the top tax bracket from 31 to 36 percent.

The president's budget was a gift to Gingrich, who successfully stigmatized his modest proposal as a traditional liberal "tax and spend" budget. "To Newt, Clinton was not the moderate New Democrat he had promised during the campaign but just another old liberal Democrat who campaigned as a moderate/conservative," wrote Mel Steely.[20] Gingrich managed to get the entire Republican conference to oppose the budget because it included a tax increase. Many moderate Democrats in the House and Senate agreed, and refused to support the bill. In August, after months of public wrangling, the final bill passed the House by only two votes. In the Senate, Bob Kerrey delivered a decisive vote for the plan only after giving a speech attacking it as timid. Vice President Gore was forced to cast the tie-breaking vote. The struggle, reported Balz and Brownstein, "left a lasting image of chaos."[21] Clinton managed to pass his budget, but Republicans "felt strength in unity and had a weapon for the next election to use against those Democrats who had supported the President."[22]

The budget battle made clear to the president and his close advisors that Gingrich had emerged as the de facto leader of the Republican Party in the House. On September 13, 1993, Clinton used the historic meeting between Palestinian Leader Yasser Arafat and Israeli Prime Minister Yitzhak Rabin to spend some time alone with Gingrich. Clinton invited Gingrich to join him on the Truman balcony after the handshaking ceremony. It would be the first private meeting between the two men.

The president wanted to figure out what made Gingrich tick. By all accounts, the president possessed a remarkable ability to read people—to scan them for points of vulnerability, but most of all, to probe for areas of agreement and compromise. Clinton later told colleagues that he saw a more complicated figure than the highly partisan, combative, right-winger he had watched eviscerate Democrats over the years. Although Gingrich was the leader of the reactionary forces in Congress, he did not fit the president's stereotype of a typical Republican reactionary: he was smart, well read, exceptionally bright, and sophisticated. Unlike most of the conservatives Clinton had dealt with in Arkansas, Gingrich seemed interested in the future, not the past, and he enjoyed talking about new ideas. While most conservatives focused solely on limiting government, Gingrich shared a passion for imagining how technology and science could serve as vehicles for transforming society. Like Clinton, he recognized that the nation was experiencing an information revolution with profound implications for public policy. Clinton also sensed a soft side to his pugnacious opponent. He understood that Gingrich needed to be seen as a rebel, but that he also wanted to be taken seriously as a member of the Washington establishment. The president saw something of himself in his opponent. He sensed that, despite his tough public posture, Gingrich was in many ways very needy and eager to please.

For now, Clinton wanted to communicate a clear and simple message to Gingrich: "I am not a pushover," he warned. "Do you know who I am? I'm the big rubber clown doll you had as a kid, and every time you hit it, it bounces back. That's me—the harder you hit me, the faster I come back up."[23]

The encounter revealed a key difference between the two men and underscored an important advantage that Clinton would exercise over the next few years. Clinton possessed a much higher emotional intelligence. The president peeled Gingrich like an onion: he stripped away the layers of heated rhetoric and populist anger until he discovered a soft core that he could exploit. It was not a conscious strategy on his part. It was instinct—over the years he developed finely tuned intuitive skills. Gingrich lacked Clinton's human touch. He could read a room full of people but he became tone deaf when it came to one-on-one encounters. Clinton felt he understood Gingrich, and his empathy, which baffled even his closest advisors, gave Clinton the upper hand in his dealing with Gingrich.

In their private meetings, Clinton would often let Gingrich do most of the talking, trying to underscore points of agreement, letting pass points of contention. While Clinton played the role of skilled poker player, rarely revealing his hand, Gingrich always opened negotiations by placing all his cards on the table. Gingrich often misinterpreted Clinton's willingness to listen as an indication that he had not made up his mind and read his occasional nods of approval as agreement. Instead, Clinton was simply playing to Gingrich's ego, learning as much as he could about his position to see how far he would have to go to compromise. Clinton "could relate to someone else's point of view in a way that made that person feel not just heard but understood," observed Treasury Secretary Robert Rubin. The problem was that he "listened so sympathetically that people who were unaccustomed to him often took it as duplicitous when he later came out against their positions." Gingrich fell into that trap.[24] Gingrich judged whether a meeting with Clinton succeeded or failed based on how forcefully he communicated his message to the president. It never occurred to him to use the opportunity to get into Clinton's head, search for his soft spots, and understand the psychology behind his actions. For that reason, he completely missed the message Clinton was sending him.

The following month, Republicans elected Gingrich as the minority leader in the House, making official what was already obvious to the White House. Fortunately, he assumed his new role just as Congress was about to begin debate on the president's effort to pass the North American Free Trade Agreement (NAFTA). With organized labor and many congressional liberals opposed to the measure, Clinton needed Republican votes to get the measure passed. As of October 19, just a month before the deadline, the White House lacked the votes it needed. Gingrich described the president's efforts to lure Democratic votes as "pathetic" at the same time he insisted on changes that would make it harder to win them over. Stephanopoulos complained to the president that "Newt's trying to have it both ways. He's setting up a situation where he gets the credit if NAFTA wins and we get blamed if it loses." The president called Gingrich and insisted that Republicans drop some of their demands. The president hung up the phone saying, "Dealing with that guy is like hugging an eel."[25] Gingrich, however, kept his end of the bargain and delivered the necessary Republican votes. "If NAFTA passes," observed *USA Today,* "Clinton will owe thanks to Minority Whip Newt Gingrich."[26] In the end, he delivered 132 GOP votes, more than half of the 234 needed for passage.

It proved to be a rare moment of cooperation between the two men. Although Clinton wanted to continue the cooperation by proposing another issue that he had campaigned for and could win Republican votes for—welfare reform—the Democratic leadership in Congress convinced him to pursue health care reform instead. The president placed the First Lady in charge of the task force and charged it with producing a comprehensive plan. In separate meetings, Gingrich advised the president and the First Lady against developing a comprehensive plan. "Don't try to write a big bill, don't try to write a grand all-purpose plan from Washington." He suggested an incremental approach that would tackle one problem at a time. "If he did that for four years in a row, he could run for re-election having passed four consecutive, positive bills."[27]

Clinton ignored this advice and tried to push through a comprehensive bill, which he presented to Congress in November. Gingrich slammed it as "culturally alien to America" and consisting of "1,300 pages of red tape."[28] As the legislation floundered, Gingrich worried that Clinton would negotiate with moderates and come up with a slightly revised version. To prevent that from happening, he opposed any amendments designed to improve the bill. The First Lady wanted the president to go on national television and pressure Congress to pass the measure. But he decided it was a losing cause and pulled the bill before it could come to a vote on the floor. In the end, he came to believe that Gingrich's advice about pursuing an incremental approach had been sound. "We made the error of trying to do too much, took too long, and ended up achieving nothing," the president admitted.[29]

The failure of the health care bill played into Gingrich's strategy for the upcoming midterm elections. He wanted to paint the president as a typical out-of-touch, big-government liberal. Even when the president won, as on the budget, Gingrich hoped to muddy the waters enough to create the impression that Clinton and the Democratic Party were incapable of governing. Over and over again the president played into his hands. Gingrich believed the biggest miscalculation was not health care, but crime. Since the 1960s, Republicans had defined the Democrats as being soft on crime. The infamous Willie Horton ad that the Republicans used during the 1988 campaign against Michael Dukakis underscored the Democrats' vulnerability. In 1992, Clinton had successfully neutralized the issue by supporting the death penalty and talking tough on crime. Shortly after the health care debate, he brandished his crime-fighting credentials by proposing a comprehensive crime bill that called for adding 100,000 new police officers. "You have a chance to seize one of the most powerful realignment issues (along with health care) that will come your way, at a time when public concern about crime is the highest it has been since Richard Nixon stole the issue from the Democrats in 1968," his domestic policy advisors told him.[30] The White House saw the president's crime bill as a "vehicle to communicate to the public a set of strongly-held values that the President embraces, as well as the President's tough stance on crime and criminals."[31]

Gingrich assumed the president would eventually get a bill through Congress, but he hoped to reframe the debate by focusing instead on other controversial provisions in the bill, including a ban on assault weapons and $7.3 billion on so-called "anti-crime prevention programs," which many conservatives dismissed as liberal pork projects. An odd coalition of conservatives opposed to the weapons ban and liberals who complained that the provision expanded the number of crimes eligible for the death penalty joined forces to block passage. Clinton fought back ferociously. Using the National Association of Police Officers in Minneapolis as backdrop, he vowed to stand firm behind the weapons ban. Later at the White House, the president, his voice raspy and hoarse from hours of phone calls and negotiating, pledged to "fight and fight and fight until we win this battle for the American people."[32]

The president often complained that Gingrich had a "Jekyll and Hyde" personality, and he saw both during the debates over the crime bill. On the stump, Gingrich attacked the bill, charging, falsely, that it "would release over 10,000 drug dealers who are currently in prison."[33] Yet, behind the scenes he was helping moderate members of his own party craft a compromise with the White House. Mel Steely noted that Clinton "had now seen the two Newts, the reasonable parliamentary leader willing to work to pass needed legislation and the partisan guerrilla leader...."[34]

In the end, the president got his bill; Gingrich got his blood. Clinton wanted to use the bill to highlight his toughness on crime, but Gingrich hijacked the debate, focusing instead on the question of gun control. By successfully directing public attention to the portion of the bill that would infuriate his conservative base, Gingrich prevented Clinton from getting the political credit he deserved for putting police officers on the street. The bill, Gingrich reflected, "enraged rural America," and was seen "as an anti-gun bill and symbolic of a leftwing administration that despises rural America."[35] Gingrich even managed to get some positive press for crafting the final compromise. The *Boston Globe*'s Thomas Oliphant told liberals that "we owe Gingrich a respectful nod for letting a bipartisan, centrist majority work its will against his own."[36]

In just his first few months on the job, Gingrich had outmaneuvered Clinton on every front. Even when Clinton won—on the budget, NAFTA, and the crime bill—Gingrich either managed to share the credit with the White House or force the president to pay a heavy political price. Whether the president won or lost, as on health care, Gingrich skillfully shaped the debate and discussion to create the impression that the White House was both incompetent and out of touch with mainstream voters. He never doubted that he could dominate Clinton, but he never imagined it would be this easy. After passage of the crime bill, Gingrich sent a message to the White House that amounted to an ultimatum: "If you want to avoid this kind of train wreck, you're going to call us in at the beginning of a bill and you're going to have conferences that are honest and you're going to share the report language with us and we're going to do this thing with dignity. And if you don't, every chance I get to wreck the train I'm going to wreck it. And then when you get tired of looking stupid in public we'll talk."[37]

While the partisan wrangling annoyed Clinton, it was the drumbeat of attacks on his character and the constant investigations of his administration that bothered him most of all. In addition to all the gossip about infidelity, drug use, and draft dodging, Clinton had been haunted by rumors of corruption, specifically that he had received favorable treatment from a local bank for a real estate investment he and his wife made in an area of northern Arkansas known as "Whitewater." As Steely noted, Gingrich "kept a relatively low profile" on Whitewater, but, when pressed, would insist that it be "thoroughly investigated by outside authorities and Congress."[38] Clinton viewed Whitewater as little more than a partisan witch hunt designed to undermine his administration. He believed that after controlling the White House for the past twelve years, and for twenty of the previous twenty-four years, Republicans refused to accept the legitimacy of his presidency. "They thought these were their parking spots at the White House for life," he often told aides. He was convinced that Gingrich was helping to orchestrate the drumbeat of criticism, keeping the issue alive, not because he believed it was true, but solely because it would sully the administration and provide Republicans with a political advantage.

Week after week, Gingrich and other Republicans in Congress, aided by their conservative allies in the press, relentlessly pursued the Whitewater issue, opening numerous investigations and calling for the appointment of a special prosecutor. The idea was to get the mainstream media and "good government" groups to support the investigation. Whether there was any wrongdoing was secondary—the investigation and the charges themselves would create the impression of impropriety, distract attention from the president's agenda, and erode his moral authority. Convinced the charges were politically motivated, the White House stonewalled reporters, was slow in turning over information, and offered conflicting statements—all of which contributed to the impression they had something to hide. When Vincent Foster, Hillary Clinton's former law partner and counsel to the president, committed suicide, conservatives spun wild yarns, even going so far as to suggest that the White House had tried to silence him. Around the same time new reports surfaced that Arkansas state troopers had procured women for Clinton when he was governor.

In January 1994, the *Washington Post* added its voice to the chorus of calls for the appointment of a special prosecutor. In the end, the president gave in to the pressure. "It was the worst presidential decision I ever made," he reflected, "wrong on the facts, wrong on the law, wrong on the politics, wrong for the presidency and the Constitution."[39] Clinton felt that the burden of proof had been shifted: instead of critics having to produce evidence of wrongdoing, he was forced to prove his innocence. On the first anniversary of Clinton's inauguration, the attorney general appointed Robert Fiske, a respected Republican lawyer, to conduct "a complete, thorough, and impartial" investigation. After only a few months on the job, however, he was replaced by Kenneth Starr, a partisan figure who was determined to bring down the Clinton administration. Little did he know at the time, but Clinton had ignited a chain reaction of events that would over time nearly destroy his presidency and bring about the end to Gingrich's career in Congress.

By 1994 there were more news stories on Whitewater than on all facets of Clinton's domestic agenda combined. Hillary observed, "If you believed everything you heard on the airwaves in 1994, you would conclude that your president was a Communist, that the first lady was a murderess and that together they had hatched a plot to take away your guns and force you to give up your family doctor (if you had one) for a socialist health-care system."[40] By March 1994, polls showed that 50 percent of the public believed the Clintons were lying about Whitewater; nearly a third suspected they had done something illegal. Gingrich "knew there was nothing" to the Whitewater investigations, Clinton reflected. "It was all politics to him. It was about power."[41] But the attacks served their purpose by eroding support for the administration and distracting the president's attention. "I have to confess that Whitewater, especially the attacks on Hillary, took a bigger toll on me than I thought it would," he later admitted.[42]

Although Gingrich believed that Whitewater was fair game, he was uncomfortable with the efforts to expose Clinton's sexual peccadillos. Many of his Republican colleagues were salivating when Paula Jones, a former Arkansas state employee, filed a lawsuit charging the president with sexual harassment. Gingrich, however, complained that Republicans were being hypocritical, arguing that they needed to keep focused on developing a positive legislative agenda. "Republicans who were screaming about Anita Hill are hardly in a position to turn now and run around brandishing Paula Jones," he charged in a rare public rebuke of his colleagues. "Ninety-five percent of Republican energy should go into creating a series of reform proposals and communicating those reform proposals. The country is so exhausted by the politics of personal destruction that it is eager for someone who says we have serious problems and who focuses on serious solutions, even if they are controversial."[43] It is impossible to know whether Gingrich would have expressed the same reservations about the "politics of personal destruction" if he had not been vulnerable to the same charges of infidelity. He conveniently defined issues that were potentially harmful to him as "destructive," but believed that just about everything else was fair game.

However unfair, the Republican attacks worked because they hit a nerve with the public, tapping into doubts about Clinton's character and integrity. "What threatens this President seems to be much larger than mere partisanship," observed journalist Michael Kelly. "There is a level of mistrust and even dislike of him that is almost visceral in its intensity."[44] Once again, Clinton's style and personality, and his history, weighted him down. "Clinton's life trails him like a peculiarly single-minded mugger," Kelly wrote, "popping out from the shadows every time it seems the President is for a moment safe—to whack the staggering victim anew."[45] Conservatives had successfully made Clinton a metaphor for the 1960s—a decade that produced a generation that rejected mainstream values, lacked a moral core, and was incapable of distinguishing right from wrong. Clinton provided them with plenty of ammunition. It was not just that he avoided the draft, experimented with drugs, and cheated on his wife, but also that he seemed incapable of accepting responsibility for his actions and waffled on the truth. Conservatives did not have to make their case against the 1960s anymore; Bill Clinton was doing it for them.

At the midpoint in his first term, Clinton presided over peace and prosperity but was having trouble getting above 50 percent in the opinion polls. In September, unemployment dipped below 6 percent for the first time in years, and the economy was producing 250,000 new jobs a month with modest inflation. Many observers agreed with Federal Reserve Chairman Alan Greenspan that Clinton's decision to tackle the budget deficit contributed to the expansion. According to the Congressional Budget Office, the estimated 1995 deficit dropped from $284 billion to $171 billion in response to Clinton's efforts. "The joke on Wall Street," observed a British newspaper, "is that Clinton is the first conservative Republican president in the White House."[46] While taking credit for cutting the deficit and expanding the economy, the administration enacted an Earned Income Tax Credit, which provided a tax cut for millions of people at or below the poverty line. "He's breaking all precedents," Frederick T. Steeper, a Republican pollster, said. "He should be at 60 per cent approval." Yet a Democratic pollster rated his odds of re-election in 1996 as no better than even.[47]

Part of the problem was that media coverage of Clinton's first 18 months in office was overwhelmingly negative. A study by the Center for Media and Public Affairs found that 62 percent of the evaluations of the Clinton presidency on the network evening newscasts were negative. "There's a feeling that this guy is a scoundrel because there's such a hostile media environment," said the center's director, Robert Lichter. "He's had the misfortune of being president at the dawning of an age that combines attack-dog journalism with tabloid news."[48] As a *Washington Post* reporter noted, Clinton was only a few years older than many of the reporters covering him. "Because he was so emphatically human in his strengths and foibles, he had narrowed the gap between leader and public. In the process, he surrendered some of the aura traditionally attached to his office."[49]

On the eve of the midterm elections, *U.S. News and World Report* discovered that many Americans viewed Clinton as ineffectual and as a big spending liberal. "What is new," however, "is that much of it is intensely personal, fueled by the belief that the president is a libertine and a liar." What united the strongest critics was "a sense that America's traditional family values are declining and that Clinton is a symbol of—perhaps even a catalyst for—the decay." The survey found that 90 percent of his opponents complained "about a lack of moral leadership in government." Half of the "Clinton haters" identified themselves as born-again Christians. It was a nerve that Gingrich kept hitting. He called Clinton "the enemy of normal Americans," citing his appointment of a lesbian, Roberta Achtenberg, as an assistant secretary of the Department of Housing and Urban Development, and a strong sex education advocate, Dr. Joycelyn Elders, as Surgeon General.[50]

As he looked toward the midterm elections, however, Clinton nonetheless professed to be optimistic. Although polls were showing growing public doubts about his leadership and style, he knew that congressional elections were often shaped by local issues and by broad issues of peace and prosperity. On that score, the Democrats should have been in good shape: the economy had rebounded, the deficit was falling, and the nation was at peace. Newt Gingrich, however, had one more surprise planned for him.

| The Revolution

ON TUESDAY MORNING, September 27, 1994, Newt Gingrich, smiling broadly, strutted across the west lawn of the Capitol, stopping occasionally for photographs and to greet bystanders. "You made us proud, Newt!" shouted an admirer. "Way to go, Mr. Speaker," said another. "Not yet," he responded. "We've still got an election to win." A few minutes later he joined 350 Republican House candidates gathered on a three-tiered stage constructed on the steps of the Capitol for the signing of the "Contract with America." After a prayer and the Pledge of Allegiance, Gingrich took the podium. He could barely contain his enthusiasm at the prospect that Republicans had a fighting chance of picking up the forty seats needed to gain control of the House. "Clinton is in such trouble with the American people that our job is to go out and offer a clear, positive alternative," Gingrich told the crowd. He pledged that if the Republicans won the majority, within the first 100 days they would bring to the House floor bills based on each of the ten items in their highly touted "Contract with America." For Gingrich, however, the goal was much more grand. "Today on these steps we offer this contract as a first step towards renewing American civilization."[1]

The ceremony, like the contract itself, was designed for the media. GOP congressmen gripped tiny American flags while the obligatory brass band played patriotic music. Organizers shuttled congressmen across the stage four at a time to sign their names, giving local television stations "back home" plenty of good action shots. The contract consisted of poll-tested ideas, many of them left over from the Reagan years—various tax cuts, welfare reform, congressional term limits, capital-gains tax cut, increased defense spending, a balanced budget amendment, line-item veto, tougher law enforcement, and tort reform—repackaged with catchy titles. A balanced budget amendment became "The Fiscal Responsibility Act." Republicans refitted the capital-gains tax cut and renewed calls for business deregulation as "The Job Creation and Wage Enhancement Act." The "American Dream Restoration Act" called for a child tax credit; the package of amendments to the Clinton crime bill, the "Taking Back Our Streets Act." Gingrich insisted that the statement include ten items and all had to be "60 percent issues" that could gain quick popular support. He fought off attempts by social conservatives to include controversial issues such as abortion and school prayer, claiming they would alienate moderates and allow opponents to brand them as intolerant.

Gingrich believed that Clinton had handed Republicans a great opportunity to finally achieve what he had been pushing for more than a decade: Republican control of the House. But to accomplish that goal, he was convinced that they needed to do more than simply run a negative campaign against Democrats: they would need to present a compelling alternative. "I'll give Newt a lot of credit for this," said Kerry Knott, who served as chief of staff to Texas Congressman Dick Armey. "He said we can run a purely negative campaign against Clinton in '94 and pick up a decent number of seats, but somewhere along the way it switched to where we thought, 'Hey, if we were to put a positive agenda together with the negative attacks on Clinton that might be enough to actually make it all the way there.'"[2] Gingrich believed that the Republicans needed something dramatic to break through the regular news cycle. "You had to have something of this scale to beat the Democratic majority," he reflected years later.[3]

Clinton was not impressed by the contract. While some of the particulars were appealing, "the contract was, at its core, a simplistic and hypocritical document," he reflected. "I agreed with many of the particulars of the contract," and was already on record supporting welfare reform, tougher child-support enforcement, and the line-item veto. What angered him most of all was that Republicans were "trying to abolish arithmetic."[4] It was the same old supply-side myth: you could cut taxes, increase defense spending, and still balance the budget. He had used up a great deal of political capital in his first budget trying to undo the damage done during the Reagan years and he received no credit for his efforts. Now the same people who gave the nation multibillion-dollar deficits were campaigning as budget-balancing hawks.

Postelection surveys raised questions about the importance of the contract. A CBS/*New York Times* poll the week of the election showed that 71 percent of respondents had never heard of the contract, and only 7 percent said it made them more inclined to vote Republican.[5] The contract was important, however, not for how it shaped public perceptions, but for how it encouraged Republicans to campaign using the same script—a script written and designed by Newt Gingrich. "The Contract was a great high," recalled Arizona Congressman J.D. Hayworth. "We were coming in with a unity of purpose, and I can't begin to explain how gratifying and emotionally satisfying that is."[6]

The contract turned Tip O'Neill's dictum that "all politics is local" on its head. Instead, Gingrich nationalized 435 local races, turning them into a referendum on Clinton. It was not important that most people had never heard of the contract. The fact was that the Republican candidates in 1994 were all speaking the Gingrich mantra of tax cuts, balanced budget, and stronger military, and it turned the election into a choice between the Republican agenda and the failures of the Clinton administration. According to Clinton aide Doug Sosnik, "The contract gave a symbolic and substantive vehicle for the Republicans to make this a change-versus-status-quo election."[7] Since he was the primary author of the contract, and the man most likely to be elected Speaker if the Republicans gained the majority, many people viewed the election as a contest between Clinton and Gingrich. In Indiana, GOP challenger John Hostettler, running against incumbent Frank McCloskey, dubbed his opponent "Frank McClinton." McCloskey returned the compliment, dismissing Hostettler as "John McGingrich."[8]

Gingrich masterfully used alternative media, especially talk radio, in the months leading up to the election. In 1960, only two radio stations had talk formats. By 1995, there were 1,130. It was an audience that spoke his language. The most popular hosts were overwhelmingly men, and nearly 70 percent of listeners were conservative. By the time of the 1994 elections, 20 million Americans were listening to Rush Limbaugh's mixture of personality with bombast on 659 radio stations.[9] His late-night television show was syndicated to 225 stations, and his two books topped the bestseller list. Gingrich nurtured his relationship with Limbaugh, faxing him information, which Limbaugh then read on the air. "Without C-Span, without talk radio shows, without all the alternative media, I don't think we'd have won," Gingrich told reporters. "The classic elite media would have distorted our message."[10]

Gingrich's influence, however, went far beyond masterminding the contract. Using GOPAC as a recruitment and training organization, Gingrich spent more than $8 million identifying the strongest potential Republican challengers and providing them with the themes, the "wedges and magnets," to use against their Democratic opponents. Every month, GOPAC would send tapes to Republican candidates with ideas, tips, and advice from Gingrich. "It was like subscribing to a motivational course, with Gingrich a cross between Norman Vincent Peale and a marine drill sergeant."[11] Gingrich also encouraged incumbents running in safe districts to donate money to the National Republican Campaign Committee to help support candidates in close races. "Newt turned us into a team," said Representative John Linder, chairman of the National Republican Congressional Committee. "One reason for such a reservoir of loyalty towards Newt is because of his tireless efforts on behalf of his G.O.P. colleagues," a Gingrich ally told the *New York Times*.[12] The efforts paid off. According to one study, 130 of the 178 House incumbents made contributions totaling $5 million, compared to only $50,000 in 1992.[13]

Having won election in 1992 in a heavily Republican new sixth district, Gingrich faced only token opposition in his race for re-election, leaving him plenty of time to travel the nation raising money for Republican candidates. He visited about one-third of the House's 435 districts in the last two months of the campaign, energizing Republicans with his own fiery brand of take-no-prisoners oratory. "I am the most serious, systematic revolutionary of modern times," he said in Alexandria, Virginia. He told Republican audiences that a GOP takeover in November would mean nothing less than "the first decisive step back to create a century of freedom for the entire human race."[14]

With Gingrich tying his domestic agenda in knots, Clinton found himself focusing more attention on foreign policy, an area where presidents have traditionally exercised greater freedom. It was also an area where he would encounter less friction from Gingrich. "We were surprisingly similar in the way we viewed the world," Clinton reflected. Both rejected isolationism and embraced a muscular internationalism that called for using military might to protect American interests abroad. Not only did they share similar views, but Gingrich also subscribed to the belief that politics stopped at the water's edge. He was simply less willing to politicize foreign policy issues. While Gingrich believed Congress needed to play a role as a coequal branch of government on domestic issues, he was willing to defer to the president when it came to foreign policy. "Newt supported me in virtually all of my foreign policy initiatives," Clinton said.[15]

Initially, with the Cold War over and no obvious foreign threat on the horizon, neither made foreign policy a high priority. Foreign policy issues were not the ones that got Clinton elected president, nor would they elevate Gingrich to the speakership. Both men remembered how the public punished George Bush for appearing to spend an inordinate amount of time on world affairs and not enough on affairs closer to home. They were determined not to repeat the mistake. There was a very practical political reason for keeping foreign policy off the front burner: they both struggled with coalitions that were more isolationist, less willing to assert American power, and still scared from Vietnam. It was hard in the post–Cold War era to build a coalition in favor of foreign involvement, so they both kept their attention focused on issues closer to home. By 1994, however, Clinton was looking abroad to bolster his standing at home.

Early on, the president's cautious and uncertain approach to world crises underscored public doubts about his ability to function as a successful commander in chief. Clinton inherited a difficult and confused American military operation in the Horn of Africa. In 1992, Bush had ordered nearly 30,000 troops to Somalia on a humanitarian mission to restore order and secure relief efforts. When local clan chiefs started blocking the shipments, Clinton expanded the military's mission to include taking on the clans. In October 1993, eighteen U.S. Army Rangers died in a bloody firefight with a gang of Somalis. A horrified nation watched television video of an American soldier being dragged through the streets of Mogadishu to the cheers of local crowds. Clinton retreated, withdrawing the remaining America forces. Within a week, he was forced to back down again when a pistol-wielding mob prevented an American ship from docking in Port-au-Prince, Haiti. After lingering for a few days off the coast, the ship turned around and went home. On the other side of the world, in the former Yugoslavia, when the Serb-dominated federal government headed by President Slobodan Milosevic launched a vicious campaign of "ethnic cleansing," the administration waffled. Secretary of State Warren Christopher described Bosnia as the "problem from hell." The president sent confusing signals: "I will not let Sarajevo fall," he told Congress. Then he added, "Don't take that as an absolute."

By 1994, however, the president scored a number of foreign policy victories. In Haiti, the administration organized an international effort to restore the democratically elected government of Jean-Bertrand Aristide, applying diplomatic pressure and convincing the United Nations to impose economic sanctions. The military regime showed no interest in giving up power voluntarily until Clinton decided to flex his military muscle, threatening to use the marines to expel the junta. With American warships looming off the coast, Haiti's military leaders backed down. He used the threat of military action with similar effectiveness in Iraq, where Saddam Hussein made threatening moves toward Kuwait. Acting decisively, the administration deployed 54,000 troops to the Gulf and threatened to attack any Iraqi troops moving toward the border with Kuwait. After his tough stand in Iraq and Haiti, the pugnacious New York *Daily News* front-page headline read: "Clinton 2, Bullies 0."[16] While flexing his military muscle, Clinton also worked the back rooms of diplomacy, negotiating a complicated deal with North Korea to abandon its nuclear weapons program in exchange for diplomatic recognition and increased trade.

Ironically, on the eve of the midterm elections, the president was hoping that his foreign policy accomplishments would help his party at the polls. In October, a *Wall Street Journal*/NBC News poll showed that 45 percent approved of Clinton's handling of foreign policy, a thirteen-point jump in one month.[17] Acting to capitalize on the good news, the president traveled to the Middle East to witness the signing of a peace accord between Israel and Jordan and make controversial calls on Syrian President Hafez Assad and Palestine Liberation Organization Chairman Yassir Arafat.

Clinton returned from the Middle East with a few weeks left before the election. His pollster, Dick Morris, had conducted a survey suggesting that the president stay off the campaign trail and remain "presidential." "Go back to the Middle East," Morris said, jokingly. "Don't campaign for anyone; it will lower your approval ratings, and you will drag everyone down to defeat." In his memoirs, Clinton said he accepted the advice and told his staff that when he returned from the Middle East he "should stay at work and make news rather than go back on the campaign trail." His schedule, however, was already filled with appearances across the country for Democratic candidates. "Apparently, when my own poll numbers started rising, Democrats around the country asked that I campaign for them." According to Morris's account, the president rejected his advice. "I've got to help them after what they did for me," he recalled Clinton saying, "voting for my economic plan and my health-care package." Even if Clinton agreed intellectually with Morris's assessment, emotionally "he needed the crowds, the cheers, the mirror."[18]

In the run-up to election day, Clinton criss-crossed the country in a breakneck seven-day journey, attacking Republicans for trying "to bury us in a mountain of negativism." Campaigning in Boston, he implored voters to say " 'no' to the negativism," and say " 'yes' to hope." Many pundits believed that the president's efforts on the campaign trail, which raised more than $50 million for Democratic candidates, combined with recent foreign policy successes that boosted his ratings, would help the party avoid disaster at the polls. His goal was to turn out the party faithful. "Don't let them sucker you," Clinton told a raucous crowd of Democrats in Michigan. "Show up on Election Day."[19]

———

On election night, Gingrich sat in his Atlanta headquarters waiting for the results. "How are we doing?" he asked one of his advisors. "Do you want the good news or the bad news?" the advisor responded. "Both," Gingrich said. "The good news is that we are going to pick up a lot of seats." Gingrich then asked for the bad news. "Wait until you meet them," the advisor responded. "You won't believe what a bunch of ideologues you are going to have to deal with," he said, predicting: "They are going to kill you."[20] By the end of the night, Gingrich knew that he would be the next Speaker of the House. He won his home district with 64 percent of the total, his highest margin ever. "This was clearly Newt Gingrich's victory—not just in Georgia but across the nation."[21]

The election results sent shock waves across the nation. The journalist James Traub later called the 1994 election "the most consequential non-presidential election of the 20th century."[22] Not a single Republican incumbent for Congress or governor was defeated. Republicans seized control of both houses of Congress for the first time in 40 years. In Senate races, they won all nine open elections and defeated two incumbent Democrats. The day after the election, Senator Richard Shelby of Alabama switched to the Republicans, increasing their edge to fifty-three to forty-seven. Republicans also scored well in the states, where they controlled the governor's mansions in eight of the nine most populous states. Democratic gubernatorial stars Mario Cuomo of New York and Ann Richards of Texas went down to defeat. For the first time in history an incumbent House Speaker, Tom Foley of Washington, was defeated.

The new freshmen were "Gingrich's children," and they reflected his combative style of politics. They were young—over half were under the age of 45. They viewed themselves as outsiders, not professional politicians. In reality, they were not much different from many of their colleagues: more than 60 percent had served in government in some capacity, and about the same percentage had previously run for public office. Since they all won election in 1994 campaigning on the same platform of balancing the budget, reforming welfare, and cutting taxes, they were convinced they had a mandate to change the way politics was practiced in Washington. They were going to force change, not make deals. "The freshmen see themselves as different," said Gil Sutknecht, a member of the class from Minnesota. Many new members came with an added sense of urgency. They had promised to serve only a few terms, so they wanted to make their mark as quickly as possible.[23]

As columnist Fred Barnes pointed out, what united "Team Gingrich" was a desire to wage war on the 1960s. "They're the flip side of the '60s Generation" he observed, the ones who did not dodge the draft, protest the war, or join the counterculture. Until the mid-1960s, Gingrich told reporters, "there was an explicit, long-term commitment to creating character. It was the work ethic, it was honesty, right and wrong, it was not harming others, it was being vigilant in the defense of liberty. It was very clear and we taught it."[24] All that changed beginning in 1965. "The 1960s produced a cultural civil war," he argued, because it gave birth to a left-liberal elite, including Bill and Hillary Clinton, that espoused "a set of values" that attacked all forms of authority. The results have been obvious and pernicious. "No civilization can survive for long with twelve-year-olds having babies, fifteen-year-olds killing one another, seventeen-year-olds dying of AIDS, and eighteen-year-olds getting diplomas they can't read."[25] His goal, beyond enacting the details of the Republican agenda, was to restore the authority of "the bourgeois system which has dominated the country for 200 years."

His closest allies shared this agenda. Gingrich ally Robert Walker often served as a pro-Vietnam spokesman on campus rallies at Millersville State College. A student at the University of Houston, Tom DeLay attended antiwar rallies to shout down the protestors. Robert Livingston, whom Gingrich appointed to head the powerful Appropriations Committee, served two years in the navy and described himself as a "counter-revolutionary." Majority Leader Dick Armey, who earned a Ph.D. in economics from the University of Oklahoma, summed up the sentiment of the new Republican leadership: "To me," he said, "all the problems began in the '60s." They were now in a position to institutionalize the "counter-revolution."[26]

Many felt indebted to Gingrich, who actively recruited them to run, offered campaign advice and money, and was the leader of their revolution. "It would be difficult to overestimate his role," said fellow Georgia Republican Congressman Bob Barr, "and hard to come up with the words to describe it. He provided the vision that allowed us to win."[27] Steve Gunderson, a moderate Wisconsin Republican, called Gingrich "the vision, the intellect, the emotion, and the motivation of the party." David Drier, who first won election in 1981 but had never served in a Republican-controlled House, summed it up: Gingrich, he said, "is the single person who brought us to majority status."[28]

Gingrich called the election "the most shatteringly one-sided Republican victory since 1946." For once he was not exaggerating. "He could with truth have made an even larger claim," noted journalist Godfrey Hodgson, that "the Republicans had ended a Democratic hegemony in American politics that had lasted, with only brief and partial interruptions, since the Great Depression."[29] The election represented the culmination of a process that began at the end of World War II when the Democratic Party moved toward supporting civil rights, and accelerated after Lyndon Johnson signed the Voting Rights Act of 1965. While the white South voted solidly Republican in presidential elections, it continued to support Democratic candidates on the local and state level out of habit. Since his first campaign in 1974, Gingrich realized that the key to Republican success in the South was to break those old habits. He finally broke through in the 1994 election. Nineteen of the forty-nine House seats Republicans picked up came from thirteen Southern states—the eleven states of the Confederacy plus Kentucky and Oklahoma. Most of the seats came from districts that tended to vote Republican in presidential elections but had continued to elect Democratic congressmen. For the first time since Reconstruction, Republicans controlled a majority of southern governorships, senators, and congressional seats. In less than a generation, the Republicans turned the solidly Democratic South into the securely Republican South. Texas, home of Sam Rayburn and Lyndon Johnson, now had two Republican senators and a Republican governor. Republican members of Congress outnumbered Democrats by two to one in Florida, Georgia, Kentucky, North Carolina, Oklahoma, and South Carolina.[30]

Gingrich's efforts to accelerate an electoral realignment in the South received a boost from an unlikely coalition of Republicans and liberal Democrats. Under President George H.W. Bush, the Justice Department filed suits against Democratic-dominated legislatures, requiring them to develop reapportion plans that would increase the representation of African Americans in Congress. The plans gained the backing of powerful liberal groups and the National Association for the Advancement of Colored People (NAACP). The creation of majority black congressional districts, however, left the surrounding districts whiter and more Republican. The result was a dramatic increase in the number of primarily liberal African Americans elected to Congress, and a corresponding rise in the number of conservative Republicans, but a decline in moderate Democrats. In 1990, the thirteen southern states sent three blacks to Congress. After 1995, there were seventeen southern blacks in Congress. There were, however, fewer Democrats and many more Republicans. After 1994, Republicans for the first time since Reconstruction outnumbered Democrats, seventy-three to sixty-four. Just four years earlier, Gingrich had been the only Republican member of the Georgia delegation. There had been nine Democrats—eight white and one black. When the new Congress assembled in January, there would be seven Republicans and four Democrats, of whom three were black.[31]

Clinton was distraught at the election results. Aides found him surprisingly passive in the days following the election, as if he were in a state of shock. Bitterly disappointed in himself and his staff, he withdrew into himself, refusing to communicate or give clear direction. Hillary was more emotive. "I don't know which direction is up or down," she said, weeping to

Dick Morris. "Everything I thought was right was wrong." After listening to the president whine about the election results, Mickey Kantor, the president's trade negotiator, offered some frank advice: "Stop feeling sorry for yourself." Things were not as bad as they appeared. Although still unable to see how he would work with a Republican Congress, Clinton did see the positive prospect of having Newt Gingrich as the next Speaker. "Maybe he'll overreach," Clinton said.[32]

While the Republicans were waging a national campaign, the Democrats were fighting district by district, failing to articulate a coherent national message to counter the Republicans. The result was that "we got the living daylights beat out of us," the president concluded. "The nationalization of midterm elections was Newt Gingrich's major contribution to modern electioneering," he observed. "From 1994 on, if one party did it and the other didn't, the side without a national message would sustain unnecessary losses." The president accepted partial blame for the Republican victory. "I had contributed to the demise by allowing my first weeks to be defined by gays in the military; by failing to concentrate on the campaign until it was too late; and by trying to do too much too fast in a news climate in which my victories were minimized, my losses were magnified, and the overall impression was created that I was just another pro-tax, big-government liberal, not the New Democrat who had won the presidency."[33] Clinton was determined to return to his "New Democrat" roots and to turn the tables on Gingrich.

"Somehow," he reflected, "I had forgotten the searing lesson of my 1980 loss: You can have good policy without good politics, but you can't give the people good government without both. I would never forget it again." He knew he had the advantage: the economy would continue to improve, and the deficit would fall. Most of all, he understood that Gingrich was more conservative than the rest of the nation. In order to fulfill their tax-cut promises, Republicans would need to advocate large cuts in popular programs for education, health care, and the environment. He was determined "to hold them to the laws of arithmetic."[34]

At a victory party later that evening, Gingrich sounded a bipartisan tone, saying he would be "Speaker of the House, not Speaker of the Republican party." He said that the Republican success in the elections proved that Americans wanted the party's "Contract with America" enacted, but he said, "At least half of our contract are things that the President supports, that we should be able to work on together." He emphasized the theme of bipartisanship in interviews with the flock of reporters who followed his every move. "We want to work with the President of the United States," he told Dan Rather of CBS. "You only get one President at a time. And we ought to be able to take one year off, it seems to me, from Presidential politics and spend 1995 actually trying to pass things working together for America."[35]

This generosity of spirit proved short-lived. Later that evening, Gingrich returned to one of his favorite themes, attacking the legacy of the 1960s. He described the president and First Lady as "counterculture McGovernicks" and the White House as a circle of "left-wing elitists." His mandate, he told reporters later, was to replace the failed policies of Lyndon Johnson's Great Society. "They are a disaster," Gingrich said. "They ruined the poor. They created a culture of poverty and a culture of violence which is destructive of this civilization, and they have to be replaced thoroughly, from the ground up." His mandate, he declared, was to uproot the permissive 1960s culture, and the elites who supported it, and replace it with a new culture that stressed moral character.[36]

Clinton understood that Gingrich's calling him and Hillary "counter-culture McGovernicks" was "his ultimate condemnation." When asked about the comment at a press conference a few days later, the president responded, "I'm a middle-aged man who's worked very hard in his life to be a mainstream American." And, he concluded, "I think I've done a reasonable job of it."[37] While Gingrich tried to tie him to the counterculture, Clinton believed that Gingrich reflected "the self-righteous, condemning, Absolute Truth-claiming side of white southern conservatism." Clinton had seen many of these people growing up in the South. "Since I was a boy, I had watched people assert their piety and moral superiority as justifications for claiming an entitlement to political power, and for demonizing those who begged to differ with them, especially over civil rights."[38] Some in the White House wanted Democrats to make Gingrich the face of the new conservatism during the campaign, but dropped the idea after their polling showed that only 42 percent of the public had ever heard of him. Although he had made himself a force to be reckoned with inside the Washington beltway and had emerged as a key Republican strategist, Newt Gingrich was not yet a household name. "They will learn about Gingrich after the election," observed a White House aide.

CHAPTER NINE

Fighting Back

T HE 1994 ELECTION MADE Bill Clinton and Newt Gingrich the two
most powerful men in America. *Time* referred to them as "the famous
fraternal twins of American power, yin and yang of the Baby Boom, polar
extremes of Pennsylvania Avenue."[1] Most contemporary observers viewed the
two men as a study in contrasts: the hard-driving, conservative revolutionary
versus the embattled liberal president. What was most striking to people
who knew them and worked closely with them, however, were their similarities. "Even though they had very different politics both were very similar
in personality and temperament," reflected White House Chief-of-Staff Leon
Panetta. "They loved talking about books they had read. They were constantly coming up with new ideas about how to solve problems. They shared
an upbeat, optimistic view that problems could be solved."[2] "There were
more similarities than differences in the way that they operate," reflected
Gingrich media advisor Jim Farwell. "Both of them are intellectuals. Both
are very interested in ideas. Both are future oriented. Both are remarkably
open to new ideas—and that is a very rare quality. For most people in politics
being open to new ideas is a posture, not a philosophy. Both of them have
endless intellectual curiosity. Both are by nature coalition builders."[3]

Panetta saw something else the two men shared: they were both very
practical politicians who looked for points of compromise. He knew Clinton
was accommodating—sometimes too accommodating. What surprised him
was that for all his bombastic rhetoric, behind closed doors, Gingrich could
also be very reasonable. "What I saw of the private Gingrich was a very
pragmatic politician," recalled White House congressional liaison John
Hilley.[4] "Deep down the president felt that he could deal with Gingrich,"

Panetta told me.[5] "The truth is that for all the posturing they both liked each other," said Farwell.

Despite their contrasting political backgrounds and viewpoints, they were both clearly products of the 1960s. They shared with other members of their generation a sense of impatience with established institutions and a willingness to challenge the system—although that trait was always more evident in Gingrich than Clinton. Growing up in a world shaped by television images, they were skilled in using the conventions of mass media to their advantage. Most of all, they were shaped by the civil rights movement and by the post-1960s revolution in social attitudes in America. They came of age in an America where it was no longer acceptable to espouse any form of prejudice. It was an easy transition for both men. Clinton had always made racial healing one of his central messages, and he possessed an innate bond with the African American community, which had always been his strongest, most loyal constituency group. Gingrich came to power as a pro–civil rights Republican in a segregationist South. His support for civil rights was not the product of political calculation. Instead, it grew out of a genuine belief in racial equality and strong opposition to any form of discrimination. "Newt doesn't have a racist or prejudiced bone in his body," reflected Chip Kahn, who managed his early campaigns for office.[6]

On specific public policy issues, Clinton and Gingrich were never as far apart as their rhetoric suggested. Both men challenged the traditional politics of their parties and called for a "third way"—a new approach to thinking about problems that challenged conventional liberal and conservative notions. Gingrich was frustrated with Republican politics in Congress and pushed his party to adopt new ideas and a more confrontational style. Clinton was eager to distance himself from the liberal excess of his party's recent past while keeping alive the tradition of activist government. During the late 1980s many of Gingrich's advisors mixed with the Democratic leadership crowd, compared policy notes, and talked about the frustrations of challenging the establishment of their own parties. "There was the same sense of intellectual ferment and hunger," reflected Reed. "We were rebels with different aims but we overlapped in many ways. We had similar objectives."[7]

Both men were skeptical of claims that Washington alone could solve most problems. Clinton recognized the importance of incorporating market principles into government programs. While he wanted to maintain programs to protect the poor, he was willing to experiment with new arrangements. His goal was to make government more efficient and less wasteful. Unlike most conservatives, Gingrich never abandoned his belief that a strong federal government was necessary. Washington needed to perform fewer roles, he believed, but it needed the power to perform successfully the tasks it had chosen. "We were like center-right and center-left graduate students in a seminar where we broadly agreed on more than we disagreed on," Gingrich reflected. "We could get together and have conversations that were almost endless." Over time, "we actually had much deeper fights with our own allies than with each other."[8]

Although they were political adversaries, in an odd way they needed each other. Clinton's victory in 1992 made Gingrich's Republican revolution possible. Having a moderate Republican in the White House would have prevented the conservative takeover of the party, muted their message, and kept Gingrich out of the political spotlight. Clinton's early miscues allowed Gingrich the chance to fulfill his dream of taking control of the House. "Could the Republicans have won in 1994 without Clinton's blunders?" a reporter asked him. "Let me give you a clear, unequivocal answer," Gingrich responded, "no."[9] Ironically, Gingrich's revolution may have saved the Clinton presidency by freeing him from the control of his party's more liberal base in Congress, giving him the opportunity to return to the moderate message that helped him win election in the first place. It was Gingrich who changed the language of American politics and forced Clinton to play the game on his turf. But it was Clinton who ultimately got the credit and emerged as the decade's most popular leader. Whenever it seemed that the public was ready to turn on the president, he could always count on Gingrich to serve as his foil, making him appear presidential by comparison. "What kept us close to the president was the Republicans," said Democratic Congressman Charles Schumer of New York. "Their extreme nastiness pushed Democrats into Bill Clinton's arms, even those who didn't like him very much."[10]

They were unusual political figures in Washington—both former professors who shared a detailed knowledge of policy and a fascination with politics. "A conversation with Gingrich can sound an awful lot like one with the president," observed Joe Klein. "Both are fascinated by the information age, the global economy and government's role in the new order."[11] Although both men possessed powerful intellects, Clinton was more disciplined, and in many ways more conventional. Gingrich, in the words of journalist James Traub, "preserved the eccentricity and unpredictable enthusiasms of a small-town autodidact."[12] Gingrich viewed every issue, no matter how trivial, through the lens of his grand scheme of history. Clinton appreciated the big picture but he was more likely to get drawn into the subtle and nuanced details of policy. As governor, Clinton had developed a detailed knowledge of how federal policies worked, and sometimes failed to work. Gingrich had mastered the intricacies of complicated issues, especially defense, immigration, and welfare. "They both saw themselves as policy wonks, as transformational figures, as visionaries, as partisans who could rise above partisanship," recalled Bruce Reed. "Clinton was more gifted at all those things except the partisan battling where Gingrich could more than hold his own."[13]

Gingrich faced many obstacles as he prepared to assume the responsibilities of Speaker. Although he seized control of the political agenda, Gingrich had a difficult time adjusting to the intense media scrutiny. Shortly after the 1994 election, Gingrich suggested that the nation could reduce its welfare burden by placing the children of welfare mothers in orphanages. In the past as an outsider he developed the habit of getting media attention by making outrageous statements. Now, the media not only reported, but also analyzed and dissected his every word. Press Secretary Tony Blankley recalled the first speech Gingrich gave after the 1994 election. When he got to the room where Gingrich was going to speak, "it was a mob scene, hundreds of reporters and boom mikes in his face," he reflected. "We'd never prepared for that level of intensity. . . . A newly elected president gets a slower rise than that, but Newt shot up like a skyrocket. It was disorienting, and it couldn't sustain itself." Gingrich agreed that many of the skills he learned as a bomb-throwing back bencher worked against him when he became Speaker. "It's like the difference between a Broadway stage and a movie," he noted. "On a Broadway stage you need to make big gestures so people in the back row can see you. But the same gesture in a movie looks grotesque."[14]

The same week her son was to be sworn in as Speaker, Gingrich's mother told reporter Connie Chung that he often referred to Hillary as a "bitch." Both Newt and his mother apologized for the comment. Hillary decided to take a different tack with Gingrich, one that her husband would use successfully in later years. She invited him and his wife, mother, and sister to the White House for tea. At one point, the president made a courtesy call. Gingrich, embarrassed about the whole episode, apologized for his mother's salty language. "Don't worry about it," Clinton responded with a laugh. "I've called her a lot worse than that."[15]

The biggest challenge Gingrich faced was figuring out how to manage his inexperienced and unwieldy coalition. Not a single member of the Republican Party had been in Congress the last time they were the majority party. Over half of the members of the 104th Congress had been elected in the 1990s. The freshman class was both ideologically cohesive and large, making up 32 percent of their party.[16] While they respected Gingrich and felt indebted to him, none was personally close to him. "We've all got respect for him, but he's not the warm and fuzzy type," said Florida's Joe Scarborough.

They also worried about Gingrich's high profile. While he was a successful revolutionary, he was not always the best public face for the party. Many Republicans believed he was no match for Clinton when it came to charm. Scarborough remembered the first time he met Bill Clinton, whom he described as "the singular object of my hatred for over a year." He got the classic Clinton treatment: "He would touch, squeeze, joke, and chuckle," he wrote. "He was charming, electric, and perfectly built for onetime encounters with voters in the snows of New Hampshire or Iowa." The week before meeting Clinton, he had stood behind the Speaker for nearly an hour. The only memorable thing about Newt, he noted, "had to do with the mounds of gray hair sticking out of his ears. And any political analyst worth his weight in salt can tell you, personal charisma trumps ear hair every day of the week." He could come to only one conclusion: "We were screwed."[17]

At the same time, Democrats orchestrated an effective counteroffensive, using many of Gingrich's tactics against him. In the first of a series of ethics charges they would file against him, Democrats pointed out that he signed a two-book deal with Harper Collins, owned by conservative media magnate Rupert Murdoch, for $4.5 million—the largest advance given to a political figure while still in office. Initially, Gingrich accused his opponents of orchestrating "a systematic smear campaign," but then he grudgingly backed down and accepted a $1 advance. It was a costly and risky decision since his agent insisted on being paid a percentage of the original $4.5 million sale price of the book.

On January 4, a few weeks before Clinton gave his State of the Union address, the House of Representatives elected Newt Gingrich as the first Republican Speaker since Joe Martin of Massachusetts in 1954. As Gingrich strolled down the center aisle, joyful Republicans leaped to their feet, chanting, "Newt! Newt! Newt!" One lawmaker shouted above the cheers, "It's a whole Newt world." Minority Leader Richard Gephardt had the unfortunate duty of handing over the gavel to the new Republican Speaker. "With resignation but with resolve," Gephardt said, "I hereby end 40 years of Democratic control of this House." The media covered the event as if it were a presidential inauguration. "Officially the ceremony marked the opening of the 104th Congress," opined *Time,* "but more important, it marked the beginning of an extraordinary period in American history in which the president of the United States will in effect share power with the speaker of the house."[18] As a symbol of his new power, Gingrich decorated his office with a five-foot replica of a *Tyrannosaurus rex* head. The unusual placement of the *T. rex* simply represented his life-long interest in dinosaurs, but some in the White House saw it as a reflection of Gingrich's desire to be seen, like the *T. rex* in its time, as the dominant and most ferocious creature in the universe.

Not everyone was convinced by the public demonstrations of power. A member of the Republican leadership, who worked closely with the Speaker, recalled standing on the House floor listening to Gingrich deliver "that god awful, excruciatingly long speech" on accepting the speakership. He noticed that Gingrich was constantly looking to his left and up into the gallery. "Finally I realize that he was trying to tell someone in the gallery behind me something," he said. "I look up in the gallery and there was his stepfather literally sitting with his back to the Speaker's podium facing the rear of the chamber with his arms crossed." His body language conveyed a clear message: "I don't care who that kid thinks he is. He's not convincing me." This congressman felt that the episode revealed a great deal about Gingrich. "I didn't have a Ph.D. historian who was just elected Speaker in front of me," he recalled. "I had a little boy who was still trying to get the approval of the old man."

Gingrich's first step in assuming control was to consolidate power in his office. Since the congressional reforms of the 1970s, power in the House had gravitated away from the Speaker and toward the committee chairs. Gingrich was determined to reverse that process by reigning in the chairs, making sure that the entire party apparatus in the House reported directly to him and remained focused on achieving his agenda. He gained control of the policy-making process by creating a Speaker's advisory group, made up of loyal lieutenants, to shape all legislation in the House. He bypassed the seniority system to appoint faithful deputies to be committee chairs, and even required GOP members of the Appropriations Committee to sign a written pledge to support his budget plan. With gavel in hand, Gingrich and his Republican troops moved methodically through the key points in the contract. On the first day they passed a series of procedural reforms designed to highlight their break with the "imperial Democratic" Congress of the past.

By early February, the House had passed nearly half of the contract. It gave the president a line-item veto, allowing him to remove objectionable spending requests from appropriations bills without vetoing the legislation. It passed legislation preventing the federal government from passing on "unfunded mandates" to the states and approved a package of reforms dealing with crime, welfare, tax cuts, and economic growth. "It was," said Elizabeth Drew, "the greatest legislative onslaught on the executive branch in modern history."[19]

While Clinton faded into the background, Gingrich and his troops took over Washington. The 1994 election and his selection as Speaker represented the culmination of a 12-year campaign to redefine the language of American politics and reshape the competition between the two parties. In the first 100 days he altered the course of government and earned the distinction of being the most powerful House Speaker since the legendary Sam Rayburn, and perhaps the most effective lawmaker since Lyndon Johnson.

The media could not get enough of him. "It was as if a new king or new president had been elected," recalled Robert Reich, who watched the spectacle from the Clinton cabinet.[20] "Newt is king of the world. I don't think there was any doubt that he was trying to signal that he, not Bill Clinton, was the most powerful person in Washington," reflected White House economic advisor Gene Sperling.[21] "The news was all Newt, all the time," observed the *Washington Post*.[22] "Newt Gingrich obsesses the city," wrote columnist Mary McGrory. "It hangs on his every word."[23] *Time* named Newt Gingrich "Man of the Year for 1995." "Gingrich has changed the center of gravity," the magazine opined.[24] According to the *Almanac of American Politics,* "Gingrich set the legislative course and political agenda as no other legislative leader— and few presidents—had in the 20th Century."[25] For those first few months, Gingrich seemed to be setting the pace in Washington. A typical headline from Mary McGrory read: "Clinton Running Hard to Keep Up With Gingrich."[26]

Initially, Clinton was unsure how to respond to the Republican election and legislative success. "There was a feeling of plummeting, and not knowing when your feet would touch bottom, if ever," presidential speechwriter Michael Waldman wrote of 1994.[27] "We were floundering," reflected White House Communications Director George Stephanopoulos. "As Newt Gingrich was orchestrating House passage of the contract with America, we were responding with a symphony of mixed signals."[28] According to aides, Clinton felt trapped by the election result, "torn between his desire to lash out at the Congress, his natural instinct for conciliation, and his dismay at his opponents' occupying the political high ground."[29] He realized that he had lost control of the political debate. While focusing so much attention on the details of his legislative program, he lost sight of how the public perceived him and his administration. He told reporters that he was shocked by "the intense partisanship of the congressional Republican leadership." What surprised him most of all, however, was "the fact that they got away with it, and they hadn't been punished" for their mean-spirited and often inaccurate portrayal of his actions.[30]

Although he admired Gingrich's ability to stay on message and to push the contract through Congress, Clinton also realized that the Speaker was repeating many of the mistakes he himself had made during his first term as governor: he overpromised, raising expectations that he could never satisfy. Having spent his entire public life in executive positions, Clinton understood the delicate balancing act between making promises and delivering results. Gingrich, on the other hand, had spent sixteen years as a member of the minority party in Congress, where he was never required to be accountable for his words or his actions. Now it was Clinton's turn to set a trap for Gingrich.

Clinton had another major intellectual advantage over Gingrich. He had come to understand the conflicting views of the American public that both detested government but also demanded its services. F. Scott Fitzgerald once said that the test of a real intellect "is the ability to hold two opposed ideas in the mind at the same time and still retain the ability to function." Gingrich, in his desire to find unifying beliefs and systems to explain behavior, could not accept that contradiction. He was convinced that Republicans had a mandate to cut back on government and he was determined to accomplish that goal. Clinton understood the tension between the public's abstract disdain for Washington and its appetite for programs that directly benefited them. He planned to walk that delicate tightrope: promising to protect popular programs while calling for smaller, leaner government. It was a juggling act that only someone as skilled as Bill Clinton could pull off.

The months following the elections witnessed a pitched battle in the White House for the political soul of the president. On one side stood Dick Morris, the first pollster Clinton had ever used, who returned to help the president craft a message and regain his political footing. "Bringing back Morris in late 1994 was Hillary's effort to return the President to his political senses," said aide Sidney Blumenthal.[31] Hillary said that Morris had "the people skills of a porcupine," but he served a useful purpose: "With his skeptical views about politics and people, Morris served as a counterweight to the ever optimistic Bill Clinton. Where Bill saw a silver lining in every cloud, Morris saw thunderstorms."[32]

Realizing that his presence would anger the president's more liberal staff members, Morris decided to stay in the shadows. Working under the code name "Charlie," for the disembodied voice from the television show *Charlie's Angels,* Morris sat in Room 205 of Washington's Jefferson Hotel and sent faxes directly to the White House residence. Morris's advice was simple: "fast-forward the Gingrich agenda." He wanted Clinton to endorse the most popular aspects of the Republican agenda—reducing the deficit, overhauling welfare, streamlining government. Doing so would neutralize the most positive aspects of the Republican agenda and focus public attention on the pain: cutting spending for the environment, education, and Medicare.

Morris's strategy clashed with the views of the president's more liberal advisors and most of the Democratic congressional leadership, who wanted him to stand firm, label the Republicans as reactionary, and stress fairness over budget balancing. For those first few months after the election, "we had two White Houses," recalled Bruce Reed, "the Morris White House that was trying to work out a bipartisan approach to allow Clinton and the Democrats to recover from the '94 debacle; and the Panetta/Stephanopoulos wing which felt the opposite."[33] They wanted to do for the Democrats what Gingrich had done for the Republicans: define the real ideological differences that separated the parties by espousing a potent message of economic populism. The Democrats needed to label the Republicans as the party of the rich and powerful while showing that the Democrats were fighting for the financial well-being of typical American families.

Although Panetta and Stephanopoulos were the most vocal advocates of this approach within the White House, the chief spokesman was Richard Gephardt, the Democratic leader in the House. Gephardt saw no reason to compromise with the Republicans or to blur the real ideological differences between Democrats and Republicans. "Our focus, our obsession, was one thing, and one thing only," recalled Gephardt chief political strategist Steven Elmendorf, "which was trying to get back the majority. We believed that we needed to make the case that the House Republican leadership was bad for America on all fronts," he said. "We wanted always to paint them as trying to cut spending for poor people. Whatever it was, it was bad for voters. It was never in our interest to give the Republicans running the place any credit. It was in the White House's interest to give them credit to show that Clinton was above partisan politics."[34]

By the time weary Republicans went home for a long break that marked the end of the 100 days, they had developed two dozen bills based on the ten-point contract. Only two relatively minor bills had made their way into law. The only major item defeated was a constitutional amendment to limit congressional terms. Most of the legislation faced an uncertain future in the Senate. Even if provisions of the contract survived the Senate, they faced the possibility of a presidential veto and the difficulty of marshaling a two-thirds majority needed for an override. Despite these obstacles, Republican leaders felt they had accomplished a great deal. "Let's not be shy about it," majority leader Dick Armey wrote his troops, "the Contract has been a great success."[35] Gingrich declared the first 100 days a success, telling reporters that he had promised to bring items up for a vote, not necessarily to make them into law. Massachusetts Democrat Barney Frank poked fun at the claim, saying

Gingrich's comment was similar to a used car salesman saying, "I didn't promise to sell you a car, I promised to show you a car."[36]

In April, both CNN and CBS granted Gingrich's request for the opportunity to address the nation at the 100-day mark. Normally, only a president, marking important occasions, would be granted this air time, but the decision revealed just how much the balance of power had shifted in Washington. "The Gingrich festival was agony for Clinton," observed the *Washington Post*'s John Harris. Clinton watched the self-congratulatory Gingrich give his prime-time speech, bragging about creating a "new partnership with the American people" and reducing "bureaucratic micromanagement from Washington," promising to "give our children and our country a new birth of freedom." Clinton was not impressed. "To hear him tell it," he said later, "you would think the Republicans had revolutionized America overnight, and in the process changed our form of government to a parliamentary system under which he, as prime minister, set the course of domestic policy, while I, as President, was restricted to handling foreign affairs."[37] Gingrich had attracted lots of media attention, but Republicans had only passed "three relatively minor parts of their contract, all of which I supported. The hard decisions were still ahead of them." Gingrich was aware of the challenges. It was impossible to reach his stated goal of a balanced federal budget in seven years and provide the big House-passed tax cuts without making cuts in politically sensitive programs.

The president's liberal advisors wanted Clinton to keep a low profile so as not to draw any more attention to the success of the Republican Congress in voting on all ten items and passing nine. But the president was restless "to get back in the game," and followed the advice of Dick Morris that he should give his own address offering a point-by-point rebuttal. At a speech for the American Society of Newspaper Editors in Dallas, Clinton tossed aside prepared remarks about education and used the occasion to set a new tone. He laid out some of the themes—campaign and lobbying reform—that he had neglected in deference to Democratic leaders in his first two years, pointing out a willingness to compromise, but refusing to cut popular programs like education, immunization, and school lunch programs. He was conciliatory, saying that he did not want "a pile of vetoes" and was willing to work amicably with Congress. As the *New York Times* noted, "the major purpose of his speech was to mount a counterattack to the Republicans and to indicate that Mr. Gingrich's unchallenged moment in the spotlight had come to an end."[38]

Liberal House Democrats were unhappy with the speech, feeling that it was too accommodating, but it seemed to strike the right note with the public. By April 1995, Clinton had regained his political footing. Surveys showed that Gingrich's popularity had been rising from October through the November elections, but had fallen steadily from January through March. A *Washington Post*/ABC News poll asked which was more dangerous: congressional Democrats going "too far in keeping costly government services that are wasteful or out of date" or Republicans going "too far in helping the rich and cutting needed government services that benefit average Americans as well as the poor."[39] On January 4, 1995, the public was evenly split: 43 percent felt the Democrats were more dangerous, 45 percent to the Republicans. By March 19, however, 59 percent of the public felt the Republicans were "going too far," while only 34 percent feared the Democrats. While voters supported the general themes of the contract, they were skeptical about specific items.[40]

On the night of April 18, at a press conference, when asked about whether his voice was being heard, Clinton responded, "The President is relevant here." The press ridiculed the comment, but it was quickly forgotten because the next day an explosion ripped through the Alfred P. Murrah Federal Building in Oklahoma City. At the time, it was the worst terrorist attack on American soil, killing 168 people—19 of them children—and injuring hundreds. Clinton scrapped a planned speech at Michigan State University and substituted a speech that made a connection between Oklahoma City and the Republican Revolution. "There is nothing patriotic about hating your country," he told graduates, "or pretending that you can love your country but despise your government."[41]

Four days after the bombing, Clinton traveled to Oklahoma City to appear at a packed memorial service. "It was the nation's first exposure to Clinton as mourner in chief," recalled speechwriter Michael Waldman. "For many people, during those days, for the very first time, he truly became a president."[42] A poll by NBC News and the *Wall Street Journal* found that 84 percent of the public approved of the president's response to the bombing.[43] Clinton believed that the bombing put Gingrich and his conservative supporters on the defensive. By prompting millions of Americans "to reassess their own words and attitudes toward government," the bombing "began a slow but inexorable moving away from the kind of uncritical condemnation that had become all too prevalent in our political life."[44] The president was relevant again and he was about to flex his political muscle.

| Budget Battles

"THE BUDGET FIGHT for me is the equivalent of Gettysburg in the Civil War," Gingrich told reporters in August 1995.[1] Although he was not as fond of military metaphors as Gingrich, Clinton would have agreed with the point: the party that won the battle over the budget would likely win the ideological war. For many observers, Bill Clinton and Newt Gingrich personified the larger struggle between the two parties about the role of government in American life at the end of the twentieth century. "At the apex of the budget drama," observed the journalist Major Garrett, "it was as if the entire Democratic Party, past, present, and future, lived within Bill Clinton, and the entire Republican Party—not the doddering, pliant, feeble legislative weakling of yore, but the rippling, youthful, proud, and intemperate majority of today—lived and breathed through Newt Gingrich."[2]

During the winter, Gingrich and Dole held a series of meetings to discuss the Republican budget strategy. They agreed that the government needed to move toward a balanced budget while also pressing for a massive tax break. Budget Committee Chairman John Kasich and Appropriations Committee Chair Robert Livingston warned Gingrich against issuing a deadline for achieving a balanced budget, realizing that doing so would force them to produce specific numbers about the politically painful cuts that would be required in popular programs, including Medicare. They suggested he promise to put the budget on course to be balanced at some point in the future. The Republican troops were restless after an exhausting first 100 days and needed a break. Dick Armey said his troops were suffering from "greater good fatigue." They were conscious of the polls, which showed the president's popularity on the rise and Gingrich's on the decline. Nearly half of the public—47 percent—disapproved of his handling of his job. Republicans were also facing increased pressure from social conservatives to address their red meat issues: school prayer and abortion. This was not a good time, they argued, to draw a line in the sand on the budget.

Gingrich ignored this advice. He was convinced that the 1994 election represented a sea change in American politics and the public had given him a mandate to make significant cuts in federal spending. In the past, when confronted with the need to make politically costly budget cuts, Gingrich believed his party had always backed down. Reagan went along with tax increases in 1982; Bush made a deal with Democrats in 1990. "This is where Stockman and Darman blinked. I will not blink," he declared.[3] He believed that he needed a victory on the budget to complete the revolution he started. Moreover, he was convinced that he had the upper hand. In his politically weakened condition, Clinton could not afford to be viewed as responsible for shutting down the government, and, he assumed, the public always blamed the president, not Congress, for shutdowns. Gingrich insisted that the president and Congress work toward a balanced budget in seven years using figures supplied by the Congressional Budget Office (CBO). In order to reach their target date and fulfill promises for a tax cut, Gingrich needed to cut the future growth of Medicare and Medicaid by an estimated $270 billion, along with slashing spending on education and numerous other programs. Since he was proposing cuts only in the growth of Medicare, Gingrich claimed the GOP was trying to "preserve, protect, and defend" the system, not destroy it.

It was a politically risky move—the most aggressive conservative assault on popular middle-class social programs in modern times. Gingrich felt that he could use the threat of a government shutdown to force the president to submit to his demands. His whole strategy was based on his unquestioned belief that Clinton lacked the backbone for a budget battle. "Remembering Clinton's unpopularity in November and secure in the knowledge that presidents cave rather than shut down the government when presented with unpleasant budgets," Steely wrote, "Newt thought he was in the driver's seat."[4] His own instincts were buttressed by reports from Senator Trent Lott, who maintained close ties with Clinton pollster Dick Morris. The word going back to Gingrich was that Clinton wanted to make a deal. Gingrich always gave himself wiggle room. Even if he did not get everything that he wanted, Gingrich was confident that Clinton would have to move so close to his position that the public and press would view it as a major Republican victory.

Clinton was sending mixed signals, trying to balance his opposition to the Republican cuts with his desire to avoid a shutdown. The question for

Clinton was whether to stand firm against cuts in Medicare or to propose his own plan. Clinton was convinced that the Gingrich cuts were part of a larger Republican assault on government. "The Gingrich revolution represented the ugly face of Republicanism with the mask ripped off," Clinton told his aides.[5] But Clinton also wanted to re-establish his credentials as a "New Democrat" and did not want to cede the balanced budget issue to the Republicans. He wanted to avoid a government shutdown, fearing that the public would direct their anger at him and not the Republicans. "How far can I go without appearing to have totally capitulated," he mused privately.[6]

Many of Clinton's advisors, including Leon Panetta and George Stephanopoulos, worked closely behind the scenes coordinating strategy with Gephardt, who supported a policy of confrontation with the Republicans. Gephardt, and the House Democratic leadership, thought the Republicans had handed them a great political issue. They had scored points earlier by attacking Republicans for cutting school lunch programs "to pay for tax cuts for the wealthy." Now they planned to use the same tactic with Medicare. Polls showed that much of the public did not know that the Gingrich budget cut Medicare benefits at the same time that it was cutting taxes on the rich. Congressional Democrats asked the president to wait until later in the summer or the fall before proposing his own balanced budget proposal. In the meantime, Democrats, according to David Obey of the House Budget Committee, wanted Clinton to "use the megaphone of the White House to pound home" the message that "there was a real difference between us and them in how to balance the budget."[7]

Believing that Democrats and the president were succeeding in painting him as an angry reactionary, Gingrich decided to soften his image. On June 11, he shared a stage in New Hampshire with the president. Gingrich relished the opportunity to point out that never before in history had a president and Speaker appeared at the same event to debate issues of the day. The *Washington Post* noted that "Gingrich heaped so much praise on Clinton, in fact, that he almost could have been mistaken for Vice President Gore."[8] In one dramatic moment the two men leaned across their chairs and shook hands, agreeing to appoint a blue-ribbon panel to propose political reforms of campaign finance and lobbying rules. Many of the Speaker's conservative advisors, and certainly many of the members of the new freshman class, were shocked by the cordial tone of the meeting and felt Gingrich missed a chance to confront the President and push for their agenda. Instead, Gingrich seemed tame, almost intimidated by Clinton. The incident made Clinton aware of Gingrich's delicate political situation. Any public hint of compromise on the Speaker's part would incur the wrath of his conservative base.

If they were going to make deals, the president reasoned, they would need to be done behind closed doors.

Shortly after the meeting in New Hampshire, Clinton decided that in order to be credible, he needed to offer a realistic plan of his own for balancing the budget. On June 13, he gave a five-minute speech from the Oval Office in which he announced his own budget plan. He promised to balance the budget in ten years without raising taxes. Clinton proposed cutting Medicare by $128 billion instead of the GOP's $270 billion. He insisted that the budget be scored by the Office of Management and Budget (OMB) instead of the CBO. The difference was significant: since its forecast of economic growth was more optimistic, the OMB required overall cuts of only $750 billion to balance the budget. The CBO put the figure at $1.2 trillion. In addition, while the Republicans threatened to turn over responsibility for Medicaid to the states, Clinton wanted to keep the responsibility in Washington. Hoping to build on the amiable meeting the previous weekend, Clinton concluded: "We ought to approach it in the same spirit of

In June 1995, Clinton and Gingrich shared a stage in New Hampshire. Conservatives were outraged that Gingrich was so civil, and that he seemed to genuinely enjoy the president's company. He would not make the same mistake again. (AP Photo/Elise Amendola.)

openness and civility [as] when the Speaker and I talked in New Hampshire last Sunday." The original draft contained a friendly mention of "Newt." The First Lady insisted that he remove it in favor of a more formal reference to "the Speaker."

The combination of Clinton's meeting with Gingrich and his early concession on the budget angered Democrats. "The worst thing for House Democrats was the Sunday event with Gingrich," a leading Democrat told Elizabeth Drew. "He'd thrown dirt at Democrats for years, and there he was being treated like he's Mother Teresa."[9] Connecticut's Rosa DeLauro complained that she felt "betrayed" by the president. There was no political advantage to calling for a balanced budget. Obey issued a statement that stung the president: "Most of us learned some time ago that if you don't like the president's position on an issue you simply need to wait a few weeks."[10]

Gingrich, however, responded positively to the president's speech. "It changes the whole model of the debate," he said. "He agrees that the budget needs balancing, he agrees that medicare needs change, he agrees there should be tax cuts, he agrees domestic spending should be restrained, he agrees defense has been cut deeply enough." He felt that the president had accepted the major premise of their budget. "Now we're arguing detail." At a meeting with the White House budget team, Gingrich even offered a potential compromise, saying they could probably agree to eight years. A Republican colleague quickly reined him in: "Newt, don't start negotiating here."[11] In meetings with his own caucus, he insisted, often to applause, that he would hold the line on a seven-year balanced budget deal. But he also made clear that it was likely that any deal would involve making concessions to the White House, especially on spending for education and the environment. But they were in no mood for compromise. "To tell some of these freshmen they have to come more toward the middle is like telling them they have to shoot their daughters," said moderate Sherwood Boehlert.[12]

They both recognized that the key to success in politics was delivering results. "Even though we were in the midst of bitterly divided government, both Clinton and Gingrich saw that it was in their interests, and to a larger degree, in their parties' interests, to work together," said Bruce Reed.[13] Gingrich's strategy was to talk tough in public, keeping the pressure on the White House, while trying to work out a compromise in private. In large meetings, surrounded by congressional colleagues and White House staffers, Gingrich would posture, delivering what amounted to an ultimatum to the president. "The two of us can do great things. We can make history together," a White House aide recalled him saying. "But if you don't do it my way, I will just have to run over you." In smaller gatherings with just the president and his chief of staff, Gingrich set a different tone. "Behind the scenes he [Gingrich] was working to avoid the shutdown," reflected White House Chief-of-Staff Leon Panetta. "In private conversations Gingrich would often say that he would like to get things done," Panetta recalled. "He was more accommodating in private than in public."[14]

Both Clinton and Gingrich were kept in check by their followers. Congressional leaders and his own staff limited the president's options; Gingrich was constantly frustrated by his hard-charging freshmen. White House officials worried that Clinton would agree to cuts that he could not sell to congressional Democrats; Republican leaders fretted that Gingrich would accept spending levels that were anathema to his caucus. "You put both these guys in a room together and you're not quite sure what's going to happen. Both could influence each other in ways we never understood," Panetta reflected.[15] A White House aide referred to the private meetings between Clinton and Gingrich as "tossed salad." The problem, he said, "was you never knew where the lettuce would fall."

In many ways, however, Gingrich exacerbated the problem with his bellicose language. Clinton used to tell aides that "Gingrich's biggest problem was that he couldn't get the people around him to stop believing all the nonsense he taught them to get there," recalled Bruce Reed. Gingrich became a captive of his own rhetoric and his own revolution. He understood the difference between public posturing and private negotiating, but most of his young followers did not. His rhetoric limited his negotiating room and prevented him from making a deal with the president. "Often times we felt that while Gingrich would be willing to find some kind of a solution, he was restrained by this band of younger members who controlled whether or not he would be Speaker," Panetta recalled. "He knew that his survival depended on being seen as the leader of a revolution." The problem was that it also limited Gingrich's range of options. "He was constrained by the politics that he helped to create."[16] In the end, he wanted a deal. But he underestimated the power of his own words, the zeal of his followers, the obstructionism of the president's advisors, and, most of all, the political skill of his adversary in the White House.

The key, they both realized, was to sit down together, with as few people as possible in the room, and hammer out their differences. Clinton's strategy was to get Gingrich away from his ideological followers, negotiate a deal, and then let him sell it to his caucus. He understood Gingrich's delicate political position: he was the leader of the revolution and he needed to inspire his followers, but he was also a pragmatic politician who wanted to make deals. Gingrich believed that if he could only isolate Clinton from House Democrats, he could convince him to accept the major outlines of a Republican budget. "He thought that if he could get the president away from the House Democrats he could work something out with him," observed Mel Steely.[17]

They wanted to deal with each other alone because they were confident in their ability to manipulate the other. In their private meetings, "Clinton would get Gingrich on the couch in the Oval Office and make his pitch," recalled a senior White House aide. He appealed to Gingrich's ego, his feeling of being an outsider battling the Washington establishment, and his willingness to take political risks. "Isn't it amazing that two guys from Hope, Arkansas, and Harrisburg, Pennsylvania, are sitting here leading the nation?" he would say. "We can do this. We can make it happen." Gingrich, on the other hand, appealed to Clinton's intellect, his willingness to think out of the box, and his ingrained skepticism about federal bureaucracy that he developed as governor of Arkansas. "I have no doubt the two of them sitting alone in a room together could have solved most of the world's problems," recalled a White House official.

Republicans complained, sometimes publicly, that Gingrich was mesmerized by Clinton's charm. They felt that the president was a much better poker player than Gingrich. The joke among House conservatives was that Clinton and Gingrich were like characters from the 1950s television show *Leave it to Beaver*. Clinton was the well-mannered but manipulative Eddie Haskell; Gingrich was the naive and gullible Beaver. "The Clinton White House figured out how to play Newt," said Tony Rush, Tom DeLay's chief of staff. "They would put the *Time* magazine cover with Newt as the 'Man of the Year' on the coffee table in front of where they would have Newt sit. Newt would come back into leadership meetings from the White House and tell us how the White House understood his significance. And people would look around and say to themselves, 'Have you lost your mind?' "[18]

What Republicans did not know at the time was that the White House had similar fears about Gingrich. Robert Dole was considered the Republicans' most skilled negotiator, but everyone in the White House knew Clinton could handle him. "It was only Gingrich that the White House feared," recalled Panetta.[19] The president "saw Newt as an intellectual soul mate with whom it was fun to match wits," reflected Dick Morris. "He looked forward to talking with Gingrich and often came back from their calls with a shy smile on his face."[20] Clinton sometimes seemed so hypnotized by Gingrich's intellect that his staff would give him a "Miranda warning" before he entered a meeting with the Speaker. "Remember, Mr. President," his aides would say to him, "anything you say in that room can and will be used against you." Aides marveled about how the two men would carry on extended, and often irrelevant, conversations about the impact of technology and globalization on the future of the workplace. "When the two of them would start engaging each other on issues of mutual fascination, both of their advisors would feel a panic that each was forgetting they were in a room with political opponents who might use any word they said against them," recalled White House economic advisor Gene Sperling. For aides on both sides it was proof of the unpredictable bond they shared and reinforced the need to keep them apart or under tight supervision. "This isn't a seminar," the president's staff would remind him. "This guy wants to destroy you."[21]

Throughout the summer and fall they talked often by phone and met occasionally in private to discuss the budget, along with other issues. There were regular high-level staff meetings where they laid out the parameters of a potential deal. Gingrich made clear that he needed a general commitment to a balanced budget and a large tax cut. Clinton wanted a guarantee that basic Democratic programs would be protected. Gingrich had staked out a tough public line, but in these conversations he left some room to maneuver. Both sides were reasonably optimistic about finding some common ground and working out a budget compromise. "My sense in September was that we were on the edge of a deal that would have been worked out and been done by Thanksgiving," Gingrich told Elizabeth Drew.[22]

In private, Clinton was moving closer to the Republican position, over the objections of many of his staff members and House Democrats. In public, however, he was exaggerating the differences between himself and the Republicans, trying to define the debate in stark terms. In many ways, Clinton was playing the same game as Gingrich, assuming a tough pubic position while trying to be more flexible in private. In late September, Morris convinced Clinton that scaring the public about Republican cuts in Medicare would be good politics. It would boost his standing as the defender of a popular social program at the same time that it tapped into public suspicions that Gingrich and his revolutionaries were outside the American mainstream. Clinton dipped into his $42 million war chest, which he originally created to ward off potential challenges in 1996, and authorized an aggressive air war against the proposed Republican "Medicare cuts."

The ads depicted Gingrich and the Republicans as heartless zealots robbing old ladies to give tax cuts to the rich. The formula was to show an inspiring "morning in America" image while an announcer talked about the differences between right and wrong. The tone switched, as the camera panned to a picture of Gingrich and presumptive Republican presidential nominee Bob Dole, warning of their plan to "cut Medicare." Switching back to Clinton, the announcer intoned: "President Clinton . . . doing what's moral, good and right by our elderly." Titled "Moral," "Protect," "Slash," "Cut," and "Wither," the series aired in "secondary markets" around the country to avoid media scrutiny.[23] But millions of Americans saw them and the president watched as his approval ratings began to tick up from the mid-40s to the mid-50s by December. One spot showed a middle-aged couple debating what to do with grandma if Congress succeeded in cutting federal health care benefits, while grandma sat in the next room crying.

The ads infuriated House Republicans, making them less willing to make a deal. Gingrich saw the ads as desperate demagoguery, but, initially, did not believe they would impact the negotiations. "Think about a party whose last stand is to frighten 85-year-olds, and you'll understand how totally bankrupt the modern Democratic Party is," he fumed.[24]

In October, when word leaked that Gingrich was having private meetings with the president, many conservatives forced him to break off the discussions. In order to keep the two men in line, the Republican conference insisted that tough-talking Texas Majority Leader Dick Armey chaperone all meetings between Gingrich and Clinton. White House officials asked Vice President Al Gore to play a similar role. Both sides were caught in a good cop/bad cop routine. In the key meetings leading up to a potential shutdown, Clinton and Gingrich would start discussing possible points of compromise, clearly reaching out to each other. Before the discussion could gain momentum, Armey would undermine the Speaker by saying the leadership would not support any compromise Gingrich might negotiate. At the same time, Gore, who sat next to the president, would back away from any compromise on the president's part. "It was remarkable to watch," said one Republican participant. "Clinton would get excited about an idea that Gingrich raised and lean forward in his chair and Gore would physically reach out and pull him back into his seat."

Gingrich recalled one moment in particular when they were all in a conference room going over the details of the budget. The Speaker raised a point, suggesting a possible compromise. Clinton responded positively, saying "We can cut that deal." Leon Panetta, who was standing in front of the room with an easel, snapped at the president: "You can't do that. We lost control of the Congress fighting for this program. You cannot give it away." Gingrich was stunned. "I had never seen a staff member, in front of the other team, so directly hammer a president," he recalled.[25]

Realizing that his aides were limiting access to the Speaker, Clinton turned to his favorite form of communication—the phone. According to Gingrich, he spoke by phone with the president "at least once a week." During intense legislative negotiations or a foreign crisis, they talked every day, sometimes a couple of times a day. Clinton often used the conversations to elicit as much intelligence as possible from the Speaker, while offering little insight into his own thinking. Occasionally, their discussions strayed from the topic at hand to books they had read or items in the news. On one occasion in 1995, with rumors circulating that Gingrich was planning to run for president in 1996, Clinton offered advice on steps he needed to take to become a viable candidate. It was during these private conversations that the two men had their most revealing and useful discussions. Clinton recalled that in these discussions Gingrich was "frank about what his caucus was really up to." The Speaker would explain the political pressures he faced to maintain a tough line with the White House, while pointing out his own willingness to reach reasonable compromises. "He was also very candid with me about his political objectives. And he, in turn, from time to time, would get in trouble with the right wing of his own caucus because they said I could talk him in to too much."[26] In meetings with his staff, Clinton often responded to their complaints about Gingrich by saying, "It's not Newt that's the problem. It's the right wingers in his caucus that we need to worry about." The comment puzzled staffers, who thought Gingrich was a "right-winger."

In many ways, these private conversations laid the foundation for their future alliance. They reinforced Clinton's perception that he could work with Gingrich, that under the right political circumstances he and the Speaker could forge areas of agreement. But he also realized that compromise was unlikely as long as Gingrich was beholden to his party's powerful right wing. He thought Gingrich was at heart a political moderate trapped by his own grandiose ambition and by his overzealous followers. Clinton also realized that Gingrich could be highly volatile with a vicious political streak, so he needed to handle him with care. At the same time, Gingrich came slowly to appreciate the president's political skill, and he was learning the hard way that Clinton could not be easily pushed around. But he also realized that Clinton was more conservative than most of the Democratic leadership in the House. As the governor of a small state, Clinton had first-hand experience with the fraud and inefficiency that sometimes characterized federal social programs. He would often complain about the problems with federal mandates and express sympathy for conservative proposals for giving more power to the states. In some ways, Gingrich's view of Clinton was a mirror image of the president's view of him: he saw him as a political moderate trapped by the ideological leanings of his party.

There was one critical element missing from their relationship. "There was no trust in the relationship," reflected Erskine Bowles. "Neither ever saw the goodness of the other. They were political enemies who respected the other's insights, intellect, and vision. But they believed the one was out to destroy the other."[27] Clinton distrusted Gingrich, but never disliked him. "Clinton had a much deeper dislike of someone like Dick Armey or Tom DeLay than Gingrich," recalled Bruce Reed. "He saw Gingrich as a bit of an opportunist, someone who imagined grand historical happenings and himself in the middle of it."[28] Most White House officials made similar observations. "I never heard Clinton express deep personal animus toward Gingrich," recalled Waldman. [29]"I remember being struck by the lack of personal animus on Clinton's side," reflected Robert Reich.[30] "He respected Gingrich as one successful politician respects another." Clinton felt that Gingrich was driven solely by a lust for power, and would do or say just about anything to achieve it. He would also destroy anyone who stood in his way. The key to managing Gingrich was to convince him that cooperation, not confrontation, offered the best pathway to power. For his part, Gingrich enjoyed the president's company, and he viewed him as a skilled tactician who lacked a strong ideological core. The best way to handle him, Gingrich felt, was to define the choices and limit the options from which he could choose.

With the threat of a shutdown looming, the White House and congressional leaders met on Wednesday, November 1. In the days leading up to the meeting, the president's advisors spent hours discussing what strategies to use to keep Clinton from negotiating a deal with Gingrich. They tried intercepting Gingrich's calls to Clinton, and joked about disconnecting the president's phone to keep him from talking to Gingrich and working out a deal. Panetta tried to limit the president's options by telling the *Washington Post* and the House Democratic caucus that the president believed that "no deal is better than a bad deal." As they gathered for the meeting, the White House staff surrounded Clinton in what Stephanopoulos said "had the feel of a family intervention." The goal was to diminish Gingrich and convince the president that the Speaker could not be trusted to negotiate in good faith. "Newt will lie and Newt will leak to force your hand," Stephanopoulos told Clinton. He told the president that he needed to keep up his guard. "In this case," he concluded, "a failed meeting is a successful meeting."[31] Stephanopoulos received unexpected support from Gore. "George is exactly right about that," the vice president said.

The meeting was already tense when Gingrich started complaining about the negative television ads Democrats were running claiming that Republicans were trying to cut Medicare. Panetta responded by reminding him of all the terrible things he and other Republicans had said about the president:

"Mr. Speaker, you don't have clean hands."[32] Vice President Gore added, "At least we didn't accuse you of drowning those little children in South Carolina," referring to a comment Gingrich made earlier suggesting liberals were responsible for the actions of a mentally ill woman who drowned her own children. Gore's counter-punch "rocked Gingrich and fortified Clinton," Stephanopoulos claimed. "Watching Gore coldcock Newt tapped the competitor in Clinton," he observed. As Gingrich pleaded for concessions, the president held firm. Gingrich told Clinton that his followers were looking for a showdown and he needed to agree to a seven-year balanced budget plan. Clinton refused, complaining that he had agreed in principle to all the Republican agenda—balancing the budget, reforming welfare, saving Medicare—but the GOP had not compromised on a single issue.

Both Clinton and Gingrich were shaken by the meeting. They had assumed all along that they would be able to find a way out of the impasse: Gingrich was convinced that Clinton would blink and accept terms close to what he proposed; Clinton was certain that he could use his powers of persuasion to push Gingrich away from his hard-line position. The reality was they were never far apart. The combination of misunderstandings, blunders, and the stubbornness of hardliners on both sides had limited the negotiating room and allowed both sides to blunder toward a shutdown. After the meeting, for perhaps the first time, both men realized that a shutdown was inevitable.

At one point during the meeting, Gingrich looked at the president and said, "You know, the problem here is you've got a gun to my head. It's called the veto. But what you don't understand is that I've got a gun to your head and I'm going to use it. I'm going to shut the government down. We are coequal branches of government, and I'm going to use my veto, which is shutting the government down." After Gingrich left, Clinton turned to Gephardt and Senate Minority Leader Tom Daschle and said, "Jesus Christ, is he going to do this? Do you really think he's going to do this?" Gephardt, who had been trying for months to convince Clinton that Gingrich and his conservative followers were more ideological than he realized, responded, "Yes, I've been trying to tell you this for days. They're going to do this. This is what they came to do."[33]

White House staff members were thrilled with the president's tough line. They gathered around a television set and watched the coverage of Gingrich leaving the White House, preparing to meet with reporters. "Newt was stunned," said one. It was clear that the always confident Gingrich now looked "shaken." He had no plan B. He had never expected to get to this point. Both sides were now locked into their positions, leaving little room for compromise.

In the days leading up to a potential shutdown, Gingrich made one of a series of critical mistakes that would damage his position. The president had asked Republicans to send him a "clean" continuing resolution, essentially asking for a resolution to keep the government open without attaching any additional demands. Instead, they sent over to the White House a resolution that included a provision eliminating a scheduled drop in Medicare premiums. The White House and congressional Democrats pounced, saying Republicans were trying to balance the budget by cutting Medicare benefits. "Hitting that one back was like batting practice," reflected Stephanopoulos.[34] On November 11, in his weekly radio address, Clinton compared Republicans to greedy bankers. "The banker says to the family, 'I'll give you the loan, but only if you'll throw the grandparents and kids out of the house first.' Well, speaking on behalf of the family, I say, 'No thanks.' "[35] The president, Stephanopoulos observed, "was the picture of stern compassion. America's dad," compared to Gingrich, who "looked more like America's brat."[36]

On Monday, November 13, Clinton vetoed the Republican bills, claiming they were trying "to impose their priorities on our nation." Gingrich refused to cede any ground. "We were elected to change politics as usual."[37] The tone between the two men was more cordial when they met in private in the White House a few hours before the scheduled shutdown at midnight. Dole opened the meeting asking for both sides to present their bottom lines and try to work toward a compromise. Gingrich agreed, suggesting they work to avoid the shutdown. Majority Leader Armey, however, played the role of bad cop, attacking Clinton for scaring old people, including his mother-in-law, with his Medicare ads. The president, who had endured brutal Republican attacks for two years, was in no mood to listen to Armey's complaint. "Don't look for any pity from me," he shot back. "Look," he said, "you guys don't get it. If you want a president to sign your budget, you're going to have to elect someone else to do it. If you want your budget, you'll have to get someone else to sit in this chair," gesturing toward his chair in the Oval Office.[38] "Even if I drop to 5 percent in the polls," he would never sign their budget. He added, "You may not believe this, but I'm willing to lose this seat rather than take a budget like this. I'll let Bob Dole do that if he's in that chair."[39] (Afterward, Clinton joked with Gore that "If we drop to 4 percent, I'm caving.")

The Republicans left the White House as midnight approached, and the shutdown commenced. It was a high-risk gamble for both sides. No one really knew how the public would react. "None of us who were involved had any idea of which side was going to get blamed," recalled Robert Reich.[40]

"The day that the government shut down we were scared," reflected White House economic advisor Gene Sperling. "We thought everyone would sink [in the polls] and the public would say 'curse on both your houses.'" Clinton took the high road, canceling a planned trip to Japan to stay on top of the situation. "I was afraid they'd get away with it, given their success at blaming me for the partisan divide in the '94 election," reflected Clinton.[41] He got a break the next morning, however, when Gingrich told reporters that he had sent a tougher version of the budget bill to the White House because Clinton failed to negotiate with him and Senator Dole on a long plane ride to Israel to attend the funeral of Yitzhak Rabin. "It's petty, but I think it's human," he said. "You've been on the plane for twenty-five hours and nobody talked to you and they ask you to get off the plane by the back ramp. . . . You just wonder, where is their sense of manners? Where is their sense of courtesy?"[42]

Gingrich's childish verbal tirade was a public relations disaster for the Republicans. Coming in the second day of the shutdown when public opinion was still malleable, it made the Republicans seem petulant and stubborn, while allowing Clinton to appear presidential by comparison. "The ultimate question the press was focused on is what is the character of these two men as they enter the showdown that will affect the nation," recalled Reich. "Who do you trust?" They were both under the spotlight. "When the beam of light is on each of these men so intensely it was an error of the first degree for Gingrich to sound so petulant," he said. The press jumped all over the incident. "Cry Baby," said the *New York Daily News,* next to a picture of Gingrich in a diaper. That afternoon the White House released a photograph of Clinton, Dole, and Gingrich chatting on the plane. "With one self-indulgent remark, he punctured his credibility and ensured that the American people knew to blame Congress, not the Administration, for the government shutdown. The fight was not over, but the field was shifting," the First Lady later observed.[43]

What Gingrich did not know at the time was that the president's advisors were continuing to manage their relationship, still fearful that, if left alone, the two would strike a deal. Realizing that the long plane ride would provide lots of opportunity for the two men to interact, Clinton's aides intentionally loaded the president with work to keep him distracted. They suspected that Clinton would want to use the time to talk with Gingrich, but they were determined to make sure that conversation never took place. "We didn't want them hanging out unsupervised," said White House congressional liaison Patrick Griffin.[44] "We *did* deliberately avoid discussion of the budget on Air Force One," Stephanopoulos confessed, "because of our continuing worry that Clinton would cede too much in a private negotiation with

On the second day of the budget shutdown, Gingrich said he took a tough stance because the president had refused to talk to him during the long plane ride to Israel to attend the funeral of Yitzhak Rabin. After the Gingrich outburst, the White House released this photograph showing the president engaged in casual conversation aboard Air Force One with Dole and Gingrich. (AP Photo/ White House.)

Gingrich or Dole."[45] Leon Panetta was charged with preventing any budget talks from taking place during the trip. Gingrich had planned to release an upbeat statement at the conclusion of the trip. "If they can make peace in the Middle East, we can get together in the US on the budget." Instead, he managed to make a deal less, not more, likely.

The Speaker's self-destructive comments not only bolstered the president's position, but they also badly damaged his relationship with his troops. He would never fully recover from the incident. "He picked the wrong bloody moment to take out a .357 and shoot both kneecaps off," said a House Republican.[46] At just the time he needed the support of his troops to present a united front with the White House, many House freshmen were losing faith in him. After being hailed as a brilliant strategist, Gingrich was running into strong opposition from a stubborn president and from angry conservatives in his own party. Gingrich had proven that he could lead a rebellion, but did he possess the skill and political dexterity to manage a coalition, and, most of all, could he go toe to toe with the wily Bill Clinton? Many of his own supporters were beginning to have serious doubts.

While Gingrich may have permanently damaged his speakership with his words that morning, Clinton would almost destroy his presidency with his actions that night. With the White House operating with a skeleton staff because of the shutdown, there was greater opportunity for presidential mischief. On the evening of November 15, 1995, Clinton invited Monica Lewinsky, a flirtatious twenty-two-year-old White House intern, into his private study for the first of a series of sexual rendezvous. Perhaps relieved that he scored a major victory in his political fight with Newt Gingrich, the president lost the personal struggle with his private demons. "I was involved in two great struggles at the same time," Clinton reflected, "a great public struggle over the future of America with the Republican Congress and a private struggle with my old demons."[47] Ironically, Clinton saved his presidency and destroyed his reputation on the same day.

The events of November 15 revealed another shared unflattering characteristic: a certain recklessness and immaturity. At one moment Clinton and Gingrich were sophisticated, thoughtful leaders making crucial decisions that would shape the entire nation; the next, they could be immature little boys unable to curb their basic urges. Gingrich was often unable to contain his anger; Clinton found it impossible to control his libido. Gingrich was the brilliant strategist who led Republicans to control of the House, shaped the public debate about government for the decade, and forced a sitting president on the defensive. But he also through his verbal excess and harsh demeanor reaffirmed public perceptions that the Republicans were mean spirited and incapable of governing. Clinton had neutralized Democratic vulnerability on the social issues, allowing them to recapture the presidency. Yet, through his personal acts of indiscretion, he also created a new set of moral concerns that would plague his party long after his presidency ended.

Both men complained that the other had a Jekyll and Hyde dimension to his personality, but were oblivious to the quality in themselves. Once when asked by a reporter how he felt about the Speaker, Clinton responded: "It depended on which Newt showed up."[48] Gingrich complained bitterly that Clinton seemed to change his positions on a daily, sometimes hourly, basis. Those who knew both men experienced first-hand their split personalities, which they rationalized as the product of their similar childhoods, growing up in dysfunctional families, trying unsuccessfully to win the approval of an abusive stepfather. Whatever the reason, the result was the same: they were often unpredictable and frequently self-destructive. *Newsweek*'s Jonathan Alter described Clinton's two personalities as "solid and squalid. Cautious and reckless. Supersmart and superdumb." During the day he was "Dr. Clinton—helping to heal the American economy and tap a vein between mindless liberalism and heartless conservatism." At night, he became "Mr. Bill—a doughy, needy mass of uncurbed appetites and fits of irrationality." For Gingrich, there was "Bright Newt," the "political visionary" and "broad-minded conversationalist" who loved ideas and was a skilled and "flexible negotiator." Gingrich, he wrote, "only plays an ideologue on TV." Then there was "Fright Newt," who "slanders promiscuously and waxes megalomaniacal."[49]

Clinton, who participated in intensive family therapy in the 1980s after his brother Roger was arrested and sent to jail for selling drugs, was better equipped than Gingrich to analyze his own emotions and more open about discussing them. He wrote in his memoirs that from an early age he learned to live "parallel lives," where his public affability often masked inner turmoil. Gingrich, on the other hand, seemed incapable of probing beneath the surface of his subconscious. He viewed himself as a man with a historic mission, but never doubted that mission or questioned his motives.

———

With Gingrich nursing his self-inflicted wounds, Bob Dole decided to fill the power vacuum. At seventy-two, Dole was the senior statesman of the party and the frontrunner for the Republican nomination in 1996. He never cared for Gingrich, whom he found abrasive, arrogant, and self-absorbed. Dole complained that Gingrich and his followers enjoyed the attention they received, but they never had a strategy for victory. "They always lived for the day," recalled Dole advisor Scott Reed. "They were sprinters not marathon runners." Throughout the budget battle, Dole would ask Gingrich, "What's our endgame?" Gingrich never had an answer. "They were intoxicated by being invited to the White House," said Reed. "Intoxicated by parading in front of the press corps. Intoxicated by reading their quotes in the papers and watching themselves on the news."[50] They walked right into Clinton's trap. Dole, gearing up to challenge Clinton in November 1996, shuttling almost daily between Washington and New Hampshire, feared that he would pay a political price for Gingrich's antics. But he also needed the support of conservatives to win the Republican nomination. For many House conservatives, Dole was the face of the old party: the moderate, deal-making, centrist wing they came to Washington to replace. Like Gingrich and Clinton, he was now looking for a graceful way to end the logjam without losing face.

White House staff members were giddy following the Speaker's self-destructive comments, convinced that the Speaker had given the president a major tactical advantage in the battle over the budget. With public opinion moving decisively against the Republicans, they assumed the president would stand firm. Some of the president's aides could not pass up the opportunity to mock Gingrich. When told of the Speaker's comments about the Air Force One incident, White House Press Secretary Mike McCurry said sarcastically, "Maybe we can send him some of those little M&Ms with the presidential seal on it." Clinton, however, was not amused. "Mike, why did you do it?" he yelled. "Don't kick him when he's down," he warned. "We have to be very conscious of Gingrich's standing. He's the only one that can pull it together. If we get something, and we put it together, he's got to be able to sell it."[51] Clinton understood better than his aides that while Gingrich could be bombastic and mercurial, he was more flexible than any of the men who would potentially take his place. The president was still convinced that he could win over Gingrich, and that only the Speaker could bring enough Republican votes to make a deal.

Instead of driving a harder bargain, Clinton moved in the opposite direction. Over the next few days, Dole and Clinton made enough concessions to bring about a temporary end to the shutdown on November 19. Clinton indicated that he would accept a seven-year timeline, but insisted that Republicans protect necessary social programs. Dole agreed to use updated, and more optimistic, estimates from the Congressional Budget Office. Both sides claimed victory. Gingrich was able to say that the deal was "a very historic achievement" since Clinton agreed to their timetable. But Clinton could brag that the Republicans agreed to his condition that the balanced budget "must protect future generations, ensure Medicare solvency, reform welfare, and provide adequate funding for medicaid, education, national defense, veterans, agriculture and the environment."[52]

Clinton went into the next round of budget negotiations with a decidedly stronger hand when the talks resumed after the Thanksgiving break on Tuesday evening, November 28. A group from the White House and the Congress assembled in the Mansfield Room across from the Senate chamber. The discussions never got off the ground. The only weapon Gingrich had in his arsenal was the threat of a government shutdown. But with polls showing the public siding with Clinton in the budget battles, Gingrich knew his threat had little credibility. He was trapped between two immovable objects. Buoyed by polls, Clinton had even less incentive to compromise. On the other side, however, his freshmen were angry about losing the first round of the fight, less trustful of their leadership, and more willing to provoke a confrontation. Gingrich was desperately looking for a way out of a confrontation that he had manufactured.

Gingrich returned to Washington after the Thanksgiving break determined to assume a lower profile in the budget battles. The message he was getting was loud and clear. As one Republican leader said: "All the members [had gone] home and heard the same thing: 'Keep it up, don't back down and tell Newt to shut up.'" In early December, Gingrich told a closed door meeting of House Republicans that he had "thrown one too many interceptions" and that it was time for him to "sit on the bench for a while." He turned over the management of the negotiations to Majority Leader Armey and Budget Committee Chairman Kasich. "We want him to pay more attention to his personal conduct," said Christopher Shays of Connecticut, "and don't give Democrats ammunition."[53]

In the middle of the budget struggle, Gingrich received more bad news. On December 6, he received a telephone call while he was sitting in the office of his chief of staff. He learned that the Federal Election Commission (FEC) had dismissed most of the ethics charges that had been filed against him. But one charge remained—that Gingrich had received illegal support from GOPAC in 1990 at a time when it was barred from participating in federal elections. It was likely that the FEC ruling would pressure the House Ethics Committee to appoint a special prosecutor to investigate. It was a difficult time for other reasons. In October, he had learned that his stepfather, Bob Gingrich, had an advanced case of lung cancer. He died a month later—on November 20, the same day that Gingrich was nominated again as Speaker.

One afternoon, while in his office surrounded by staff and a few close colleagues, the burden of his stepfather's death, combined with the stress of the past few months, proved overwhelming for Gingrich. Tears started streaming down his face as he complained that "no one knows what my wife and kids have gone through for two and a half years of charge after charge after charge."[54] His second wife, Marianne, whom he married shortly after his divorce to Jackie, embraced him. He began sobbing uncontrollably. It was a revealing moment for a man who rose to power by using ethics investigations to highlight the corruption in the Democratic Party. Had he ever stopped to consider what impact his numerous ethics crusades on Democrats had on their families? It revealed that Gingrich had a soft chin. During periods of enormous stress, Clinton was often at his best. Gingrich, on the other hand, became irritable, uncertain, and volatile.

While Gingrich was saddled with questions about his judgment and character, the president was showing renewed strength in his handling of foreign policy. For the past two years, the president had watched from the sidelines as the Serbs, undeterred by empty NATO threats of military action, continued their policy of ethnic cleansing, murdering thousands of innocent men and boys in Srebrenica and tightening their grip over Sarajevo. Despite gruesome televised pictures of atrocities, the American public did not want to risk sending U.S. troops. In August, however, the president had authorized the use of American air power to force the Serbs to the negotiating table in Dayton, Ohio. In November, the presidents of Bosnia, Croatia, and Serbia signed a peace agreement that solved territorial differences and brought an end to hostilities. As part of the agreement, Clinton promised 20,000 American troops to join a multinational force to keep the peace. Senate Republicans, led by Dole, expressed qualified support for the president's plan, but it was a different story in the House, where many new freshmen opposed using the American military for humanitarian purposes. Privately, Gingrich supported the measure, but remained noncommittal in public. Clinton would have to win this one on his own. After a powerful Oval Office speech that mixed idealism with compassion, and an effective lobbying campaign, the president managed to convince both a reluctant Congress and a skeptical public to support the mission. More important, his decisive action, and his willingness to buck public opinion, made him appear strong and statesmanlike. Polls showed that nearly two-thirds of the public expressed confidence in his ability to handle the situation in the Balkans.[55]

While Gingrich remained largely absent from the Bosnia debate, he found it impossible to sit on the sidelines of the budget battles. After all, this was his fight. If Congress and the president did not reach a deal, or if Congress would not authorize a new continuing resolution, the government would run out of money and shut down again on December 16. Gingrich worried about the backlash that would come from closing down the government right before the Christmas holidays. He had no desire to play the Grinch to Clinton's Santa Claus. He suggested that his conference pass the resolution, agree not to close the government until after the holidays, and then pass targeted spending bills that would only fund the parts of the government the Republicans favored. The Republican caucus was in no mood for compromise. "This is the most defining moment in 30 years in this town, and the question is, is it going to be business as usual, or are we going to do the right thing for our children?" asked GOP Conference Chairman John Boehner.[56]

Many of the freshmen were still convinced that public sentiment was with them, despite the polls, and that it was imperative to continue the fight. "Newt would have been much more flexible than the rest of us," a Republican leader told Elizabeth Drew.[57] Gingrich came up with another plan for opening the government. "We all just laughed," said a member. "We told him there isn't any way."[58] A few days later in a meeting with the president, Clinton asked Gingrich for a continuing resolution (CR) to continue funding the government until they could work out a compromise. "If I go back and

In November and December of 1995 the key players—Clinton, Gingrich, Senate Majority Leader Robert Dole, and Vice President Al Gore—held a number of meetings at the White House to try and iron out their differences. This picture was taken on Tuesday, December 19. (AP Photo/White House.)

try to get a long-term CR without a budget from you, the next time you'll be dealing with Speaker Armey," he said.

The second shutdown started on Saturday, December 16. Since employees considered "essential" were allowed to stay on the jobs, the impact was less severe. The Republican leadership, however, showed no sign of backing down. "I believe we are in the middle of one of the defining battles of our nation's history," Armey wrote his colleagues. "If we don't see this through and win, we may never get another chance. When will there ever be another group of 235 men and women with this much courage and this much unity?" The polls may have been against them, but Armey showed no sign of compromise. "I believe we are right. I believe the country agrees with us. And I believe we can muster the stamina, the courage, and the resolve to finish this fight and win on our terms." [59]

House Republicans possessed an abundance of resolve; what they lacked was a strategy. Clinton was riding a political high when the talks resumed on December 22 at the White House. "I am not going to let them hurt our children," Clinton told reporters. The pressure was creating tension in the Republican ranks. The next day on the Senate floor, Dole took aim at the House Republicans. "I think it's time for adult leadership," he said. Clinton's tough stand placed Gingrich in an untenable position. He desperately wanted to work out a deal with the White House, and he was under intense pressure from Dole and other moderates to end the shutdown. But he also did not want to risk alienating his conservative base among House Republicans. On the first day of the shutdown, Gingrich sent a memorandum designed to stiffen the resolve of Republican leaders. "The White House has crossed the line," he wrote. "We want them to understand that if they want a long-term stand-off, we are prepared to stay the course for as long as it takes."[60]

It must have been apparent at the time, however, that Republicans lacked the political will for another prolonged shutdown. Adding to their problems, many observers blamed the shutdown for a precipitous 100-point drop in the stock market on December 18. Clinton allowed the pressure to build before reaching out to the Republicans. The talks resumed on December 22 at the White House. "We would get together in Dole's office before going over to the White House. We would agree that we were not going to give ground on anything," recalled Ken Keys, a member of the Republican negotiating team. "So we would all go down to the White House and Newt would make some concession to Clinton. Everybody on the Congress side would be asking 'What is he doing?'" After the meeting they would go back to Dole's office for a postmortem on the meeting. The team would often quiz Gingrich about why he broke ranks and started making concessions. "I like the guy so much I want to do a deal with him," Gingrich confessed.[61]

Even then, after two shutdowns, and despite all the stress and pressure of the moment, close aides marveled at the cordial, almost playful relationship between the two men. "My most vivid memory of the two of them together was during the budget negotiations after the second government shutdown just before New Years in 1995," reflected Bruce Reed. "Throughout the meeting Clinton and Gingrich were whispering to each other, nudging each other at points people made."[62] Behind the scenes, Gingrich was pleading with his negotiating team to deal in good faith with the White House—even as he accused Clinton of lying. He complained that with Dick Armey as his constant shadow, his negotiations were turning into an amateurish good cop/bad cop routine. "We must honestly practice listen, learn, and help and try to meet all their legitimate concerns," Gingrich wrote in a private note to the other members of the negotiating team. "We must hold our tempers, cheerfully seek new solutions and push to get an inch of progress each hour," he wrote. "No bad cops—I need to be honest cop."[63]

The president, however, was not budging. On December 30, Gingrich and Armey met with Dole in his office. They realized the battle was over. At one point during the meeting, Clinton called asking for a new round of face-to-face negotiations. According to Armey, Gingrich, "who had been sort of sitting there, stewing, jumped up and grabbed the phone." "Give me the damn phone," he said to Dole. Gingrich, convinced that Clinton's misdirection, and not his own failed strategy, was responsible for the impasse, shouted "at the loudest level of volume" at the president: "You're a goddamn lying son of a bitch!" The president, sitting in the Oval office with a few aides, held the phone receiver at arms length away from his body and rolled his eyes until Gingrich finished his tirade.

The incident revealed the unstable and explosive nature of their relationship. One day, they could be surprisingly playful; the next, inappropriately combustible. Unfazed by the comments, Clinton tried to calm Gingrich down. "Come on, Newt, lighten up!" he said. Referring to a recent edition of *Time* magazine, he noted, "You're Man of the Year." Dole was stunned by the exchange. He told Gingrich that he had never heard anyone speak to the president of the United States that way before. Gingrich responded, "Well we've never had such a lying son of a bitch as president before."[64]

On January 2, Dole, believing his party had paid a high price and with his own poll numbers tumbling, rammed a bill through the Senate reopening the government through January 12. "Enough is enough," he said. Gingrich realized it was time to throw in the towel. He came to the realization "that it was very likely going to prove to be impossible to get to an agreement." He concluded, wrongly, that the president never wanted a deal in the first place and actually wanted the government shutdown. That evening, after another day of fruitless negotiations, Gingrich recommend that his caucus agree to a continuing resolution opening the government. He confessed to making a number of strategic and tactical mistakes. He said he had anticipated their poll numbers dropping, but had failed to "calculate that a surge in Clinton's numbers would cause him to dig in even more."[65] His caucus, however, was still unwilling to concede defeat.

With Senate Republicans already on record supporting a resolution ending the shutdown, and House moderates threatening to vote with Democrats, Gingrich realized it was time to force conservatives to face political reality. On Friday morning, January 5, Gingrich met again with his troops. This time he told them he was not taking any questions. The time had come to end the shutdown. End of discussion. Conservatives were outraged by his action. "If you don't like the way we're doing it, run for leadership yourself," he told them.[66] The House passed a new measure by a lopsided 401–17 margin that funded the government for three weeks. On Saturday, January 6, Clinton signed the budget bill that ended the twenty-one-day shutdown. Three days later the budget talks broke down again. They struggled over the next few weeks, but Clinton won the debate. Gingrich knew he could not shut down the government again.

Gingrich had misjudged Clinton. "We made a mistake," Clinton remembers Gingrich saying. "We thought you would cave."[67] Gingrich could have declared victory at a number of points, especially when Clinton declared his support for a balanced budget in ten years or when he agreed to a seven-year timetable if the Republicans gave up their goal for deep spending cuts. Gingrich's hubris help do them in. "I'll tell you what killed us," Armey said. "In '93 and '94 the Democrats killed themselves because they were too full of themselves, and [in] '95 and '96 we killed ourselves because we were too full of ourselves."[68] Gingrich misinterpreted the results of the 1994 election and oversold the revolution. He had always thought of himself as a "transformational" figure. He thought this was his moment. It was not. "At the beginning a lot of us new conservatives who were elected in 1994 wanted to do too much too quickly," reflected Bob Barr. "We looked at the election of '94 as a mandate to dramatically change government and it really wasn't. It reflected a desire for change, but a lot of it was simply anti-Clinton. The country was simply not yet ready based on that one election, as important as it was, for the deep changes we were advocating." Gingrich made the mistake of reinforcing that view. "Our leadership could have done a better job of reminding us that simply because we won the election doesn't mean that we can start dismantling government. Change has to be much more incremental and gradual."[69]

Gingrich led the Republicans into battle with a deeply flawed plan. When the president put up more resistance than he expected, Gingrich had no alternative strategy. He was inconsistent and unpredictable, firing up his troops one day with militant speeches, then desperately searching for compromise behind closed doors. "You don't go into a battle and fight and then back down," reflected Barr. "If you are going to back down, don't engage in the first place." His handling of the budget would create lasting doubts about his leadership ability.

Gingrich possessed a near messianic drive to end Democratic hegemony in Congress and to create a new Republican majority. In the process of gaining power he created a militant, often simplistic framework for defining the differences between Democrats and Republicans, and he recruited a generation of conservatives who embraced his moralistic worldview. Once he achieved his goal of becoming Speaker and made the Republicans the majority party, he wanted to switch gears and negotiate many of the same deals that he had scorned his predecessors for making. Gingrich used fire and brimstone to lead his followers to the political promised land, but once they arrived he tried to instruct them in the art of negotiation and compromise. He was always more complicated than his rhetoric would suggest, but his followers were not attracted to him because of his nuanced view of public policy. They followed him because he hated the same things they hated. Clinton understood this tension in Gingrich's worldview and exploited it brilliantly.

The battle over the budget may have been the turning point of the Clinton presidency, but it was an inadvertent one. Clinton had not wanted to force a shutdown, but his Medicare ads, which grossly exaggerated the real differences between his administration and the Republicans, limited Gingrich's bargaining room at the same time that his aides steeled his resolve for confrontation. Using his back channel to Lott, Morris lulled the Republicans into believing that Clinton would negotiate a compromise at the same time that he launched the ads that convinced them to fight. "You couldn't have bought a better disinformation campaign if you tried," gloated Stephanopoulos. Once the shutdown began, Gingrich dutifully played the role that Clinton had scripted for him. "Let's face it," Stephanopoulos said. "Gingrich saved our butt."[70]

Although Gingrich clearly had political momentum on his side, Clinton possessed an institutional advantage. Clinton was the head of the executive branch, and the titular head of the Democratic Party. He had been elected by popular vote. Gingrich, on the other hand, was appointed by other House leaders. He lacked the firm foundation on which to lead his revolution. "Gingrich didn't understand," observed the *National Review*'s Richard Lowry, "that he was elected Speaker rather than Prime Minister."[71] Gingrich had never run for office outside his largely, white, educated, upper-middle-class congressional district, which never represented a cross-section of America. His style of politics was popular with his constituents, but he often had a deaf ear about how it played out in other parts of the country.

Gingrich emerged from the budget showdown in the worst of all political positions. His actions and overheated rhetoric allowed the mainstream media and Democrats to successfully label him as an uncompromising right-wing extremist. Public approval of the Republican House sank from a high of 52 percent in December 1994 to less than 30 in January 1996. Gingrich's personal approval rating plummeted to only 27 percent. By January 1996, Gingrich's unpopularity ratings rivaled Richard Nixon's at the depth of the Watergate crisis.

Yet on Capitol Hill, he lost the trust of conservatives who viewed him as being too accommodating and too eager to strike a deal with Clinton. Many of the freshmen were deeply disillusioned with Gingrich's handling of the budget negotiations. "He's been weakened in his ability to convince us that his political judgment is always wise," said Mark Souder of Indiana.[72] While most of the nation believed that he had been extreme, the freshmen felt he had sold them out. "We made a commitment last fall to stare down the president, and we blinked. We turned over the agenda to the president, and that's why we got sent up here. . . . We were sent here to force the president to balance the budget," said Florida's Joe Scarborough.[73] Many freshmen felt betrayed when Gingrich tried to blame them for his failed strategy. "The leadership didn't want to take the rap for a failed strategy, and in a classic Washington maneuver they blamed the freshmen," fumed David McIntosh of Indiana. "The freshmen class didn't want to back down, and they were told by Newt Gingrich: 'I will not back down,' but they were let down by Gingrich and Dole, when they decided they had to back down."[74]

The budget battles left Gingrich shaken and weakened; Clinton was invigorated and strengthened. "He had been a progressive governor in a conservative state. He was comfortable as a counter-puncher, challenging the boundaries of how far he could push the conservative consensus," reflected speechwriter Michael Waldman.[75] It was through his battles with Gingrich that Clinton tested and probed the limits of what was possible. He understood the weaknesses in the other side, the extent to which the public would support progressive measures, the best way to frame reform proposals, and how to define his opposition. He came away more sure of himself and his ability to handle the Republicans in Congress.

Clinton was not gloating over his victory over Gingrich. Instead, he felt that it opened up new possibilities for the future. If he were to create a new center in American politics, he would need to build coalitions between moderates in both parties. Gingrich could play an important role in his plans. On the one hand, he was an ideal foil. Clinton had so successfully stigmatized Gingrich as an uncompromising right-winger that Democrats planned to make him the face of the Republican Party. Clinton knew that he could stymie any conservative efforts to derail his agenda by attaching Gingrich's name to it. On the other hand, he believed in his efforts to rehabilitate his image, Gingrich would be even more accommodating, eager to prove that he was a responsible leader. Having Gingrich supporting a piece of his agenda would provide political cover for moderates and other conservatives. "It's an institutional version of only Nixon can go to China," said Waldman. "If Gingrich makes a deal with a Democratic president, then it's really hard for the right wing to complain too much."[76]

CHAPTER ELEVEN

Winning Re-election

B Y THE WINTER of 1996, the relationship between Gingrich and Clinton had hit bottom. In addition to the bad feeling created by the budget battles, both had grown weary of the constant stream of investigation and invective hurled at each other. As Clinton had feared, Republicans used their oversight function to investigate every aspect of his presidency. The strategy was developed by the Speaker's closest advisor, Joe Gaylord, who suggested that Republicans engage in an orchestrated effort to "indict the Clinton administration." Specifically, he recommended that the Republicans use their "oversight function" to keep the administration on the defensive. "Change the battlefield to one where Democrats are on the defensive by attacking personal ethics, attacking individual legislative records, forcing Dems to defend Clinton administration." Part of the plan was to put pressure on the White House to get House Democrats to back off their investigations of Gingrich. "Get the Clinton administration under special prosecutor problems and have the Clinton administration get the House Dems to back down."[1]

It would seem unlikely that the party would embark on such a strategy without at least the implicit approval of the Speaker. In describing Gaylord's role, Gingrich said earlier that he was "empowered to supervise my activities, set my schedule, advise me on all aspects of my life and career. He is my chief counselor and one of my closest friends."[2] Republican committee chairs had followed the Gaylord strategy over the past two years, hauling hundreds of government officials before investigative panels. Few presidents had faced the sheer number of inquiries as the Clinton administration. Congress called witnesses and issued subpoenas over the improper collection of FBI files by the White House, drug use in the White House, and the firing of seven White

House permanent employees of the Travel Office. Committees examined Hillary Rodham Clinton's commodities trading in the 1980s and investigated the travel activities of Energy Secretary Hazel O'Leary.

If Clinton was upset by the investigations, Gingrich was seething at the ads that the White House started running in 1995 making him the face of Republican extremism. Gaylord estimated that the White House ran 180,000 ads featuring Gingrich. "Week after week, month after month, from early July 1995 more or less continually until election day in 1996, 16 months later, we bombarded the public with ads," wrote pollster Dick Morris.[3] "At first, I think neither man thought the fighting was real," recalled Morris. "But when Newt saw his reputation and his career destroyed by our ads and Clinton's saw how close to home the Whitewater and FBI files scandals' shells landed, each reconsidered and came to dislike the other."[4]

Through the summer and fall of 1996 Gingrich tried to rehabilitate his public image. A friend referred to it as "Newt's sweater phase, when he wanted to show the kinder, gentler Newt." Working with a team of consultants, he tried smoothing out his rough edges and bolstering his sagging approval ratings. The goal was to show a warm, fuzzy side to the Speaker. There was one problem: Gingrich did not have a warm, fuzzy side. He petted squealing pigs on the *Tonight Show* with Jay Leno. He developed phrases that would make him sound as nonthreatening as possible. He posed with people with disabilities and with the elderly. He even tried the obligatory "kissing baby" photo shoot. Instead of kissing the baby, however, Gingrich lectured her about the Republican legislative record.[5]

Unlike Clinton, who possessed a natural charm and comfort in these informal settings, Gingrich often appeared awkward and out of place. "The problem is, you can't make someone look like something he's not," confessed a friend involved in the makeover effort. He had risen to power by manipulating the media behind the scenes, feeding newspaper reporters juicy quotes, framing issues for editors and reporters, and popping up on television to deliver a scathing attack and then quickly disappearing. Now, prolonged exposure on television exaggerated his worst qualities. It accentuated his large head and unkempt hair and added extra pounds to his already expanding waistline. Television liked to personalize stories, something Clinton learned during the 1992 campaign when he transformed himself from "Slick Willie" to "the man from Hope." But Gingrich did not have a compelling story to tell, and felt little need to manufacture one.

The master of wedge politics had become a wedge himself, used to drive moderate and independent voters from the Republican Party. Clinton played the Gingrich card throughout the 1996 presidential campaign. In 1948,

Harry Truman defeated his moderate Republican opponent Thomas Dewey by tying him to the "do nothing 80th Congress." In 1996, Clinton planned to undermine support for Republican nominee Senator Robert Dole by tying him to the conservative "Gingrich Congress." In campaign ads, Clinton replaced Dole's running mate, the popular former pro football quarterback turned congressman Jack Kemp, with Newt Gingrich. The president turned Gingrich's successful 1994 strategy on its head. He wanted to make 425 congressional elections into a referendum on Gingrich. "The story is, two candidates are running for reelection," said liberal Massachusetts Congressman Barney Frank: "Clinton and Gingrich."[6]

The president's campaign created a new political creature—the "three-headed Gingrich monster"—Dole, Kemp, and Gingrich. "Clinton realized that the entire campaign season could be unraveled by pulling on the Gingrich thread," recalled Dole campaign manager Scott Reed. "It made Dole look weak." Dole's relationship with Gingrich went through a series of phases, Reed recalled. It started out as "I guess that I have to work with him." But it quickly degenerated to "I can work with him," to "he's starting to hurt us," to "he's fucking killing us."[7]

Dole initially wanted to demonstrate his leadership skills by running the Senate while he ran for president. His so-called "rotunda strategy" made him vulnerable to the obstructive tactics of Democrats and the internal divisions within his own party. If he remained in the Senate, the public would view him as the titular head of the party and blame him for the gridlock that would inevitably follow. Eventually, he realized that his only chance of winning the election was to separate himself from Capitol Hill. In May, Dole dramatically announced that he was resigning his Senate seat to seek the presidency full time. "I will seek the presidency with nothing to fall back on but the judgment of the people of the United States and nowhere to go but the White House or home," Dole said during an emotional farewell.[8]

If he had any chance of winning in November Dole would need to energize the conservative base of his party, and for that effort he needed Gingrich's support. But he was not the only candidate in the race courting the Speaker. While sparring with him on the campaign trail, Clinton was actively wooing Gingrich in Washington. He realized that in modern times there was no clear precedent to build upon in trying to work with a powerful Speaker of the opposite party. No president ever had to deal with a Speaker as combustible as Gingrich and who wore so many hats: Speaker of the House, titular head of his party, and leader of the conservative movement in Congress.

For now, Clinton was convinced that Gingrich's desire to be more statesmanlike, to establish his credibility as a leader, would make him more accommodating, more willing to work with the White House. When asked what he hoped to hear the president say in his 1996 State of the Union address, Gingrich mockingly responded, "Thank you and goodnight." Clinton, however, was determined to take advantage of the moment. After the Speaker introduced him to the packed House chamber, the president handed him a copy of his address with a small note scribbled on the front page: "Is there room for common ground Mr. Speaker?"[9] He was reaching out to the Speaker because he was redefining and refocusing his message, hoping to attract more Republican votes, possibly at the expense of the liberal wing of his own party. Sullen Republicans sat in stoned silence as Clinton co-opted their rhetoric and their agenda, mixing a message of economic and cultural populism with perfect pitch. Declaring that "the era of big government" was over, he called for a new "values" agenda that focused on small, nonthreatening issues, such as curfews and school uniforms.

Despite the tensions in their relationship, the reality was that the two men shared a similar political objective in 1996. Clinton wanted to win reelection and cared little about House Democrats; Gingrich wanted to maintain control of the House and felt Dole had little chance of victory. In a sense, they both were triangulating, looking for legislative victories to convince voters to maintain the status quo. "Dole felt the only way he could succeed in 1996 was to make sure that Clinton failed," reflected Bruce Reed. "Gingrich, on the other hand, was determined to pass as much of the Contract as possible."[10]

Dole's departure elevated Trent Lott to the position of Senate majority leader. "Our accomplishments in 1996 were aided mightily by Lott's ascendancy to Senate leader. Like the Clinton White House, he was eager to demonstrate the ability to govern," recalled White House congressional liaison John Hilley.[11] Lott was a conservative with a soft touch, a partisan who valued civility, an ideologue who liked to make deals. He lacked Gingrich's imagination and intellect, but he also carried little of his political baggage. Gingrich wanted to be a revolutionary on the stump and a statesman in private. Lott melded the two roles. Where Gingrich was sometimes unpredictable and moody, Lott was steady and controlled. Using Dick Morris as an intermediary, Lott and Clinton started discussing a range of bills they could work on together. Morris, who played both sides of the aisle, sent messages back and forth and also served as a cheerleader.

Although Lott took the lead in the negotiations with the White House, Gingrich supported the strategy in the House. "Newt played second fiddle," reflected John Hilley. "Lott was our man in '96."[12] The first battle was over a Democratic proposal to increase the minimum wage to $5.15 an hour from

$4.25. With polls showing nearly 80 percent of the public supporting an increase, neither Dole, looking for votes, nor Gingrich, hoping to rehabilitate his battered image, wanted to stand in the way. House conservatives opposed to the increase rallied around Armey, Tom DeLay, and Budget Committee Chairman John Kasich. "I would much rather go down fighting for the principles of less government and lose the majority than to cave in to polls," DeLay lectured Gingrich. But moderates were breaking ranks, looking for compromise. "The revolution does not ask us to be martyrs," said Connecticut's Christopher Shays. "As long as the minimum wage is around our necks, the revolution will fail."[13] In the end, Gingrich supported the increase but obtained in return $21.4 billion in tax cuts over 10 years for small businesses.

In the days leading up to the Republican Convention in August, Clinton signed two other important pieces of legislation. On health care, Congress and the president agreed to legislation guaranteeing people the right to take their health insurance with them when they change jobs and making it more difficult for health providers to deny coverage to patients who had a history of illness. The legislation had been held up for weeks because of Republican insistence on including a provision for tax-free Medical Savings Accounts. In the end they agreed on a limited program capped at 750,000 policies.

Welfare reform was the biggest, and most controversial, initiative. The president, who had campaigned promising "to end welfare as we know it," had made welfare reform central to his New Democrat message. Clinton believed that reforming welfare would save money over the long haul as recipients moved into the workforce, but it would initially require increased spending on training and education to allow them to make the transition. He also believed that legal immigrants should be entitled to all the benefits granted to citizens. Republicans agreed with the goal of ending welfare, but opposed money for retraining and wanted to bar immigrants from collecting any money. The president was trying to walk a political tightrope. "Almost everybody likes your welfare plan," Bruce Reed told the president in December 1993. But, he warned, "this wonderful bipartisan coalition that likes our welfare plan so much begins to fall apart on the issue of how to pay for it." Liberals, he pointed out, wanted "to raise taxes and not cut existing programs," while conservatives wanted to spend less money and punish immigrants. Spelling out the delicate balancing act, Reed said the administration will "get clobbered from the L and the R if we don't split the uprights."[14]

For the first few years the White House struggled to "split the uprights," and twice the president vetoed Republicans bills he considered too punitive.

As they moved into an election season, the politics of welfare reform became central to both campaigns. Dole wanted to prompt a third veto so he could continue to depict Clinton as a big-spending liberal on the campaign trail. But both Gingrich and Lott were interested in protecting their majorities in Congress and believed they would be in a stronger position if Republicans could go home being able to tell their constituents they passed a popular reform measure.

During 1996, the Republicans inched closer to the president's position. In July, Bruce Reed wrote Clinton: "We have already won the battle on virtually every issue that is central to moving people from welfare to work."[15] For months, Lott had been promising the White House that he would be able to remove the few offending provisions from the Republican initiative and give the president a bill that he could sign. On July 30, however, Lott called the president to inform him that, while he was able to get some changes, the provision barring immigrants from collecting benefits remained in the legislation that was making its way to the president's desk. Clinton was furious. "This is not about welfare," he shouted to an aide after hanging up the phone. "This is about screwing immigrants and screwing me."[16] The Republicans had maneuvered Clinton into a box: he could veto a popular, but flawed bill, further blurring his "New Democrat" image and providing Dole with a wedge to use against him. Or he could sign the legislation and bolster his centrist image, but risk the wrath of liberals, including some in the White House. On July 31, the president assembled his close advisors and hashed out the arguments, both political and substantive, for and against. After two and a half hours of debate, Clinton announced, "Let's do it. I want to sign it."

The bill represented the most sweeping change in federal welfare policy since the New Deal. It set a five-year lifetime limit on benefits for most recipients and forced able-bodied adults to go to work within two years of receiving aid. It abolished the Aid to Families with Dependent Children (AFDC) program and provided states with block grants to set up their own programs. It tightened eligibility requirements for the federal food stamp program and limited benefits to three months a year. At a Rose Garden signing ceremony just a few weeks before the Republican Convention, Clinton signed the legislation, even as he promised to amend it by restoring benefits for legal immigrants and providing more incentives for businesses to hire poor mothers.

As expected, the legislative flurry boosted Clinton's standing in the polls, but in another revealing example of how the two leaders' fates had become inexorably intertwined, it may also have strengthened Gingrich's position as Speaker. Passing welfare reform, Gingrich believed, would mute Democratic attacks that Republicans were obstructionists and thus increase GOP prospects of maintaining control of the House, and improve his own chances of winning re-election as speaker. At some level, Gingrich realized that his own power was enhanced by having Clinton in the White House. He wanted the president to be strong enough to win re-election and appear threatening to conservatives, yet weak enough to be dependent on Republican support to pass his agenda. If Dole won the election, power would shift from the House to the White House, and a moderate Republican would be less threatening, and less needy, than a moderate Democrat.

The experience with welfare reform in particular also underscored how much the Clinton White House needed Gingrich. Despite months of private conversations, and constant back-channel discussions with Dick Morris, Lott could not deliver on his promise to give the president an acceptable welfare reform bill. Lott, the president complained, frequently promised more than he could deliver. "He could not deliver the votes," reflected a White House aide. While Clinton would have preferred to deal with a Democratically controlled Congress, that seemed unlikely, so his best option was to deal with a chastened but still strong Gingrich. In their private meetings, Gingrich provided the president with accurate information about his caucus and more precise vote counts than Lott. For all his flaws, the Speaker possessed the political and intellectual firepower to win over conservatives on tough votes.

Both men shared something else in common: they paid a heavy political price with their most ideological supporters for cooperating on passing legislation. Gingrich's makeover campaign, combined with his growing willingness to avoid confrontation with the president, complicated his relationship with conservatives, both in and out of Congress. "Suddenly the daring thinker with the 50-year time horizons was tailoring his language to the poll results of the previous week," complained David Brooks. "He set out to be a Thatcher, but has succeeded so far as a superior Bob Dole."[17] At the same time, liberals chastised the president for his decision to sign the welfare reform bill. Representative Maxine Waters, a California Democrat, said at the time, "It is not plausible that Americans will stand by and watch hungry children starve because their mothers did not meet a two-year deadline."[18] Half of the House Democrats—including Minority Leader Richard Gephardt and Minority Whip David Bonior—voted against the Republican-sponsored bill. The liberal view of Clinton was a mirror image of how conservatives saw Gingrich—as a political opportunist driven by polls who lacked strong principles.

One of the reasons Lott was playing a bigger role in dealing with the Clinton administration was because Gingrich was tied up at home trying to hold on to his seat in Congress. In 1996, Gingrich faced a spirited campaign from Michael J. Coles, a self-made millionaire and cofounder of the Great American Cookie Company. Coles focused his critique of his opponent on his role in the government shutdown and his efforts to cut popular education programs. Worried about a possible backlash, Gingrich spent more time at home in his district than in most of his previous campaigns.[19] Coles, however, faced an uphill battle. The district was one of the most Republican in the country and, while Gingrich's national poll figures were low, he remained popular with his constituents. "We realize that sometimes he sticks his foot in his mouth and he has problems at the national level," said the Cobb County GOP chairman. "But they don't elect him; we do."[20] Gingrich labeled Coles a big-spending liberal and warned of the dire consequences if the Democrats took control of the House, hammering away at the prospect of "Speaker Dick Gephardt." "The people he would put in power are liberals," he said.[21]

Dole, a World War II veteran and certified member of the "greatest generation," tried turning his campaign into a referendum on the "baby boom generation." In his acceptance speech in San Diego, Dole offered an elegant evocation of a simpler time, of America before the 1960s. "I remember," he told an enthralled crowd, a time when things in America were better, a time of "tranquility, faith, and confidence in action." He accused the president's generation of being "an elite who never grew up, never did anything real, never sacrificed, never suffered, and never learned." On the same night, Bill Clinton was in fashionable Jackson Hole, Wyoming, celebrating his fiftieth birthday party by singing Beatles songs.[22]

He may have been a moderate behind closed doors, but on the campaign trail Gingrich was a fire-breathing conservative who threw political "red meat" to his audiences. In July, he called President Clinton "a charming character of almost zero credibility" who was running "a scandal-ridden" administration.[23] His unpopularity with the public made him even more attractive to conservative audiences since they viewed it as proof that he was willing to take controversial positions and support the conservative agenda regardless of the political consequences. The reality was far more complicated, but Gingrich relished the role and played it to perfection before packed houses. "In almost every case where Newt appeared," the *New York Times* reported, "the event was sold out or had to be moved to a larger venue. People want to come to see him."[24] Despite the prospect of a close election at home, Gingrich traveled to nearly 150 House districts, and raised more than $7.9 million for House GOP incumbents. One party official estimated that Gingrich raised more than $100 million, if the solicitations that used his name, image, or voice were added to the total. A popular item: for a $250 donation, a supporter could get an "official replica" of the gavel Gingrich used as House Speaker.

The Republicans received an expected lift from the convention, but Dole still lagged far behind the president in national polls as the Democrats gathered for their coronation. Clinton's presidential train, the "21st Century Express," snaked its way through the battleground states of Ohio and Michigan on its way to Chicago. While Clinton talked about the future, his mind was probably still focused on the past. Democrats were returning to the Windy City for the first time since the bloody riots of 1968. A young Bill Clinton had watched the Democrats' debacle while sitting in a hotel room in Shreveport, Louisiana. He remembered the convention as one of a series of events that year "that broke open the nation and shattered the Democratic party."[25] For Clinton, the campaign was about more than winning an election. By crushing Gingrich, scaling back the Republican Revolution, and returning to his New Democrat roots, he hoped to complete the unfulfilled mission of Robert F. Kennedy. He had devoted his public life to repairing the party's tattered political fabric. Now he was leading the party back to Chicago, to the place where it all came apart, to show that a new party could emerge from the ashes of the old. He was returning as an incumbent president holding a double-digit lead over his opponent in the polls. Unlike the last time they gathered in Chicago, the Democrats focused their attacks on their Republican opponents and not on each other. In 1968, students chanted "the whole world is watching," said Dan Rose, an old antiwar activist. In 1996, "the whole world will be yawning."[26] Vice President Al Gore set the tone for the convention, declaring that there is "a profound difference in outlook" between Dole and Clinton. "In his speech from San Diego, Senator Dole offered himself as a bridge to the past. Tonight Bill Clinton and I offer ourselves as a bridge to the future."

Gingrich, once the toast of the town, found himself relegated to a minor role at the Republican Convention in San Diego, but he was the star of the Democratic gathering in Chicago. Dole allocated the Republican Speaker of the House only five minutes. Gingrich used his time to talk about two local Georgia-based charities, and to praise Martin Luther King Jr. He never mentioned the word Congress. In Chicago, however, Democrats invoked his name nearly as often as Dole. Senator Edward Kennedy called the Republican ticket the "trio of reaction—Dole, Kemp and Gingrich." The Speaker was the mastermind of the Republican Revolution, "but Bob Dole swallowed it hook, line and sinker," Kennedy told delegates. "He is an extraordinary figure in the opposition camp—at once worst enemy and best friend," observed the

Washington Post. "The Democrats say the country can get along without him. The question is whether they can."[27]

"It's the economy, stupid," had been the mantra of the Clinton campaign in 1992, and many of his advisors planned to revive it for 1996. Two new pollsters recruited by Dick Morris, who was forced out by a sex scandal during the Democratic convention, offered the president a different message. Mark Penn and Doug Schoen argued that anxiety over values, not the economy, was motivating voters, especially middle-class suburban parents. Clinton, dogged by character issues his entire public life, relished the opportunity to be a spokesman for traditional family values. He supported a host of bite-sized initiatives, from banning assault rifles to supporting school uniforms and V chips, which allowed parents to control the shows their children watched on television. His speeches were littered with value-laden rhetoric, highlighting how Republicans "violated," "ignored," and "trampled" on American values, and how he "cherished" them.

While Clinton was soaring, Dole continued to fumble, his disorganized campaign unable to articulate a consistent theme. Although Dole was trying to distance himself from Gingrich, the Speaker did not hesitate to offer unsolicited campaign advice. Nearly all the advice he gave Dole centered on exposing the president's "lies." He proposed an "expose the Clinton falsehoods" campaign modeled after the television show *America's Funniest Home Videos.* Contestants would submit videos that highlighted campaign lies, with Dole choosing a national winner in October. "If people understand how routinely dishonest the Clinton campaign (and Clinton) are then their last wave of lies will have dramatically less effect," he wrote.[28] In October, he suggested that Dole adopt a Harry Truman "Give 'em hell" campaign. "We should NOT go negative. We should NOT raise the 'character issue' We should NOT 'slash and burn' We should NOT attack." Instead, he said the campaign should be focused on highlighting how Clinton "deliberately lies and misleads" about anything "that suits his purposes." It wasn't clear how Dole was supposed to call Clinton a liar without raising the character issue or avoid being negative.[29]

With polls in the final weeks showing Clinton with a sizeable lead, many pundits predicted that the Democrats would take back control of the House and were openly speculating about the possibility of a Gephardt speakership. Those scenarios changed dramatically in the final weeks of the campaign, after the *Los Angeles Times* reported that the Democratic National Committee (DNC) had returned an illegal $250,000 contribution by a South Korean company. The controversy centered on donations raised by the DNC's John Huang, a former official with an Indonesian financial conglomerate. Huang raised millions for the party from foreign sources, suggesting that American foreign policy was for rent to the highest bidder.

Over the next few weeks, voters learned that the president appeared to be auctioning the White House off to the highest bidder. Clinton, believing he needed to raise large sums of money to rehabilitate his image after the 1994 elections, provided donors with unprecedented access, including numerous "coffees," lunches, dinners, and sleepovers in the White House. Investigators discovered that a shadowy network of Asian fundraisers and donors had access to the White House. Huang visited the White House more than sixty-five times. Insiders called the White House "Motel 1600." A DNC brochure even included a price list: a $25,000 contribution would get an event with Al Gore. A meeting with the president cost twice that amount. For $100,000 a donor could attend a private dinner with the president at the Hay Adams Hotel.

The stream of reports that Clinton was selling access to the White House distracted attention from the Democrats' message and slowed their progress at the polls. The Dole campaign, unable to get traction on any other issue, latched on to the potential scandal, accusing Democrats of laundering money from overseas sources. "They've got their own laundromat, pumping out money," Dole said. "Now they are out raising money at Buddhist temples where they take a vow of poverty," he said.[30]

Gingrich, who was convinced Clinton was one scandal away from being forced from office, thought this may be the one. "What we're seeing here is the opening phase of what will turn into being the largest scandal in American history," he said with typical hyperbole, "because it involves foreigners being directly involved in the American political system, the American government, the American criminal justice system."[31] Of all the Republican investigations into Clinton's "scandals," the investigation of campaign finance abuse in the 1996 campaign was personal for him. He stoked the fires of Whitewater and Travelgate for political advantage, but on campaign finance he took a direct, almost daily interest. He believed that the money paid for the ads that Clinton used to destroy his reputation. When Clinton first started airing ads in 1995, Gingrich was not concerned, because he did not think the Democrats had enough money to sustain the effort long enough to change public attitudes. "Our assumption in 1995 was that they could never sustain their advertising campaign because they couldn't pay for it. We underestimated the amount of foreign money they received," he recalled with some bitterness nearly a decade later.[32]

The charges seemed to have little impact on the presidential race, however. In the final days, Clinton had a choice: he could campaign in the big states of New York, California, and Pennsylvania in the hope of running up his popular vote margin; or he could concentrate on a handful of states with close House and Senate races. He decided to try and influence some key races, hoping that if he could turn the tide in a few close races, Democrats could gain control and keep the congressional investigating committees out of GOP hands.

On election night, the public sent a mixed message. As expected, Clinton defeated Dole, 49 to 41 percent—independent Ross Perot garnered just 8 percent—and piled up 379 electoral votes to Dole's 159. Clinton became the first Democrat since Franklin Roosevelt to win a second term. But, as the *Washington Post*'s John Harris noted, "It is a reminder of the precarious state of Clinton's fortunes for most of his term that the man regarded as the most skilled Democratic politician of his generation never commanded more than a plurality in a national election."[33] As expected, Gingrich won his race by a comfortable 57 to 43 percent margin. Overall, Republicans lost ground in the House, but retained a slim majority, and boosted their Senate margin. Republicans suffered a net loss of nine seats, leaving them with a 225–207 balance in the House. In the total popular vote for the House, Republicans managed a narrow 48.9 to 48.5 percent plurality, a sharp decline from their 52 to 45 percent margin in 1994.[34]

Although they retained control of both Houses, many Republicans expected to win seats and blamed Gingrich for dragging down many promising Republican candidates. At the same time, many Democrats felt the campaign finance scandal slowed Democratic momentum and prevented them from winning back the House and possibly the Senate. "That really hurt the party, but House Democrats felt they paid the political price, not Clinton," said Begala.[35]

Both men felt the election results justified their strategies. Gingrich took pride that, for the first time since 1928, the GOP managed to hold Congress for two successive elections. Clinton also saw the election as a vindication of his presidency and his return to his "New Democrat" message. "After the 1994 elections, I had been ridiculed as an irrelevant figure, destined for defeat in 1996. In the early stages of the budget fight, with the government shutdown looming, it had been far from clear that I would prevail or that the American people would support my stance against the Republicans."[36] The president was confident that he had found a new middle ground in American politics. On election night he announced: "Tonight we proclaim that the vital American center is alive and well. It is the common ground on which we have made our progress."

The election outcome underscored how the two men had influenced and shaped each other in ways that neither fully appreciated. Clinton campaigned against a cartoon version of Gingrich even as he adopted much of his agenda. Gingrich, who came to office promising a revolution, retained control of the Congress by practicing moderation. They found themselves closer to each other, and further from the ideological fringe of their respective parties, than ever before. How would he work with President Clinton? reporters asked Gingrich after the election. "Carefully," he said. Do you trust him? they asked. "No," he responded, but added, "we don't have to like each other," pointing out examples in American history when powerful elected officials— he used the example of Jefferson and Hamilton—put their personal feelings aside and worked together for the good of the nation. "We should transcend our personal feelings," he said, although he could not restrain from pointing out that Clinton won re-election because he "consciously sold out liberalism and became a conservative."[37]

In 1996, Trent Lott took the lead in helping the White House break the legislative logjam. After the election, however, Clinton wanted to move more aggressively to develop new legislation and tackle bigger problems. He and his advisors knew that he needed Gingrich as his partner. The White House needed someone who could both count votes and change minds. After 1996, observed Erskine Bowles, "all roads ran through the Speaker."[38]

| "We Can Trust Him"

O N JANUARY 20, 1997, a triumphant Bill Clinton took the oath of
office for a second time. He placed his hand on the same family Bible
as he did four years earlier. To underscore what he hoped would be the theme
of his second term, he had the Bible open to Isaiah 58:12, which said: "And
they that shall be of thee shall build the old waste places: thou shalt raise
up the foundations of many generations; and thou shalt be called, The
repairer of the breach, The restorer of paths to dwell in." "His fondest
goal," recalled political consultant Paul Begala, "was to heal the country, to
unite the country, and he chose that passage from the Bible to represent his
aspiration."[1]

Standing under sunny skies, the president delivered a hopeful address
about the possibilities of bipartisan cooperation. "The American people returned to office a president of one party and a Congress of another," said
Clinton. "Surely, they did not do this to advance the politics of petty bick-
ering and extreme partisanship they plainly deplore. No, they call on us
instead to be repairers of the breach and to move on with America's mission.
America demands and deserves big things from us, and nothing big ever came
from being small."[2] What was not in the speech revealed something about the
breach that existed between Clinton and his own party. The original version
included the line: "The voters elected a president of one party and a Congress
of another party with eyes wide open." A few hours before he delivered the
speech, his congressional liaison removed the phrase "with eyes wide open,"
fearing it would antagonize House Democrats.[3]

During the inaugural ceremonies, Clinton made a number of overtures to
Gingrich. During the brief limousine ride to the ceremony, underscoring his

theme of healing, Clinton told Gingrich, "There's a moment [in life] to breach the differences." Later, during a luncheon in Statuary Hall after the swearing-in, while dining on a meal of shrimp, oyster, and scallop pie and beef a la mode, the president went out of his way to offer a toast to Gingrich. The embattled Speaker reciprocated the feeling of bipartisanship. While presenting the president and vice president with flags that had flown over the Capitol earlier in the day, he remarked: "We want each of you to, on occasion, look and remember that while we may disagree about some things, here you're among friends. And as Americans, we cherish and wish you Godspeed in your administration."

The next day, January 22, 1997, Gingrich sat alone in his office watching maintenance workers disassemble the inaugural platform while his peers debated a reprimand and fine, having found him guilty of using tax-exempt money for political purposes. The special counsel issued a scathing, meticulously detailed account of how Gingrich repeatedly violated federal tax law by laundering political contributions through tax-exempt foundations. The charges revolved around a college class and, later, a series of televised town hall meetings that Gingrich developed to spread his message. The special counsel concluded that in both cases, "there was an effort to have the material appear to be non-partisan on its face, yet serve as a partisan, political message for the purpose of building the Republican Party." When the $500,000 price tag for the class, "Renewing American Civilization," stretched GOPAC's budget, Gingrich decided to continue the program as a charity. The charity he selected was the Abraham Lincoln Opportunity Foundation. Although originally created to serve inner-city youth in Colorado, the organization moved to Washington and took up space in GOPAC's offices and was run by GOPAC chairman Howard Callaway. When questioned about the cozy relationship between his political organization and the nonpartisan charity, Gingrich denied any connection existed. The Ethics Committee, however, unearthed hundreds of documents proving that GOPAC was actively involved in developing and funding the classes, and criticized the Speaker for submitting information that he "knew or should have known was inaccurate, incomplete, and unreliable."[4]

Confronted with overwhelming evidence, Gingrich had reluctantly reversed course and admitted that he had brought discredit on the House by submitting incorrect information to the Ethics Committee. Even his supporters on the committee were convinced that Gingrich was guilty of skirting the law and misleading the committee. "Newt put up a reasonable defense" before the Ethics Committee, a sympathetic GOP member said. "But to buy it completely, you have to buy the difficult notion that he's not smart or engaged."[5] The House voted overwhelmingly, 395 to 28, to reprimand Gingrich and order payment of a $300,000 fine. "This is a sad day for the House," said one member after another during the 90-minute debate. The *Atlanta Journal-Constitution* concluded that Gingrich's actions were "motivated by his thirst for power and by his own delusions of grandeur."[6]

The ethics charges against Gingrich led to a minor revolt in the party and called into question whether Gingrich could win re-election as Speaker. After a frantic lobbying campaign, Gingrich convinced all but nine House Republicans that his ethical violations should not deprive him of another term. It turned out to be a useful exercise, because while surveying members, he discovered that many had lost faith in his ability to lead the party. "The members don't like you and don't support you. They will turn on you. It is not ethics but you personally," a staff member reported to him.[7] An apologetic Speaker expressed gratitude after being sworn in. "For those who agonized and ended up voting for me, I thank you," Gingrich said in an uncharacteristically brief speech. "Some of this difficulty, frankly, I brought on myself. . . . To the degree I was too brash, too self-confident or too pushy I apologize. To whatever degree and in any way that I brought controversy or inappropriate attention to the House, I apologize."[8]

The revolt against Gingrich diminished some of the Speaker's power at the same time that it enhanced the position of party moderates who were determined to take control back from the hard-driving conservatives. By disbanding the Speaker's advisory group, Republicans allowed committee chairs to assume many of their old powers. After the election, Gingrich polled members of the conference, asking them for advice on strategy for the new session. Moderates advised Gingrich to move away from his hard-line public stance against the president and focus on achieving tangible results. Most members stressed that he should avoid partisanship, improve communications within the conference, and keep himself out of the media. Gingrich's notes of his conversations reveal the tone of the comments:

Fred Upton: "We must reach out to the moderate Democrats."

Doc Hastings: "Smile a lot, don't take on the national media to their face, work at communicating better. . . . If we emphasize that if Clinton governs as he campaigned we can work together. However we should investigate him when it is appropriate but in a low key solid manner."

Jim Sensenbrenner: "Be careful about going after Clinton and let it be done calmly and methodically."

Joel Hefley: "We probably were too hard and had too harsh an edge in retrospect. . . ."

Jim McCrery: "Keep up the new softer, smarter less confrontational approach with Clinton."

Dennis Hastert: "Be cautious and bipartisan."

Mike Castle: "We need more moderates in the room for leadership meetings. The current leadership is simply too conservative. . . ."

Jim Longley: "We need to be sensitive about how Sunbelt conservatism comes across in the northeast."[9]

Clinton kept his distance from the debate over Gingrich. "I could have urged the Justice Department or the U.S. attorney to investigate the charges of tax evasion and false statements to Congress," he wrote. Instead, he tried to stay above the fray, perhaps hoping that Gingrich would do the same and back off on his investigations. The House should handle it, he told reporters, "and then we should get back to the people's business."[10] But more important, he needed Gingrich. "If he loses power, the crazies will take over," he told aides. "Gingrich is actually a moderating force these days."

Clinton, too, started 1997 under a cloud of scandal. In addition to dealing with the ongoing Whitewater investigation, Clinton confronted new charges that he sold access to the White House to unsavory characters in order to pay for his re-election campaign. Gingrich reacted angrily when reporters compared the charges against Clinton for campaign finance irregularities with his problems with the House Ethics Committee. At one point, Gingrich instructed his staff to write letters to the editors of major newspapers to "point out the desperation of the elite media in seeking moral equivalency." He claimed that if a Republican cashes a check "and a Democrat robs a bank the story begins 'the two parties withdrew money from a bank today.'"[11]

Gingrich's complaint revealed another similarity between the two men: both were capable of bouts of self-pity, convinced they were victims of a "biased" media. A White House aide told *Newsweek* that Clinton believed there was a "tacit conspiracy between the press and the Washington in crowd, which has always believed that Clinton is a rube, and that it is their duty to bring him down." In private, the president would often explode in anger when the press failed to respond warmly to a new initiative or seemed to be preoccupied with scandal. "They're screwing me," he would shout.[12] Gingrich suggested that "elite media," which at various times seemed to include everyone except Rush Limbaugh, opposed him because they were part of the liberal establishment he set out to destroy. Clinton could not understand why the media seemed so focused on his private life but failed to expose the hypocrisies of his leading critics. At the same time, Gingrich complained that the media were protecting Clinton, refusing to debunk the "lies" he told during the government shutdown or expose his campaign finance scandals. He complained that the news media were engaged in a "passive conspiracy" to aid Clinton's efforts to "misuse the office of the presidency to mislead instead of lead."[13]

By the winter of 1997, both men had moved toward the center of American politics. Gingrich believed that the Republican takeover of Congress had pushed the political debate to the right. While he would not win on every issue, he had set the parameters of discussion. With the exception of a handful of liberal Democrats, few elected officials in Washington raged at the wisdom of the Republican emphasis on smaller government, tax cuts, and deficit reduction. The debate was more over means than ends. Clinton, who understood the public mood better than congressional Democrats, was comfortable negotiating within those restraints, realizing that he could use his influence to push for specific programs that were important to him. "By '97 you have two adversaries who are very good at sizing each other up who have to make deals if the system is going to work," Gingrich later reflected. In a clear break with the past, Gingrich stressed the need to work together with Democrats to find "common ground." "If the last Congress was the 'Confrontation Congress,' this Congress will be the 'Implementation Congress,'" he told fellow House members.

Both men had been chastened by political realities. Clinton had overreached in his first two years, trying to push through an ambitious agenda on a slim majority. Rocked by the Republican takeover of Congress, he focused on passing small, symbolic initiatives that would re-establish his credibility with the public and allow him to regain his political footing. He now felt confident enough to launch another round of reforms. This time, however, instead of relying solely on congressional Democrats, he would build a bipartisan coalition among moderates in both parties. Gingrich spearheaded the Republican takeover of Congress, but quickly discovered the difference between mobilizing opposition and leading the majority. Not only was Clinton a far more wily opponent than he had imagined, but he also discovered that the American public embraced the rhetoric of change but often recoiled from its consequences.

Privately, both men worried about how history would view them. "It was legacy time," reflected Joe Gaylord.[14] Clinton knew that he had a limited amount of time to establish a substantial legislative record—a standard litmus test in evaluating presidential greatness. In August 1996, Clinton had agreed with Dick Morris's assessment that he was a "borderline third tier" president. He often said that he wanted to emulate Thomas Jefferson and

Theodore Roosevelt, two predecessors who ushered in new centuries by re-defining the role of government. His challenge was to find a "synthesis" between liberal notions of "big government" and conservative belief in "no government." Gingrich realized that without some major achievements he would be remembered as little more than a conservative rebel. But Gingrich was a revolutionary who wanted to be remembered as a statesman, a populist who desperately needed the respect of the establishment. *Time* magazine once called him an "establishment guerrilla," who rose to power by "attacking the institutions he badly wants to lead."[15]

The balance of power between the president and the Speaker had clearly shifted in Clinton's favor. "By 1997 Clinton felt that he had the upper hand," reflected speechwriter Michael Waldman. "He felt that he had won the public debate."[16] The election results forced Gingrich to deal with Clinton with fewer votes and less power. "Gingrich's victory can be the Republican Party's undoing," White House pollster Mark Penn wrote the president after the election. "On the one hand, the need for Gingrich to rehabilitate his image may drive him to agree to a balanced budget and other legislation, giving us a more workable Congress. On the other hand [voter] dislike of Gingrich provides the 1998 target."[17]

The president decided to move aggressively to take advantage of the moment. "Because he felt he had the upper hand he believed there was an opportunity to work with Republicans to reframe the debate about govern-ment in progressive terms," recalled Waldman.[18] Clinton gathered his eco-nomic team after the election and told them his top priority was passing a balanced budget bill. "After he won reelection in 1996, I'm sure some De-mocrats were hoping he would de-emphasize his commitment to balancing the budget," recalled economic advisor Gene Sperling. "But a balanced bud-get agreement was central to his effort to gain the public's trust that Demo-crats could seek big progressive goals and still be the party of fiscal respon-sibility." He believed that he had risked his presidency in 1993 on trying to balance the budget in a "responsible" way with his first budget, but never got credit for his effort. Now that he had the upper hand he could have walked away from the tough choices involved. Instead, recalled congressional liaison John Hilley, "he was anxious to finish the job." The debate with Gingrich was not over whether to balance the budget, but on what timetable. "It wasn't Republican pressure that was forcing his hand," said Sperling.[19]

Clinton reshuffled the White House staff to make a budget deal more likely. By 1997 many of the liberals were gone, replaced by moderate "New Democrats." In the most significant move, Clinton replaced Chief-of-Staff Leon Panetta with Erskine Bowles, a genteel, soft-spoken, North Carolina investment banker with close ties to southern Republicans. Bowles, according to Sidney Blumenthal, "was a negotiator, a manager, and a New South Democrat."[20]

Bowles met Clinton for the first time in 1992 when he agreed to help raise money for the governor's presidential campaign. He vividly recalled one of their first encounters, sitting in the back seat of a car following an event. That morning, Bowles's oldest son, who was diabetic, had suffered a wrenching seizure. Clinton seemed to sense his mood and asked what was bothering him. Bowles told Clinton about his son, and angrily denounced President Bush's decision to ban fetal tissue research, which offered a possible cure. Clinton listened passively. "He never said a word to me," Bowles recalled. "But then, about a month and a half later, somebody from the Juvenile Diabetes Foundation called me and said Clinton had mentioned Sam in a speech on health care and vowed that if elected, he'd end the ban on fetal tissue research."[21] Later, as president, when he lifted the ban by executive order, Clinton gave Bowles the pen he used to sign it. Bowles was deeply touched by the gesture, which solidified a growing friendship. Bowles offered to leave his lucrative business practice and come to Washington to work for the administration. Clinton appointed him to serve as head of the Small Business Administration and then deputy White House chief of staff. He left the White House to return to the private sector in 1995.

After the 1996 election, Clinton asked him to return as chief of staff for one year to help him get a balanced budget deal. In keeping with the spirit of businessmen who served in government during World War II, Bowles accepted an annual salary of $1. Clinton realized that he needed someone who could work with conservatives, who lacked both a history in Washington and existing political commitments. Panetta, although theoretically a budget hawk, had close ties to people on Capitol Hill and fought to keep his pet programs. Clinton needed someone whom he trusted, but also someone who could quickly establish relationships with Trent Lott and Gingrich.

Although he supported a balanced budget, Gingrich was uncertain whether Clinton was serious, and even if he was, whether he could trust him to negotiate in good faith. He interpreted Bowles's appointment as a clear signal that the president was serious about working together. Gingrich recalled that in his first meeting with the new chief of staff, Bowles said, "Look, I came back [to Washington] to get a balanced budget, and as soon as I get it I've done my job. I wouldn't be here if this wasn't real."[22] Bowles assured him that he had the authority to speak for the president in their discussions, and that when he made a commitment, he would keep it. Gingrich was convinced. "We can trust him," he told his colleagues.[23]

Bowles became the liaison between Clinton and Gingrich, shuttling back and forth brokering deals between Capitol Hill and the White House. Neither man trusted the other, but both trusted Bowles, and he became the key figure in their evolving relationship. "You cannot underestimate the role that Erskine played," recalled Joe Gaylord. "He and Gingrich liked each other. They trusted each other."[24] Bill Archer, the powerful head of the House Ways and Means Committee, also felt comfortable with Bowles. "He was not ideological. He was not pushing a big left agenda. He was there to make things happen between the White House and a Republican Congress."[25] Later, Gingrich would call his appointment "decisive," and a turning point in his relationship with the White House. "It is the one brief period when you have a significant adult whose experience transcends Washington, who understands making deals and getting business done, and who has a center-right bias in fiscal policy," he said. "He had the ability to bridge the White House and my party in Congress."[26]

Before he could begin tackling the budget, Bowles needed to establish priorities and bring order to an often chaotic policy process. "Clinton's problem was that he had a thousand visions, which was like having none at all," he recalled. In one of his first acts as chief of staff, Bowles ordered a

Chief-of-Staff Erskine Bowles talks with the president and vice president. Although neither man trusted the other, both Clinton and Gingrich had complete faith in Bowles, who served as the liaison between them. (William J. Clinton Presidential Library.)

complete review of how the president used his time. "It is our most valuable resource," he said. Based on the results, he focused the president on a handful of high-priority items and delegated the rest to the senior staff. "Erskine's greatest strength was in bringing some control and some regularity and some linear thinking to the policy process," recalled Waldman.

In order to navigate the rocky relationship between the two principal players, Bowles had to understand both men. He learned quickly that there was no love lost between them: each was convinced the other was out to destroy him. But he was struck as much by their similarities as he was by their differences. "They suffered from many of the same strengths and weaknesses," he recalled. Both were visionaries who were intellectually curious. "They had a sense of history and could examine problems from many different perspectives." Unlike most politicians in Washington who understood issues only from the talking points handed them by aides, "they were the most well-informed, thoughtful, and insightful people in a meeting." It was clear to him that the investigations had taken a toll on both men, and on their views of each other. "They both had political toughness," he observed. "You could challenge their policies, but they got personally hurt very easily when you challenged their character." They responded to attacks in different ways. "When someone would strike out at Clinton it would hurt him. He would try to bring him back in and win him over. Gingrich, on the other hand, would just as easily be hurt, but his reaction was to bury them."[27]

While Republicans warmly greeted news of Bowles's appointment, Democrats saw it as an indication that Clinton was going to abandon the Democratic leadership and start making deals with the Republicans. "Erskine did not come from our world," reflected Steve Elmendorf, chief political advisor to Richard Gephardt. "He was a business guy who wanted to get things done."[28] In private conversations with Bowles and congressional liaison John Hilley, Democratic leaders complained that by trying to make deals with Gingrich, the White House was helping congressional Republicans and preventing Democrats from regaining control of the House. "You guys are screwing us," they were told.

House Democrats could barely constrain their anger with the White House. Many blamed Clinton for their minority status. They charged that his early failures allowed Gingrich to take control of the House in 1994. Instead of working with them to defeat Gingrich, the president "triangulated" and used them as foils to save his presidency. They were on the way to retaking the House in 1996 until the campaign finance scandals provided Republicans with some last-minute political traction. "That really hurt the party, but House Democrats felt they paid the political price, not Clinton," said Begala.

"On top of that, Clinton has Erskine cutting deals with the guy who is trying to kill them."[29] House leaders grilled Bowles and Hilley in private meetings. "I had more contentious meetings with House Democrats than with Republicans," Bowles reflected.[30] One Democrat who participated in the meetings said that members "addressed Bowles like you would talk to a dog."[31]

Gephardt, who had to deal the most with Gingrich, was incredulous that Clinton could still delude himself into thinking he could trust the Speaker. "He is going to try and kill you," he warned, pointing out how as Speaker he had empowered House committees to investigate every aspect of the White House, including a two-year investigation of the president's Christmas card list. "From Gephardt's perspective, Newt was undermining everything that he got into public life for: social security, medicare, caring for the poor, a decent society," reflected Begala. "And my party's president, my leader, is sitting down and cutting deals that disadvantage me and my party."[32]

For liberals, the only remaining ally in the White House was Hillary Clinton. While she was an influential voice in the first few years, she was largely excluded from policy discussions after the health care fiasco. She was much less generous toward Gingrich than her husband, viewing him as part of the right-wing conspiracy that was out to destroy his administration. But she was largely absent from the inner circle after 1994, directing her attention outward, traveling around the world, condemning policies that discriminated against women. Her most high-profile domestic initiative after the health care debacle was a book about the White House pets called *Dear Socks, Dear Buddy*. Bowles gracefully made clear to the president that he would prefer she keep a low profile during the second term.

Clinton, who liked to keep all his political options open, wanted to reach across the aisle and work with Gingrich without precipitating a full-scale rebellion within his own party. He was engaged in a delicate juggling routine, keeping the Republican ball in play without dropping the Democratic ball. In order to keep Gephardt and the House leadership in the game, he sent senior staff members to Capitol Hill every Friday for private meetings where they could reassure anxious Democrats of his good intentions while giving them the opportunity to vent their frustrations. "We felt it was really important to go to them," reflected Begala, who was part of the White House team. "The feelings among House Democrats toward Newt were extraordinarily raw and bitter," he recalled. "Newt didn't only take power away from them after 40 years of dominance, he was hard edged and brutally dominating. He was no Nelson Mandela."[33]

Bowles was convinced that the two sides could have come to an agreement in 1995, but that neither really wanted to find common ground. The president's advisors were too wedded to preserving existing Democratic programs and too closely tied to the House leadership. Gingrich was too much a captive to his own rhetoric and the ideological leanings of his freshmen troops. Bowles was determined to avoid the mistakes that led to the shutdown in 1995. His first move was to limit the number of people involved in the discussions. "You put them in a room together and they could both talk forever," he said of Clinton and Gingrich. They would accomplish more with fewer people because "there was no one to show off to."[34] That also meant excluding the House Democratic and Republican leadership. There would be no chaperones this time around. Bowles was looking to make a deal, not score points. The decision only added to the anger and the anxiety on Capitol Hill. House liberals feared that Clinton would make short-term compromises on the budget that would boost his standing, but in the long run, undermine the party. "I did not want Clinton to commit us to budget reductions that we would not be able to deliver on over the long haul," said David Obey.[35]

Next, Bowles removed Clinton and Gingrich from the details of the negotiations, but turned to them when the negotiators reached an impasse. "When we got stuck, we appealed to Mount Olympus," recalled Gene Sperling, who was part of the White House negotiating team. "This isn't '95," Clinton reminded the team. "They are trying to work with us now. Fight as hard as you can for everything we want—but don't overplay your hand."

Gingrich sent similar signals to his team. "The reason it happens is that the guys at the top wanted it to happen," said Sperling. "The atmosphere in the room was completely different from 1995," reflected Ken Keys, a Republican staff member involved in the negotiations. "In 1995 people were talking but not negotiating. In 1997 the focus was clearly on getting a deal."

Clinton was not the only one taking a big political chance by reaching across the aisle. Gingrich was engaged in the riskiest juggling act of his career—trying to keep conservatives in line while negotiating with a president despised by many members of his party. Conservatives wanted to wage an all-out war to destroy the Clinton presidency, and they found it unconscionable that Gingrich, the architect of the Republican Revolution and the most fierce and effective congressional partisans of the past decade, was working with the president. The man who taught Republicans how to gain power by polarizing now was trying to teach them to exercise power by compromising. It was not an easy transition for Gingrich or for his party. Gingrich had learned his lessons about dealing with Clinton, but conservative members of his party had not.

There were also rumblings within the Republican caucus that Gingrich was still traumatized by the government shutdown and so desperate to repair his sagging public image that he was no longer willing to take unpopular positions. "After the government shutdown, Newt changed," said Congressman Lindsey Graham. "He decided he was going to be a deal-making politician." Joseph Scarborough, the Florida congressman later turned television pundit, complained to the *New York Times* that "our leadership remains shell shocked from the government shutdown a year and a half ago. Most of us are ready for them to start leading again rather than sitting back and reading from Clinton's song sheet."[36]

In June 1997, Republicans loaded a disaster relief bill with partisan riders, believing that Clinton would not dare veto it. The $8.6 billion emergency spending bill included $5.6 billion to flood-ravaged regions of thirty-five states in the Midwest and West. House Republicans decided to tack on two unrelated provisions. One would have prevented a government shutdown in the event of a future impasse on the budget; the other would prohibit the Commerce Department from using statistical sampling techniques to estimate inner-city populations in the 2000 census. Gingrich pleaded with conservatives not to hand the president a loaded gun. "You know how good Bill Clinton is at this stuff," he admonished them. "Why are you sticking your head up and letting him beat on you?"

The move was a public relations disaster for the Republicans. The president stuck to the high road, vetoing the measure and returning it to the Capitol in less than 30 minutes. "Despite the obvious and urgent need to speed critical relief to people in the Dakotas, Minnesota, California and 29 other states ravaged by flooding and other natural disasters," congressional Republicans added "unacceptable provisions," Clinton said in a letter to the House. After weeks of media criticism and poignant pleas from flood victims, House Republicans were forced to back down. The White House gloated that the Republicans had self-destructed, again. "They just seem to keep touching third rails," one administration official told the *Washington Post.* Said another: "Every once in a while the Hezbollah wing of their party gets a hold of the steering wheel and drives right off the cliff." This time, Gingrich had seen the train wreck coming, and not only did nothing to encourage it, but he also tried, but failed, to stop it.[37]

The incident exacerbated Gingrich's relationship with conservatives and led to an abortive coup attempt later that summer. Gingrich's chief antagonist was Tom DeLay of Texas. They had never been especially close. According to DeLay biographers Lou Dubose and Jan Reid, DeLay "thought Gingrich was as full of shit as a Christmas turkey."[38] He viewed Gingrich as "a thinktank pontificator and a flake."[39] The Texas congressman complained that Gingrich suffered from "the classic academic's dysfunction: He thought that ideas alone were enough." The Speaker, he wrote in his memoirs, "knew nothing about running meetings and nothing about driving an agenda."[40]

Their differences, however, went beyond tactics and reflected a growing rift within the party over how to deal with a popular president. Since Ronald Reagan's election in 1980, conservatives had been united behind a common goal of undermining support for the Democratic Party, electing more Republicans, gaining control of the Washington establishment, and passing key elements of their agenda. After their victory in 1994, many viewed Clinton as the last remnant of a dying Democratic order. His resilience, however, and his growing popularity exposed deep fissures on the Right. Gingrich had pursued power as a means of discrediting liberalism, creating an opening for new, mostly conservative ideas and different approaches to governing. DeLay saw power as an end in itself. He was less interested in winning the war of ideas than he was in distributing the spoils of victory. For him politics was not about practicing the art of the possible; it was about waging total war and settling for nothing less than unconditional surrender. For DeLay, victory was not possible as long as Clinton was in power. He was, like many conservatives, driven by a visceral hatred of Clinton. "It isn't just that he is a liberal," he reflected. "What sent me over the top about Clinton is that his brand of liberalism had an almost anti-American feel to it."[41] Gingrich, he charged, had gone soft on the president by making too many deals and by compromising on key components of the Republican platform.

Gingrich, who now viewed himself more as a reformer than a revolutionary, believed that conservatives had already won the key struggle in the battle of ideas, forcing Clinton to fight on their turf. If they pushed too hard and appeared too rigid and uncompromising, they risked losing all their hard-fought gains. Gingrich warned conservatives not to "pick artificial fights" with the president at a time when he was embracing much of their agenda. "If he wants to take our plays, hand them to him," he said. "Don't make it hard for him. If he wants to join our huddle, welcome him in."[42]

Behind the scenes, DeLay started organizing conservatives in an effort to undermine Gingrich's control of the party. He found that many members of the leadership were ready to make a move. In July, Armey, DeLay, and Bill Paxon met in Lindsay Graham's office to plot strategy. While many of the participants have offered conflicting accounts of their roles in the attempted coup, they all agreed to call for a vote of no confidence in the speaker. They divided, however, over who should replace him. At one point Armey, perhaps disappointed that he could not win the support of the caucus to fill the Speaker's chair, told Gingrich of the plot. Gingrich moved quickly, calling a meeting of the entire Republican conference to listen to their complaints and defuse a tense situation. "Oh, I hear we have a problem," he said with a tone of sarcasm. Just in case they had any doubt, he underscored that he planned to stay on as Speaker and that he was the one calling the shots. As Speaker, he said, "I am in essence the head coach of the House Republicans."[43]

The coup quickly evaporated, the plotters running for cover, pointing accusatory fingers at each other.[44] If the coup was designed to send a warning signal to the Speaker about moving toward the center and working with Clinton, it had the opposite impact. According to Steely, it "changed the way Newt dealt" with his troops, making him more willing to work with the president and to pursue accommodation over confrontation. Just as Clinton had come to distrust his left flank, Gingrich had learned that he could not count on the continued loyalty of his conservative base. "Newt," he observed, "was working to moderate his public statements and make them sound less angry and threatening."[45] The coup, however, was a warning shot, revealing Gingrich's fragile hold on the speakership.

In August 1997, after months of intensive negotiations, a combination of moderate Republicans and conservative Democrats passed a balanced budget bill. The legislation contained something for both sides. "In a year when the stock market landed on Mars and inflation became a fugitive, Washington embraced a new politics of abundance," observed *Time,* "that gives away something to just about everyone."[46] A growing economy allowed them to achieve the seemingly impossible: a balanced budget for the first time in 30 years, the largest tax cut in 16 years, while providing $24 billion in new health care programs for children. "We got 95 percent of the new investments I had recommended in the State of the Union, and the Republicans took two-thirds of the tax cut figure they had originally proposed," Clinton observed.[47] The budget bill also restored disability and health benefits to legal immigrants that had been left out of the welfare reform bill, included targeted benefits to help single mothers join the workforce, and dramatically boosted spending on education, including a tax cut for college tuition. According to Michael Waldman, the legislation represented "the biggest single federal investment in higher education since the GI bill after World War II."[48]

On August 5, 1997, with the band playing "Hail to the Chief," Gingrich and Clinton strolled proudly across the White House lawn to boast to reporters about the new spirit of cooperation in Washington. Clinton later described the mood as "euphoric." "I certainly hope we can tap this spirit of cooperation and use it to meet and master the many challenges that remain before us," Clinton said. Gingrich hit an optimistic note, saying the budget deal proves that "the American constitutional system works. Slowly, over time, we listened to the will of the American people. We reached beyond parties, we reached beyond institutions and we found ways to get things done." Vice President Gore even asked the Speaker's wife, Marianne, to stand and be applauded by the crowd. "With all the sweetness and light at the White House that day, it was hard to remember that we'd been at each other's throats for more than two years," Clinton reflected.[49]

In many ways, the balanced budget bill represented a historic legislative achievement, revealing how much Gingrich had altered the way Washington worked. For once he was not exaggerating when he gushed to reporters: "Four years ago we were raising taxes and moving toward government-run health care. Now we're balancing the budget and cutting taxes. It's fair to say if you were to look at our speeches in 1994 and what passed today and will pass tomorrow, you'd have to say the world is a lot closer to what we campaigned on than to what anybody else did."[50] But it also revealed how much Gingrich had overreached. In 1995, Republicans passed a budget that called for $245 billion in tax cuts, the elimination of four Cabinet-level agencies, and steep reductions in Medicare. This budget deal slowed the growth of government but also institutionalized many of the programs that had been earmarked for elimination, including a new $24 billion health program for uninsured children. "In 1993, Republicans and talk radio went tooth and nail with the administration on Hillary Clinton's health care package," blustered radio host Michael Reagan. "Now they're implementing it one piece at a time."[51] Gingrich defended the compromises as a necessary part of effective governing. "I made a very conscious decision that it was better for America and better for the Republican Party to prove that we could govern," he told the *Washington Post*. "We decided that four years of incremental achievement in our direction are superior to four years of obstruction while we scream about values."[52]

Both men had reason to celebrate the victory. "They saw it as a personal vindication of a policy stance they had been working on for a long time," recalled Hilley, who helped broker the deal. Clinton believed that his efforts to balance the budget in his first year had cost the Democrats control of the House and Senate in 1994 and almost destroyed his presidency. Gingrich also felt he paid a heavy political price for his efforts to balance the budget in 1995. Years later, Gingrich would claim that the balanced budget bill re-presented the final chapter of the budget shutdown. Some Republican leaders also convinced themselves that the shutdown forced Clinton's hand and eventually led to the balanced budget bill. But Clinton pursued the issue after he had won the debate and when he held the strongest hand. As the journalist Joe Klein observed, the president's doggedness in pushing the legislation contrasted with his "feckless public image." He was persistent, he noted, "in the service of his political beliefs, not his ambition," and his efforts produced "the most important substantive achievement of his presidency; a government that had dramatically improved the lives of millions of the poorest, hardest-working Americans."[53]

Internal polls showed that the public gave both men credit for the deal. Gingrich's polls, which showed his approval rating as low as 15 percent in the heat of the ethics investigation, rebounded to nearly 24 percent after the signing. Some polls showed that more than 60 percent of the public gave Congress a favorable rating. For the first few years, both men had based their political strategy on the assumption that their conflict was a zero-sum game. One side had to destroy the other in order to declare victory. Now they had proof that they could help themselves by working together. According to his pollster Linda DiVall, after the success of the balanced budget bill, Gingrich realized that if he and the president "worked together and put aside the partisanship, they would both benefit."[54] That realization would produce a major turn in their relationship. The *Atlanta Journal-Constitution* applauded the "new, improved Newt," claiming that "Newt the Right-wing Warrior has become Newt the Moderate."[55]

Trying to build on the momentum of the balanced budget bill, Clinton and Gingrich pushed Congress to pass fast-track legislation, which limited Congress to a yes-or-no vote on any trade deal presented by the president. It was a major miscalculation. According to Waldman, the debate over fast track threatened "an open break between the congressional Democrats and the White House." Clinton wanted to reassemble the same coalition he had forged on North American Free Trade Agreement (NAFTA). "This is a no-brainer on the merits," the president told his aides.[56] Politically, however, it was complicated for House Democrats. Organized labor, which was fiercely opposed to Clinton's trade policies, provided large sums of money to Democratic candidates, even as its ability to turn out voters had declined. Union political action committees (PACs) made up 48 percent of all PAC contributions to Democratic congressional candidates in 1996, up from 36 percent in 1994. At the same time, under the aggressive leadership of John J. Sweeney, the American Federation of Labor and Congress of Industrial Organizations (AFL-CIO) was dramatically increasing its spending on television advertising.[57]

Gephardt headed the opposition to the bill, showing members of Congress photographs of open sewers and ramshackle huts in Mexico, vivid reminders of poverty set against the backdrop of high-tech U.S. factories. He was so angry that he had the White House phones removed from the majority leader's office. Presidential politics also muddied the waters. Gephardt was considering a run for the presidency in 2000, realizing that Al Gore would be his leading primary opponent. "If Gore and Clinton are trying to capture the center, the place to go after Gore is to run to the left," observed Bruce Reed. "You had to convince the base that Gore is screwing you."[58] In the end, Gephardt won the debate. White House tallies showed that only 42 of 205 House Democrats supported the president. Gingrich promised to deliver 170 Republican votes, but the total fell short of the 218 needed for a majority, so Clinton reluctantly withdrew the legislation instead of risking an embarrassing defeat. "Dick Gephardt just ate Bill Clinton's lunch," observed the *Washington Times,* "and it's Al Gore who has indigestion."[59]

Despite the failure on fast track, Clinton felt that he had found a political formula that worked. It depended on Gingrich staying in power. "By late 1997, when Clinton talked about Gingrich," reflected Waldman, "it would be with a wry smile, not a scowl."[60] The "scowl" was reserved for his party's leader in the House. The feeling was reciprocal. In December, Gephardt gave a highly publicized speech at the John F. Kennedy School of Government, which was clearly directed at Clinton's new centrist politics. "We need a Democratic Party where principles trump tactics," Gephardt said. "We need a Democratic Party that is a movement for change, and a movement for values, and not a money machine." Echoing many critics of Clinton, Gephardt blasted "poll-driven" politicians who have failed to make major changes in policy. "Too often our leaders seem enamored with small ideas that nibble around the edges of big problems," he said. When he spoke those words, Gephardt had no idea that the president had already laid the foundation for a bold new initiative to tackle a "big problem."[61] The House minority leader, and the rest of the Democratic leadership, had been kept in the dark as Bill Clinton and Newt Gingrich plotted the next step in their efforts to transform partisan politics in America.

CHAPTER THIRTEEN | "You Ain't Seen Nothing Yet"

AFTER SUCCESSFULLY NEGOTIATING the balanced budget bill, Bowles believed he had completed the job for which the president had hired him. He informed Clinton that he planned to step down as chief of staff and return to his highly profitable, and more enjoyable, private-sector position. The president had different ideas. Over the next few months, the president aggressively courted Bowles, trying to convince him to stay on for at least another year. In December, the president and First Lady asked Bowles to join them on Air Force One for a Christmas trip to visit American troops stationed in Bosnia. On the return flight, they surrounded him and made a joint pitch for him to stay. They assured him that the congressional investigations into Whitewater were dying out and they had a unique window of opportunity to make history. "We are going to do great things," he promised.[1]

With the exception of the giddy first few days of his presidency, Clinton had never been more confident than he was in the fall and winter of 1997. "There was a real sense of excitement," recalled John Hilley.[2] For most of his presidency, Clinton had been on the defensive. He started out resisting pressure from congressional Democrats trying to impose their priorities on him. After 1994, he was fighting to preserve his presidency from the Republican onslaught. Now all that had changed. His personal popularity remained high. Most of all, he and the people around him finally felt they had figured out how to make it all work: how to maneuver legislation through a Republican Congress, how to use the media to shape public opinion, and how to make the most effective use of their greatest asset—the president's remarkable political skills. Under Bowles, the White House was functioning like a well-oiled machine. The staff was making better use of the president's time, not pulling him in a hundred different directions at the same time. "The second-term White House had settled into a rather placid middle age," Waldman noted. "Meetings were orderly, lines of authority were clear, decisions were made on time. The bracing liberal-centrist quarrels of earlier years were over."[3]

The president had reason to be optimistic. It appeared that the independent counsel might be on the verge of filing a final report finding no crimes or cause for impeachment hearings, and closing up shop. In February 1997, Starr had announced he would leave his post in the fall to become dean of the law school at Pepperdine University in California. Hounded by conservatives, Starr decided to stay, but his willingness to leave was a clear sign that he had turned up no incriminating evidence on the Clintons.

Prosperity allowed Clinton to once again plan big, new initiatives. By 1998, the combination of a healthy, growing economy, fiscal restraint, and the end of the Cold War had solved the budget crisis that had plagued Washington since the early Reagan years. Years of low inflation cut the government's cost of borrowing and held down spending on programs such as Social Security and Medicare. At the same time, the strong economy and stock market generated a rising tide of tax payments. In 1992, the annual deficit had soared to $290 billion, leading politicians of both parties to warn that the United States was destined to leave its children a mountain of debt. In 1997, the economy grew at a robust 8.2 percent, generating billions of dollars in additional tax revenue. The federal government was reporting a $70 billion surplus—the first in three decades—and projected a $4.4 trillion surplus over the next 15 years. *The New York Times* called erasing the deficit "the fiscal equivalent of the fall of the Berlin Wall."[4]

With budget surpluses, Clinton believed that he could once again make a strong case for progressive government. Prosperity provided the president with "another chance for a new beginning," observed Waldman. "After three years of treading lightly, seeking to rebuild confidence in government, he could propose a more ambitious program." His plan was to use the 1998 State of the Union "to persuade the public that government could do big things again."[5] Clinton viewed 1998 as a critical year, perhaps the most important since 1968 when conservatives hijacked political debate in America, labeled liberals as out of the mainstream, and captured the hearts and minds of the American middle class. By balancing the budget, Clinton once again demonstrated that a Democrat could be trusted with the public purse, purging the party of the ghosts of LBJ and Jimmy Carter. Since the days of Lyndon Johnson's "Great Society," Republicans had painted Democrats as the party of high taxes and wasteful spending. Clinton managed to maintain popular government social programs while also balancing the budget—a goal that had eluded all of his recent predecessors, including Ronald Reagan. "FDR saved capitalism from itself," he told his aides. "Our mission has been to save government from its own excesses. So it can be a progressive force."[6]

In addition, he had an historic opportunity to change the terms of debate between the two parties. By developing a language of politics that stressed rights and responsibility, he could articulate a vision of America that transcended the sum of its parts. Clinton believed that for the past three decades the Democrats had failed to articulate a broader, national message that appealed to basic American values. While they had become the party of the "special interests," Reagan taught the Republicans to appeal to higher ideals of patriotism and self-reliance. Under Gingrich, however, the Republicans had become the party of radical individualism. The Democrats needed to take advantage of that opportunity by capturing the high ground, redefining the party in the tradition of Woodrow Wilson, Franklin Roosevelt, and John F. Kennedy. As was often the case, when talking about his goal in politics, Clinton returned to the unfulfilled mission of Robert Kennedy. "We took what Bobby Kennedy was trying to do in Indiana in 1968, and we pulled it off," he said, referring to the senator's ability to develop a message that transcended race and class differences.[7]

Clinton believed that great presidents solved big problems: Lincoln won the Civil War; Teddy Roosevelt tamed the excesses of industrialism; FDR restored hope during the depression and defeated the Nazi threat. Clinton wanted to tackle one of the most difficult problems facing his generation: Social Security. "The president felt that we had solved the structural problems associated with the budget, but we had not faced up to the generational problems of Social Security, Medicare, and Medicaid," recalled Bowles.[8]

On August 14, 1935, surrounded by lights and motion-picture cameras, Roosevelt had signed the Social Security Act into law. The measure, he said, was "the cornerstone in a structure which is being built but is by no means complete—a structure intended to lessen the force of possible future depressions."[9] Over the next few decades it emerged as the government's largest, most enduring, and most popular entitlement program. "When future historians review the social legislation of the first two centuries of American history," observed the economist Henry Aaron, "they are likely to hail the Social Security Act as the most important piece of legislation in the entire period, with the possible exception of the Homestead Act." The centerpiece was a long-range old-age pension system to be financed by a payroll tax on employees and a payroll tax on employers.

The ink had barely dried on the original bill before critics began calling for changes. From the moment Roosevelt submitted his proposal to Congress, liberal critics had raised questions about the huge reserve fund needed to support old-age pensions, withdrawing money from the economy at a time when many people were struggling to survive. In 1937, the government began deducting 1 percent from the already depleted paychecks of workers, even though no one would receive benefits until 1942. Surpluses may have been financially necessary for the long-term future of the program, but they were politically unpopular. Roosevelt's enemies were quick to go on the offensive. Alfred Landon, the Republican nominee in 1936, described Social Security as "unjust, unworkable, stupidly drafted and wastefully financed."[10] In 1939, Roosevelt sought to shore up political support for his social insurance program by liberalizing benefits and moving up the schedule for paying benefits.

In 1949, Harry Truman tried to add a national health care provision, but ran into a wall of opposition from the American Medical Association. Following his massive landslide in 1964, Lyndon Johnson made the cause his own. On July 31, 1965, he traveled to Truman's birthplace of Independence, Missouri, to sign Medicare and Medicaid into law. Medicare expanded the Social Security's old-age pension program to cover certain medical expenses and was paid for through wage deductions and employee contributions to the Medicare trust fund. Medicaid, paid for from general tax revenue, provided health care for the needy and poor.

In the 1980s, faced with the prospect of an aging population and rising health care costs, Congress accepted the recommendations of a bipartisan commission to shore up Social Security well into the next century. A coalition of Democrats and Republicans supported the politically painful steps that included reducing the annual cost-of-living increases, raising the taxable income base, delaying the age for full benefits from 65 to 67, and boosting payroll taxes. President Reagan said the package "assures the elderly that America will always keep the promises made in troubled times a half-century ago." Despite these changes, a number of independent reports and analyses signaled the deepening crisis in the long-term health of Social Security and Medicare. In the 1990s, both the Social Security and Medicare trustees, along with projections from the Office of Management and Budget and the Congressional Budget Office, agreed that both systems were out of balance and required a major overhaul.

The main culprit was the aging of the baby boom, the massive cohort of 78 million Americans born between 1945 and 1964. By 2030, the number of Americans over 65 would double, draining the Social Security reserves. When the government issued the first Social Security check in 1940, there were twelve workers supporting every pensioner. By 1960, that ratio had dropped to five to one; by 2030 that ratio was projected to drop to three to one. By some estimates, by 2012, spending on Social Security and Medicare, along with interest on the national debt, would consume the entire federal budget. The Congressional Budget Office estimated that Congress would either need to cut benefits or approve a significant tax increase to keep the programs viable, and the cost of fixing the program increased every year. "If policy-makers delayed action . . . for five years, the cost of resolving those problems would increase by about 15 percent," the Budget Office warned. "If action was delayed for 20 years, the total costs would shoot up by about 60 percent."[11]

In 1994, the Health and Human Services secretary, Donna Shalala, appointed a thirteen-member advisory council on Social Security. The commission included three representatives from organized labor, three from business, and a handful of policy experts. By the time the panel issued its final report in 1997 it was deeply divided, split into three factions. One group advocated a private-sector approach, investing half of payroll taxes into personal savings accounts (PSAs), with the other half being controlled by the Social Security Trust Fund. These ambitious privatization plans were supported by conservatives, business groups, and think tanks funded by Wall Street. On the other side, a faction headed by labor and many liberal groups suggested only minor changes while maintaining the current benefit structure. They called for further study about whether to invest part of funds in a government-managed stock fund. A third group called for a 1.6 percent increase in the payroll tax, with the additional money going into individual retirement accounts and the government giving individuals limited choices for investment options.[12]

Despite their differences, there were also signs of an emerging consensus. All agreed that the program needed to be reformed. All accepted that some portion of Social Security revenue should be placed in investments other than low-paying U.S. Treasury bonds. They agreed that benefits must be trimmed, that the retirement age should be pushed back, and that state and local government workers should be required to participate. But they split sharply over whether to continue the pay-as-you-go system, in which current workers basically pay benefits to current retirees, or to move closer to a true pension system, in which workers are required to put aside money in advance for their own retirement. Despite their different approaches and formulas, all three recognized that some privatization would eventually be necessary. The debate was over how much, who would control the funds, and whether the money was to stay as part of the system or be invested in individual accounts.[13]

While there were dozens of reform plans circulating around Washington, ranging from minor tinkering to radical overhaul, there was a growing consensus around "middle ground" proposals that combined some structural changes in the retirement age with some form of private accounts. A growing number of influential Democrats, such as Senator John Breaux of Louisiana and Congressman Charles Stenholm of Texas, accepted the individual-account concept. Senator Daniel Patrick Moynihan added his powerful voice to the debate, endorsing a modest plan to allow 2 percent of annual wages to flow into private accounts. Moderate Republicans, such as Congressman Jim Kolbe from Arizona, were already working across the aisle trying to build some consensus. Even a few conservatives were willing to join the effort. North Carolina Congressman Mark Sanford, a member of the Class of 1994, supported a radical scheme that would shift two-thirds of the Social Security payroll tax into personal retirement accounts, but he was willing to go along with a more moderate approach. "Our system of government is built on marginal or incremental change," he said.[14]

There were also hopeful signs in 1997 that the public was ready for a serious discussion about Social Security reform, even though it was the most sensitive, potentially explosive issue in American politics. An August 1997 survey by Clinton pollster Mark Penn found that 73 percent of Democratic voters favored some form of privatization, and support was especially strong among younger workers. Independent polls also showed that many young people believed that without significant change the programs would not be able to provide for them in their old age. There was now some political benefit to a reform plan that guaranteed the program's survival for future generations, even if that meant some sacrifices now. The chief political strategist of the powerful American Association of Retired Persons (AARP) told the *Washington Post* that this was "an opportune time to take on the longer-term challenges" facing Social Security. "The stars are in alignment," he said.[15]

The prospect of spearheading a drive to reform Social Security proved too tantalizing for Bowles, who agreed to stay on and assist the president. Bowles was key, not only because of his effective management style, but also because of his relationship with Gingrich. Given the high risk involved, Clinton realized that he could not undertake this without bipartisan support, and, Bowles reflected, "He knew to do this he needed to work with Gingrich."[16] He was confident that he could hold moderate and conservative Democrats and bring enough Republicans to the table to make significant reform. "Both President Clinton and Speaker Gingrich realized that there was not enough of a consensus that one party could agree to that could become law," recalled former Congressman Stenholm, a moderate Democrat who would play a key role in any effort.[17]

The danger, however, was that Republicans would seize the surplus and use it for tax cuts. Some of Clinton's advisors suggested that he make a surprise announcement of a total overhaul of Social Security in the 1998 State of the Union Speech. Mindful of the health care debacle, Clinton rejected this option, believing it was important to bring Gingrich and other Republican leaders into the discussions. He also wanted to engage in a public education campaign that would make people aware of the sacrifices that would be necessary, building political support for a bipartisan solution. Instead of coming out with a detailed plan, he would use the bully pulpit of the presidency to establish guidelines for the discussion. "Save Social Security First" was the slogan he developed to describe his strategy, making clear that he would reserve all of the budget surplus until Congress produced a viable reform package.

The president reached out early on to two of the most powerful Republicans in the House: Gingrich and Bill Archer. As chair of the House Ways and Means Committee, Archer would have control over any plan to reform Social Security. Clinton invited Archer to the White House for an early morning meeting during the week between Christmas and New Year's. Archer had a carefully prepared fifteen-minute presentation, which he was determined to deliver. As he was making his points, he noticed Clinton slumping in his chair, appearing almost to fall asleep. When he finished, however, Clinton sat up and responded to each of Archer's points in the exact order he had raised them.[18]

Archer was interested in tax reform, but Clinton steered the discussion toward entitlement reform. "There are actually two things that I want to talk about," Clinton said. "I want to solve the Social Security problem and I want to solve the Medicare problem." Archer responded that he would be excited to work with him. "I'm prepared to take the political heat to provide political cover for the Republicans," Clinton declared. "I will support proposals that are politically very difficult to do." Archer was impressed. "I did not doubt for one minute that Bill Clinton was totally serious and sincere when he raised the issue of solving Social Security." As he was leaving the White House, Archer, who was nearly seventy, turned to an aide and said, "I would never want my constituents to hear this, but that is probably the smartest man who has been president in my lifetime."[19]

While Clinton talked privately with Archer, Bowles reached out to Gingrich. "I'm confident that these two guys can work together and solve a lot of problems," Bowles recalled. "Yes, there was still going to be fights. They are never going to be friends. They are never going to completely trust each other. But can they do things that can really make a difference long term? You bet."[20]

Initially, Gingrich, who had been burned before on Social Security, was reluctant to get out in front on the issue. "They were much more forward leaning on the issue," reflected Gingrich Chief-of-Staff Arne Christenson.[21] Polls showed that Social Security was the most popular federal government program. By large majorities most Americans trusted Democrats to preserve it since they had used it effectively against Republicans in the past. In the 1982 midterm elections, Democrats used the threat that Republicans wanted to abolish Social Security to make major gains, picking up twenty-six seats. In 1986, Gingrich ignored the advice of his ideological soulmate Jack Kemp, who said that any Republican who dares tamper with Social Security "is a candidate for a prefrontal lobotomy," and proposed a radical overhaul of the system. Two years later, his Democratic opponent made Gingrich's plan the centerpiece of his attacks on him.[22]

The signing of the balanced budget bill in August 1997 signaled an important change in the relationship between the two men. They realized they could accomplish more by working together, even if that meant abandoning the liberal and conservative wings of their respective parties. (William J. Clinton Presidential Library.)

It did not take long, however, for Gingrich to recognize the potential of a possible Social Security reform package. Bowles provided Gingrich with the same assurances that the president offered to Archer. The president would take the political heat for controversial proposals. His goal was to pass legislation, not to give Democrats an issue for the upcoming 1998 congressional elections. To Gingrich, those assurances meant more coming from Bowles than they did directly from Clinton.

Politically, the president and the Speaker were closer than anyone realized. They recognized that their parties needed to change in response to new circumstances. "The part of Gingrich that Clinton admired and that he tried to emulate was the Alvin Toffler visionary approach," reflected Waldman.[23] He tried to frame the debate over Social Security in language that was familiar to most Americans, calling it a "choice revolution." Nearly all Americans welcomed the consumer revolution and the range of economic possibilities it offered. Clinton believed that the greatest legacy of the 1960s was to expand that choice revolution to the realm of culture and lifestyle. While most conservatives welcomed the expanding range of economic options, they wanted to restrict cultural choices. Allowing people to pick among hundreds of different car sizes and shapes was evidence of a healthy economy; giving people the ability to decide whether to have an abortion, or live openly gay lives, was the reflection of moral decline. Many liberals, on the other hand, welcomed the cultural revolution of choice, but stubbornly refused to rethink their attitudes toward government, giving it the flexibility to respond to changing economic conditions.

Both men acknowledged that government could no longer offer Americans an industrialized age, one-size-fits all set of choices. "We were trying to think through the necessary reforms to modernize America to move into the twenty-first century," recalled Gingrich. "It was very conscious on that level."[24] They both believed that any effort to update Social Security would require government to incorporate some measure of choice, and that meant some form of privately managed account. "We always knew that finding common ground on Social Security wasn't terribly difficult from a policy standpoint," recalled Bruce Reed. "There was really only one plausible policy compromise. That was to have private accounts on top of security. That would give the Republicans what they wanted but leave Social Security intact. The policy differences were always the easiest to bridge."[25]

The exact details would have been worked out later, but the broad outlines were clear. Gingrich was willing to give up the tax cut for a proposal that included private investment in Social Security. "The balanced budget bill was act I," Gingrich reflected. "This was act II. . . . We were going to have a very workmanlike, very intense, remarkably creative two or three years."[26] Clinton congressional liaison Larry Stein noted that what was unique about 1997 was that "a Republican speaker who was eager to accomplish something, a Democratic president who was eager to accomplish something, and the available resources all came together in a fortuitous alliance."[27]

Instinctively, both men still wondered whether the other was setting a trap in preparation for the upcoming 1998 elections. Would Clinton leak word that Gingrich was once again trying to tamper with Social Security and Medicare, reinforcing his image as hostile to the old and poor? Would Gingrich tell reporters that the president was ready to accept the centerpiece of Republican proposals for Social Security: privately funded accounts?

The political possibilities were just too tantalizing to ignore. Despite all the forces pulling the nation apart, Clinton and Gingrich believed there was enough political support in Congress to create a lasting centrist coalition. If Clinton could reach out to moderate and conservative Democrats, and Gingrich could bring along a sizable number of moderate Republicans, they could create an enduring legislative majority that could address real problems. The Senate might be an obstacle, but they felt they could create momentum that would allow Trent Lott and Senate Minority Leader Tom Daschle to work something out. The American public would reward them for their success, creating an incentive for other political leaders to reject partisanship and participate in a bipartisan coalition. "It would not have been a slam dunk, but you would have had the legislative process working in a way in which you ultimately would have gotten a bill that would have done a good job of fixing Social Security," recalled Congressman Charles Stenholm.[28]

Bowles realized that it was important for the two men to sit face to face. "We worked like crazy" to lay the groundwork for the meeting, he reflected. "It was not easy to get them together in that room. They had to be convinced that the other guy was not going stab them in the back." According to Arne Christenson, "They were both calculating whether there was an opportunity for something big that would be in their interests, but also enough in the other person's interest, that they could make a deal."[29]

The president made the final decision about where to hold the meeting and who should be invited. He decided to hold the meeting in the Treaty Room, which he used as a private study. Clinton had hired a designer to create a historic Civil War atmosphere, furnishing the room with many Civil War–era pieces, including Ulysses Grant's original cabinet table and an antique table originally purchased by Mary Todd Lincoln. He filled the bookshelves with his private collection of biographies of world leaders, including a large number of books about JFK. With its fourteen-foot ceilings and stunning view of the South Lawn, the Treaty Room had been a favorite of presidents dating back to Andrew Johnson. The room had been the site of a number of important treaty signings over the years, including the 1963 Nuclear Test Ban Treaty. Clinton may have liked the symbolism: if old adversaries like the United States and the Soviet Union could put aside their differences, then certainly he and the Speaker could find some common ground for the future.

It was imperative that House Democrats not learn of the meeting. "It was our experience that it was virtually impossible for Gene Sperling to have a secret meeting with Bill Archer on Social Security without the Democratic caucus going off the deep end," reflected Bruce Reed, who learned of the meeting for the first time in 2007.[30] Clinton also kept it a secret from his own vice president. The president felt that Gore lacked the personal skills to negotiate directly with the Speaker. "Gore was not a good poker player," recalled a senior White House aide, and "this meeting was all about political poker." More important, he knew that Gore would oppose the whole initiative. "Clinton did not have a deep aversion to private accounts done outside Social Security," recalled Waldman. "Gore did."[31] Politically, tampering with Social Security made no sense to Gore. He knew that liberal Democrats would oppose the plan, and that his greatest challenge in the 2000 Democratic primaries would come from the left, probably from Gephardt. The last thing he wanted to do in his final years in office was to give a potential opponent traction by handing him the Social Security issue. "Gore knew he would have to win the Democratic primary, and challenging Democratic orthodoxy was a risk he had no desire to take," said Reed. Gore was more interested in reframing the debate over Social Security as a continuation of the budget battles from 1995. He preferred to freeze the discussion, claiming that Democrats wanted to "Save Social Security First" while the Republicans wanted to use the money for a tax cut for the rich.

By the time they sat down for their secret meeting on the evening of October 28, both men had seen their views of each other evolve over time. "By 1997 you have two adversaries who are very good at sizing each other up who have to make deals if the system is going to work," Gingrich said.[32] They were, as Gingrich titled his memoir of the period, *Lessons Learned the Hard Way*. It would have been a fitting title for Clinton's experience as well.

Clinton had once viewed Gingrich as an ideological bomb thrower, a reckless, power-hungry right-winger who was willing to destroy anyone who dared stand in the way of his grand schemes for "saving western civilization," which he saw as little more than an intellectualized repackaging of poll-tested conservative attacks on liberal ideas and the Democratic Party. While he still considered Gingrich temperamental and unpredictable, Clinton also believed

On October 28, 1997, Gingrich and his chief-of-staff, Arne Christenson, met secretly with the president, White House Chief-of-Staff Erskine Bowles, and congressional liaison John Hilley in the Treaty Room to talk about Social Security reform and their plans to create a centrist "political coalition." (William J. Clinton Presidential Library.)

that deep down inside Gingrich wanted to be remembered as a statesman, not a rebel. He had a creative, if unconventional, mind, and was willing to think about issues outside of traditional partisan binders. His hubris, so evident in his first two years as Speaker, had been tamed by the budget showdown and by an ethics investigation that had weakened his grip on power. Instead of being seen as the leader of a conservative revolution, Gingrich needed to prove to moderates that he could pass legislation and regain the public's trust.

Gingrich's views of Clinton had undergone the most dramatic change. He came to the speakership convinced he could dictate terms of surrender to the new president. He learned that Clinton possessed more backbone than he had imagined, and that he was a skilled political fighter. He also over time disabused himself of the idea that Clinton was a "closet liberal." By 1997, he appreciated that Clinton "was a much more complicated person. . . . With the exception of his McGovern period, Clinton really is a southern Baptist populist," he reflected years later. "As a result, he can accommodate reality."[33] In his mind, reality meant that he needed to work with a Republican Congress and incorporate their ideas into his agenda.

Convinced there was an opportunity to work together, the two men agreed to the secret White House meeting. While the discussion focused on their plans for Social Security and Medicare, the president and Speaker also tried to unblock obstacles presented by other contentious issues that threatened to derail the budget negotiations. Much of the conversation revolved around the horse trading on bills necessary to pass the 1998 budget. They focused on two controversial issues: Clinton's ongoing efforts to pass fast-track legislation, which would give the president greater authority to negotiate trade agreements, and appropriations for the United Nations. Highlighting why it was so difficult for Democrats to support the fast-track initiative, the president shared the comments of one congressman who complained that a vote would cost him $200,000 in union contributions for his re-election campaign. According to one participant, Clinton grimaced when the Speaker told him that Minority Leader Richard Gephardt had tried scheduling China-bashing votes to coincide with the visit of Chinese President Jiang Zemin, who had arrived earlier in the day. The discussion underscored an important new political reality: on some of his major legislative initiatives, the president was closer to Gingrich than he was to the leadership of his own party.

The two leaders worked together to neutralize other hot-button issues. The Speaker made clear that he needed a deal on the census. Democrats wanted to replace the traditional approach the government used to count people for the census with a new method based on statistical sampling. Republicans blocked the change, claiming that sampling favored Democrats. Realizing there was no easy answer, Clinton and Gingrich looked for a way to "kick it down the road"—coming up with a short-term solution that would placate all sides. The question of abortion in international aid, according to a White House official, "was always the last issue at 7:00 AM after you've been up two straight nights." Although the abortion issue was important for the large contingent of social conservatives in his party, Gingrich viewed it as a bargaining chip that could be used to exact concessions from Democrats on issues that were more important to him, such as increased spending for defense and space exploration. Neither he nor Clinton wanted it to block their larger agenda. "How do we punt this thing?" they asked. Clinton raised the issue of "school testing." In his 1997 State of the Union, Clinton had included provisions for fourth-grade national testing in reading and math, but majorities in both houses voted against it by a veto proof majority. Clinton wanted to revive it in the budget negotiations, where he had more leverage, and Gingrich offered constructive advice on the best way to proceed.

After the hour-long meeting, Clinton provided his guests with a brief tour of the Lincoln bedroom before rushing off to dinner. Both men left feeling confident about the possibilities of success. There were still some major hurdles. There was enough distrust between the two men that neither was ready to fully let down his guard. The "coalition" was real, but fragile, capable of unraveling from the sheer weight of their mutual distrust. "This isn't like Sears and Roebuck," Christenson recalled, describing the new relationship between the president and his boss. "This is more like the Soviet Union and the United States during World War II."[34] From Gingrich's perspective, the two men recognized that they shared common interests on some major policy initiatives. But they were "not going to be buddies for the rest of their lives."[35] Bowles was the glue that kept the coalition together. Throughout the fall and early winter, he continued his shuttle diplomacy, reassuring both men of the good intentions of the other.

Clinton and Gingrich were both taking big risks by working together and by pushing such an ambitious agenda. Politically, Gingrich was taking the bigger gamble, since he faced the possibility of a rebellion that could cost him his speakership. There would be no deal without Gingrich, and White House aides worried whether he could maintain his grip on power. The Speaker had no doubts. While a handful of disgruntled members were bashing him in the media and conservatives were in revolt, he felt that the balanced budget bill had strengthened his position with party moderates—the very people he would need to both stay in power and push through entitlement reform. For now, he talked about creating an "echo chamber" by getting a small number of influential members to speak out early and often in support of the reform effort to insulate himself from the inevitable conservative backlash. The president had to contend with some political perils of his own. He knew that the initiative would not be popular with some members of his administration. The situation was further complicated by Al Gore, who now viewed administration initiatives through the prism of his own campaign for president less than two years away.

The real problems would be on Capitol Hill, however, where the president's efforts would once again pit him against the leadership of his own party in the House. While the Senate had often been the graveyard of efforts to reform Social Security in the past, Clinton had a close relationship with Majority Leader Tom Daschle and with Republican Majority Leader Trent Lott. Relations between the parties were more cordial, less partisan in the Senate, making it easier to build a centrist coalition of Democrats and Republicans. That was not the case in the House, where Clinton's relations with Gephardt had turned frosty after passage of the 1997 balanced budget bill, and where the Democratic and Republican leadership were barely on speaking terms. Clinton hoped to bypass the party's liberal leadership and reassemble the coalition of suburban "New Democrats," who tended to be socially liberal but fiscally conservative, and "Blue Dogs," largely rural, southern conservative Democrats, who passed the balanced budget bill.

Despite being pushed by the two most powerful political figures in America, a massive overhaul of Social Security would be an uphill fight. "No one ever lost money betting against Social Security reform," recalled Begala.[36] In their efforts to build a truly bipartisan coalition, would the successful effort to pass the North American Free Trade Agreement (NAFTA) be the model, or the failure of fast track? Clinton always said that he needed at least 100 Democratic votes in the House to support a bill. Could he muster that many votes on an issue as controversial as Social Security? Could Gingrich, who had already suffered one rebellion and seen his hold on power seriously eroded, bring along enough moderate Republicans to seal the deal? All the key players—Clinton, Gingrich, Bowles, John Hilley, and Bill Archer—were cautiously optimistic. "It wasn't crazy for them to think that if they could do the impossible and pass welfare reform and the balanced budget bill, they could do Social Security," reflected Bruce Reed.[37]

The plan was for Clinton to make his bold initiative for reforming Social Security and Medicare the centerpiece of his State of the Union address in January 1998. Gingrich would follow the president's speech by making positive comments about the initiative. He would then ask Archer's Ways and Means Committee to make specific recommendations in just a few months. Both sides would try to keep the issue off the table in the 1998 congressional elections, before pushing it through a lame-duck Congress in December. In the meantime, the president would use the bully pulpit to frame the terms of debate and prepare the public for the initiative. The president asked two powerful groups, the American Association of Retired Persons (AARP), the largest organization of senior citizens, and the Concord Coalition, an influential lobbying group that advocated fiscal discipline, to organize four regional forums to discuss the issue. The national "dialogue" would conclude with a White House conference on Social Security in December 1998—the same time that Congress would be voting on a reform proposal.

The president had decided to use the congressional winter recess in December 1997 to start leaking information about his agenda, generating media coverage of important items, hoping to frame the debate before Congress returned in January. "We had figured out how to get things done," Bowles reflected. "We were all feeling very confident."[38] "The State of the Union used to be a speech," White House advisor Rahm Emanuel told the president. "Now it's a month." Near the end of the month the president conducted the longest press conference of his presidency, where he told reporters that he was ready to tackle the "long-term problems of the country, the long-term challenges." John Harris, who covered the White House for the *Washington Post,* reflected that the ninety-minute session "left an impression, accurately, of a still young and still creative president eager to make the most of the remaining three years of his presidency."[39] As he headed for his annual Renaissance Weekend retreat for New Year's, Clinton had reason to feel good about the future. "I looked back on 1997 with satisfaction," he reflected, "hoping the worst of the partisan wars had passed in the wake of all that had been accomplished."[40]

In January, just weeks before the State of the Union address, the administration started preparing the public and Congress, signaling that it would support some form of privatization. "Given that we have to work with the Republicans, it's hard to see a plan passing without some individual-account piece," a Clinton advisor told *Business Week.*[41] Gingrich revealed his hand in a speech at a local Cobb County event. Years later he described it as "a precursor to the State of the Union." The goal was to strike a bipartisan note while positioning himself to come out in favor of Clinton's Social Security agenda. "There's no crisis, but there's a long, steady problem unless we invent a better model," he said while calling for "a dialogue about creating the best retirement system in the world."[42] When asked about his plans for the future, Gingrich responded, "You ain't seen nothing yet."

Gingrich's speech caught the attention of *Washington Post* reporter E.J. Dionne. "It was an important speech because it marked how far the world has come in less than four years" since the Republican Revolution. Talk of revolution, he observed, "has given way to the era of Republican incrementalism, gradualism, caution." Dionne noted that Gingrich's ideas sounded "remarkably similar to those a certain character in the White House has been proclaiming since 1992." Dionne concluded by noting, "If the story of 1995 was about the adjustments President Bill Clinton made to a new conservative climate, the story of 1998 will be about the adjustments Gingrich and his colleagues are making to the practical climate of the post-deficit world."[43]

While moving quickly on Social Security, Clinton and Gingrich set Medicare reform on a slower track. On January 16, working closely with Trent Lott in the Senate, the president and Speaker managed to convince two allies to serve as cochairs of the National Bipartisan Commission on the Future of Medicare. Clinton friend John Breaux, a moderate Louisiana senator known for his ability to forge compromise, was appointed chairman, and Gingrich colleague Bill Thomas, powerful head of the House Ways and Means subcommittee on health care, agreed to serve as administrative chairman of the seventeen-member commission. Gingrich and Clinton worked hard behind the scenes to create the committee, believing that it could provide political cover for any controversial recommendations they may need to push through Congress. "You don't ask John Breaux to head a committee unless you are looking for a deal," reflected Bowles. The president and Speaker charged them with producing a set of recommendations by March 1999, which would still give them enough time to get a bill through Congress before the 2000 presidential campaign moved into full swing.

By mid-January 1998, Bowles believed everything was on track. The administration had been leaking its agenda to the media over the past few months, defining the issues and dominating the debate. Clinton and Gingrich had agreed on the broad outlines of a Social Security plan, and they had set up a bipartisan committee that promised to lay the groundwork for a major overhaul of Medicare. The president and the Speaker were looking forward to the annual State of the Union address, scheduled for January 27, when they would make public the plans they had carefully laid over the previous months. No one, however, was prepared for what happened next.

CHAPTER FOURTEEN | "Monica Changed Everything"

E ARLY ON WEDNESDAY MORNING, January 21, Erskine Bowles arrived at his office in the White House at his usual 7:00 AM starting time. He liked to spend a few hours getting caught up on the news in preparation for his daily 9:00 AM briefing with the president. The day was already packed with events, and Bowles was trying to wrap up the details of the State of the Union address scheduled for the following week. While some White House officials had learned the previous evening that the *Washington Post* was running a story about the president having an illicit affair with an unnamed White House intern, Bowles learned about it for the first time when he opened the paper sitting on his desk. There across four columns at the top of the paper read the headline: "Clinton Accused of Urging Aide to Lie; Starr Probes Whether President Told Woman to Deny Alleged Affair to Jones's Lawyers."[1]

The story, and investigations that followed, revealed the intrigue taking place behind the scenes to bring down the Clinton presidency. After their initial encounter on November 15, 1995—the second day of the government shutdown—the president and Monica Lewinsky continued their clandestine meetings for the next twenty months. After the lovesick Lewinsky was transferred to work in the Pentagon, a conniving Linda Tripp befriended her and cajoled her to share the tales of her sexual trysts with the president, which she secretly taped. Eventually, there would be seventeen tapes covering twenty hours of conversation. Through an interlocking network of conservative lawyers and activists, Tripp managed to tip off the attorneys for Paula

Jones, who had a sexual harassment suit pending against the president, and to turn the tapes over to Kenneth Starr. On January 17, 1998, when he gave his deposition in the Jones case and denied a sexual relationship with Lewinsky, Clinton had unknowingly stepped into a legal trap. What made this incident different from all the other allegations was that it raised the possibility that the president had committed an impeachable offense. Among the possible crimes was that he suborned perjury, perhaps committed perjury himself, and obstructed justice.

When Bowles asked the president about the story that morning, Clinton denied it. "Erskine," he said, "I want you to know that this story is not true."[2] Bowles was crushed by the alleged charges, which he assumed were untrue. He was also devastated that a potentially great moment had been lost. Whether true or not, he understood the political implications: all of their hard work in building the alliance with Gingrich had been destroyed. "It was game over," he recalled. Bowles believes that the Lewinsky affair "was one of the seminal events in American history." There was no doubt in his mind that Clinton and Gingrich would have created a plan for reforming both Social Security and Medicare that year and, perhaps, set the stage for a new period of bipartisanship. "Gingrich wanted to do it; Clinton wanted to do it. It was a real missed opportunity," he said. "Monica changed everything."[3] John Hilley, who played a key role in developing a legislative strategy for Social Security reform, shared Bowles's disappointment. "The scandal effectively undermined the bipartisanship that had accomplished so much in 1996 and 1997."[4]

That morning, Bowles assembled the staff for the daily meeting. His "face was pale, his voice subdued," observed White House aide Sidney Blumenthal. "Now everything about his body language and tone conveyed that he wished he were anywhere but where he was." He told the staff to focus on their work, but he was clearly disgusted by the whole story.[5] "I think I'm going to throw up," he said after a meeting with lawyers and the political staff.

Gingrich was in Detroit when he learned the news of the Lewinsky affair. His aides told him that if he tried to make any public comment they would tackle him. Like everyone else, he spent much of the day on Wednesday trying to piece the story together. "It was obvious that this was not an issue of the President having another affair," Gingrich recalled. "There was an issue of perjury involved." He knew immediately, however, that the scandal would derail their grand plans for reform. "I knew that for him to survive he had to go to the left because the only way he could survive was to keep his left wing furious with us." Gingrich reflected. "He couldn't do anything to offend the left. I knew it was over. At point we were in a cycle where it was just going to grind down."[6] For now, Gingrich planned to keep a low profile and he told his colleagues to proceed with caution in the coming days.

It is likely that a number of considerations other than generosity informed Gingrich's muted response. For one thing, he believed that the charges against Clinton were so serious there was no need for him to comment. "His attitude was, I don't need to add any fuel to this fire," recalled Arne Christenson. He was convinced that Clinton would want nothing more than to confuse the public by politicizing the issue, making it look like another petty power struggle between Democrats and Republicans in Washington, and he was determined not to say anything that would allow the White House to shift public attention away from the scandal. Although he has refused to talk about it publicly, he must have realized that he was vulnerable to similar charges. Already rumors were swirling around Capitol Hill that his marriage was on the rocks and that he was having an affair with a woman in his office. Perhaps for that reason, Gingrich, who often framed the smallest issue in the grandest terms, later developed a narrowly legalistic interpretation of the Lewinsky affair. It was not about personal behavior, he said. "This is about perjury in a federal civil case."

What no one knew at the time was that Gingrich had tied his political fate to that of the president. The Lewinsky scandal forced Gingrich to shift gears. He woke up on the morning of January 21 believing that he and Clinton were going to work together to forge a political realignment. He went to bed that night knowing there would be no Social Security or Medicare reform, and no centrist political coalition. Clinton's self-destructive actions may have inflicted a mortal blow to his own ambitions to be remembered as a great statesman. That was a serious blow to a man who from the time he was a teenager wanted to be a "transformational" figure. Instead of building a bipartisan coalition, Gingrich would now focus on winning as many seats as possible in the upcoming elections.

It seemed like a realistic goal. He was convinced that the weight of the investigation into Clinton would be an albatross for the Democrats. How could it not? A president's party always lost seats in the off-year election of a second term, and it was likely that voters would want to send the president a clear signal that they disapproved of his actions. The president was enjoying high approval ratings, but Gingrich was certain they would drop as more information was revealed. The scandal provided Republicans with an opportunity, but it also posed real danger if they overplayed their hand.

The media certainly did not need any prodding from Gingrich to keep the story on the front pages. The network news anchors started the day in Cuba where they were covering the Pope's visit, but by midday they were on private jets back to the United States to cover one of the biggest news stories of the decade. In the first few days, the story drowned out all other news items, as the press clamored to learn new details. Talk of resignation and impeachment filled the airways. The public complained about the media saturation even as they soaked it up on 24-hour cable news shows, which witnessed a big boost in ratings. "It's been a sad moment for America, a fine moment for Fox news," said a network's vice president.[7] From January until the trial in the Senate the following winter, the Associated Press assigned twenty-five full time reporters to the story, who wrote 4,109 pieces. That represented an average of eleven stories per day. The evening news broadcasts on the three major networks devoted 1,931 minutes to the scandal—more than the next seven topics combined.[8]

Despite the public fascination with the story, the president was determined to push forward with the original plan for his State of the Union address. "I thought that if I could survive the public pounding for two weeks, the smoke would begin to clear, the press and the public would focus on Starr's tactics, and a more balanced view of the matter would emerge," Clinton reflected. "I went on doing my job, and I stonewalled, denying what had happened to everyone."[9] Many of those who were close to the president were surprised that he never fully appreciated how the story, especially the potential charges of perjury and obstruction of justice, had altered the political calculus. "It was an ironic but undeniable fact that the only place in America where you could have a two-hour conversation about Bill Clinton and the name Monica Lewinsky did not come up was in the White House itself."[10]

The media frenzy revealed how technology had altered the way reporters covered politics and limited the president's ability to control his message. The Lewinsky affair dealt a fatal blow to the already beleaguered standards of objective journalism, which required reporters to cover stories without being part of them, and to construct a firewall between gossip and truth. "This was the first big story since journalism changed," observed ABC pundit Cokie Roberts. "We never had a story like this, with three 24-hour channels and all the 'dot coms.' None of us knew how to operate in that world."[11] The competition with 24-hour news networks, and a host of Internet cites, led most major news outlets to abandon rules that every story had to be confirmed by two sources. Now, breathless reporters rushed on to the air to report the latest gossip and rumors, newspaper and magazine editors loosened the rules of evidence, and conservative Web sites circulated wild stories of White House intrigue. At the same time, a new breed of celebrity reporters made the rounds on news talk shows to offer opinions about the scandal, discuss the latest rumors, and make predictions about the future.

Each day the situation grew bleaker, as journalists, amid the rumors and speculation, uncovered new evidence. By the weekend, there were reports that an unnamed White House worker had witnessed a private encounter between Clinton and Lewinsky. Word also surfaced of the existence of a dress containing the president's semen. Both the *New York Post* and *Daily News* ran the same headline on Monday, January 26: "Caught in the Act." Pundits openly predicted the end of the Clinton presidency. George Will called it "dead, deader really, than Woodrow Wilson's was after he had a stroke." While most observers predicted impeachment proceedings, ABC's Sam Donaldson raised the possibility of a presidential resignation. "Mr. Clinton, if he's not telling the truth and the evidence shows that, will resign, perhaps this week," he opined.[12] As Paul Begala noted, however, "anyone who knew Clinton, knew that the only way he was leaving office was with his feet up."[13]

The reaction to the developing scandal was so overwhelming that Bowles feared it might be necessary to cancel the State of the Union speech. Would the president's critics use the occasion to embarrass him? he wondered. Would they refuse to stand when he walked into the House chamber? On the morning of the speech, the First Lady gave voice to her husband's thoughts, and added fuel to the media fire, when she offered a spirited assault against his attackers on NBC's *Today* show. The charges, she protested, were created by a "vast right-wing conspiracy" hellbent on destroying his presidency. "Bill and I have been accused of everything, including murder, by some of the very same people who are behind these allegations," she said.

On January 27, less than one week after the Lewinsky story broke, the president entered the House to deliver his State of the Union address. A few hours before the speech, Gingrich had warned his colleagues not to insult the president, saying the public wanted more patriotism and less partisanship. As Clinton walked into the chamber, he was greeted with applause, whistles, and cheers. "Ladies and gentlemen, the state of the union is strong," Clinton announced, prompting a standing ovation. "We have a smaller government, but a stronger nation." He then sketched out the outlines of his plan for Social Security, proposing to set aside $200 billion over the next five years while leading a bipartisan effort to preserve and strengthen the troubled retirement program. "Let us say to all Americans watching tonight, whether you're 70 or 50, or whether you just started paying into the system, Social Security will be there when you need it," Clinton declared. "Social Security First."[14]

Most observers gave Clinton high marks for his performance. The *New York Times* noted that the president "performed brilliantly in the midst of extraordinary adversity," pointing out that he "sounded a note of dignity and sobriety."[15] As originally conceived, the speech was supposed to set in motion a string of bipartisan gestures, but nearly everyone in the hall that evening involved in the discussions understood how the politics of Social Security had shifted in just one week. "You would have to be blind to not realize that the whole political environment had changed," reflected Charles Stenholm.[16] The affair polarized both the Left and Right, making any possibility for consensus moot. "Clinton realized that he could not lose his left without losing his office," recalled Christenson. "Gingrich realized that with the Right in a full-throated roar, he could not appear indifferent to things that were driving them crazy. Both sides realized their future viability depended on sticking with their base."[17] As the *Washington Post*'s David Broder observed, "The State of the Union, originally seen as the peak of a drive to put the president clearly in control of the national agenda, became under the altered circumstances an effort to salvage a bad situation."

According to the original script, Gingrich was to follow with the Republican response, expressing his support for the president's Social Security initiative. Instead, he said nothing. Trent Lott delivered the formal Republican response in a televised response titled "Family, Faith and Freedom," which repeated the traditional conservative litany of tax cuts, family values, and strong national defense. There would be no reaching across the aisle to build a bipartisan coalition. Most Republicans followed the Speaker's advice, letting the media take the lead in discussing the possibility of impeachment or resignation. Only hardline conservative Bob Barr strayed from the strategy, announcing that he was drawing up articles of impeachment against the president.

After the speech, the president went on a campaign-style trip to sell his initiatives. His spirits were lifted by warm and enthusiastic crowds and by overnight polls showing public approval of his job rating at the highest levels of his presidency. A *Washington Post* poll showed that 67 percent of the public gave him high marks for job performance; six in ten said the nation was "headed in the right direction."[18] The polls buoyed Clinton's belief that public support would intimidate Republicans out of pursuing impeachment hearings while encouraging Democrats to stand united behind him.

House Democrats who had fought Clinton on many of his major legislative proposals rallied around him now. Just a few months earlier, Clinton was willing to abandon the leadership of his own party to make legislative history. Now he was completely dependent on them to avoid making history in a very different way. Political calculation, not affection, bound congressional Democrats to the president. "For our own self-interest it was important for us to stay together because if we scattered I felt it would doom us even more," recalled Michigan's David Bonior.[19] "From that point on Clinton was the hero of the Democrats and the Democrats were the great defenders of Bill Clinton," observed Paul Begala. "The more liberal you were, the more likely you were to defend him."[20] Most Democrats supported Clinton because they saw it as an opportunity to drive a wedge between the president and Gingrich. According to Larry Stein, who assumed the job of White House chief congressional liaison on the day the Lewinsky story broke, "the Democrats got the double benefit of being the president's chief defenders while also vilifying the Republicans for attacking the president."[21]

Congressional Democrats made the case that the entire sordid affair was the logical outgrowth of Newt Gingrich's desire to demolish his presidency. "You see, Mr. President, now you see how this right-wing power run-amok has been going after us all these years," they told him. For years they had watched in frustration as Clinton worked deals behind their backs with Gingrich. They had tried to convince him and his staff that Gingrich was simply biding his time, waiting for an opportunity to destroy Clinton's presidency. They believed that Clinton was the ultimate nightmare for conservatives: an articulate, effective moderate who possessed an instinctive feel for the political center. Even if conservatives could not remove him from office, they could sully his reputation. "The entire impeachment was not so much about removing the president from office as it was sullying his reputation to the point he would not be the icon that Ronald Reagan would become," recalled Congressman Victor Fazio.[22] Although Gingrich was largely quiet about the affair, Democrats made the case that he was pulling the strings behind the scenes. "Clinton learned that no matter how much he and Gingrich were fascinated by each other's intellect that in the end, Gingrich's permanent political posture is an exposed stiletto," reflected David Obey.[23]

The strong Democratic response cemented the White House strategy for managing the politics of the scandal. The plan was to make it the second act of the government shutdown saga: show the president hard at work solving real problems while his small-minded and partisan opponents waged an increasingly nasty and personal vendetta against him. They never wanted the spotlight to stray too far from Gingrich, who would be the perfect partisan foil for the congressional phase of a possible impeachment battle. They knew that Gingrich was not driving the process, but they saw the political benefit of making him the congressional face of impeachment. "Gingrich is the best bogeyman any Democrat has had in the modern era," reflected Peter Baker, who covered the White House for the *Washington Post*. "They loved to have Gingrich out front."[24] The key was also to focus the discussion on sex, not on the possible issue of perjury. "The whole premise governing the Democratic strategy was to paint the Republicans as unfair," observed Baker, "to make a case that they were being partisan."[25]

Gingrich was not the only foil. Initially, the White House worked to undermine the credibility of the tone-deaf special counsel Kenneth Starr. "There's going to be a war," said James Carville, the president's feisty political consultant. Clinton and Starr emerged on opposite sides of the 1960s cultural divide. The owl-faced special prosecutor was born 28 days before Clinton in the neighboring state of Texas. Both men grew up in humble circumstances, went east to college and law school, and stayed home during the Vietnam War (Starr had a medical deferment for psoriasis). Starr met President Kennedy the day before he died, but, unlike Clinton, did not shake his hand. His idol was Richard Nixon. While Clinton identified with the decade's youthful experimentation, Starr clung more tenaciously to his fundamentalist faith and strict values. While Clinton worked his way up the ranks of the Democratic Party, Starr established his credentials as a conservative jurist, serving as solicitor-general under President George Bush before accepting appointment as special prosecutor investigating allegations of Clinton wrongdoing in the Whitewater affair. Over the previous three years, Starr had expanded his probe far afield from the original Whitewater investigation.

Starr's strong-armed tactics and self-righteous demeanor made him an easy White House target. Hillary Clinton called him "a politically motivated prosecutor who is allied with the right-wing opponents of my husband." Harold Ickes, a former Clinton aide, said Starr was a dangerous moralist who viewed the Clintons "like Sodom and Gomorrah and is hellbent on running them out of Washington." An unnamed administration official told the *New York Times* that the White House's attacks were "part of our continuing campaign to destroy Ken Starr." The public seemed to agree with the White House view of Starr. By March, the president's approval rating had soared to over 70 percent, but only 11 percent of the public had a favorable view of Starr.[26]

While the Lewinsky story forged an unprecedented unity between House Democrats and the Clinton White House, it divided, confused, and frustrated Republicans. The Lewinsky affair exploded just as conservatives were launching a major initiative designed to "take back" the "values and morality" agenda, which they believed the president had successfully hijacked during the 1996 campaign. Majority Leader Armey led the values charge, calling for an aggressive campaign to energize the conservative base while also reaching out "to a much broader segment of Americans."[27] "I believe the issues of values and morality will be the dominant issues of 1998 and 2000," Armey wrote his colleagues less than a week before the Lewinsky story broke.

"We need to be better role models, we need to communicate our values successfully, and we need to shepherd a legislative agenda that gives parents and individuals the freedom to live their lives and raise their children in a safe, moral environment."[28] News of the president's affair only underscored conservative concern about the nation's spiritual health, proved their suspicions that Clinton was unqualified to serve as the nation's moral leader, and energized them to force him from office. Conservatives not only wanted Gingrich to respond to the White House public relations offensive, but they also pushed him to start impeachment proceedings without Starr. "Gingrich could order Congress to proceed on its own," declared activist Paul Weyrich. "Since the appointment of the independent counsel, they've deferred to him. It's essentially political cover."[29]

Many party moderates, however, were looking at the polls and getting nervous, fearing they were headed toward another losing confrontation with a popular president. Trent Lott wanted Starr to present his evidence and get the whole affair behind them as quickly as possible "He's had enough time, and its time to show his cards," said Lott in March. "He needs to wrap it up, show us what he's got."[30] Whether they wanted to move aggressively to impeach the president or were looking to get the issue behind them as quickly as possible, most Republicans were uncomfortable with the prospect of another Gingrich–Clinton confrontation. Memories of the budget shutdown were still fresh on their minds. The more the president turned impeachment into a personal struggle between himself and the Speaker, the more likely it was that he would be able to thwart a full investigation.

The rapidly changing environment baffled Gingrich, who seemed uncharacteristically uncertain from the beginning of the crisis about how to respond. He understood that the president's survival strategy depended on politicizing the issue and that it was essential that Republicans avoid falling into the trap. At the same time, however, he relished the opportunity to turn the Lewinsky affair into a Democratic version of Watergate, make major gains in the 1998 elections, and then recapture the presidency in 2000. "I don't think he was the driving force in propelling impeachment forward," reflected journalist Peter Baker. "But he believed that impeachment was both a necessary process and one that would be good for the Republican caucus. He was not a passive bystander."[31]

Torn between a conservative base that favored moving full-speed ahead on impeachment and moderates wanting to distance themselves from Starr and the whole Lewinsky matter, Gingrich tried to buy time by telling everyone to wait for the Starr report. The law required that the independent counsel inform the House of "any substantial and credible information" that could serve as grounds for impeachment. "I've said for three months nothing matters until Judge Starr reports," he repeated over and over in interviews.[32]

While counseling patience and caution, Gingrich sent mixed signals to his caucus and to the White House that left nearly everyone confused about his intentions. For weeks he had been advising colleagues to avoid even mentioning the "I" word. But in a February 4 meeting with Republicans, he made numerous references to impeachment, saying that he wanted to see all of the documents from Starr's four-year investigation, not just those related to Lewinsky. The comment raised eyebrows. Was he indicating that he wanted a wider investigation into the president's activities, or was he raising the bar on impeachment?

The following evening Hillary sat Gingrich next to her at a dinner in honor of British Prime Minister Tony Blair. She hoped "to glean Gingrich's thoughts on the latest Starr charges." The specter of impeachment was being raised. "Gingrich was the key: If he gave the go-ahead, the country was in for a rough ride." According to the First Lady, Gingrich leaned in toward her and said, "These accusations against your husband are ludicrous. And I think it's terribly unfair the way some people are trying to make something out of it. Even if it were true, it's meaningless. It's not going anywhere." She was surprised but relieved by his comments, saying it provided evidence "that Gingrich was more complicated and unpredictable than I had thought."[33] It is likely that the comments revealed that Gingrich was "more polite," and not necessarily "more complicated" than she had thought. He had made clear from the day the story broke that the issue of a president committing perjury was serious. He probably was uncomfortable having a conversation with the president's wife about Clinton's rumored, but still unproven, infidelities.

Gingrich's indecisiveness fed the frustration of caucus conservatives who believed that Republicans needed to develop a coherent response to the unified message coming from the Clinton White House and the Democratic congressional leadership. In February, Gingrich polled conservatives to find out why they were so anxious and angry, and why they were dissatisfied with his leadership. There were many different complaints, but they all added up to the charge that he had gone soft on the president. The top complaint was that the "Democrats are always striking out at the Republicans, there is never a response from the leadership." While Democrats were speaking with a single voice, Republicans were "bashing" each other in the press. They complained that Gingrich was "compromising with Clinton on issues." There was a general sense that Democrats were on the offensive and that Gingrich was so eager to make deals with Clinton that he failed to articulate a compelling alternative Republican message. They wanted him to speak out "in support of Barr's impeachment inquiry," and they insisted that he keep public attention focused on other White House "scandals."[34]

Throughout the winter and early spring of 1998, Gingrich could barely contain his anger as the president skillfully demonized Starr and made sex, not perjury, the central issue in the case. But he felt trapped: if he spoke out, he would only play into the White House strategy. He felt that he was doing everything possible to maintain a spirit of bipartisanship, but the Democrats were constantly stonewalling, fighting for partisan advantage, and over-simplifying issues in the press. "We haven't found Howard Baker yet on the other side," he lamented, referring to the Tennessee Republican senator who worked with Democrats during the Watergate hearings.[35]

With his frustration building, Gingrich finally exploded on April 27 at the annual GOPAC meeting. This was a gathering of the conservative party faithful—the loyal troops who raised money and motivated the base. They expected "red meat" and Gingrich decided to give them what they wanted. "What we have lived through for two and a half long years is the most systematic, deliberate obstruction of justice cover up in an effort to avoid the truth we have ever seen in American history," he said with typical exaggeration. The Lewinsky investigation, Gingrich said, is "not some silly thing about some college intern," but "is about the rule of law." Said Gingrich: "This is the heart of America. This is what the Constitution means. . . . In a republic, by definition, we are all subordinate to the law. That means you can't claim executive privilege for frivolous reasons. It means you can't abuse the law. It means you can't abuse power." He concluded by making the pledge that most conservatives wanted to hear: "I will never again as long as I am Speaker make a speech without commenting" on the Lewinsky scandal.[36]

The speech produced the thunderous applause that Gingrich wanted, but it also served to undermine his deliberate strategy to stay off the Lewinsky radar screen. It was a public relations gift to the White House, producing front-page stories in leading newspapers and appearing to prove that he was the mastermind behind the drive for impeachment. The *Philadelphia Daily News* columnist Sandy Grady warned: "Head for the fallout shelter! Nuclear Newt is Back."[37] Even though he knew that attacking the president would play directly into his hands, he simply could not control his anger and his self-righteousness. "Newt just couldn't help himself," said his former chief-of-staff Dan Meyer. "He got in front of a rabid partisan crowd, and they just loved his red meat."[38] Questioned about his reaction at a press conference, the president responded by seizing the high road. "I think it would not serve the American public well for me to waste my time" responding, the president said. "I think I need to be focused on the public issues that affect them, and that's what I intend to do." Press Secretary Michael McCurry went so far as to suggest that the White House would no longer work with Gingrich until he "comes back and sits down and does the work as Speaker that he needs to do."[39]

While lambasting the president in public, Gingrich was trying to lay the groundwork for dealing with any report that Starr would send to the Congress. In the spring, the Speaker floated the idea of creating a special panel to investigate the charges. Gingrich feared the prospect of a train wreck in the Judiciary Committee, which, consisting of twenty-one Republicans and sixteen Democrats, was perhaps the most ideologically divided, partisan committee in the House. Its membership reflected the extremes of the cultural divide in America. The majority of Republicans were white male Christian conservatives from predominately suburban or rural areas. On the Democratic side were six Jews, five African Americans, three women, and one gay man— all representing urban areas. Whether liberal or conservative, the overwhelming majority were lawyers trained in adversarial combat, representing safe districts, feeling little incentive to moderate their views or seek compromise.

The suggestion of creating a special committee put Gingrich at odds with the committee's territorial seventy-four-year-old chairman, Henry Hyde. Unlike the Speaker, who was despised by most Democrats, Hyde had earned the trust and respect of his colleagues across the aisle. Jesse Jackson Jr. called him "a voice of moderation, a fair person, with a judicious temperament."[40] The chairman emphasized that he wanted the proceedings to be bipartisan. Despite his demeanor of reasoned nonpartisan, Hyde was convinced that Clinton should be removed from office and never wavered from the belief that it was his obligation to make that happen. "I hate the son of a bitch," Hyde said. "I want to get him. But I want to get him in the right way."[41]

Hyde forced Gingrich to retreat from his plans to create a more ideologically balanced committee. He told the Speaker privately that any charges presented by Starr fell under his jurisdiction. To make sure Gingrich got the point, other members delivered the same message publicly. Florida's Charles Canady called Gingrich's suggestion "an unprecedented and unprincipled act of partisanship," ignoring the fact that Gingrich made the plan to prevent the impeachment from becoming partisan.[42] More than half of the Republican members of the committee wrote Gingrich complaining that a special committee would "abruptly break" with the precedent set by the impeachment of Andrew Johnson and the process that led to Richard Nixon's resignation. Republicans also wanted to make Hyde, not Gingrich, the face of the party on impeachment. They feared a new committee would increase both the power and visibility of the Speaker, since he would be responsible for picking the Republican members. The more the press and public focused on Hyde and the less Gingrich popped up in news stories about impeachment, the harder it would be for Democrats to dismiss the entire proceeding as partisan. The creation of a select committee, they claimed, "could easily be misinterpreted as partisan maneuvering."

Until July, the focus of the story had been on the abstract question of whether a sexual encounter had even taken place. Clinton denied it; his accusers claimed it happened, but offered no proof. That changed on July 28, when Lewinsky reached an agreement with Starr to tell the story of her relationship with the president. She also turned over to the prosecutors a dark blue dress containing the president's "genetic material." The president now faced a host of difficult personal, political, and legal questions. What would he tell the upcoming grand jury? How would he explain that he had lied to the nation, and to his wife? On the evening of August 15, the president confessed the tawdry details of his affair to his wife.

Two days later, Clinton sat for four hours in the Map Room of the White House testifying by closed-circuit television before the grand jury investigating the Lewinsky affair. The same room where FDR had once followed troop movements in Europe during World War II was now the scene of a humiliating presidential confession. Faced with conclusive DNA evidence, he was forced to admit after seven months of denial that he had a sexual relationship with Lewinsky. But along the way, he masterfully blurred the issues in the case, obscuring what the prosecutors believed was a clear definition of what constituted "sexual relations." "It depends on what the meaning of 'is' is," Clinton said at one point, nitpicking at the prosecutor's use of language. As the *Washington Post*'s John Harris noted, the grand jury proceeding, like the entire Lewinsky debate, "was a contest between Starr's absolutism and Clinton's relativism." Starr, like many conservatives, "believed there were truths and lies." Clinton, on the other hand, believed that "truth is often not black and white." Like many liberals, Clinton maintained that since "no one could possess absolute truth, judgement should always be tempered by generosity and tolerance."[43]

That evening, Clinton went on national television to tell the nation about his testimony. A solemn president admitted to the nation that he had misled his wife and the public, confessing to "inappropriate intimate physical contact" with Lewinsky. "It was wrong," the president said. "It constituted a critical lapse in judgment and a personal failure on my part for which I am solely and completely responsible." The president, however, seemed more defiant than contrite, insisting that the "matter is between me, the two people

I love most—my wife and our daughter—and our God," he said. "It's nobody's business but ours. Even Presidents have private lives." He complained that the investigation had "gone on too long, cost too much and hurt too many innocent people."[44]

The following day, Gingrich again suggested caution, saying that the Clinton confession was "part of a much bigger story" and added that "everyone would be best served if they waited for Judge Starr's report and found out what all the facts were." Later, Gingrich told reporters that he believed only "a pattern of felonies" and not "a single human mistake" would constitute grounds for impeachment. "I don't think the Congress could move forward only on Lewinsky, unless he [Starr] had such a clear case, such an overpowering case," Gingrich said. "But I think we would be better served to know the whole story."[45] "There's a high value to stability in our system," he said. "I don't like the idea of changing who the president is capriciously." Realizing that both he and Starr were politically radioactive, Gingrich now tried to reassure the public by making clear that the Judiciary Committee and its chairman, Henry Hyde, would conduct any investigation. "Get it away from me and get it away from Starr," he said. "Get it to Henry, who . . . even the Democrats have sort of set . . . up as the perfect person to preside over this. I think Henry will then have to make the decision."[46]

His words were reassuring to Democrats, but they worried conservatives, who were having trouble figuring out exactly where Gingrich stood. He seemed to have a different standard every week. He went from blasting Clinton in April for being the most corrupt president in history to giving him a free pass in August. House Majority Whip Tom DeLay decided that he needed to take charge of the Republican response to the affair. He told his aides that it would be his mission to drive Clinton from office. "This is going to be the most important thing I do in my political career," he told his aides. "As of today, I want a war room. I want a communications strategy. I want a political strategy. I want you to work day and night."[47] At the end of the day he issued a statement calling for Clinton's resignation. His office would serve as the clearinghouse for the impeachment drive, effectively marginalizing Gingrich and the rest of the Republican leadership. "The Campaign," as his aides dubbed it, would put him on a collision course with the president.

The president, however, was more concerned about the Democratic response, realizing that his fate lay in the hands of his friends, not his enemies. "Republicans are never going to be able to remove you," advisor Doug Sosnik told him, "but Democrats can."[48] Given his rocky relations with his own party, that message was not reassuring. On August 25, Gephardt gave a speech raising the possibility of impeachment. The White House saw it as a warning sign of deep trouble. Even his former close aide George Stephano-poulos, now a commentator for ABC News, reacted angrily to Clinton's call for privacy. "It's bad enough that Bill Clinton defiled his presidency by having sex with an intern of the Oval Office; bad enough that he humiliated his wife and daughter. But President Clinton turned his personal flaws into a public matter when he made the whole country complicit in his cover story," he wrote in *Newsweek*. "This was no impulsive act of passion; it was a coldly calculated political decision."[49] When Democratic Senator Joseph Lieberman followed up on September 3 with a denunciation of Clinton's behavior as "disgraceful" and "immoral," Clinton called a meeting with members of the House and Senate to apologize to them personally.[50]

Clinton's survival strategy included personally accepting blame and re-peatedly apologizing for his lapse of judgment. He told a group of religious leaders at the White House that he agreed "with those who have said that in my first statement after I testified I was not contrite enough," Clinton said, referring to his August 17 address to the nation. "I don't think there is a fancy way to say that I have sinned." At the same time, however, he allowed his lawyers to rigorously defend him while also assailing Starr's tactics. The centerpiece was to demonstrate to the public that he was focused on per-forming the substantive duties of his office. "That is the plan," said Press Secretary Joe Lockhart. "The third part is the most important—and the most important to him. If he took his eye off the ball, if he stopped doing what the voters elected him to do, that's when people would lose faith in him."[51]

With the exception of his brief outbreak in April, Gingrich had stayed above the partisan fray, but by the fall his anger was again getting in the way of his low-key strategy. As was often the case, he was pulled in opposite directions. The statesman wanted to keep a low profile and stay out of the crossfire, yet as the leader of the conservative revolution and the fundraiser-in-chief for the party, he needed to fire up the party faithful. Gingrich was walking a political and ideological tightrope, trapped between the divisions within his party, the confused role that he played as both party leader and Speaker, and a campaign strategy that required that he emphasize Democratic scandals without focusing on the president's sex life. As his friend Mel Steely observed: "How could he balance the moral character question with a pre-sentation of the issues that would appeal to both moderates and independents and at the same time appeal to the republican base to be sure they would turn out?"[52]

By September, press reports suggested that the White House was going to highlight the hypocrisy of the president's accusers by exposing their sex lives. *Salon* quoted "one close ally of the president" in charging that "die-hard

Clinton loyalists" were raising "the threat of exposing the sexual improprieties of Republican critics." Among those mentioned were Gingrich.[53] On September 2, 1998, Bowles sent Gingrich a note refuting a newspaper account that someone in the White House was delving into his personal life. "If I find a single instance of this I will fire that person," he wrote.[54]

The investigations took a personal toll on Clinton. During the summer of 1997 when the right wing was revolting against him, Gingrich confessed to a friend that he felt like "half of his body was dead." At the time, when told the remark, Clinton did not understand it. But now he did, and he used the same phrase to describe himself. The two men, who just a few months earlier were planning to forge a political coalition and launch an ambitious reform program, were now engaged in mortal combat, both fighting for their political lives. Their cordial relationship had turned decidedly frosty. As recently as October, they had been meeting privately to plot strategy. Now, they were barely on speaking terms and friendly banter had given way to angry recrimination. Clinton's behavior, and Gingrich's inability to get traction in dealing with it, left many people questioning the judgment of both men. The key question, suggested Michael Kelly, is, "Will Bill Clinton's failings trump Newt Gingrich's?" The answer, he wrote, "will determine not only the fall elections but, to a significant degree, whether the Democrats or the Republicans dominate national politics in the years ahead."[55]

| "Because We Can"

A T 4:00 PM ON September 9, a white Ford Windstar and a blue Dodge Ram pulled up to the Capitol and unloaded two copies of the 445-page Starr Report, along with 36 boxes of supporting materials related to the independent counsel's investigation of the president. Gingrich, who had no advance warning that Starr was sending over his report, was attending a Republican leadership meeting at the nearby Library of Congress. After delivering the boxes, Starr's representatives, trailed by eighteen armed police officers and a phalanx of reporters, delivered the documents that formally transferred the materials from the special prosecutor's office to Gingrich and to Minority Leader Gephardt, who was in his Capitol office. "It is in their custody and control now," Starr's spokesman said."[1] With those words, the impeachment drama moved from the grand jury room to the halls of Congress and the White House focus shifted from Kenneth Starr to Newt Gingrich.

The Starr Report, along with all the supporting evidence, was locked away in a secure room on Capitol Hill so no one could view it. The House now needed to write the rules for how to proceed without even having a chance to see the report. Gingrich and Gephardt spent a frantic day trying to prepare the House for the next phase of the impeachment struggle. In many ways, the president's fate was in the hands of two men who disagreed on just about everything except their distrust of him. Politically, they were constant combatants and polar opposites. "They hated each other," recalled *Washington Post* reporter Peter Baker.[2] Gephardt entered the House in 1976, two years before Gingrich, as a prolife conservative. During the 1980s, as he contemplated a run for the presidency, he moved gradually to the left. Gingrich started in politics as a moderate but eventually became the leader of a conservative revolution. Gephardt was low key, with telegenic features and icy blue eyes; Gingrich was bombastic, better suited for close encounters than for television. For the past few years, they maintained a professional relationship, but never pretended to enjoy the other's company. Now they were forced by circumstance to work together on the biggest issue either had ever faced: the possible impeachment of the president. Both had been courted and burned by Clinton. Neither trusted him, but Gephardt was determined to save his presidency as much as Gingrich was now set on destroying it.

Later that day, Gingrich huddled with Gephardt; Hyde; John Conyers Jr., the ranking Democrat on the Judiciary Committee; and the two chief investigators: David Schippers for the Republicans and Abbe Lowell for the Democrats. Both sides pledged to work in the spirit of bipartisanship. "This is as serious a thing as we'll ever do" was how Gingrich opened the meeting. Gephardt promised cooperation. "I'll go halfway and even more to reach a sensible goal," he said. "I don't have any partisan goals or objective here." Both Hyde and Gingrich assured him that bipartisanship would guide all of their actions in the difficult months ahead. "This will ultimately fail if the Democrats don't get on board," Hyde told the group.[3]

The first question the House needed to consider was how to handle the materials that Starr provided. Most Republicans wanted the summary report released immediately. Democrats hoped to give the president's lawyers two days to review the material before it was released. "If the Republicans want to be nonpartisan they may be persuaded to give the president some reasonable period of time" to review the material, Gephardt insisted. He pointed out that the House had given Gingrich an advance look at the report when he was being investigated for ethics violations. Democrats eventually scaled the request down to an hour, but Gingrich and the Republicans held their ground. He feared Clinton's lawyers would leak the most damaging information, spinning it in the most positive light. In a party-line vote the House Rules Committee defeated the request and sent to the full House a resolution to allow immediate release of the Starr Report.

The debate moved to the full House, where Gingrich gave a rare speech from the floor imploring lawmakers to abstain from personal attacks. "Members engaging in debate must abstain from language personally offensive toward the president," he said. Republican leaders hoped to have the report summary on the Internet within an hour of the vote. Some Democrats condemned the "lynch mob" mentality of the Republicans, claiming they had ignored the issue of "fundamental fairness" by denying the president access to the report. Not knowing what was contained in the report, however, they were unwilling to align themselves too closely with Clinton. When the debate ended, most Democrats, not wanting the public to view them as obstructionists, joined with Republicans, and the House voted by an overwhelming 363 to 63 vote to publish the summary. They agreed to make public eighteen boxes of supplemental material on September 28, after the Judiciary Committee removed unnecessary or offensive references.[4]

Many Americans were appalled, and fascinated, by the level of sexually explicit detail in the Starr Report. America Online reported that its members spent a record 10.1 million hours online the day the report was released. The file was downloaded 750,000 times, and most major newspapers reprinted the full 112,000-word text.[5] The narrative report read, according to the *Washington Post*'s Peter Baker, "more like a bad Harlequin romance than a legal document."[6] It revealed, in graphic detail, that over a fourteen-month period beginning in November 1995, Clinton had nine sexual encounters with Lewinsky and fifteen phone-sex conversations, and then lied about it to his aides, to the country, and under oath. The summary claimed "substantial and credible information . . . that may constitute grounds for an impeachment in four categories: perjury, witness-tampering, obstruction of justice and 'abuse of power.'"[7]

Gingrich had hoped that the report would change minds by proving that Clinton had indeed lied under oath. Realizing that he was perceived as a highly partisan figure, Gingrich went out of his way in the days and weeks following the delivery of the Starr Report to assure just about anyone who would listen that he was taking a back seat in the proceedings and deferring to Judiciary Committee Chairman Hyde. Gingrich avoided making headlines as much as possible, and when he did speak about the proceedings, his words were carefully measured and balanced. Even his hometown newspaper, which was often highly critical of him, noticed a decided change in the Speaker's tone and language. "In another time, Newt Gingrich would have relished an all-out attack on President Clinton as much as any other Republican in the House of Representatives," noted the *Atlanta Journal-Constitution.* "He would have scoffed at party elders who tried to rein in his speeches on the House floor, speeches that first made his national reputation. Gingrich would have regarded his more reticent colleagues as too timid at a time when they should have been pressing their partisan advantage. But in 1998, as the Speaker of the House, Gingrich is managing the most delicate issue of his long career in Congress by publicly urging caution and forgoing by the dozen opportunities to speak out."[8]

While Gingrich was keeping a low profile, Gephardt was taking charge of the president's defense in the House, carefully orchestrating strategy with the

White House. It was ironic that the man Clinton had planned to abandon just a few months earlier was now responsible for trying to save his presidency. Gephardt adopted a page from the Gingrich handbook. In the first two years of the Clinton presidency, Gingrich tried to muddy the political waters by making the president appear incompetent and out of touch, often turning legislative victories into public relations defeats. Now, Gephardt hoped to undermine public faith in the impeachment process by painting the Republicans with the brush of partisanship. The Democrats did not have to win the votes; they just needed to make the Republicans look like bloodthirsty partisans. "We're going to win by losing," Gephardt said.[9]

As the nation was digesting the Starr Report, it prepared for the next steamy delivery: "Bill and Monica, The Video"—specifically, four hours of videotapes of Clinton's August 17 grand jury testimony scheduled to be released with the next batch of material on September 28. The rumor circulating on Capitol Hill was that the video provided an unflattering picture of a president who was angry, defensive, and evasive. Republicans wanted it released; Democrats were nervous. In addition to the videotapes, there were boxes of potentially explicit material that both sides agreed needed to be reviewed since it contained confidential FBI interviews and other materials that should remain sealed. Lawyers for both sides combed though the material, identifying information that should be removed. Realizing they agreed on most of the redactions, the Democrats decided to go back and intentionally expand the list in the hopes of provoking a fight with the Republicans.[10]

While fighting over the release of the additional material, *Salon* magazine revealed that Henry Hyde had had an extramarital affair some thirty years earlier. "Ugly times call for ugly tactics," a *Salon* editor explained.[11] The redaction battle and the accusations against Hyde, which Republicans mistakenly assumed had been orchestrated by the White House, poisoned the atmosphere and killed any hope of bipartisanship. "The result is an environment with all the subtle niceties of a prison race riot," observed the *National Journal*.[12] Gingrich asked FBI Director Louis Freeh to investigate the matter, writing that "there is credible evidence than an organized campaign of slander and intimidation may exist," and even naming White House aide Sidney Blumenthal as a possible source.

On September 18, the Judiciary Committee voted again along party lines to release the videotape of Clinton's grand jury testimony, along with 2,800 pages of additional material. The two sides agreed on 120 deletions, but Republicans voted to deny 11 additional redactions. The closed-door sessions were followed by dueling press conferences where Republicans described the meetings as "civil" and "bipartisan." Democrats blasted Gingrich and the Republicans for orchestrating a smear campaign against the president. "This is a public relations campaign for impeachment," complained Barney Frank.[13]

Gephardt had manufactured a partisan confrontation, and the Republicans played right into his hands. It was ironic that Gingrich, a master of partisan intrigue, was caught flatfooted, pleading for bipartisanship, while his Democratic rivals elbowed for political advantage. The public was clearly siding with the Democrats. On September 21, an estimated 22 million Americans watched the president's testimony on television. Millions more read transcripts published in special sections of newspapers and magazines, or watched on the Internet. Instead of producing a backlash against Clinton, the release of the videotape elicited sympathy and support. Many Americans empathized with a man defending himself against a humiliating intrusion into his private life. In his more than four hours of testimony, Clinton appeared both contrite and defiant. "I'd give anything in the world not to have to admit what I've had to admit today," he said. While admitting to "inappropriate intimate contact" with the onetime White House intern, he insisted that he had not lied when he denied having "sexual relations" with her.[14] Oral sex, he declared, did not fit under the restricted definition provided by the prosecution. Knowing that the tape would eventually make it into the public, Clinton never lost his composure.

As much as Republicans tried to make the debate over the rule of law, for most Americans it was all about sex. The release of the evidence that was supposed to convince the public that Clinton should be removed from office had the opposite impact: it bolstered his already formidable approval ratings as high as 68 percent in a CBS survey. Democrats also successfully painted Starr as an overzealous, partisan prude determined to bring down the president. Even more discouraging for Gingrich, a *New York Times* poll revealed that many Americans were focusing their anger not at Clinton for his actions, but at Starr and the Republicans for making them public. Nearly 75 percent disapproved of the way the Judiciary Committee was handling the affair, and three-quarters said it was a mistake to release the video. Only 27 percent wanted Congress to go forward with impeachment, while 43 percent wanted the whole matter dropped.[15]

There was also a growing popular belief that, despite his public professions of bipartisanship and claims of maintaining his distance from the mechanics of the investigation, Gingrich was still the man calling the shots behind the scenes. Even some Republicans expressed public doubts. "He calls the shots," a committee chairman told the British newspaper, the *Observer*. "If tapes are going to be released, it's his decision. If hearings are going to be held, he'll decide. He consults and listens, but makes the calls." The *Observer* saw the battle over impeachment as another phase in the ongoing Clinton–Gingrich wars. "There is a sense, emerging from the fray, of Clinton and Gingrich now engaged in mortal combat in which Gingrich—adopting a statesmanlike demeanor but waging partisan warfare—seeks to wreak his revenge for playing second fiddle to his political nemesis."[16]

Emboldened by the poll numbers, the president's supporters took the partisan gloves off. The key to keeping Democrats together was to focus their anger at Gingrich, not Clinton. "If you ask a House Democrat how they feel about Bill Clinton, you'll get a broad range of answers," said a Democratic strategist. "But they all feel the same about Newt Gingrich."[17] Gephardt wrote a three-page letter to the Speaker, which was quickly leaked to the press, warning that the House investigation had "veered seriously off course," and blaming the Speaker for the problem. He cited the refusal to give Clinton an advance look at the report, along with the "unnecessary release of graphic sexual material" that was included in Starr's report as evidence of a "failure of earnest bipartisanship."[18] Democratic political operative James Carville accused Gingrich of masterminding the House impeachment inquiry and arm-twisting Republican lawmakers. "This entire thing has been under the orchestration, supervision and direction of Newt Gingrich and independent counsel Kenneth Starr," Carville said on NBC's *Meet the Press.* Referring to the Speaker's ethics problems, he called Gingrich "a sanctioned, certified, adjudicated and confessed liar." Charles Rangel joined in, telling CNN that with Gingrich leading the investigation "it's going to be a political question, and only a political question."[19]

The procedural debates about whether to release the Starr Report were all a prelude to the most significant decision: whether the evidence submitted warranted opening a full impeachment inquiry of the president. In October, the White House tried to short-circuit the impeachment process by letting it be known that the president was ready to accept some form of punishment short of removal from office—likely a censure by Congress combined with a financial penalty. The censure option provided the Democrats with an alternative to impeachment that was more in line with the public mood: it would allow them to express their disapproval of the president's behavior without removing him from office. The White House made it clear that if Republicans failed to go along with censure, Gingrich would bear the blame for a process that could "drag on and on and on endlessly."[20]

When asked about the prospect of a deal that would avoid a full impeachment hearing, Hyde told reporters that such a decision was "above my paygrade." Gingrich, however, quickly rejected the move. "For anybody to talk about doing anything before we finish the investigative process simply puts the cart before the horse," he said.[21] The White House jumped on the comments, saying they offered proof that Gingrich, not Hyde, was calling the shots on impeachment. "Those who are trying to bring this matter to closure by putting forward what are reasonable ideas are getting drowned out by those who seem to want to let this matter go on and on," said White House Press Secretary Michael McCurry.[22] The following day, Hyde held a press conference to reassert his control. "I was selected to chair this committee, presumably not as a delegate of the Speaker's office, but as a person who has some autonomy." While Hyde was reasserting his power, Gingrich went back into mute mode, refusing to make any public comments about the investigation. At one point, while listening to a Republican debate about censure, Gingrich stuffed his tie in his mouth and bit it—a sign of his frustration at keeping silent on an issue about which he felt so strongly.

But the damage had been done. Every time that Gingrich's name or face appeared in the news, it reinforced the message from the White House: impeachment represented another effort by the highly partisan, and personally vindictive, Speaker to accomplish what he failed to achieve in the budget shutdown—the destruction of the Clinton presidency. "Politically it's pretty clear what the White House is trying to do," a Republican strategist told the *Washington Post,* "which is to make this a referendum between Clinton and Gingrich."[23]

The highly public squabble between Hyde and Gingrich distracted attention from the growing rift between Gephardt and the White House over how to handle the upcoming vote on whether to open an impeachment investigation. Clinton wanted House Democrats to shut down the investigation. The Republicans, he believed, would eventually have to face the reality that the public did not support impeachment. Gephardt rejected the White House strategy and instead announced that he would support an abbreviated impeachment inquiry that would have a specific deadline—December 31—and be limited in scope to matters referred to Congress by Starr. The move surprised Clinton and angered some of his supporters. James Carville complained that if the Republicans accepted the Democratic alternative, it would undermine the strategy of making the whole process appear partisan. "How can you be so goddamn stupid?" Carville shouted. White House advisor Rahm Emanuel reassured him, pointing out that the Republicans were so set on impeachment that they would never accept the offer. "Their stupidity will never allow them" to take the offer, he said.[24]

Emanuel was right. Although polls were showing that a majority of the public supported a vote for censure and opposed impeachment, a combination of personal anger and political calculus led Gingrich to support widening the scope of the investigation into Clinton's actions. Gingrich insisted that the debate not be limited to the Starr Report, but instead include the panoply of Clinton "scandals"—from Whitewater to Travelgate. Although Starr had found no evidence of wrongdoing on any of these issues, Gingrich did not want to let go. He believed that Clinton was one scandal away from impeachment. Lying under oath in a federal court proceeding should have been enough, but the president had skillfully redefined the debate and stigmatized Starr and the House Republicans. Seeing the Lewinsky story in the broader context would make the president's character, and not his sexual escapades, the central issue. Gingrich also refused to let go of the campaign finance investigations. Not only was he still angry that Clinton used the money to run thousands of ads demonizing him, but also the committee looking into the issue suspected the administration may have given China the technology needed to upgrade its long-range nuclear missiles in exchange for campaign contributions. "Newt thinks we can hang Clinton on this one," a GOP aide told *Roll Call*.[25]

On October 8, with Gingrich wielding the gavel, the House debated the Republican motion to authorize the Judiciary Committee to undertake a formal impeachment investigation. Hyde implored his colleagues to remember their "duty," claiming "this isn't about sexual misconduct any more than Watergate was about a third-rate burglary." While Republican speakers spoke solemnly about their responsibility for upholding the judicial system and the "rule of law," Democrats claimed that impeachment was more about partisan politics than about high principles. "The president betrayed his wife," said Robert Wexler of Florida. "He did not betray the country."[26]

By the time the debate over whether to proceed with impeachment had ended, Clinton joined Andrew Johnson and Richard Nixon as only the third American president to face an official impeachment investigation. The House vote, largely along partisan lines—256 to 178—lacked the bipartisan moral authority of the sweeping 410–4 consensus for an impeachment inquiry against Nixon. Only thirty-one Democrats, mostly first-year members facing tough re-election challenges and representatives from swing districts in the South, voted with the Republicans. The vote authorized the House Judiciary Committee to take whatever time it needed to investigate the president, and gave it the right to examine every aspect of the administration, from Lewinsky to campaign finance abuse. Afterward, a contrite Clinton said that he had "surrendered" to whatever fate Congress intended for him. "I hope that we can now move forward with this process in a way that is fair, that is constitutional, and that is timely," Clinton said. "It is not in my hands. It is in the hands of Congress and the people of this country, ultimately in the hands of God. There is nothing I can do."

Despite the obvious historical comparison to Watergate, most observers were struck by the differences in both tone and substance between the debate over Clinton's transgressions and Nixon's crimes. "The Nixon crisis, at least as we remember it, was full of grave figures making grave decisions," noted *Newsweek*. "The atmosphere in the House last week had all the grandeur of Ft. Lauderdale at spring break. As the allegedly momentous vote approached, seats were empty and rhetoric nearly so."[27] In one of the more tense moments, Democrat Nancy Pelosi drew a round of partisan cheers and hisses from the opposition when she accused Republicans of a double standard. She looked straight at Gingrich, who was presiding over the debate, and reminded him that in early 1997 he had admitted lying under oath to the House Ethics Committee and had not been deposed. "We all agree that lying is wrong. But why the double standard?" Pelosi asked. "How inconsistent, Mr. Speaker, for this Republican majority to move to an impeachment inquiry of the president about his personal life."

In retrospect, the partisan vote represented a major victory for the president, and a serious problem for Gingrich. As Nancy Gibbs and Michael Duffy observed in *Time,* by embracing the Democratic alternative, Republicans could have appeared "fair and statesmanlike . . . and awakened on Friday to headlines saying that more lawmakers had voted to investigate Bill Clinton than Richard Nixon." Instead, "they handed the Democrats the chance to tar the whole process as a vendetta." In exchange for a few small concessions, the Republicans would have involved the Democrats in the impeachment process. The burden would have been on Democrats to show the process unfair, rather than on Republicans to prove it fair.[28] Once again, Gingrich played into their hands. If Gingrich had been less a polarizing figure, if he had developed more goodwill toward House Democrats, Republicans might have been more successful in focusing public anger at Clinton rather than drawing it toward themselves. The move guaranteed that the public would view the entire impeachment proceeding as little more than a partisan exercise—precisely what Clinton wanted. "I wasn't surprised," Clinton reflected, "we were just a month away from the midterm elections and the Republicans were running a single-issue campaign: get Clinton."[29]

When he needed him most, Clinton could always count on Gingrich to save his presidency by trying to destroy it. Unwilling to get into another battle with the president, Gingrich had initially placed all his faith in Starr, but he later realized that the special prosecutor misplayed his hand by focusing on sex. "If Starr had written a twenty-five-page report on the meaning of felony, and not said a word about sex, it would have been infinitely worse for the president," he reflected years later.[30] By October it was clear that the president had successfully defined the issue, and the public had lost interest in impeachment. For now, Gingrich wanted to keep the issue on the front burner for the elections in November. Some aides speculated that if the Republicans made a respectable showing, Gingrich would have pushed his party to reach some compromise and avoid a long, costly impeachment trial. Gingrich, however, was always better at provoking confrontation than he was at preventing it. "As the impeachment combat begins," noted *Time*'s Karen Tumulty, "the challenge for Clinton and Gingrich will be to avoid each other's traps—and their own. Because if their past as sparring partners offers any lesson, it's that they need each other to survive."[31]

The impeachment battle brought out the worst qualities in both men, revealing their penchant for self-pity and self-denial. They personalized the impeachment struggle, oversimplified the issues involved, and, perhaps most of all, turned each other into one-dimensional caricatures. Once again, their misunderstandings led to miscalculation. By viewing impeachment as part of a Gingrich-led conspiracy to remove him from office, Clinton dismissed the legitimate concerns of many Republicans and moderate Democrats who were genuinely outraged by his actions. Gingrich came to believe his own conspiratorial rhetoric and convinced himself that the president, to whom he had hitched his own political fortunes just a few months earlier, was engaged in a systematic campaign to corrupt the Constitution. In reality, the Lewinsky affair left both men with less power. Clinton was fighting to keep his presidency alive; Gingrich was struggling to maintain his delicate juggling act as both Speaker and leader of the Republican Revolution.

By the fall of 1998, Gingrich was unable to control his anger, despite overwhelming evidence that the public wanted to end the debate over impeachment and put an end to the Lewinsky matter. Polls showed that most people agreed that the president lied about the affair. Yet his approval ratings climbed, support for impeachment dropped, and anger at Starr and the House Republicans spiked. It seemed Clinton rose higher in the polls with each new revelation of wrongdoing. "He was befuddled," observed Mel Steely. "He had seen his own approval ratings nose dive, now the President was guilty of far greater offenses, and he seemed to rise in stature."[32]

Down Pennsylvania Avenue, Clinton complained about the hypocrisy of Gingrich and the Republican leaders. The House Ethics Committee had found Gingrich guilty of lying, but they voted for a reprimand. In his case, they pursued impeachment. Why? "This was about power," he wrote, "about something the House Republican leaders did because they could, and because they wanted to pursue an agenda I opposed and had blocked."[33] Although Clinton possessed a remarkable ability to collect facts and to synthesize information, he seemed incapable of changing self-destructive aspects of his character. He protested that his sex life was private, but he knew from the Gary Hart affair in 1987 that the rules governing how the press dealt with questions previously considered private had changed. Whether fair or not, he knew better than anyone the intensity of the opposition to him, and how his opponents had always used sex as a marker to demonstrate that he had rejected mainstream values. According to his biographer David Maraniss, "The reality that Clinton never seemed willing to deal with was that his risk was not his alone; that his actions had consequences not just for himself and his family and friends, but also for millions of people, some who believed in him, some who cared about his policies, some who despised his enemies and did not want them to prevail, some who just wanted to think positively about human nature."[34]

Privately, he complained that the Speaker and many other Republicans were holding him to a higher standard than they held themselves. It was a constant source of puzzlement for Clinton and his allies that his behavior was always open to public scrutiny, but his critics were held to a different standard. "We were aware of a degree of hypocrisy on the other side," a White House official confessed. Unlike Clinton, who had his entire sex life exposed in excruciatingly embarrassing detail, Gingrich was never forced to confess his sins, or even to account for his past behavior. In 1995, the year Gingrich was elected Speaker and was arguably the second most powerful political figure in America, author Gail Sheehy had painted a revealing portrait of the "inner" Gingrich for *Vanity Fair.* She interviewed a woman, Anne Manning, who claimed to have had an affair with Gingrich in 1977. "We had oral sex," Manning told Sheehy. "He prefers that *modus operandi* because then he can say, 'I never slept with her.'" She also claimed that Gingrich warned her not to tell anyone about the affair. "If you ever tell anybody about this, I'll say you're lying."[35]

The rumors of Gingrich's affairs did not end with Manning in 1977. In 1994, the investigative reporter David Corn followed up rumors that the soon-to-be Speaker was having an affair with House congressional aide Calista Bisek. At the time he was fifty and she was twenty-seven, only a few years older than Lewinsky. Corn worked with a tabloid television show to stake out Gingrich's apartment, hoping to catch a glimpse of Bisek coming or going at unusual hours. She never showed up. "My guess at the time was that Gingrich, just weeks away from being handed the speaker's gavel, realized he was under intense scrutiny, and may therefore have been acting with more caution than previously had seemed necessary to him," Corn recalled. He, and the rest of the press corps, dropped the story. The story remained the subject of gossip and rumors until 1999 when both the *New York Post* and the New York *Daily News* published stories about the affair. "Newt's Fooling Around with His Girl on the Hill," the *Post* shouted.[36]

Gingrich had usually brushed off questions about his infidelity, and the press rarely pursued the issue. In 1994, when questioned by the *Washington Post* about infidelity during his first marriage, he said, "In the 1970s, things happened—period. That's the most I'll ever say."[37] When asked about the similarities between his behavior and the president's, he simply responded, "I haven't led a perfect life," often followed by, "I did not lie to a federal judge under oath." He never formally acknowledged his affair with Bisek, whom he later married, until March 2007 when he confessed in a telephone call with Focus on the Family leader James Dobson. At the time, Gingrich was testing the waters for a possible 2008 presidential run and needed to win the support of conservative voters. "There were times I was praying and I felt I was doing things that were wrong but I was still doing them," he said. "I look back on periods of weakness that I was not proud of."[38]

Why did the press give Gingrich such wide latitude, while being so aggressive in pursuing questions of Clinton's infidelity? Since he never ran for national office, journalists were reluctant to raise, or pursue, questions about his private life. More important, although rumors of his various affairs dated back to the late 1970s, the press never took Gingrich seriously enough to treat his indiscretions as a major issue. Until 1994, they saw him as a conservative gadfly, a distinctly local figure. "Newt wasn't important enough to have his private life be a focal point for the national media," observed Chip Kahn.[39] After the Gary Hart incident, it was considered fair game to highlight the private lives of prominent national politicians, but even then reporters were reluctant to probe too deeply into the sex lives of congressional candidates, and when they did, it was often difficult to prove infidelity. Even the Lewinsky investigation was the product of unique circumstances: the president's reckless actions, a zealous special prosecutor, an ongoing high-profile case of sexual harassment, and the unusual alliance among inveterate "Clinton haters."

Even when the press did report on rumors of Gingrich's infidelity, the mainstream national media paid little attention. In part, the differences in media coverage reflected a contrast in personal style. "Sexuality was part of Clinton's persona," observed a Gingrich associate. "It was never part of Newt's persona. Newt is still basically a nerd." As one Clinton watcher said, "It's not that Clinton seduces women. It's that he seduces everyone."[40] Oddly enough for an advocate of traditional values, Gingrich was helped because eventually he divorced and, on two occasions, married the women with whom he had affairs. In that sense, Clinton was paying a heavy price for maintaining his marriage.

―――

The struggle over impeachment provided a backdrop to the negotiations over the budget. In the previous budget deal, Clinton and Gingrich worked out compromises that angered liberal House Democrats and many conservative Republicans. This time Clinton and the Democrats forged a united front. It was a sign of weakness, not strength. With hopes of a coalition with Gingrich dead, and Republicans determined to remove him from office, Clinton needed to keep his party united behind him. In the past, he and the House leadership had engaged in bitter fights over the budget priorities. Now, the president used the budget process to win back the support of disaffected Democrats. "We had no leverage in '98," recalled Bowles. "The whole strategy in '98 was 'rope a dope.'"[41]

The president may have lacked political weight to score points against the Republicans, but he still possessed a powerful counterpunch in the threat of another government shutdown. In August, Bowles delivered the blunt message: produce a budget that "maintains fiscal discipline" while also expanding "the critical investments" the president deemed necessary or face a shutdown. "There is no need for a government shutdown," he warned, "but if there is one it will be because Republicans have either not done their job on time and finished the budget or have decided to short-change critical investments in our nation's future."[42]

On October 9, the day after Democrats voted against the Republican impeachment plan, Clinton invited forty House and Senate Democrats to the White House to discuss strategy for the budget. According to an account in *Newsweek*, Clinton "told them he wanted to face down Gingrich on the budget—would they be willing to stay in Washington for a protracted battle?" Most members were initially skeptical. They wanted to get home and campaign and did not want to be stuck in Washington debating details of the budget. The president made clear that despite impeachment, he had the upper hand because Gingrich could not afford to provoke another shutdown so close to an election. If the Democrats held firm, he believed they could extract significant concessions. To help entice Democrats still reluctant to put their political faith in him, Clinton sweetened the pot, promising to fight for additional money for popular environmental and education programs. After the meeting, the leaders marched together before the television cameras as a defiant Clinton made clear that he wanted $1.1 billion to hire 100,000 new teachers.[43] One Democrat roamed the halls telling colleagues to get what they needed, because "Christmas has come early."

Clinton's audacity shocked Gingrich, who could not understand why Democrats who had opposed the president in the past would rally behind him now. "People can't figure it out," said South Carolina Republican Mark Sanford. "How this guy can be down and out, and now he's the one calling the shots?" Many conservatives wanted to stay in Washington and fight, but Gingrich decided to accommodate political reality. He realized that the president could use the threat of a veto to hold Republicans in Washington right up until election day. Not only would such a move prevent Republicans from getting back to their districts to campaign, but it would keep the debate focused on issues that helped Democrats, such as the environment and education. Gingrich decided to make concessions. "They're basically bringing money to us in a wheelbarrel," Clinton joked.[44] In the end, Gingrich won $9 billion in extra funds for defense programs and provisions against Internet porn, but gave into Clinton demands for $1.1 billion for new teachers.[45]

The press declared Clinton the winner in the budget battle. The *New York Times* said the "biggest victory" went to Clinton, "who demonstrated his power to influence Congress even as Congress considers whether to impeach him." The best Republicans could brag about "may have been their ability to get out of town without drawing blame for disrupting the Government."[46] The White House not only won the public relations war, but they also managed to deflate and divide the opposition at the same time. "We had seven bad months and seven good days," joked a Clinton aide. Conservatives viewed the contest as another defeat for Gingrich. For many young conservatives, the 4,000-page, $500 billion budget resulted from the kind of horse trading they had come to Washington to reject. Barr, who dismissed the budget as "a bloated, pork-laden, spending bill," recalled how Gingrich went around to every member in a close race and asked what they needed in the bill to help win. "That is exactly what the Democrats used to do," he said. "It left conservatives feeling uneasy."[47]

On October 20, having completed the successful budget negotiations, Clinton announced that Erskine Bowles would be stepping down as chief of staff. With no more deals to be made, Bowles no longer had a purpose in the White House and he was eager to return to private life. He suggested John Podesta fill his position. A former trial lawyer and political consultant, Podesta had started out as the White House staff secretary in Clinton's first term. He became the administration's "scandal man," leading an in-house investigation into the Travel Office firings and closely monitoring the Whitewater probe. He left the administration briefly before the 1996 election, but Bowles hired him back as deputy chief of staff in 1997. Once the Lewinsky story broke, he served as the White House political point man, coordinating strategy and helping define the message. Clinton initially resisted, fearing that Podesta was a political warrior, someone you brought in to burn bridges, not build them. Eventually he relented. House liberals welcomed the change, viewing it as proof that triangulation was dead.

———

Gingrich was confident that the Lewinsky affair could only help Republicans in the fall elections. A president's party always lost seats in the off-year election of a second term, and it was likely that voters would want to send a signal of their anger to the administration by voting against its party in the elections. If nothing else, the scandal would leave Democrats so dispirited that they would stay home. At best, it would produce a backlash that would push Democrats to vote for Republican candidates. In addition, Gingrich believed that the Starr Report would produce outrage among Christian conservatives and drive them to the polls in record numbers. "When things happen that make one side's partisans unhappy, they stay home. When they stay home, they stay home for the whole ticket," Gingrich told a crowd of Young Republicans in suburban Atlanta. "I believe this fall we're going to see a surprisingly big Republican victory almost everywhere in this country," Gingrich predicted.[48]

As they looked to the elections, both Clinton and Gingrich were playing to their base. The elections were turning into a clash of wills between the two men, who less than a year earlier had tried to reach across the aisle and form a centrist coalition. "Forget sex. Forget lies. Forget videotape. Forget redactions, the Linda Tripp tapes, Ken Starr, Al Gore, Richard Gephardt, Henry Hyde, John Conyers, and all the bit players on the Judiciary Committee. From now to Election Day there's only one story line," wrote Major Garrett in U.S. News and World Report: "Clinton versus Gingrich."[49]

Although Gingrich did not want to allow Clinton to hold Republicans hostage in Washington and refocus the debate on issues favorable to Democrats, he also feared that Republicans were going to get caught in the trap of talking only about impeachment and morality. Republicans risked a backlash if they appeared preoccupied with Lewinsky and failed to put forward a positive agenda that would highlight the broader ideological differences between Democrats and Republicans. On the campaign trail in the final weeks, Gingrich never mentioned the word "impeachment," and instead touted the Republican record of welfare reform, tax relief, and increased defense spending. Campaigning in Wisconsin, Gingrich told a crowd gathered for a football game between the San Francisco 49ers and the Green Bay Packers that the election was "a choice between two teams. One that believes in higher taxes, bigger Government and more power in Washington. The other believes in lower taxes, smaller Government and more power in Wisconsin." When asked by reporters about the possibility of impeachment, he blamed the media for its "maniacal fixation" on the Lewinsky affair. "It's not about gossip and scandal in the White House," Gingrich told the crowd. "This election is about major policy questions and two very different directions the country could go in."[50]

Clinton believed that the party with the best national message would win, and in this case, it was the Democrats who were on message, focusing on their agenda of saving Social Security, putting 100,000 more teachers in the schools, and passing a Patients' Bill of Rights.[51] Democrats once again used Gingrich to help fire up the party faithful. For example, in Maryland, Democratic Senator Barbara Mikulski attacked her Republican challenger, Ellen Sauerbrey, claiming at a Halloween rally that she was "masquerading" as a moderate. "When she takes off the mask, takes off the makeup, she's nothing but Newt Gingrich in high heels and earrings," she said.[52]

The Republicans raised the political stakes in the final weeks leading up to the elections when the Republican Congressional Campaign Committee (RCCC) produced a controversial ad campaign, "Operation Breakout," which focused on the president's character. The RCCC was responding to pressure from conservatives, who felt the party had failed to lay down clear ideological markers for the public. As earlier, they believed that by compromising with the president on so many issues, Gingrich had conceded many critical Republican issues to the Democrats. Clinton could brag that he had balanced the budget, cut taxes, ended welfare, and placed more police officers on the streets. Unable to get ideological traction on standard Republican issues, conservatives believed the party needed to make Clinton's character and behavior the central issue. "In every election, there is a big question to think about," said one of the ads. "This year, the question is: Should we reward . . . Bill Clinton? And should we reward not telling the truth?"[53]

There was a serious debate whether to air the ads. Pollster Linda DiVall told Gingrich not to air them, saying that her focus groups showed that the spots excited conservatives but alienated moderate and independent voters, who were going to decide many key elections. "Many of the ads I strongly recommended not be run were," she recalled.[54]

The Clinton White House jumped all over the story, claiming that Gingrich orchestrated the $10 million campaign focused on the Lewinsky scandal. A gleeful Al Gore called a news conference to denounce the attacks, which he claimed were "personally devised by Speaker Newt Gingrich." He described them as "more personal ads, more personal attacks, more partisan investigations, more of the politics of personal destruction." Gephardt sent the Speaker a letter, released to the public, saying that by masterminding the ad campaign Gingrich had "forfeited" his "legitimacy as Speaker." Once the ads proved controversial, even some Republicans saw the benefit of dumping the whole issue on Gingrich's lap, telling the press that the Speaker had detailed knowledge of the ads and had specifically authorized their use.[55] The press picked up on the theme, suggesting that Gingrich focused on Lewinsky because he had run out of ideas. "Gingrich looked to Monica as his deliverance from having to come up with a new, new Republican Revolution," observed *Time*'s Margaret Carlson.[56]

The reality, however, was much different. "Newt had only vague knowledge of the ads," claimed Joe Gaylord, who as head of the National Republican Campaign Committee (NRCC) was directly responsible for the decision to develop and air them. The Speaker's press secretary, Christina Martin, truthfully responded to the criticism by stating that Gingrich "was aware but not involved in either the scripting or the execution of the ads." She added, "Newt Gingrich was no more a part of these ads than Al Gore was a part of Bill Clinton's inappropriate behavior." In addition to exaggerating the extent of Gingrich's involvement in the campaign, the White House magnified both the cost and the personal nature of the ads. Only three of the twenty-nine spots crafted as part of the $10 million campaign focused on Clinton's integrity, and they were scheduled to air in small markets in specific congressional districts around the country. The spots were originally designed to fly under the national radar screen, targeting conservatives without antagonizing moderates. In addition, the three ads did not dwell on the fact that the president had engaged in an inappropriate sexual relationship, but instead focused on his efforts to cover it up. One ad showed the infamous video clip of Clinton wagging his finger as he denied the Lewinsky affair. But like the LBJ "daisy ad" from 1964, which contrasted images of a young girl picking daisies with the countdown toward a nuclear explosion, the anti-Clinton spots attracted national media attention. They were featured on all the leading news networks, dominated discussion among television pundits, and made the front page of the *New York Times*. Most of the news coverage repeated the White House charges, reinforcing the perception that Gingrich was once again out of control, leading a highly partisan witch hunt.

The flap over the ads did little to dampen Gingrich's expectations about the election. Interviewing him just a week before the election, *Washington Post*'s Dan Balz reported that Gingrich's "confidence appears boundless," saying that he was predicting an across-the-board sweep. "Only Republicans cowed by the liberal news media and a Beltway mentality fear President Clinton," he declared. "I don't know a single policy debate he's won this year. So why are we afraid of him? This is not 1996."[57] A few days later, Gingrich told the *Atlanta Journal:* "If everything breaks against us, my guess is we'll be about plus 10. If everything breaks for us, will be much closer to plus 40."[58] According to James Rogan, a Republican member of the Judiciary Committee, "Gingrich was telling us in October that we would pick up twenty or thirty seats—plus. We were going to come back with a windfall of seats."[59] As late as the afternoon of election day, Gingrich was confidently predicting a gain of twenty seats.

As the election results trickled in that evening his spirits sunk. "It was a morose night," his press secretary recalled. Republicans lost five seats in the House and made no gains in the Senate, making them the first party since the Civil War to lose seats to a party of an incumbent president in his second term. Gingrich tried to put a positive spin on the disappointing news. At 9:30 PM he entered the ballroom to celebrate his landslide re-election and bragged that Republicans would retain control of the House in three successive elections for the first time in seventy years. A half hour later, he went on CNN. When asked "what happened," he responded, "I don't know." One of the ways he had held on to power was by maintaining the belief that he was smarter than anyone else. "When he admitted on television that he did not know why they had lost, he lost a key advantage," recalled an advisor.

It was a different story at the White House, where President Clinton viewed the election as a repudiation of Gingrich. According to aides, the president was "euphoric" after the election, convinced that the voters had "vindicated" him, sending a clear signal to House Republicans to stop the march toward impeachment. "The American people sent us a message that would break your eardrums if anyone was listening," the president said. "The important thing is, we have to get back to doing the people's business."[60]

The next morning, Gingrich rose early to appear on the morning talk shows. He appeared defensive, blaming the media's "All Monica All the Time" fixation for preventing Republicans from getting their positive message across to voters. Later, in a conference call with several dozen congressmen, he again blamed the media, saying that he had little to do with the anti-Clinton ads that produced the backlash. Most GOP members were not buying it, however. They were angry that Gingrich seemed unable to chart a clear course. That evening, Louisiana Republican Robert Livingston called Gingrich and suggested he step aside. If he did not voluntarily resign, Livingston threatened to run against him for Speaker.

Gingrich worked the phones on Thursday trying to take the temperature of the caucus. He realized he was in trouble. He had helped make the Republicans the majority party in Congress, but now many of his closest supporters refused to endorse him. For Gingrich the biggest blow came when Christopher Shays, a Connecticut moderate who had stuck with him through the ethics fight, told him, "I don't think I can do this anymore." Shays felt the party was paying too high a price defending him. "There was a developing feeling within the Republican membership that he was a drag on the party and their re-election," reflected Bill Archer. Compounding the situation were rumors that Gingrich was having an affair. "Many Republicans felt that with the party about to impeach the president, they could not have as the leader of their party [one] who was so morally flawed," recalled Archer. "There was too much of a contradiction."[61]

On the evening of November 6, 1998, Gingrich announced that he was stepping down as Speaker and resigning his seat in the House at of the end of his term. "He never made himself a figure to the loved," reflected Joe Gaylord. "What he promised were results. When he was unable to produce those results in 1998, he no longer had any purpose."[62]

Gingrich had become a metaphor for excess and partisanship—the very qualities that many Americans disliked most about Washington. He helped set the standards for demonizing his opponents. Clinton, the skillful counter-puncher, used those same tactics against him. "The policies he used to get power were then turned against him once he was in power," recalled Steely.[63] Gingrich never learned to reconcile the expectations of change that he created with the realities of the legislative process. "Ultimately he had difficulty dialing back that rhetoric to the kind of realistic expectations that can be produced by the legislative process," reflected a colleague. "You don't fire up a crowd by telling that politics is the art of the possible. You don't talk about transitional changes. You talk about huge generational shifts in politics." Gingrich was brilliant at getting power, but not good at keeping it. He was a political entrepreneur, not a manager. He repeatedly claimed that im-peachment was not about the president's sex life, but instead about com-mitting perjury, but that seemed like a Clintonesque parsing of words for a man who claimed his mission in life was to "save western civilization" from moral decline. In the end, Gingrich was undone by the politics of moral absolutism that he helped to create. "The man who decried what he called 'a multicultural, nihilistic hedonism that is inherently destructive of a healthy society,' and who blamed liberals for Woody Allen's affair with his step-daughter and for Susan Smith's murder of her two children, can't expect much sympathy when the chickens come to roost on his own bedpost," observed Jay Bookman, editorial writer of the *Atlanta Journal-Constitution.*"[64]

Clinton was visiting friends when he heard the news that Gingrich had resigned. He must have had mixed feelings. He no doubt felt satisfaction that the man who he believed was spearheading the drive to remove him from office had instead been forced to give up his own job. That feeling would have been balanced by a sense of loss at what he and the Speaker could have accomplished had the circumstances been different. Clinton was not only losing a talented adversary, he was losing his favorite foil.

The next day a gracious Gingrich congratulated Clinton on the election, calling it a truly historic victory. The two men had a pleasant conversation. The president told aides that he wanted to send a warm letter to the Speaker, but Gephardt objected to an early draft, claiming it was too effusive. He saw no reason to mourn the Speaker's demise. With aides unable to work out language, Clinton and Gephardt tried to reconcile their differences and finalize the letter over the phone. Gephardt convinced the president to remove a paragraph praising Gingrich for his work on the 1997 balanced budget bill, but Clinton refused to alter the overall tone of the message. "Newt Gingrich has been a worthy adversary, leading the Republican party to a majority in the House, and joining me in a great national debate over how best to prepare America for the 21st Century," the statement read. "Despite our profound differences, I appreciate those times we were able to work together in the national interest, especially Speaker Gingrich's strong support for America's continuing leadership for freedom, peace and prosperity in the world."[65] Gingrich appreciated the gesture. "We in the Speaker's office found it to be a very gracious statement at a time when there was a lot of acrimony in the air," recalled Arne Christenson.[66] Later, the president claimed to have "mixed feelings" about Gingrich's decision to resign. "He had supported me on most foreign policy decisions, had been frank about what his caucus was really up to when the two of us talked alone, and, after the government shutdown battle, had shown flexibility in working out honorable compromises with the White House," he wrote in his memoirs.[67]

A few weeks later, however, Clinton saw the other side of the Speaker—the vengeful, pugnacious side. Gingrich admitted to Erskine Bowles that while most moderates would have preferred to pass a resolution of censure and get the whole Lewinsky affair over with, conservatives were forcing the impeachment vote. The election results sent a clear signal that the public did not want to see a prolonged impeachment trial. Despite all that, Gingrich said they were going ahead with the impeachment vote. A puzzled and always practically minded Bowles asked him why they would continue down that road when the public opposed it, many members of his own party did not support it, and there was no way they could win a trial in the Senate. Gingrich's response stunned him and, later, the president. "Because we can," he said.

CHAPTER SIXTEEN

The End of Reform

S HORTLY AFTER 9:00 AM on Friday, December 18, Illinois Republican
Ray LaHood gaveled the House Chamber to order. Gingrich did not want
his last act as Speaker to be presiding over the impeachment of a president,
and Speaker-designate Robert Livingston did not want it to be his first act, so
they selected LaHood for the task. The chaplain opened the session with a
brief prayer: "Where there is hatred, let us sow love; where there is injury,
pardon; where there is discord, union; where there is doubt, faith; where there
is despair, hope; where there is darkness, light; where there is sadness, joy."

The proceedings were pushed back by a day following the president's
announcement that he was ordering a military strike on Iraq for violating its
agreement on arms inspections. The military maneuvers only added to the
tension in the hall. Republicans were convinced that Clinton had ordered the
strike to distract attention from the impeachment proceedings; Democrats
were angry that Republicans would attempt to undermine the authority of
the commander in chief while American troops were still in harm's way.
While most Republican leaders questioned the timing of the attack, Gingrich
supported the president's decision. "We have a chance today to say to the
world: no matter what our constitutional process, whether it is an election eve
or it is the eve of a constitutional vote, no matter what our debates at home,
we are, as a nation, prepared to lead the world."[1]

At 9:50 AM Henry Hyde stood at a lectern and began making the Republican case for impeachment. "The question before this House is rather
simple," he said. "It is not a question of sex. Sexual misconduct and adultery
are private acts and are none of Congress's business. It is not even a question of
lying about sex. The matter before the House is a question of lying under

oath. This is a public act, not a private act. This is called perjury." Before voting on the four articles against the president, Livingston shocked the House by announcing that he would leave Congress because he was also guilty of having an adulterous affair. He challenged the president to follow his example and resign. "I say that you have the power to . . . heal the wounds that you have created. You, sir, may resign your post."[2]

President Clinton was trying to ignore the proceedings and to go through the motions of a normal day. He was still in shock that Republicans had gone ahead with the impeachment proceedings. Polls showed that a majority of Americans opposed impeachment, and it was clear that the Senate would never muster the two-thirds vote to convict the president. Most of all, he believed the midterm elections sent a loud signal to lawmakers that the American public wanted the whole affair to end.[3]

The president, however, had made a number of miscalculations in the six weeks between the election and the opening of the impeachment debate. Just when there appeared to be some flexibility on the Republican side of the aisle, Clinton angered members of the Judiciary Committee with his defiant response to a questionnaire they sent him on November 5. Not only did he wait until November 28 to respond, but he also continued his convoluted legal argument that the vague definition of "sexual relations" allowed him to claim that he did not have sex with Lewinsky. On other answers, he was vague and evasive. "His answers," the committee said in its report, "are a continuation of a pattern of deceit and obstruction of duly authorized investigations."[4]

The president had also overestimated the potential impact of the election on hardline members of the Judiciary Committee, and on Republicans in general. Although opinion polls showed the public opposed to impeachment and favoring some form of censure, a majority of Republicans, especially party activists, supported impeaching the president. Congressional districts were so gerrymandered that most GOP members represented districts with high concentrations of Republican voters. As a result, congressional Republicans felt little pressure to go along with public sentiment. Most representatives felt they could pursue the case for impeachment without fear of producing a backlash at home. In addition, most Judiciary Committee members were insulated from the November election results. Of the twenty Republican members up for re-election, nine ran without a Democratic opponent, and all but three scored above 60 percent.

In the past, Clinton could usually count on Gingrich to help save him from his own mistakes, but not now. Gingrich kept a low profile after the election. He refused to talk with reporters, failed to attend Republican leadership meetings, and withdrew from discussions about strategy and tactics.

Although the administration had made Gingrich the face of impeachment, his departure made impeachment more, not less, likely. Gephardt saw the problem. "Newt's sworn it off," he said. "Without him, there's no leader to stop it."[5] Oddly enough, after spending months complaining that Gingrich was orchestrating the impeachment drive, the White House and congressional Democrats found themselves publicly pleading with Gingrich to get more involved in the process. "I believe that it is incumbent on you to provide the leadership necessary to move this process forward," Gephardt wrote him. White House Press Secretary Joe Lockhart told reporters that Gingrich and Livingston "need to step up and figure out a way to get this thing resolved expeditiously."[6]

Many moderate Republicans, and even some White House officials, believed that had Gingrich remained as Speaker, even in his weakened position, he could have short-circuited the impeachment process. "Though few realized it at the time, the Democrats would come to miss Gingrich," Evan Thomas wrote in *Newsweek*. "Between bursts of bombast, Gingrich was capable of statesmanship. Had he survived, Newt might have tried to work out a compromise to punish the president short of an impeachment vote."[7] Presidential speechwriter Michael Waldman agreed, pointing out that "Speaker Gingrich's sudden abdication meant that nobody was in charge—nobody to negotiate or wave a yellow flag of caution."[8]

According to Clinton legal advisor Lanny Davis, the White House divided Republicans who favored impeachment into two camps: those who had legitimate intellectual concerns that the president had violated the law and needed to be punished, and those who were driven by a passionate hatred of Clinton. They placed Gingrich in the first group, along with South Carolina's Lindsey Graham and California's Jim Rogan. Davis believed that right after the election there was a brief window when it was possible to negotiate a censure. He was not alone. Clinton aides told *Washington Post* reporter Peter Baker that they believed Gingrich was at heart "a pragmatic politician" and "a deal cutter," who, "having gone through the government shutdown, saw the virtue in not taking things to the cliff."[9] Some moderate House Democrats felt the same way. "By this point, Gingrich is a moderate in the Republican party," reflected Democrat Charles Stenholm.

The White House may have been engaged in wishful thinking. There is little evidence that had Gingrich continued to play an active role he would have tried to derail impeachment. "In the entire time after the November elections, he never once brought up to me the idea that he would short-circuit the Judiciary Committee process," reflected his chief-of-staff Arne Christenson. "He believed the impeachment process needed to go forward and the

House needed to render its judgment."[10] He was not the one driving the train down the track, but he saw no reason to try and stop it.

While Gingrich may not have stopped the impeachment train wreck, his absence complicated the situation for the White House. Even though his replacements were far more partisan and just as determined to push impeachment, they were less well known and not as easy to typecast as Gingrich. Since the government shutdowns in 1995, observed the *National Journal,* "Gingrich had solidified his place alongside such men as Herbert Hoover, Joseph McCarthy, and Richard Nixon in the pantheon of Republicans whom Democrats love to revile. When he disappeared, Democrats were hard-pressed to shift the conversation from Clinton's behavior."[11]

The two men who moved in to fill the power vacuum were also the most ardent supporters of impeachment: Henry Hyde and Majority Whip Tom DeLay. Behind the scenes, DeLay was firing up the conservative base, appearing on dozens of talk radio shows a day, faxing talking points, asking big contributors to talk with members of Congress. "He was a partisan," observed Waldman. "He hated Clinton. And he was determined to see him impeached."[12] His biggest contribution, however, was to pressure the House leadership into blocking Democrats from presenting a censure motion. Most observers believed that had it been presented to the House, it would have won approval, thereby bypassing the entire impeachment process. On December 12, as the House geared up for the impeachment debate, the Republican leadership released a carefully orchestrated series of letters making it clear to the nation, and to moderates in their party, that censure was not an option. Hyde sent Livingston a letter asserting that censure "violates the rules of the House." Livingston followed with his own letter saying censure "would violate the careful balance of separation of powers." Gingrich released a brief letter saying he concurred with Hyde and Livingston.[13]

By the end of the day on December 19, the House had voted on four articles of impeachment against Bill Clinton. The House passed two—one alleging the president committed perjury in his August 17 grand jury testimony, the other that he obstructed justice. But lawmakers rejected the two other articles, which alleged the president committed perjury in his deposition in the Paula Jones lawsuit, and that he abused his power when he tried to cover up the Monica Lewinsky affair. Clinton sat stoically in the dining room adjacent to the Oval Office watching on television as the House voted to impeach him. New Gingrich's last vote as a member of the House of Representatives was to impeach the president. The transmittal letter that accompanied the articles of impeachment to the Senate carried his signature. In one of the last speeches he gave on the floor, however, Gingrich applauded

Clinton for bombing Iraq. It was appropriate that he would close out his formal relations with the president by sending mixed signals.

———

While Congress was laying the groundwork for impeachment, both sides continued working on a possible Social Security reform package. Throughout the year, the president kept the issue before the public, making it a topic of his weekly radio addresses, giving speeches, and holding town hall meetings. Warning that it is better to "fix the roof when the sun is shining," he pleaded for a bipartisan solution. He had hoped that his efforts would culminate in a White House summit scheduled for December, which would bring together all the interested parties, highlight areas of agreement, and provide Congress with an added incentive to pass a historic Social Security reform bill. Instead, by the time the conference was convened, Social Security reform was a minor sideshow to the larger impeachment drama taking place on Capitol Hill. The parties were profoundly divided, and goodwill was a scarce commodity. On the day the impeachment debate began on the House floor, Podesta called a meeting of the senior staff. "This is going to be a hard week," he predicted. After hearing reports from various aides, Podesta turned to National Economic Council Director Gene Sperling and asked, "Gene, how's our 'bipartisan Social Security process?' " According to Waldman, "the room erupted in laughter."[14]

The president convened his scheduled two-day White House conference on Social Security on December 8. At the same time, his attorneys were on Capitol Hill engaged in a last-minute effort to slow down a party-line impeachment vote on the House Judiciary Committee scheduled for later that week. Clinton opened the conference on a hopeful note. "The stakes are too high, the issues far too important," Clinton told more than 250 participants drawn from Congress, advocacy groups, universities, labor unions, and religious organizations. Propping up Social Security is "not about politics," he said. "It's about doing right by young Americans and older Americans and the future of America."[15] Publicly, the president remained noncommittal on private accounts and refused to endorse a specific reform proposal. He learned from the health care debate that he would be more effective if he focused on outlining the parameters of the debate but avoided specifics. In keeping with his approach, he laid out five principles: strengthening the program's guarantee of core benefits; maintaining universality and fairness; shielding benefits from market fluctuations; continuing benefits for the disabled and poor; and maintaining "fiscal discipline."

Behind the scenes, however, there was a growing policy consensus emerging between the White House and congressional Republicans in favor

By the time the president held his much-anticipated conference on Social Security in December 1998, the Lewinsky scandal had destroyed any chance of finding a bipartisan solution to the problem. (William J. Clinton Presidential Library.)

of private accounts. A White House working group, chaired by Sperling and Deputy Treasury Secretary Lawrence Summers, had been meeting weekly all year to analyze options and prepare recommendations for the president. Meanwhile, Archer had asked a former aide, Ken Keys, who had been a key player in developing the 1997 balanced budget bill, to work independently of the White House, examining all the options and proposing possible solutions. A few weeks before convening the White House conference, both sides met to discuss possible points of compromise. "It was amazing when we first sat down and put our cards on the table how close together we were on how to fix Social Security," recalled Keys. "I don't have any doubt that there was a potential deal there."[16] A later review by members of the Federal Reserve concluded "that there was more potential for substantive consensus on Social Security reform than the heated rhetoric on the topic suggested," pointing out that "proposals from the left and right seemed to be moving toward each other."[17]

According to Keys, there was general consensus that any proposal would require an increase in the retirement age to account for the fact that people were living longer and healthier lives. The well-off should pay slightly higher taxes to help maintain the system. A good deal of pain could be cushioned by applying the large budget surpluses. Any reform that included private accounts would require the government to fund current Social Security beneficiaries at their existing level while diverting revenue into private accounts. The budget surplus, projected to swell to $125 billion in 1999 and $236 billion in 2000, would allow the administration to fund the transition to a quasi-private system. "This is the most fundamental and important policy foundation that would have allowed a deal to go forward," recalled congressional liaison John Hilley. "We had the extra money to fund a transition to a quasi-private system without raising taxes."[18] As Summers said, "We've got the money now and a problem later."

The two sides had even bridged many of the differences on the controversial idea of private accounts. Everyone agreed that it was necessary to get a higher rate of return on Social Security funds, and that could only be accomplished by allowing individuals to invest in private equity funds. The administration came to the conclusion that the individual accounts would have to be built on top of Social Security; it was not politically feasible to divert existing funds into private accounts. They also accepted the Republican premise that individuals, and not the government, would invest the money. At the same time, Republicans conceded that the government needed to limit the range of options available to individuals, probably to a handful of broad index funds.

Although they were closer together on substantive issues of policy, they were miles apart on politics. The impeachment fight had sapped the president of the political strength to force compromise on his coalition. "The hard political reality was that Clinton was not going to be able to support private accounts," reflected Arizona Republican Jim Kolbe. "It was obvious, very quickly, that the ball game was over."[19] According to Hilley, "The scandal deprived Clinton of the last two years of his presidency." Because of impeachment, "he was delivered out of the middle where we had him and into the left wing."[20] Clinton's efforts to pass entitlement reform, and forge an enduring centrist coalition within the Democratic Party, rested on a fluid alliance of moderate and conservative Democrats. Many of them, however, abandoned him after word of the Lewinsky scandal leaked. The liberal groups who were mobilized to fight impeachment and to save his presidency were also the most vehemently opposed to privatization efforts, even modest ones. "We have seen an unprecedented level of outrage among working families when they learn of the benefit cuts and tax increases being proposed by those who would turn Social Security over to Wall Street," said John J. Sweeney, the president of the American Federation of Labor and Congress of Industrial Organizations (AFL-CIO).[21] Clinton, who had a strained relationship with the liberal wing of his party throughout his presidency, was now dependent on them for his political survival. They tied his hands on private accounts, preventing him from reaching across the aisle to make a deal on what would have been the most lasting legacy of his presidency.

With Gingrich no longer playing an active role, Archer became the key player on the Republican side. Archer never doubted that Clinton wanted to pass a reform package that included private accounts. However, he believed that the president now lacked the political will to pick a fight with his strongest supporters. Privately, the president's aides admitted to Archer that Clinton had been so weakened politically by the impeachment struggle that he needed every Democratic vote he could muster, making any bipartisan deal on Social Security moot. "I've stiffed organized labor on trade. I can't stiff them again," the president told Archer.[22] With Clinton unwilling to take the lead, the reform effort stalled. Archer insisted that the president go on the record supporting private accounts before the Republicans put their proposals on the table. "Without a specific plan from the president, a very difficult job will become much, much harder," he said.[23] Archer found himself going around in circles trying to get Democratic support.[24]

After raising expectations that he would push for a massive overhaul of Social Security, the president ended up making a modest proposal in his 1999 State of the Union address. The White House plan provided for a new, voluntary investment-oriented scheme similar to the 401(k) plans offered by corporations. The Universal Savings Accounts (USAs)—a separate, supplemental pension plan—would give tax credits to Americans with incomes under $100,000, to be put into these accounts. It would benefit couples earning more than $100,000 only if they had no employer-sponsored pension.[25] It was a far cry from the substantial policy proposals and difficult political decisions he promised to make earlier. "Nobody would have projected USAs as saving Social Security for all time," said Archer. "In fact, to me it was just window dressing. There was no relationship between the USAs and saving Social Security. All it did was create another tool for retirement savings."[26]

The ambitious plan to overhaul Medicare met a similar fate. By the time the National Bipartisan Commission on the Future of Medicare issued its recommendations in March 1999, Gingrich was a private citizen and Clinton was an impeached, lame-duck president. In less than fifteen months the political world had been turned upside down. Clinton had planned to use the commission to develop bold, controversial proposals, and he was willing to pressure Democrats into accepting painful compromises in order to get a deal with the Republicans. When its chairman John Breaux announced his support for a Republican proposal to make Medicare function like private health benefits, the president sided with liberals and denounced the plan. Without presidential support, the committee divided along partisan lines and the once promising goal of reforming Medicare was dead.

Whether the president and the Speaker could have pulled off a major overhaul of Social Security had it not been for the Lewinsky scandal will remain one of the great unanswerable questions of modern politics. Not everyone involved in the discussions was convinced there was a direct relationship between the scandal and the failure of Social Security reform. "Did the Lewinsky scandal harm Clinton's second term on a substantial level?" asked Treasury Secretary Robert Rubin. "My instinct is that Clinton could not have gotten more done," he argued, "even if the scandal had never struck."[27] Rubin believed that the Democratic interest groups would never have given the president the political wiggle room he needed to pass a reform that included private accounts, and congressional Republicans would not have passed any initiative that failed to include it. Some people in the White House were convinced they could carry the issue, but worried whether Gingrich had the votes. Some congressional Republicans were confident they could find the votes, but questioned whether Clinton had the political stomach for another bruising battle with his own party. Gene Sperling, who was charged with examining policy options for the White House, believed that Clinton and Gingrich shared a desire to get a compromise bill passed and agreed on a general framework, but cautioned that there were lots of specifics to be worked out, and each one had the potential to sabotage the entire effort.

There were also a number of major institutional obstacles to overcome. Bruce Reed, who had spearheaded the president's welfare reform initiative and understood the twists and turns of the policy-making process, observed that "all the natural forces in Washington work against compromise." The moderate middle, the place where Clinton and Gingrich had been trying to make an ideological home, was weakening. Clinton had spent his entire political career redefining the center and finding ways to build bipartisan coalitions. It is unclear whether Gingrich, however, was temperamentally capable of making that transition. He rose to power by pursuing a deliberate strategy of fomenting partisan divisions, but now was trying to forge a new consensus. But was it too late for him to make that transition?

Despite these obstacles, all of the major players in the White House and Congress involved in the conversations, both Democrats and Republicans, were confident that a deal was possible, and that a great opportunity had been squandered. Chief-of-Staff Erskine Bowles and congressional liaison John Hilley, the two key players on the White House side, were certain they had the strategy and the votes to pass Social Security reform. "It was close—really close," recalled Bowles.[28] Their congressional allies felt the same way. "We were very close, in my opinion, and would have gotten it done had it not been for a momentary lapse of judgment on the part of the president," said Democrat Charles Stenholm. "It's kind of the Nixon-goes-to-China theory. It takes a Democrat to do some of the hard choices in social programs."[29] When the journalist Joe Klein asked him in the final months of his administration about "the opportunity costs" of the Lewinsky scandal, especially when it came to Social Security reform, the president admitted, "I am disappointed there." "I regret we didn't get to do Social Security," he said. "I think maybe we could have gotten it if we hadn't had that whole impeachment thing."[30]

Gingrich and the leading Republicans involved in the discussions agreed. Archer looks back at the period with sadness and regret. "I don't hate Bill Clinton and I'm not bitter," he reflected. "I'm just sad. Sad that we had the opportunity to really do something to improve this country. We could have left an incredible legacy for our kids and our grandkids. It was the last chance for real bipartisanship." He had no doubt that without the partisan wars generated by the Lewinsky affair, the dream of a major Social Security reform would have been realized. "I have come to the conclusion that Lewinsky got in the way," he said. On the North American Free Trade Agreement (NAFTA), Clinton was willing to withstand the opposition of organized labor to get a bill passed. Not this time. "I'm convinced that he needed organized labor to fight impeachment, so he could not risk alienating them with a fight over Social Security."[31]

There was enough blame to go around for the lost opportunity. Publicly, many of the president's aides tried to downplay the political impact of the Lewinsky affair, saying it was a private issue that the Republicans turned into a public scandal. In the modern media age, however, the line between private behavior and public consequences has been forever blurred. The president's reckless behavior may have denied him the chance to leave behind a significant legacy of meaningful reform. At the same time, Gingrich and other leading Republicans convinced themselves they could pursue a two-track policy: holding hearings to destroy Clinton's presidency in one room on Capitol Hill while trying to build a coalition with him in another. Impeachment empowered the groups in both parties that were the least interested in reform: liberal Democrats who opposed privatization and conservative Republicans who supported large tax cuts. Clinton and Gingrich, the masterminds behind the reform initiative, had been rendered powerless. It was their vision and political skills that brought the nation to the precipice of significant reform, but once again, it was their tragic flaws that prevented them from achieving greatness.

———

On January 7, 1999, a cold, drizzly day in Washington, the Senate took up the two charges of impeachment forwarded by the House. Under the Constitution, if two-thirds of the Senate, or sixty-seven senators, voted for conviction on either of the two articles of impeachment, Clinton would be removed from office and Vice President Al Gore sworn in to replace him. After days of listening to Republican prosecutors from the House and the president's defense lawyers, the senators closed the doors, turned off the television cameras, and deliberated. At the end of the fourth day of closed-door meetings, the doors opened and curious onlookers packed the galleries and filled the aisles to hear the verdict. "Senators, how say you? Is the respondent, William Jefferson Clinton, guilty or not guilty?" Chief Justice William Rehnquist asked after a clerk read the first charge of perjury. As the clerk called each senator's name, each stood to announce his or her verdict. Ten Republicans joined a united Democratic Party in declaring the president "not guilty," making the final count forty-five to fifty-five. On the obstruction-of-justice charge, five GOP senators crossed over, resulting in a fifty–fifty vote. Clinton "hereby is acquitted of the charges," the chief justice proclaimed.

By the time the Senate reached its verdict, Newt Gingrich was a private citizen for the first time since winning election to the House in 1978. A subdued Clinton emerged from the Oval Office two hours later to apologize to the American people: "I want to say again to the American people how profoundly sorry I am for what I said and did to trigger these events and the great burden they have imposed on the Congress and the American people."[32] The president could take solace from the fact that neither of the two articles of impeachment attracted even a simple majority of senators' votes, and both fell far short of the two-thirds majority needed to convict and expel the president. Yet both he and Gingrich realized that a great moment of possibility had been squandered.

It is likely that the Clinton presidency, like the extraordinarily talented and tragically flawed figure who led it, will be remembered for its bright promise but modest achievements. By all accounts, Bill Clinton was a man of remarkable abilities. He could be a mesmerizing public speaker and a convincing behind-the-scenes negotiator who was capable of changing the minds of even his most ardent opponents. Beyond the tactical skill, however, he understood the conflicting currents of the public mood as it tried to absorb the cultural and political earthquake of the 1960s. Unlike many on the Left, he appreciated that change needed to be slow and gradual, that people longed for reform and stability at the same time. He also came to power at a unique time in the nation's history when peace and prosperity reigned supreme. By 1997, it appeared that Clinton might finally realize the full promise of his presidency. Not only had he defeated the Republican Revolution, but he had also won over Newt Gingrich, his chief nemesis, and was secretly making deals to create a new centrist coalition.

Had he succeeded in his plan to overhaul the nation's entitlement programs, Clinton could have secured the place in the history books that he so eagerly sought and provided the Democratic Party with a firm political foundation for the future. Since the 1960s, the Republicans had employed the language of cultural populism to win the affection of the white middle class, stigmatizing the Democrats as culturally alien and fiscally irresponsible. Clinton had helped neutralize that message through his successful stewardship of the economy and his ability to articulate a broad national vision that transcended the agenda of narrow special interests. Now he had the chance to reinforce the perception of Democratic Party as the spiritual home of Franklin Roosevelt and John F. Kennedy—the party of bold, progressive, and competent leadership. It was not to be: the president's promiscuity combined with conservative petulance promised that the Clinton presidency will be remembered not for what it accomplished, but for what it promised and failed to deliver. "It's hard to describe the disconnect, the contrast, between Bill Clinton the man and Bill Clinton's two-term presidency," observed the columnist Richard Cohen. "The charm, the brilliance, the sureness and all the rest somehow produced a presidency that never lived up to its potential."[33]

Social Security and Medicare reform were the major casualties of the Lewinsky affair, but many other promising initiatives were also killed. The impeachment battle ended an effort to pass legislation limiting tobacco sales to minors while raising millions of dollars for public health and education. In October 1997, in the heyday of their bipartisan dealings, Clinton and Gingrich had agreed to create an informal joint working group to craft a bipartisan compromise on tobacco. The sticking point had always been a provision that would raise money by increasing prices in return for government guarantees that would limit the legal exposure facing tobacco companies. Liberals opposed making any deals with tobacco; conservatives rejected increasing taxes on sales. Behind the scenes, Clinton and Gingrich were trying to find some common ground, even if it meant breaking with the most ideological supporters in both parties. After Lewinsky, Clinton lost his ability to forge a deal, the center collapsed, and the Left and Right moved to fill the vacuum. "It came apart because Democrats didn't really want a deal; they wanted the issue. Republicans didn't want Clinton to get an accomplishment because they were busy trying to convince people to throw him out of office," reflected Bruce Reed. "The inmates had taken over the asylum."[34]

As part of his goal to be a "repairer of the breach," the president had promised to address simmering racial problems in America. In a speech at the University of California, San Diego, in June 1997, Clinton announced an ambitious effort to answer the question, "Can we fulfill the promise of America by embracing all of our citizens of all races?" He followed the speech with an executive order creating a seven-member advisory board to make specific recommendations. By the time the commission issued its report fifteen months later, the president was burdened with impeachment, fighting for his political survival, and reluctant to launch new initiatives. "Go somewhere and try to find a trace of that initiative, and it's like yesterday's sandcastles after a long, overnight rain," reflected civil rights activist Roger Wilkins. The president's approach to the race issue served as a metaphor for his entire administration: he promised more than he could deliver, but he still delivered more than any other president in recent memory. In addition to talking frequently about racial issues, he appointed a number of African Americans to high-profile positions, and his economic policies, especially the Earned-Income Tax Credit for the working poor, helped produce historic gains in income for black households. Blacks showed their affection in the voting booths, giving him 84 percent of their vote in 1996. They also stuck with him during the entire impeachment struggle.[35]

Most tragically, the president's preoccupation with impeachment may have prevented his administration from focusing its full attention on the growing danger of global terrorism. During his eight years in office, terrorists attacked the World Trade Center, two U.S. embassies in Africa, and an American warship, the USS Cole. In the last years of his administration, intelligence officials repeatedly warned about the growing threat from Osama Bin Linden, but Clinton remained remarkably passive. Years later, Gingrich would join the chorus of critics blaming Clinton for not doing enough to prevent the attacks on September 11, 2001, charging that Clinton's "pathetically weak, ineffective ability to focus and stay focused" made him ill-equipped to thwart Bin Laden's plan. But there is no evidence that Gingrich ever pressured the president to take a stronger position against terrorism, or offered an alternative strategy. "In retrospect," he said in October 2001, "I wish I had been much more consistent in holding President Clinton's feet to the fire on this issue."[36] Ironically, both men fancied themselves as visionaries preparing America for the challenges of the next century, but they failed to anticipate with appropriate force and clarity the greatest threat facing the nation. If the test of leadership is the ability to anticipate future problems, draw attention to them, and push the nation toward a response, then the two leading political figures of the decade received a failing grade.

CHAPTER SEVENTEEN | '60s Legacies

THE PRESIDENT INSISTED the impeachment debate was about sex; Gingrich maintained it was about perjury. In reality, it was about much more. The last time the House impeached a president was in the aftermath of the Civil War, as the nation engaged in a passionate debate over the legacy of slavery and the meaning of freedom. The roots of the Clinton impeachment traced back to the cultural conflicts of the 1960s, nurtured during three decades of partisan wrangling, cultivated by a host of powerful interest groups, and brought into sharp focus by a zealous special prosecutor.

In both cases, the decision to impeach a president was part of the nation's ongoing effort to absorb the profound impact of wrenching social and cultural change. By the time the Radical Republicans in Congress voted to impeach Andrew Johnson in 1868, the war between North and South had been settled, but the nation was still fighting over the meaning of victory. In the modern culture wars there was no dramatic surrender at Appomattox, only an ongoing series of skirmishes, culminating in a constitutional crisis of epic proportions. The Civil War was fought over the lofty issue of freedom versus slavery. At the heart of the cultural civil war of the 1960s was the expansion of sexual freedom and individual expression. It was appropriate that the first representative of the '60s generation to occupy the White House would produce a heated national debate over sex. "Sex had been a label to explain a cluster of ideas and values that had upset Clinton's enemies for decades," observed Sidney Blumenthal. "He had always been a screen on which were projected conservative feelings about the 1960s, the counterculture, and race. Through it all, sex had been a tracer, a code," he wrote. "In politics, sex is rarely just about sex."[1]

For most conservatives the Lewinsky affair was a metaphor for the counterculture values that emerged from the Left during the 1960s. "Why do you hate Clinton so much?" an interviewer asked a conservative. Because, he responded, "he's a womanizing, Elvis-loving, non-inhaling, truth-shading, war-protesting, draft-dodging, abortion-protecting, gay-promoting, gun-hating baby boomer. That's why." Conservative journalist David Frum claimed that Clinton's personal behavior exemplified the pernicious legacy of the 1960s sexual revolution. "What's at stake in the Lewinsky scandal," Frum wrote, "[is] the central dogma of the baby boomers: the belief that sex, so long as it's consensual, ought never to be subject to moral scrutiny."[2] After reviewing the affair, Judge Richard A. Posner concluded that the Right hated Clinton because he "is part of the generation of the 1960s." He smoked marijuana, dodged the draft, married a feminist, and appointed gays and lesbians to high-profile positions in the government. "Now he tops it off with 'deviant' sex in the White House office complex and a cascade of lies to cover it up."[3] As the *Wall Street Journal* editorialized, independent counsel Kenneth Starr was "not just prosecuting Bill Clinton; he was prosecuting the entire culture that gave birth to what Bill Clinton represents."[4] "By purging Clinton," observed John Kenneth White, "Republicans believed they would also expunge the worst excesses of the counterculture."[5]

Morally driven conservatives could not understand why people were not outraged that the president had sex with a woman half his age and then lied about it under oath. Most surveys, however, showed that while Americans did not approve of the president's actions, they did not believe they were serious enough to warrant removal from office. Revelations about Gingrich's affair, along with the subsequent "outing" of other Clinton critics, including Henry Hyde and Robert Livingston, made many of the president's critics seem not only rigid and puritanical, but also hypocritical. The only thing most Americans disliked more than a devious middle-aged man lying about sex was moralizing, self-righteous hypocrites telling other people how to live their lives.

Conservatives used the Lewinsky affair to force a confrontation over the legacy of the 1960s. They believed that impeaching the president would help purge countercultural values from American society and restore an older set of values that stressed responsibility over freedom. What they discovered, however, was that much of the nation had already moved beyond the stale debate between the Left and Right that defined the culture wars. Prosperity, combined with the social and cultural earthquake of the 1960s, produced a revolution in the way Americans thought about sex, gender, and the relationship between men and women. The women's movement had served as the engine driving much of the change. Over the previous three decades, feminists had challenged older notions of womanhood and expanded the list of "rights"—legal abortion, no-fault divorce, equal pay for equal work. At the same time, the everyday lives of women had changed dramatically as more moved into the workforce and demanded equal treatment both at home and in the office. These changes, combined with the coming of age of the baby boomers, produced a sea change in attitudes about sex. For example, in 1965, 69 percent of women said that premarital sex was "always" or "almost always" wrong. Two decades later, only 22 percent made similar claims. The percentage of Americans supporting abortion skyrocketed from 24 percent in 1972 to 40 percent in 1996.

Polls showed that Americans celebrated the expansion of individual rights and the loosening of rules governing private behavior, but they were troubled by some of the unintended consequences of the new cultural freedom: a rising divorce rate, a dramatic rise in single-parent families and of female-headed families in poverty, the emergence of AIDS, and the spread of sexually transmitted diseases. Conservative intellectuals and New Right ministers gave voice to that unease, even as they exaggerated the extent of the backlash. Conservatives complaining about the decline in traditional values, the blurring of the line separating right and wrong, and the growing permissiveness in society promised to roll back the 1960s.

The impeachment debate revealed that most Americans had integrated the 1960s into the fabric of their lives. While comforted by the rhetoric of traditional values, they were reluctant to impose the older standard of morality advocated by most conservatives. Instead of choosing between new rights and old values, the vast majority of Americans created a shield of privacy that allowed them to avoid passing judgment on questions of personal morality. While Americans disagreed on many issues, the social scientist Alan Wolfe found one common theme running through American social attitudes in the late-1990s: "To exclude, to condemn, is to judge, and middle-class Americans are reluctant to pass judgement on how other people act and think," he concluded.[6]

The public response to the Lewinsky scandal and the impeachment process revealed that most Americans embraced a new faith in tolerance as a morally neutral middle ground. "All the detail wakes up a little piece of guilt in all of us," observed a psychiatrist. "People look at the president and say, 'There, but for the press, go I.' "[7] Polls showed that nearly 90 percent of Americans agreed that the country "would have many fewer problems if there were more emphasis on traditional family values." But nearly 70 percent agreed that "we should be more tolerant of people who choose to live according to their own moral standards, even if we think they are wrong."[8] Talking to people in the conservative, working-class town of Plainfield, Connecticut, David Brooks noted that whether they loved Clinton or hated him, they agreed "that personal behavior has no connection with public performance." Many people were willing to condemn his perjury, but few wanted to moralize about the president's adulterous affair with a twenty-one-year-old intern.[9]

Clinton, a master at empathy, played to the conflicting currents of opinion. Throughout his career, Clinton had threatened old taboos even as he reinforced traditional values. Conservatives found him so threatening precisely because he managed to push the cultural boundaries to the left even as he upheld older values. He avoided the draft, protested against the Vietnam War, smoked pot, and embraced the casual style and informality of his generation. Yet he also spoke about the importance of individual responsibility and family values, often quoting freely from scripture to underscore his message. During the Lewinsky affair, he engaged in practices not uncommon among adult men, and when confronted about it, he lied. Once trapped, however, he expressed sorrow, apologized, and asked for forgiveness. In many ways, Hillary Clinton struck the same tone. She was a strong feminist whose personality and prominence symbolized the success of the women's movement and the desire to challenge traditional notions of womanhood. Yet, during the impeachment, she adopted a more traditional stance, choosing to stand by her husband. She was nontraditional enough to tap into the strong sentiment for women's rights, yet traditional enough to reassert her role as a loyal wife supporting her husband.

The painful experience of watching Americans refuse to accept the impeachment and removal from office of a confessed adulterer forced many conservatives to acknowledge that they had lost a key battle in the culture war. Andrea Shelton, executive director of the Traditional Values Coalition, reluctantly accepted that Americans were living in a "post-Christian culture," where people "say they go to church" and claim to pray. At the same time, however, they enjoy the benefits of a "live and let live" culture that espouses a "do whatever feels good attitude."[10] Looking back on the scandal, Gingrich recognized that he "was out of sync with the culture. This is a culture that is much more open, and has gone through many more experiences, than a person of my age and my background understood."[11]

Most revealing, however, is that despite the heated rhetoric and months of debate and turmoil, the simple reality was that there was very little difference between the lifestyles and values of the chief protagonists in the saga. While Clinton embraced the new sexual freedom of the 1960s that seemed to give married men license to have affairs, Gingrich subscribed to the 1950s notion that men could cheat on their wives as long as they kept it a secret. "They were extremely disciplined about some things, but undisciplined about other areas of their lives," reflected a close Gingrich aide who requested anonymity. "Getting elected was a priority. Dominating the political scene was a priority. Being faithful to their spouses was not a high priority."

———

The debate may have been contrived, but the consequences of impeachment were real. For a brief period, Clinton and Gingrich realized that their own legacies, and the future success of their respective parties, required reaching beyond their bases to build a moderate, centrist political coalition. Like the generation they represented, both men were moving into the sunset years of their public careers, hoping to leave behind a constructive legacy for the future. Instead, they will likely be remembered not for their quiet efforts to forge bipartisanship, but for their actions, intended and unintended, in aggravating partisan differences.

Gingrich believed that he could tear down liberal government and then reassemble it under conservative rule, but he discovered that it was easier to damage the old regime than it was to create a new one. Gingrich helped bring to power a group of conservative ideologues who resisted his later pleas for moderation. Like an earlier generation of French radicals, he discovered that revolutions often devour their children. The members of the Republican class of 1994, "Newt's children," saw themselves as representatives of the "common man." They came to Washington to represent "average" Americans and to change a system that catered to the interests of a liberal elite. On impeachment, however, they viewed themselves as moral crusaders defending traditional values from the vulgar masses.

Through his indiscretions, Clinton badly damaged his lifelong effort to blur the ideological differences between Democrats and Republicans. A centrist who preached reconciliation and moderation, Clinton left office having aroused the passions of conservatives and liberals. Clinton's actions, and the impeachment process itself, placed values, not policy, at the center of public debate and discussion, and it left partisans on both sides feeling embattled and under assault. "Clinton" said journalist Ronald Brownstein, "was creator and destroyer." He made the Democrats viable by appealing to middle-class values. But then he flaunted those values. He helped the Democrats to compete again for the presidency only to see the party lose control of both the House and the Senate. He bounced back to defeat Newt Gingrich only to have his presidency tarnished by impeachment.[12]

In the end, Gingrich chose to quit rather than to fight to keep his job, yet he managed to leave behind a party that was in many ways stronger and more secure. Clinton saved his presidency, but left behind a divided and weaker party. When he took office in 1993, there were Democratic majorities in the House and Senate, and Democrats made up a majority of the nation's governors. When he left, Republicans controlled Congress and most governorships. Clinton erased Democratic vulnerability on a host of issues—that the party was soft on crime, favored criminals over victims, supported the poor but were indifferent to the middle class—but then created a new fault line on questions of morality and personal integrity.

Gingrich may have revived his party's political fortunes, but he left the conservative movement fractured and demoralized. As the Reagan Revolution started losing steam in the mid-1980s, Gingrich emerged from the shadows, providing the Right with a combative style, a potent vocabulary, and a clear, compelling agenda. Once in power, however, he made a number of costly tactical mistakes. Perhaps for the first time since 1980 when Ronald Reagan captured the presidency, conservatives lacked both a unified agenda and an inspiring leader. They also lost their unquestioned confidence that they represented the cultural values of the American middle class. In February 1999, New Right activist Paul Weyrich confessed, "I no longer believe that there is a moral majority."[13] Many conservatives, who never fully trusted Gingrich, blamed him for their predicament. "The abject disarray of the once-formidable conservative wing of the party is not entirely Gingrich's fault," observed journalist David Frum. "But it is very largely his fault," he concluded."[14] The Right complained that Gingrich muddled their message through his compromises with the president, and although many cheered him when he forced a government shutdown and pushed for impeachment, they now attacked him for picking the wrong issues on which to wage public fights. Even when he was right on the issues, he was no match for Clinton in the battle for public opinion. The president made Gingrich the face of conservatism, and as the Speaker dropped in the opinion polls, he dragged the entire movement down with him.

While it is true that Gingrich was a better rebel than leader, the problems confronting conservatives transcended the Speaker's personal failings. Gingrich never resolved how to be both the legislative leader of his party in Congress and the ideological spokesman of the conservative movement. As the leading Republican in the House, he needed to produce a record of accomplishment, which meant making deals with the president. As the spokesman for the conservative movement, however, he needed to lay down ideological markers, stand firm on principles, and inspire the faithful. It was a juggling act that would have confounded even the most adroit politician under the best of circumstances. His skilled and savvy protagonist in the White House turned a difficult task into an impossible one.

The impeachment wars that marred the final years of the Clinton presidency added partisan fuel to the generational divide, making any consensus unlikely for the foreseeable future. Clinton was the first representative of his generation to occupy the White House, but nearly all the major contenders to succeed him were also products of the tumultuous 1960s, which suggested that the battle over the legacy of the decade would continue. In the immediate aftermath of the impeachment battle, however, both Democrats and Republicans made an effort to appear nonpartisan. Under the tutelage of political advisor Karl Rove, the leading Republican contender, Texas Governor George W. Bush, developed a strategy to be a "kinder, gentler Gingrich." He referred to himself a "compassionate conservative," talked about improving education, and even appeared with a group of gay Republicans. Vice President Al Gore had a difficult time finding his voice and his message as he performed a delicate "Tennessee Two Step," trying to benefit from Clinton's policies while disassociating himself from the president's actions.

Under normal circumstances, peace and prosperity would have translated into an easy Democratic victory in 2000, but the Lewinsky affair and the impeachment that followed muddled the political waters. The scandal, combined with the intense media coverage and the highly partisan debate over impeachment, left the public deeply divided and defensive. With polls showing that nearly 70 percent of Americans felt the public had become too tolerant of behavior that was once considered immoral, and more than half believing that groups holding values similar to their own were losing influence, it was clear that many Americans were planning to vote their values, not their pocketbooks. On election night, the nation split down the middle, and it was left up to the Supreme Court to pick George Bush as the winner. According to the journalist Andrew Sullivan, the election revealed that in the post-Lewinsky world America was "two nations, as culturally and politically alien as they are geographically distinct."

Despite his initial, superficial desire to present a moderate image, Bush governed as a conservative. Gingrich and Clinton had once talked about forging a "60 percent" coalition made up of moderates in both parties. But in the polarized post-Lewinsky age, both parties played to their base. Gingrich had left government, but he cast a long shadow over Washington. The president found that many congressional leaders had been raised in the Gingrich style of "slash and burn" politics, and many insiders who filled middle-level staff positions in the White House were Gingrich proteges.[15] Once in office,

Bush abandoned any pretense of moderation, pushed for a massive tax cut, backed away from his support for the environment, and made few efforts to reach reasonable compromises with congressional Democrats. The terrorist attacks on September 11, 2001, only reinforced his inclination to see issues, both domestic and foreign, in terms of black and white.

The president's move to the right contributed to Erskine Bowles's decision to seek the Senate seat vacated by North Carolina's Jesse Helms in 2002. Bowles had always disparaged the Byzantine world of politics, professed his love of the private sector, and seemed anxious to leave Washington from the day that he arrived. So why was he spending his time, and a considerable chunk of his fortune, to return? Bowles never fully answered that question until 2006, when I showed him the notes of the secret meeting that he helped organize between Clinton and Gingrich. "That is why I wanted to go back to Washington," he said, gesturing toward the notes. "Because I saw what you could accomplish when the two sides are willing to work together."[16] Bowles lost the election.

Bowles had hoped the "two sides" could have achieved meaningful Social Security reform, an issue President Bush tried to revive, making it the top priority of his second term. But the window of political opportunity had passed. A shaky stock market, soaring gasoline prices, and worry about an unpopular and expensive war in Iraq had eroded public support for private accounts, the centerpiece of the president's proposal. The president announced a sixty-day tour to build support for his proposal, but polls showed that fewer people supported the plan at the end of the tour than when he first announced it. As Clinton and Gingrich understood, absent massive majorities, reforming Social Security required a bipartisan coalition. Democrats had little incentive to buy into the plan, and their interest groups fiercely opposed the president's privatization efforts. Fearing that Democrats would use Social Security as a political issue in future elections, many moderate Republicans backed away from the plan. "This privatization plan is sinking like a rock," said a gleeful Democratic senator.[17]

By 2004, it was obvious that the impeachment wars had marked the opening salvo in a bitter new phase of the generational wars that started in the 1960s. In this new partisan atmosphere there were no figures of the stature of Clinton and Gingrich with the skill to build coalitions, or the courage to take the political risk of reaching across the aisle. Bush, executing a strategy of "divide and conquer," played to his conservative base, tapping into cultural anxieties that the Democratic Party was out of touch with mainstream values. *Washington Post* columnist David Broder lamented that the dispute over John Kerry's Vietnam War record in the 2004 presidential contest confirmed his "worst fears" that "the baby boomers who came of age in that troubled decade" will never make peace with each other and "lead a united country."[18]

While the war in Iraq dominated public debate in the campaign, it was only one in a constellation of issues that divided the two parties. Polls showed that self-identified Democrats and Republicans were worlds apart on a wide range of economic and cultural issues. A *New York Times*/CBS News poll of delegates to the 2004 national conventions revealed that 80 percent of Democrats believed that government needed to do more to solve national problems. Only 7 percent of Republicans agreed. Nearly three-quarters of Republicans opposed abortion; a similar majority of Democrats supported a woman's right to choose. Republicans were nearly unanimous in support of the president's tax cuts—94 percent. Nearly 90 percent of Democrats were opposed. On the critical issue of Iraq, 96 percent of Republicans, but only 7 percent of Democrats, supported the decision to invade.[19]

Following Kerry's defeat in November, the Democratic Party inched further to the left. The centrist "New Democrat" message that Clinton had articulated in the mid-1990s, which blended liberal and conservative ideas, was eclipsed by the militant appeals of Democrats spoiling for a fight. New Internet-based groups such as MoveOn, flushed with money and highly motivated members, pushed the party toward a more confrontational stance with the Bush administration. "It may be in the 1990s, there was a middle; there isn't a middle now," said one of the founders of MoveOn. "You have a Republican Party that is willing to break all the rules and accept no compromises to get what they want. In the face of that, saying 'I'll meet you halfway' is as sure a recipe for disaster as I know. You have to fight fire with fire."[20] As the minority party in Washington, Democrats took a page from the Newt Gingrich book of politics, attacking the ethics of the Republican leadership, eroding public faith in the integrity of the party and its leadership. In 2006, Democrats regained control of the House and Senate by turning the elections into a national referendum on President Bush. In 1993–94, Clinton had handed Gingrich health care. In 2006, Bush provided the Democrats with a disastrous war in Iraq.

Memories of the 1960s have faded, but the generational war for the hearts and minds of the American people goes on. As they look to the 2008 election, the '60s generation seems farther apart than ever. "The looming battle between the two wings of the 1960s generation—one championing the Roosevelt heritage, the Old Order, the other championing the Reagan heritage, a New Order—explains much of the bitterness of contemporary politics," observed conservative commentator R. Emmett Tyrrell Jr.[21] Neither side saw a reason to compromise. The only glimmer of hope came from the presidential campaign of Illinois Senator Barack Obama. Many Americans, especially younger voters, reponded to his plea for moving beyond the 60s-era culture wars, but it remained unclear whether his party or the nation were ready to embrace his message of generational change.

Having fought to define the debate over the role of government and the political legacy of their generation, Bill Clinton and Newt Gingrich devoted considerable time and effort after 2000 to shaping how history will view them. Clinton told his side of the story of the 1990s in his bestselling memoirs, *My Life,* published in 2004. Since then he has devoted most of his time to a variety of humanitarian causes, including an ambitious effort to combat the spread of AIDS in Africa. Gingrich published his memoir of the decade in 1998, before impeachment. In his early retirement he retreated into the world of historical fiction, offering counterfactual accounts of the key military battles such as Gettysburg and Pearl Harbor. Perhaps because he never abandoned dreams of running for public office, Gingrich has been more proactive than Clinton about defending his record and trying to remake his image. While in 2007 Gingrich still entertained dreams of running for the presidency, Clinton was forced to live vicariously through the aspirations of his wife.

Both men see history as one of many tools to be employed in their constant effort to redefine themselves to stay politically relevant. Their views of each other, and their relationship, are still in flux, constantly under revision to accommodate the political moment. There was a brief period after the 2004 election when the two men were willing to allow the story of their past effort to work together to be uncovered, but as the Bush administration came to an end and the nation geared up for a new election season, that window closed.

Throughout his presidency, Clinton had maintained a nuanced view of Gingrich. Unlike most House Democrats, and many members of his staff, he never hated Gingrich, and he often enjoyed his company. While they disagreed on means and tactics, Clinton believed they were both reformers trying to change their parties and to help the nation adjust to the realities of a twenty-first-century world. During nearly six years of political combat, the president rarely made a disparaging personal comment about Gingrich. After the impeachment struggle, however, his mood soured. Clinton convinced himself that Gingrich had stood between him and presidential greatness. But he still seemed comfortable with allowing me to tell the story of his private dealings with the Speaker. By 2006, however, with his wife gearing up for her own run at the presidency, Clinton shifted gears. He had once seen himself as a post-partisan politician, as the man who would blur ideological differences between Democrats and Republicans. Now the master of triangulation pushed Democrats to assume the ideological offensive against Republicans. With his wife locked in a tough primary battle, the president was determined to help broaden her appeal to traditional Democratic voters. Telling the party faithful that he had once tried to form a coalition with a man most of them despised was not part of the message.

Gingrich underwent a similar transformation. Initially, the disgraced Speaker hoped to pull himself back to respectability by latching his legacy to that of the popular president. Making public that he had worked closely with Clinton behind the scenes could demonstrate that he was not the crazy right-winger so often depicted in the media. In the years after leaving office, Gingrich also seemed to mellow in his view of Clinton, whom he sometimes described as "basically a political moderate." While he openly accused Clinton of being a "liar," "fundamentally dishonest," and "corrupt," he did not blame the president for his own fall from grace, or for the declining fortunes of his party. For that he faulted his own failures and the mistakes of the Republican leadership since 1998. The Republican effort post-Lewinsky to draw moral lines in the sand, he complained, allowed the party to "stop thinking." In addition, the corruption of former ally Tom DeLay, and the ineptness of the Bush administration, had eroded support for the party and blurred the ideological differences between Democrats and Republicans. In books and on the lecture circuit, he emphasized that Republicans must once again become the party of new ideas.

By 2007, after abandoning his own plans to run for the presidency, Gingrich still hoped to shape the debate of the post-Bush Republican party. In order to be taken seriously, however, he needed to reestablish his conservative credentials, and bragging about private deals with Bill Clinton was not the most effective way to win the hearts and minds of the Republican base. As a result, he started downplaying his extensive dealings with the president, denying the numerous accounts that he had tried to avoid a government shutdown in 1995, or that he was once willing to abandon his conservative base to forge a centrist coalition with the president.

It will be many years before the full story of the Clinton presidency, and the divisive politics of the 1990s, can be told. Until the vast materials in the Clinton Library are opened to researchers, it will be difficult for scholars to use documented evidence as a check on self-serving memories. In the meantime, both men will use their considerable skills and resources to define their own role and to shape public views of the other, revealing that in history, as in life, their legacies will be forever joined.

SOURCES

Manuscript Collections

Newt Gingrich Papers, West Georgia State University
Richard Armey Papers, Carl Albert Congressional Research and Studies Center, University of Oklahoma
Tip O'Neill Papers, Boston College
Robert Michel Papers, Dirksen Congressional Center
Chip Kahn Papers (private)
Jimmy Carter Presidential Library
William J. Clinton Presidential Library

Interviews

Bill Archer, Washington D.C., July 19, 2006
Dick Armey, phone interview, November 8, 2004
Peter Baker, phone interview, March 27, 2007
Bob Barr, phone interview, July 3, 2006
Paul Begala, phone interview, March 17, 2006
Tony Blankley, Washington D.C., June 24, 2005
David Bonior, New York, November 8, 2005; phone interview, March 27, 2006
Erskine Bowles, phone interview, January 18, 2006; Charlotte, North Carolina, December 5, 2005

Arne Christenson, phone interview, June 25, 2005; June 3, 2006; Washington D.C., October 3, 2005; phone interview, January 20, 2006; phone interview, March 12, 2007

Linda Divall, phone interview, January 30, 2006

Steve Elmendorf, Washington, D.C., October 5, 2005

Jim Farwell, phone interview, March 8, 2004

Vic Fazio, Washington D.C., July 19, 2006

Rich Galen, Washington D.C., June 23, 2005

Joe Gaylord, Washington, D.C., February 12, 2004; phone interview, February 13, 2006

Newt Gingrich, Washington D.C., November 14, 2005; Washington D.C., March 31, 2006

Stanley Greenberg, phone interview, January 23, 2006

Pat Griffin, Washington D.C., June 23, 2005

John Hilley, Washington D.C., October 4, 2005; phone interview, September 7, 2006

Ken Keys, phone interview, August 15, 2006

Chip Kahn, phone interview, August 22, August 23, 2006; Washington D.C., April 26, 2007

Jim Kolbe, Washington D.C., July 19, 2006

Robert Livingston, phone interview, June 20, 2006

Christina Martin, Washington D.C., June 24, 2005

Sylvia Matthews, phone interview, January 11, 2006

Dan Meyer, Washington D.C., June 23, 2005; phone interview, January 9, 2007

David Obey, phone interview, July 21, 2006

Leon Panetta, phone interview, November 22, 2005

Bruce Reed, Washington D.C., September 22, 2006

Scott Reed, Washington D.C., June 23, 2005

Robert Reich, phone interview, March 22, 2007

Steve Richetti, Washington D.C., December 20, 2005

James Rogan, phone interview, August 22, 2006

Gene Sperling, phone interview, February 11, 2006

Mel Steely, phone interview, April 14, 2005

Larry Stein, phone interview, September 15, 2005

Charles Stenholm, phone interview, June 20, 2006

Robert Walker, Washington D.C., November 17, 2005

David Winston, Alexandria, Virginia, February 12, 2004

Ann Woolner, phone interview, August 8, 2006

NOTES

Preface

1. Erskine Bowles interview.
2. Bowles interview.
3. Bowles interview.
4. Arne Christenson interview.
5. The meeting has been recreated based on interviews and detailed notes taken by one of the participants.
6. Bowles interview.
7. Bruce Reed interview.
8. Newt Gingrich interview.
9. Bowles interview.
10. Christenson interview.
11. Gingrich interview.
12. Bowles interview.
13. Although he did not grant access specifically for this book, I did have the chance to interview the president in November 2004 for a History Channel event in New York City. In the course of that ninety-minute discussion I asked him a number of questions about his dealings with the Republican Congress, and with Newt Gingrich in particular. Some of his quotes in this book are from that interview. The president, through his aides, agreed to provide written answers to a series of questions I submitted in September 2006. As of this writing, however, he had not responded.
14. Frank Rich, "Separated at Birth," *New York Times,* January 12, 1995, A25.

Chapter One

1. Erskine Bowles interview.
2. Katherine Q. Seelye, "Gingrich's Life: The Complications and Ideals," *New York Times,* November 24, 1994, A1.
3. Dale Russakoff, "He Knew What He Wanted," *Washington Post,* December 18, 1994, A1.
4. Seelye, "Gingrich's Life: The Complications and Ideals." A1.
5. Bill Clinton, *My Life* (New York: Alfred A. Knopf, 2004), 20.
6. Meredith Oakley, *On the Make: The Rise of Bill Clinton* (Washington, D.C.: Regnery, 1994), 29.
7. Joseph J. Serwach, "Little Newtie Grows Up to be Mover, Shaker," *Rocky Mountain News,* November 18, 1994, A44; *Washington Post,* December 18, 1994.
8. Mel Steely, *The Gentleman from Georgia: The Biography of Newt Gingrich* (Macon, GA: Mercer University Press, 2000), 10.
9. Clinton, *My Life,* 58.
10. Steely, *The Gentleman from Georgia,* 8.
11. Newt Gingrich, *Window of Opportunity: A Blueprint for the Future* (New York: Tom Doherty Associates, Inc., 1984), 219.
12. Newt Gingrich, *To Renew America* (New York: Harper Collins, 1995), 17–19.
13. John Carlin, "Statesman, Fiddler, Buffoon," *Independent* (London), January 7, 1996, 4.
14. Gail Sheehy, "The Inner Quest of Newt Gingrich," *Vanity Fair,* September 1995, 149.
15. Wayne Meyer, *Clinton on Clinton: A Portrait of the President in His Own Words* (New York: Harper Collins, 1999), 2.
16. Steely, *The Gentleman from Georgia,* 6.
17. Russakoff, "He Knew What He Wanted," A1
18. Sheehy, "The Inner Quest of Newt Gingrich."149.
19. Newt Gingrich interview.
20. Russakoff, "He Knew What He Wanted," A1
21. Steely, *The Gentleman from Georgia,* 18.

Chapter Two

1. Daniel Yankelovich, *New Rules,* (New York: Bantam, 1984), 2.
2. Kenneth J. Heineman, *Campus Wars: The Peace Movement at American State Universities in the Vietnam Era* (New York: New York University Press, 1993), 5.
3. Bill Clinton interview.
4. Robert Reich interview.
5. Allan Bloom, *The Closing of the American Mind* (New York: Simon and Schuster, 1987), 314–16.
6. Dennis Kelly, "The '60s on Trial," *USA Today,* January 18, 1995, D1.

7. Reich interview.

8. Nigel Hamilton, *Bill Clinton: An American Journey* (New York: Random House, 2003), 347.

9. Hamilton, *Bill Clinton: An American Journey,* 121.

10. David Maraniss, *First in His Class* (New York: Simon & Schuster, 1996), 49.

11. Curtis Wilkie, "Perseverance: The Making of a Candidate," *Boston Globe,* June 3, 1992, A1.

12. Bill Clinton, *My Life* (New York: Alfred A. Knopf, 2004), 70.

13. Clinton, *My Life,* 117.

14. Maraniss, *First in His Class,* 96.

15. Hamilton, *Bill Clinton: An American Journey,* 133.

16. Robert E. Levin, *Bill Clinton: The Inside Story* (New York: Shapolsky Publishers, 1992), 61.

17. Dale Russakoff, "He Knew What He Wanted," *Washington Post,* December 18, 1994, A1.

18. Thomas W. Lippman and Ann Devroy, "Gingrich Takes Aim at Clinton Staff," *Washington Post,* December 5, 1994, A1; "Gingrich's Pot Mistake," *Seattle Post-Intelligencer,* July 23, 1996, A6.

19. Chip Kahn interview.

20. Russakoff, "He Knew What He Wanted."

21. "Hundreds Join Anti-Administration Protests Over 'Hullaballo' Censorship Controversy," *Tulane Hullabaloo,* March 8 and 15, 1968.

22. "MORTS Issues Election Platform," *Tulane Hullabaloo,* April 5, 1968.

23. "HERE Petition Sparks Consultation Controversy," *Tulane Hullabaloo,* March 21, 1969.

24. Phil Noble and Associates, "Background Research on Newt Gingrich," Prepared for the Democratic Congressional Campaign Committee (June 1984), Tip O'Neill Papers, Boston College, Series II, Kirk O'Donnell Files, Box 1, Folder 3.

25. Russakoff, "He Knew What He Wanted."

26. "Notes on Negro-GOP Controversy as Reported in New Orleans Press," June 27, 1968, Khan Papers; Khan to Editor of The Lessons of Victory, "An Analysis of the 1968 Election in Louisiana," n.d., Khan Papers; David Snyder, "State GOP Nears Showdown," *New Orleans Statesmen,* June 18, 1968, A1.

27. Philip Caputo responded to Herr's comment by saying, "Vietnam was what we had because we had happy childhoods." See: Caputo, *Means of Escape: Memoirs of the Disasters of War* (New York: Harper Collins, 1991), 13.

28. Hamilton, *Bill Clinton: An American Journey,* 204.

29. Carl Davidson, "Toward Institutional Resistance" (Madison, WI: SDS, 1967), 3–4.

30. Steven M. Gillon, *The American Paradox* (Boston: Houghton Mifflin, 2003), 223–24.

31. Clinton, *My Life,* 104.

32. Steven Roberts and Matthew Cooper, "Clinton, Oxford and the Draft," *U.S. News and World Report,* October 19, 1992, 36.

33. Clinton, *My Life,* 133.

34. Clinton, *My Life,* 109.

35. "The 1992 Campaign: A Letter by Clinton on his Draft Deferment," *New York Times,* February 13, 1992, A25.

36. Clinton, *My Life,* 157.

37. Newt Gingrich interview.

38. Gingrich to Kahn, September 21, 1969, Kahn Papers (private).

39. Clinton, *My Life,* 133.

40. Clinton, *My Life,* 144.

41. Gingrich interview.

42. Mel Steely, *The Gentleman from Georgia: The Biography of Newt Gingrich* (Macon, GA: Mercer University Press, 2000), 25.

43. Untitled, no date, GP-WGSU, Box 9, Folder 8.

44. Newt Gingrich, Concluding Statement for the Free University Course, "The Year Two Thousand," July 11, 1969, Kahn Papers.

45. Maraniss, *First in His Class,* 209.

46. Bill Clinton, *My Life,* 200.

Chapter Three

1. Maraniss, *First in His Class* (New York: Simon & Schuster, 1996), 298–99; Mel Steely, *Gentleman from Georgia: The Biography of Newt Gingrich* (Macon, GA: Mercer University Press, 2000), 54, 55.

2. Newt Gingrich interview.

3. "Text of Newt Gingrich Announcement Speech," April 17, 1978, Gingrich Papers (GP), West Georgia State University (WGSU), Box 25, "Announcement Speech."

4. Roy Reed, "Inflation Issues Stressed in Arkansas Race," *New York Times,* September 5, 1974, A26; Bill Clinton, *My Life* (New York: Alfred A. Knopf, 2004), 223.

5. Delta Research, "An Evaluation of Newt Gingrich's Victory Potential," Kahn Papers (private).

6. Chip Kahn interview.

7. Michel Papers, "Campaigns and Politics," Box 36, NRCC, Recruiting Committee, Southern Region. Dirksen Congressional Center.

8. Ann Woolner interview.

9. "March 20, 1974 Staff Meeting," Kahn Papers (private).

10. "Gingrich Predicts Win Tuesday," *Atlanta Constitution,* November 4, 1974, A3.

11. "Gingrich Predicts Win Tuesday."

12. Steely, *Gentleman from Georgia,* 60.

13. Kahn interview.

14. Richard Fenno, *Congress at the Grassroots: Representational Change in the South, 1970–1998* (Chapel Hill: University of North Carolina Press, 2000), 79.

15. Steely, *Gentleman from Georgia,* 61.

16. *The West Georgian,* November 8, 1974.

17. "Agenda for July 22, 1975," Kahn Papers (private).

18. Kahn interview.

19. Steely, *Gentleman from Georgia,* 71.

20. Gingrich Announcement Speech, March 22, 1976, GP-WGSU, Box 38, Folder 9.

21. Steely, *Gentleman from Georgia,* 72–73.

22. Steely, *Gentleman from Georgia,* 85.

23. "Election Statistics, 1974–76," GP-WGSU, Box 26, Folder 10.

24. "Election Statistics, 1974–76," GP-WGSU, Box 26, Folder 10.

25. "Text of Newt Gingrich Announcement Speech," April 17, 1978, GP-WGSU, Box 25, "Announcement Speech."

26. Kahn interview.

27. "Georgia 6th," Carter Presidential Library, 1978 Congressional Campaign Files, Box 201.

28. Dale Russakoff and Dan Balz, "After Political Victory, A Personal Revolution," *Washington Post,* December 19, 1994, A1.

29. "Steering Committee Report From July 12," GP-WGSU, Box 26, Folder 20.

30. Frank Gregorsky, "Great Memos I Have Known," (GP-WGSU), Box 230; Mel Steely interview.

31. "Text of Newt Gingrich Announcement Speech," April 17, 1978, GP-WGSU, Box 25, "Announcement Speech"; "After Political Victory"; Mark Hosenball and Vern E. Smith, "How 'Normal' Is Newt?" *Newsweek,* November 7, 1994, 34.

32. Dale Russakoff, "He Knew What He Wanted," *Washington Post,* December 18, 1994, A1.

33. Steely, *Gentleman From Georgia,* 65.

34. Newt Gingrich to Mack Mattingly, March 1978, GP-WGSU, Box 37; Frank and Guy to Newt, May 16, 1983, GP-WGSU, Box 230, "Great Memos I Have Known."

35. "New Faces Edge Into the National Spotlight," *U.S. News and World Report,* November 20, 1978, 33.

36. Steven M. Roberts, "New Breed of Arkansas Officials Taking Race Out of Politics," *New York Times,* December 14, 1978, A26.

37. "Clinton Enters Congressional Race," *Northwest Arkansas Times,* February 28, 1974.

38. "Four Democrats Vie for Congressional District Seat," *Northwest Arkansas Times,* May 26, 1974.

39. Maraniss, *First in His Class,* 321.

40. Kevin Freking, "Experts: Hard to Top Clinton on Vote Trail," *Arkansas Democrat-Gazette,* November 5, 2000.

41. Meredith Oakley, *On the Make: The Rise of Bill Clinton* (Washington, D.C.: Regnery, 1994), 139.

42. Clinton, *My Life,* 222.

43. Clinton, *My Life,* 223.

44. "Clinton Labels Gasoline Fee 'Outrageous,'" *Northwest Arkansas Times,* October 2, 1974.

45. "Clinton Blames Administration for Inflation," *Northwest Arkansas Times,* October 29, 1974.

46. Freking, "Hard to Top Clinton on Vote Trail."

47. David Osborne, *Laboratories of Democracy* (Boston: Harvard Business School Press, 1988), 87.

48. Maraniss, *First in His Class,* 337.

49. Clinton, *My Life,* 228.

50. Maraniss, *First in His Class,* 340.

51. "Bill Clinton to Run for State Office," *Northwest Arkansas Times,* March 17, 1976.

52. "Clinton Favors Death Penalty," *Northwest Arkansas Times,* April 23, 1976.

53. Maraniss, *First in His Class,* 351.

54. Oakley, *On the Make,* 129.

55. Maraniss, *First in His Class,* 332–33.

56. Clinton, *My Life,* 240.

57. Clinton, *My Life,* 165; David Maraniss, "Clinton & Clinton," *Washington Post Magazine,* February 1, 1998.

58. Nigel Hamilton, *Bill Clinton: An American Journey* (New York: Random House, 2003), 294.

59. Hillary Clinton, *Living History* (New York: Scribners, 2004), 52.

60. Maraniss, *First in His Class,* 344.

61. Oakley, *On the Make,* 260.

62. Maraniss, *First in His Class,* 327.

63. Hamilton, *Bill Clinton: An American Journey,* 304.

64. Clinton, *Living History,* 74.

65. Clinton, *My Life,* 257.

Chapter Four

1. "Building a Republican Team in the House," O.D. Resources (September 1979–February 1980), pp 6–7, 11, GP-WGSU, Box 40, "Project Majority."

2. Craig Winneker and Glenn R. Simpson, "Newt's Freshman Year," *Roll Call,* April 17, 1995.

3. John A. Farrell, *Tip O'Neill and the Democratic Century* (Boston: Little, Brown, 2001), 630.

4. Farrell, *Tip O'Neill and the Democratic Century,* 631.

5. William Safire, "Silent Majority's Roar," *New York Times,* November 6, 1980, A35.

6. Dole responded with an angry note: "The June 29 issue of the *Congressional Quarterly* indicates that you're at it again," he wrote. "You sound more and more like Bob Novak everyday." See Dole to Gingrich, July 9, 1985, Gingrich Papers (GP), West Georgia State University (WGSU), Box 2281, "Newt Letters."

7. Gingrich to The Oversight Committee, February 28, 1983, "Survival objectives," GP-WGSU, Box 752, "Campaign '82."

8. Mel Steely, *The Gentleman from Georgia: The Biography of Newt Gingrich* (Macon, GA: Mercer University Press, 2000), 156.

9. Steely, *Gentleman From Georgia,* 164–65.

10. Frank and Guy to Newt, May 16, 1983, "Great Memos I Have Known, vol II," GP-WGSU, Box 230, Folder 40.

11. Frank and Guy to Newt, May 16, 1983, "Great Memos I Have Known, vol II," GP-WGSU, Box 230, Folder 40.

12. Frank to Janis, September 3, 1983, GP-WGSU, Box 463, Folder 66.

13. Frank to Janis, no title, September 3, 1983, GP-WGSU, Box 463, Folder 66.

14. Paul Weyrich, "The Pro-Family Movement," *Conservative Digest,* May and June 1980, 15.

15. David Brock, *Blinded by the Right* (New York: Three Rivers, 2003), 63–64.

16. Brock, *Blinded by the Right,* 65.

17. Frank to Newt, "The Permanent Imbroglio, Resolutely Extrapolated," December 27, 1982, GP-WGSU, Box 2279, "Internal Memos."

18. Frank Gregorsky, "The Basics of Newt Gingrich," GP-WGSU, November 22, 1983, Box 230.

19. Gingrich, *To Renew America,* 7.

20. Brock, *Blinded by the Right,* 67.

21. Brock, *Blinded by the Right,* 67.

22. Newt Gingrich, *Window of Opportunity: A Blueprint for the Future* (New York: Tom Doherty Associates, 1984), 21.

23. John J. Pitney Jr., "The Many Faces of Newt Gingrich: A House Speaker Divided," *Reason,* February 1, 1997.

24. Newt Gingrich, *To Renew America* (New York: Harper Collins, 1995), 5.

25. "Finance Report," January 13, 1983, GP-WGSU, Box 752, "Campaign 84."

26. William Chafe, *The Unfinished Journey: America Since World War II* (New York: Oxford University Press, 1991), 463.

27. Gingrich letter, "Dear Friend," GP-WGSU, n.d., Box 2405, "1982 campaign."

28. "Newt Notes," n.d., GP-WGSU, Box 2281, "Newt Notes."

29. Dan Balz and Charles R. Babcock, "Gingrich, Allies Made Waves and Impressions," *Washington Post,* December 20, 1994, A1.

30. James Rogan interview.

31. In June 1983 he sent a memo to the "Whip Planning Committee," called "A Republican Majority."

32. "House GOP Majority Proposal," July 23, 1987, GP-WGSU, Box 901, Folder: "House GOP majority proposal."

33. Dan Balz and Ronald Brownstein, *Storming the Gates: Protest Politics and the Republican Revival* (Boston: Little, Brown, 1996), 145.

34. Nancy Gibbs and Karen Tumulty, "Master of the House," *Time,* December 25, 1995.

35. John Carlin, "Statesman, Fiddler, Buffoon," *The Independent* (London), January 7, 1996.

36. Farrell, *Tip O'Neill and the Democratic Century,* 635.

37. Gibbs and Tumulty, "Master of the House."

38. Farrell, *Tip O'Neill and the Democratic Century,* 636.

39. Gibbs and Tumulty, "Master of the House."

40. Rich Galen interview.

41. Jim Smith to Wednesday Lunch Group, September 16, 1987, GP-WGSU, Box 1019.

42. Gibbs and Tumulty, "Master of the House."

43. Howard Kurtz, "Spin Cycles; A Guide to Media Behavior in the Age of Newt," *Washington Post Magazine,* February 26, 1995.

44. Katherine Q. Seelye, "Gingrich First Mastered the Media and then Rose to be King of the Hill," *New York Times,* December 14, 1994, A20.

45. Kurtz, "Spin Cycles; A Guide to Media Behavior in the Age of Newt."

46. Farrell, *Tip O'Neill and the Democratic Century,* 632.

47. "The Bork Hearings," *New York Times,* September 16, 1987, A27.

48. Arthur Higbee, "American Topics," *International Herald Tribune,* January, 1993.

49. Ralph Reed, *Active Faith* (New York: Free Press, 1996), 111.

50. Robin Toner, "House Republicans Elect Gingrich as Whip," *New York Times,* March 23, 1989, B10; "The GOP's Official Troublemaker," *St. Petersburg Times,* March 24, 1989, A20.

51. Dan Balz and Serge Kovaleski, "Gingrich Divided GOP, Conquered the Agenda," *Washington Post,* December 21, 1994, A1.

52. Jean Heller and David Dahl, "Gingrich: An Outsider Working from Inside," *St. Petersburg Times,* October 6, 1990, A11.

53. Frank to Newt, January 6, 1983, GP-WGSU, Box 752, "Campaign 84."

54. Joe Gaylord interview.

55. Frank Gregorsky to Newt Gingrich, April 30, 1983, GP-WGSU, Box 2404, Past Management Memos.

56. Balz and Brownstein, *Storming the Gates,* 133.

57. Dick Williams, *Newt: Leader of the Second American Revolution* (Marietta, GA: Longstreet Press, 1995), 272.

58. Pitney Jr., "The Many Faces of Newt Gingrich."

59. Ann Woolner interview.

60. David Osbourne, "Newt Gingrich: Shining Knight of the Post-Reagan Right," *Mother Jones,* November 1984.

61. Kurtz, "Spin Cycles: A Guide to Media Behavior in the Age of Newt."

62. Brock, *Blinded by the Right,* 68–69.

63. David Obey interview.

64. Balz and Brownstein, *Storming the Gates,* 134.

65. Balz and Brownstein, *Storming the Gates,* 133.

66. Fazio interview. In 1984, Tony Coelho, the chairman of the Democratic Congressional Campaign Committee, hired a private consulting firm to investigate Gingrich's activities as a student at Tulane in the 1960s, looking for information that could be used against him. "Although he was an activist and certainly liberal, he probably could not have been characterized as a radical leftist," they concluded. Much of the information from that report, along with quotes culled from newspapers and the Congressional Record, were pulled together to create a lengthy document, "Talking Heads: A Newt Gingrich Chrestomathy," which was distributed to Democratic members of Congress in 1985. It was designed to give Democrats ammunition to use against Gingrich at the same time that it would make him aware that Democrats were willing to fight back. What is remarkable was how little they found. The goal was to make him look like a self-serving hypocrite. See Phil Noble Associates to Tony Coelho, July 6, 1984, Tip O'Neill Papers, Boston College, "Talking Heads: A Newt Gingrich Chrestomathy," Robert Michel Papers, Press Series, Box 26, "F" Subject, Conservative Opportunity Society.

67. Frank to Newt, Mel, Mary, Bob, "Two Rules for A.A. Longevity," July 7, 1983, GP-WGSU, Box 2279, Internal memos.

68. Richard Wolf, "Gingrich Hears Rumble at Home," *USA Today,* August 15, 1989, A4; Tom Kenworthy, "A Message to Bradley and Gingrich," *Washington Post,* November 8, 1990, A52; *Laura Parker, "Close Contest Brings Gingrich's Attention Back Home," Washington Post,* November 11, 1990, A12.

Chapter Five

1. Hillary Clinton, *Living History* (New York: Scribners, 2004), 82–83.

2. Bill Clinton, *My Life* (New York: Alfred A. Knopf, 2004), 263.

3. Clinton, *My Life,* 266.

4. Meredith Oakley, *On the Make: The Rise of Bill Clinton* (Washington, D.C.: Regnery, 1994), 204.

5. Nigel Hamilton, *Bill Clinton: An American Journey* (New York: Random House, 2003), 354.

6. Clinton, *Living History,* 91.

7. Clinton, *Living History,* 83–84.

8. Clinton, *Living History,* 92.

9. Clinton, *Living History,* 92–93.

10. "White Criticizes Clinton for Using 'My Theme' in Ad," *Arkansas Gazette*, October 2, 1980.

11. "Decisive Victory by White Defies all Published Surveys," *Arkansas Gazette*, November 6, 1980.

12. "'Super' Response to Ad, White Says," *Arkansas Gazette*, October 15, 1980.

13. "White Attacks Carter Remarks on Fort Chaffe," *Arkansas Gazette*, October 11, 1980.

14. "White Renews Clinton Attack," *Arkansas Gazette*, October 16, 1980.

15. "Gov. Clinton Maintains 2-to-1 Lead Over White," *Arkansas Gazette*, October 15, 1980.

16. Clinton, *Living History*, 89–90.

17. "Anatomy of a Smashing Victory," *Arkansas Gazette*, November 6, 1980.

18. "Anatomy of a Smashing Victory."

19. Clinton, *Living History*, 90.

20. Clinton, *My Life*, 286.

21. David Maraniss, "Lessons of Humbling Loss Guide Clinton's Journey," *Washington Post*, July 14, 1992, A1.

22. Dick Morris, *Behind the Oval Office: Getting Reelected Against All Odds* (New York: Rennaisance Books, 1998), 51.

23. Clinton, *My Life*, 295.

24. David Maraniss, "Clinton's Life Shaped by Early Turmoil," *Washington Post*, January 26, 1992, A1.

25. David Maraniss, *First in His Class* (New York: Simon and Schuster, 1996), 396.

26. Clinton, *My Life*, 294.

27. Maraniss, *First in His Class*, 401.

28. Clinton, *My Life*, 302.

29. Michael Kelly, "The President's Past," *New York Times Magazine*, July 31, 1994.

30. "White Relying on Strategies of '80 to Win," *Arkansas Gazette*, October 31, 1982.

31. "Clinton Plays up Democratic Support," *Arkansas Gazette*, October 30, 1982.

32. "White Offers Concession at 11:35 PM," *Arkansas Gazette*, November 3, 1982.

33. "Clinton's Life Shaped by Early Turmoil."

34. Clinton, *My Life*, 287.

35. Clinton, *My Life*, 305.

36. Oakley, *On the Make*, 274.

37. For the best discussion of Clinton's education reform initiatives, see David Osborne, *Laboratories of Democracy* (Boston: Harvard Business School Press, 1988), 88–102.

38. Osborne, *Laboratories of Democracy*, 92.

39. Barbara Matusow, "True Grit," *Washingtonian*, January 1993.

40. Jeannie M. Whayne, *Arkansas: A Narrative History* (Fayetteville: University of Arkansas, 2002), 391.

41. Osborne, *Laboratories of Democracy,* 88–102.

42. Joe Klein, "Clinton's Challenge," *Newsweek,* Winter/Spring, 1993, 26.

43. "Vote Totals," *Arkansas Democrat-Gazette,* November 6, 1986.

44. Curtis Wilkie, "Perseverance: The Making of the Candidate," *Boston Globe Magazine,* June 3, 1992.

45. David Maraniss and Eric Pianin, "The Tax Attacks," *Washington Post,* January 26, 1992, A1.

46. Wilkie, "Perseverance."

47. Steven M. Gillon, *The Democrats' Dilemma: Walter F. Mondale and the Liberal Legacy* (New York: Columbia University Press, 1992), 394.

48. Howard Fineman, "Duel of the Democrats," *Newsweek,* April 8, 1991, 32; Kenneth S. Baer, *Reinventing Democrats: The Politics of Liberalism from Reagan to Clinton* (Lawrence, KS: University of Kansas, 2000), 65–75.

49. Clinton, *My Life,* 332.

50. Hamilton, *Bill Clinton: An American Journey,* 452.

51. "On Brink of Running, Clinton Called it Off," *Washington Post,* February 7, 1995, A1.

52. "On Brink of Running."

53. Clinton, *My Life,* 341.

54. "No Title," *Arkansas Democrat-Gazette,* July 22, 1988.

55. Eric Alterman, "GOP Chairman Lee Atwater Playing Hardball," *New York Times Magazine,* April 30, 1989, 30; Anthony Lewis, "The Slime-Slinger," *New York Times,* June 8, 1989, A31.

56. Clinton, *My Life,* 344.

57. Oakley, *On the Make,* 395.

58. Oakley, *On the Make,* 399.

59. John Micklethwait and Adrian Wooldridge, *The Right Nation: Conservative Power in America,* (New York: Penguin, 2004), 104.

60. Baer, *Reinventing Democrats,* 163–64

61. Robin Toner, "Road to the Nomination," *New York Times,* July 12, 1992, A18.

62. Baer, *Reinventing Democrats,* 178.

63. Lars-Erik Nelson, "Her Lawyers Find Joy in Mudville," *New York Daily News,* May 28, 1997.

64. Godfrey Sperling, "Bill Clinton Tries to Clear the Air," *Christian Science Monitor,* September 24, 1991, 19.

65. George Stephanopoulos, *All Too Human: A Political Education* (Boston: Little, Brown and Company, 1999), 32, 38–39.

Chapter Six

1. Quoted in Christopher Madison, "Sounding Retreat," *National Journal,* November 16, 1991, 2784.

2. Newt Gingrich to President, "1992 Presidential Campaign Strategy," February 20, 1992, Gingrich Papers (GP), West Georgia State University (WGSU), Box 1891, "Memo to President"; Newt Gingrich to President, February 28, 1992, GP-WGSU, Box 3188, "Key Principles for a Successful '92."

3. Gingrich to Calio, April 9, 1992, GP-WGSU, Box 1889, Folder: "Newt and Bush."

4. Andrew Rosenthal, "The Media and the Message," *New York Times,* August 20, 1992, A20.

5. David Broder and Ruth Marcus, "Bush Charges Democratic Platform Ignores God," *Washington Post,* August 23, 1992, A14.

6. David Dahl, "Strategy: Sell Yourself, Slam Opponent," *St. Petersburg Times,* (Florida), August 20, 1992, A5.

7. David Brock, *Blinded by the Right: The Conscience of an ex-Conservative* (New York: Three Rivers, 2003), 139.

8. Dan Balz, "Harkin Asserts Clinton's Tax Policies in Arkansas Favor the Rich," *Washington Post,* January 21, 1992, A8.

9. Jeffrey H. Bimbaum, "Clinton Received a Vietnam Draft Deferment," *Wall Street Journal,* February 6, 1992, A16.

10. Martin Nolan, "Vietnam's Haunting Specter," *Boston Globe,* February 10, 1992, A13.

11. Joe Klein, *The Natural: The Misunderstood Presidency of Bill Clinton* (New York: Doubleday, 2002), 1.

12. Thomas B. Edsall, "Clinton Admits '60s Marijuana Use; 'A Time or Two' During British Stay Disclosed in TV Debate," *Washington Post,* March 30, 1992, A1.

13. Robin Toner, "Clinton's Candidacy Is Shaken, Again," *New York Times,* February 13, 1992, A25.

14. Michael Powell, "One Nation, Torn Apart," *Washington Post,* December 19, 1998, C1.

15. John F. Harris, *The Survivor: Bill Clinton in the White House* (New York: Random House, 2005), 145.

16. George Stephanopoulos, *All Too Human: A Political Education* (Boston: Little, Brown and Company, 1999), 79.

17. Richard Berke, ""Saying Clinton Is Cynical, Tsongas Goes on the Attack," *New York Times,* March 7, 1992, A11.

18. Harris, *The Survivor,* xxiv.

19. Gerald Seib and Alan Murray, "Changed Party," *Wall Street Journal,* July 15, 1992, A1.

20. Gwen Ifill, "The Party's Over," *New York Times,* July 17, 1992, A1.

21. Jerry Roberts, "Democratic Convention Ticket Stresses Shift in Ideas," *San Francisco Chronicle,* July 13, 1992, A9.

22. Marlon Manuel, "Gingrich Territory," *Atlanta Journal-Constitution,* November 15, 1998, H1.

23. William Booth, "Unknown Democrat Tests Gingrich in Newly Created District," *Washington Post,* October 27, 1992, A15.

24. Clifford Krauss, "The House Bank," *New York Times,* March 17, 1992, A18.

25. Peter Applebome, "Gingrich Faces Spirited Foe and Queries on Ethics," *New York Times,* July 21, 1992, A12.

26. Peter Applebome, "Gingrich Tries to Avoid Heat of Voter Outrage He Fanned," *New York Times,* April 18, 1992, A1.

27. Applebome, "Gingrich Tries to Avoid Heat."

28. Quoted in Richard Wolf, "New questions, district for Gingrich," *USA Today,* April 20, 1992, A2.

29. Applebome, "Gingrich Tries to Avoid Heat."

30. Tim Curran, "Ironic Reversal: GOP Whip Battles Anti-Hill Sentiment," *Roll Call,* July 9, 1992.

31. Curran, "Ironic Reversal: GOP Whip Battles Anti-Hill Sentiment."

32. Applebome, "Gingrich Faces Spirited Foe."

33. Richard Wolf, "Gingrich Nail-biter Ends on a Handful of Votes," *USA Today,* July 23, 1992, A2.

34. Mel Steely, *The Gentleman from Georgia: The Biography of Newt Gingrich* (Macon, GA: Mercer University Press, 2000), 240

35. Steely, *Gentleman from Georgia,* 241.

36. Stephanopoulos, *All Too Human,* 87.

37. A.L. May, "Clinton Jabs Away at Bush," *Atlanta Journal-Constitution,* October 21, 1992, A10.

38. "Excerpts from Clinton's Speech on Foreign Policy Leadership," *New York Times,* August 14, 1992, A15.

39. Richard Berke, "Cooking Up Some Ideas for Negative Campaigns," *New York Times,* September 27, 1992.

40. Dan Balz, "Bush, Perot Lash Clinton; Democrat Upbeat as Race Draws to Close on Negative Note," *Washington Post,* November 2, 1992, A1.

41. Andrew Rosenthal, "Bush Didn't Score Needed Knockout," *New York Times,* October 12, 1992, A1.

42. Robin Toner, "The Debate," *New York Times,* October 16, 1992, A1.

43. David S. Broder, "President Comes Out Slugging in Final Debate; Strong Show By Bush May Change Little," *Washington Post,* October 20, 1992, A1.

44. Dan Balz, "Bush, Perot Lash Clinton; Democrat Upbeat as Race Draws to Close on Negative Note," *Washington Post,* November 2, 1992, A1.

45. Gingrich, "Draft Memo: The 8 Steps to Defeating the Democratic Ticket in 1992," (GP-WGSU), Box 1889; Gingrich, "Working Our Way to Prosperity, Summary," October 28, 1991, (GP-WGSU), Box 1889.

46. "To The Wire," *Newsweek,* Special Election Issue, November/December 1992.

47. Bill Lambrecht, "Gingrich in a Fight for His Political Life," *St. Louis Post-Dispatch,* September 18, 1992, A1.

48. Booth, "Unknown Democrat Tests Gingrich in Newly Created District."

49. Katherine Seelye, "Gingrich's Life: The Complications and the Ideals," *New York Times,* November 24, 1994, A1.

50. Joe Klein, "Clinton's Challenge," *Newsweek,* Winter/Spring, 1993, 26.

51. Gary Pomerantz, et al. "Even If Bush Didn't Carry Ga.," *Atlanta Journal-Constitution,* November 5, 1992, A1.

52. Chip Kahn interview.

53. Joe Gaylord interview.

Chapter Seven

1. Newt Gingrich interview.

2. John Micklethwait and Adrian Wooldridge, *The Right Nation: Conservative Power in America* (New York: Penguin, 2004), 106.

3. Gingrich interview.

4. Michel Papers, Leadership Series, Box 17, F, Leadership Meeting Notes, January 26, 1993.

5. Newt to Mel Steely, January 26, 1993, Gingrich Papers (GP), West Georgia State University (WGSU), Box 1891, "Newt's Notes on Clinton."

6. Michael Waldman, *Potus Speaks: Finding the Words That Defined the Clinton Presidency* (New York; Simon and Schuster, 2000), 23.

7. Paul Begala interview.

8. Dan Balz and Ronald Brownstein, *Storming the Gates: Protest Politics and the Republican Revival* (Boston: Little, Brown, 1996), 84

9. Bruce Reed, "Monkey Do," *Washington Monthly,* June 2001.

10. David Brock, *Blinded by the Right: The Conscience of an Ex-Conservative* (New York: Three Rivers Press, 2004), 148.

11. Micklethwait and Wooldridge, *The Right Nation,* 107.

12. Balz and Brownstein, *Storming the Gates,* 32.

13. Balz and Brownstein, *Storming the Gates,* 28.

14. Dan Meyer interview.

15. George Hager and Eric Pianin, "Shutdown!" *Washingtonian,* April 1997, 113.

16. Begala interview.

17. Bill Clinton, *My Life* (New York: Alfred A. Knopf, 2004), 450.

18. "His Side of the Story," *Time,* June 28, 2004.

19. Balz and Brownstein, *Storming the Gates,* 95.

20. Mel Steely, *The Gentleman from Georgia: The Biography of Newt Gingrich* (Macon, GA: Mercer University Press, 2000), 257.

21. Balz and Brownstein, *Storming the Gates,* 95.

22. Steely, *Gentleman from Georgia,* 257.

23. Gingrich interview.

24. Robert Rubin, *In An Uncertain World: Tough Choices from Wall Street to Washington* (New York: Random House, 2004), 133.

25. George Stephanopoulos, *All Too Human: A Political Education* (Boston: Little, Brown and Company, 1999), 220–221.

26. *Judy Keen, "NAFTA Vote Casts a Long Political Shadow," USA Today,* November 17, 1993.

27. Margaret Maree, "Replace the Welfare State," *Atlanta Journal-Constitution,* September 2, 1993.

28. Steely, *Gentleman from Georgia,* 260–61.

29. Paul Starr, "What Happened to Health Care Reform?" *American Prospect,* Winter 1993, 20–31.

30. Bruce Reed and Jose Cerda III to the President, October 27, 1993, Domestic Policy Council, Bruce Reed Papers, Box 85, "Crime Bill—Memos to the President," Clinton Presidential Library. Only a small number of the 80 million artifacts housed at the Clinton Library have been opened to researchers. Without access to these materials it will be impossible for scholars to reach definitive conclusions about the Clinton presidency.

31. Rahm Emanuel and Michael Waldman, "Memorandum for Circulation," January 27, 1994, Domestic Policy Council, Bruce Reed Papers, Box 79, "Strategy."

32. Douglas Jehl, "Clinton Fights Back," *New York Times,* August 13, 1994, A1.

33. Bob Herbert, "Gingrich Assaults the Truth in his Crime Bill Diatribe," *St. Petersburg Times,* August 21, 1994, D3.

34. Steely, *Gentleman from Georgia,* 265.

35. Gingrich interview.

36. Thomas Oliphant, "Gingrich Leadership Tryout," *Boston Globe,* August 23, 1994, A13.

37. Steely, *Gentleman from Georgia,* 267.

38. Steely, *Gentleman from Georgia,* 255.

39. Clinton, *My Life,* 574.

40. Hillary Clinton, *Living History* (New York: Scribners, 2004), 245.

41. "Interview of the President by *Rolling Stone Magazine,*" November 2, 2000, Clinton Presidential Records, Press Office, Box 85, Clinton Presidential Library.

42. Clinton, *My Life,* 588.

43. Scott Shepard, "Gingrich Raps Scandal-based Politics," *Atlanta Journal-Constitution,* May 19, 1994, B7.

44. Michael Kelly, "The President's Past," *New York Times Magazine,* July 31, 1994, 12.

45. Kelly, "The President's Past."

46. Martin Walker, "American Diary," *Guardian* (London), October 24, 1994.

47. Burt Solomon, "Clinton, Down but Not Out," *National Journal,* October 8, 1994.

48. Howard Kurtz, "The Bad News About Clinton," *Washington Post,* September 1, 1994, D1.

49. John F. Harris, *The Survivor: Bill Clinton in the White House,* (New York: Random House, 2005), 146–47.

50. Ken Walsh, "A Polarizing President," *U.S. News and World Report,* November 7, 1994, 37.

Chapter Eight

1. Tom Brazaitis and Sabrina Eaton, "GOP Revels in Possible House Takeover," *Cleveland Plain Dealer,* September 28, 1994, A7.

2. Major Garrett, *The Enduring Revolution: How the Contract with America Continues to Shape the Nation* (New York: Random House, 2006), 71.

3. David Skinner, "Remembrance of Contracts Past," *Weekly Standard,* September 28, 2004.

4. Bill Clinton, *My Life* (New York: Alfred A. Knopf, 2004), 622.

5. Linda Killian, *The Freshmen: What Happened to the Republican Revolution* (Boulder, CO: Westview Press, 1999), 6.

6. Nicol C. Rae, *Conservative Reformers: The Republican Freshmen and the Lessons of the 104th Congress* (Armonk, NY: M.E. Sharp, 1998), 42.

7. James Traub, "Party Like It's 1994," *New York Times Magazine,* March 12, 2006.

8. Dick Kirschten, "McClinton V. McGingrich," *National Journal,* November 5, 1994, 2592.

9. Louis Bolce, et al., "Dial-In Democracy: Talk Radio and the 1994 Election," *Political Science Quarterly,* Autumn, 1996, 457–81.

10. Howard Kurtz, "The Talkmeisters," *Washington Post,* January 5, 1995, C1.

11. Dan Balz and Ronald Brownstein, *Storming the Gates: Protest Politics and the Republican Revival* (Boston: Little, Brown, 1996), 145.

12. Leslie Wayne, "Gingrich, Politically Weakened, Remains Top GOP Fundraiser," *New York Times,* March 23, 1997, A1.

13. Rae, *Conservative Reformers,* 35–36.

14. Richard Wolf, "Gingrich Ready for a Revolution," *USA Today,* October 19, 1994.

15. "Interview of the President by *Rolling Stone Magazine,*" November 2, 2000, Clinton Presidential Records, Press Office, Box 85, Clinton Presidential Library.

16. Quoted in R.W. Apple, Jr., "Threats in the Gulf," *New York Times,* October 12, 1994, A11.

17. Gerald F. Seib, "Better Opinion of Clinton Fails to Thaw Voters' Icy View of Democratic Party," *Wall Street Journal,* October 20, 1994, A24.

18. Dick Morris, *Behind the Oval Office: Getting Reelected Against All Odds* (New York: Rennaisance Books, 1998), 15–16.

19. John Aloysius Farrell, "Clinton Goes to the Wire for Votes," *Boston Globe,* November 7, 1994, A1.

20. Jim Farwell interview.

21. Mel Steely, *The Gentleman from Georgia: The Biography of Newt Gingrich* (Macon, GA: Mercer University Press, 2000), 275.

22. Traub, "Party Like It's 1994."

23. Rae, *Conservative Reformers,* 92.

24. Dale Russakoff, "Few More Bombs," *Washington Post,* November 10, 1994, A1.

25. Newt Gingrich, *To Renew America* (New York: Harper Collins, 1995), 8.

26. Fred Barnes, "Revenge of the Squares," *New Republic,* March 13, 1995.

27. Bob Barr interview.

28. Rae, *Conservative Reformers,* 33–34.

29. Godfrey Hodgson, *The World Turned Right Side Up: A History of the Conservative Ascendancy in America* (Boston: Houghton Mifflin, 1996), 278.

30. Gary C. Jacobson, "The 1994 House Elections in Perspective," *Political Science Quarterly,* Summer, 1996, 203–23; Peter Applebome, "The Rising GOP Tide Overwhelms the Democratic Levees in the South," *New York Times,* November 11, 1994, A27.

31. Applebome, "The Rising GOP Tide."

32. Clinton, *My Life,* 631–32; Leon Panetta interview.

33. Clinton, *My Life,* 629.

34. Clinton, *My Life,* 632.

35. Maureen Dowd, "Vengeful Glee (and Sweetness) at Gingrich's Victory Party," *New York Times,* November 9, 1994, B2

36. Jill Zuckman, "Gingrich Declares War on Social Programs," *Boston Globe,* November 12, 1994, A1.

37. "Remarks by the President in Announcement of Patsy Fleming as the Director of the Office of National Aids Policy," November 10, 1994, Clinton Presidential Records, Press Office, Box 20, Clinton Presidential Library.

38. Clinton, *My Life,* 633.

Chapter Nine

1. Lance Morrow, "Newt's World," *Time,* December 25, 1995.

2. Leon Panetta interview.

3. Jim Farwell interview.

4. John Hilley interview.

5. Panetta interview.

6. Chip Kahn interview.

7. Bruce Reed interview.

8. Newt Gingrich interview.

9. Robin Toner, "A Revival and a Party Transformed," *New York Times,* December 27, 2000, A1.

10. Joe Klein, *The Natural: The Misunderstood Presidency of Bill Clinton* (New York: Doubleday, 2002), 15–16.

11. Joe Klein, "The House That Newt Will Build," *Newsweek,* April 25, 1994.

12. James Traub, "Far from the Pinnacle of Power," *Seattle Post-Intelligencer,* November 5, 2000, G1.

13. Bruce Reed interview.

14. Hanna Rosin, "The Newt Deal," *Washington Post,* January 30, 2005, D1.

15. Mel Steely interview.

16. Norman J. Ornstein and Amy L. Schenkenberg, "The 1995 Congress: The First Hundred Days and Beyond," *Political Science Quarterly,* Summer 1995, 183–206.

17. Joe Scarborough, *Rome Wasn't Burnt in a Day* (New York: Harper Collins, 2004), 49–50.

18. Richard Lacayo and Jack E. White, "Master of the House," *Time,* January 16, 1995.

19. Elizabeth Drew, *Showdown: The Struggle Between the Gingrich Congress and the Clinton White House* (New York: Simon and Schuster, 1996), 21.

20. Robert Reich interview.

21. Gene Sperling interview.

22. "Spin Cycles: A Guide to Media Behavior in the Age of Newt," *Washington Post Magazine,* February 26, 1995, W8.

23. Mary McGrory, "Bye-Bye to Boswell with a Bias," *Washington Post,* January 10, 1995, A2.

24. Nancy Gibbs and Karen Tumulty, "Master of the House," *Time,* December 25, 1995.

25. Michael Barone and Grant Ujifusa, *The Almanac of American Politics, 1996* (Washington, D.C.: National Journal, 1995), 373.

26. Mary McGrory, "Clinton Running Hard to Keep up with Gingrich," *St. Louis Post-Dispatch,* December 18, 1994, B3.

27. Michael Waldman, *POTUS Speaks: Finding the Words that Defined the Clinton Presidency* (New York: Simon & Schuster, 2000), 69.

28. George Stephanopoulos, *All Too Human: A Political Education* (Boston: Little, Brown and Company, 1999), 338.

29. Waldman, *POTUS Speaks,* 78.

30. Dan Balz and Ronald Brownstein, *Storming the Gates: Protest Politics and the Republican Revival* (Boston: Little, Brown, 1996), 60.

31. Sidney Blumenthal, *The Clinton Wars* (New York: Farrar Straus, 2003), 138.

32. Hillary Clinton, *Living History* (New York: Scribners, 2004), 251.

33. Bruce Reed interview.

34. Steve Elmendorf interview.

35. Armey to Barr, March 9, 1995, Armey Papers, Carl Albert Center, Legislative File, (unprocessed collection).

36. Garry Wills, "What Happened to the Revolution?" *New York Review of Books,* 43 (1996): 10.

37. Bill Clinton, *My Life* (New York: Alfred A. Knopf, 2004), 650.

38. Steven A. Holmes, "Clinton Defines the Limits of Compromise with GOP," *New York Times,* April 8, 1995, A1.

39. Richard Morin, "Public Growing Wary of GOP Cuts," *Washington Post,* March 21, 1995, A1.

40. Ornstein and Schenkenberg, "The 1995 Congress: The First Hundred Days and Beyond."

41. Waldman, *POTUS Speaks,* 82–83.

42. Waldman, *POTUS Speaks,* 82.

43. Gerald F. Seib, "Terrorism Fear Running Deep," *Wall Street Journal,* April 27, 1995, A4.

44. Clinton, *My Life,* 654.

Chapter Ten

1. Howard Gleckman, "Collision Course," *Business Week,* August 21, 1995, 24.

2. Major Garrett, *The Enduring Revolution: How the Contract with America Continues to Shape the Nation* (New York: Random House, 2005), 123.

3. Dan Balz and Ronald Brownstein, *Storming the Gates: Protest Politics and the Republican Revival* (Boston: Little, Brown, 1996), 157.

4. Mel Steely, *The Gentleman from Georgia: The Biography of Newt Gingrich* (Macon, GA: Mercer University Press, 2000), 302.

5. Michael Waldman interview.

6. Leon Panetta interview.

7. David Obey interview.

8. Ann Devroy, "Clinton, Gingrich Play Down Disputes," *Washington Post,* June 12, 1995, A1.

9. Elizabeth Drew, *Showdown: The Struggle Between the Gingrich Congress and the Clinton White House* (New York: Simon and Schuster, 1996), 235.

10. Obey interview.

11. Drew, *Showdown,* 236–37.

12. George Hager and Eric Pianin, "Shutdown!" *Washingtonian,* April 1997, 113.

13. Bruce Reed interview.

14. Panetta interview.

15. Panetta interview.

16. Panetta interview.

17. Steely, *Gentleman from Georgia,* 308.

18. Garrett, *The Enduring Revolution,* 106.

19. Panetta interview.

20. Dick Morris, *Behind the Oval Office: Getting Reelected Against All Odds* (New York: Renaissance Books, 1998), 268.

21. Gene Sperling interview.

22. Drew, *Showdown,* 306.

23. James Bennet, "Who's on the Attack?" *New York Times,* October 22, 1996, A1.

24. Hager and Pianin, "Shutdown!"

25. Newt Gingrich interview.

26. "Interview of the President by *Rolling Stone Magazine*," November 2, 2000, Clinton Presidential Records, Press Office, Box 85, Clinton Presidential Library.

27. Erskine Bowles interview.

28. Bruce Reed interview.

29. Waldman interview.

30. Reich interview.

31. George Stephanopoulos, *All Too Human: A Political Education* (Boston: Little, Brown and Company, 1999), 401–02.

32. Bill Clinton, *My Life* (New York: Alfred A. Knopf, 2004), 682.

33. Garrett, *The Enduring Revolution*, 117.

34. Stephanopoulos, *All Too Human*, 403–04.

35. Linda Killian, *The Freshmen: What Happened to the Republican Revolution* (Boulder, CO: Westview Press, 1999), 187.

36. Stephanopoulos, *All Too Human*, 404.

37. Killian, *The Freshmen*, 188.

38. Clinton, *My Life*, 683.

39. Stephanopoulos, *All Too Human*, 402.

40. Robert Reich interview.

41. Clinton, *My Life*, 683.

42. Lars-Erik Nelson, "Gingrich Shows Pique & Volleys," *Daily News* (New York), November 16, 1995.

43. Hillary Clinton, *Living History* (New York: Scribners, 2004), 319–20.

44. Pat Griffin interview.

45. Stephanopoulos, *All Too Human*, 404.

46. Michael Weisskopf and David Maraniss, "Stung and Beset, Speaker Breaks Down and Weeps," *Washington Post*, January 18, 1996.

47. "His Side of the Story," *Time*, June 28, 2004.

48. "Interview of the President by *Rolling Stone Magazine*," November 2, 2000, Clinton Presidential Records, Press Office, Box 85, Clinton Presidential Library.

49. Jonathan Alter, "Bright Newt, Fright Newt," *Newsweek*, November 16, 1998, 49.

50. Scott Reed interview.

51. Nigel Hamilton, *Bill Clinton: Mastering the Presidency* (New York: Random House, 2007), 523–24.

52. Weisskopf and Maraniss, "Stung and Beset."

53. Michael Duffy, "Back to the Bench," *Time*, December 11, 1995.

54. Weisskopf and Maraniss, "Stung and Beset."

55. Hamilton, *Bill Clinton: Mastering the Presidency*, 552.

56. Hager and Pianin, "Shutdown!"

57. Drew, *Showdown,* 351.

58. Drew, *Showdown,* 351.

59. Armey to members, December 20, 1995, Armey Papers, Carl Albert Center, Legislative files, (unprocessed collection).

60. Gingrich to Republican leaders, December 16, 1995, Gingrich Papers (GP), West Georgia State University (WGSU), Box 2602, "Newt Memos."

61. Ken Keys interview.

62. Bruce Reed interview.

63. "Draft- Proposed Negotiating Process," December 29, 1995, GP-WGSU, Box 2602, "Newt Memos."

64. Garrett, *The Enduring Revolution,* 125; Gingrich interview.

65. Drew, *Showdown,* 360.

66. Drew, *Showdown,* 367.

67. Clinton, *My Life,* 694.

68. Dick Armey interview.

69. Bob Barr interview.

70. "Special Election Issue: "On Target," *Newsweek,* November 18, 1996.

71. Richard Lowry, "Lost Opportunity Society," *National Review,* December 7, 1998.

72. Killian, *The Freshmen,* 260.

73. Killian, *The Freshmen,* 273.

74. Nicol C. Rae, *Conservative Reformers: The Republican Freshmen and the Lessons of the 104th Congress* (Armonk, NY: M.E. Sharp, 1998), 124.

75. Waldman interview.

76. Waldman interview.

Chapter Eleven

1. Katherine Q. Seelye, "Memo Shows Strategy of Gingrich's Allies," *New York Times,* January 19, 1997, A23; Lars-Erik Nelson, "GOP Strategy; Tie Democrats in Legal Knots," *New York Daily News,* December 17, 1997; David Brock, *Blinded by the Right: The Conscience of an Ex-Conservative* (New York: Three Rivers Press, 2003), 249–50.

2. "Newt Gingrich to Gay Gaines and Lisa Nelson," October 26, 1993, Exhibit 43, "In the Matter of Representative Newt Gingrich," Report of the Select Committee on Ethics, January 17, 1997.

3. Dick Morris, *Behind the Oval Office: Getting Reelected Against All Odds* (New York: Renaissance Books, 1998), 139.

4. Morris, *Beyond the Oval Office,* 269.

5. Thomas Rosenstiel, "Newt's Looking for Love," *Newsweek,* November 6, 1995, 44.

6. Chris Black, "Democrats See a Chance to Recapture the House," *Boston Globe,* August 5, 1996, A1.

7. Scott Reed interview.

8. Jill Zuckman and Michael Kranish, "The Candidate's Name Is Mr. Dole," *Boston Globe,* May 16, 1996, A1.

9. Notes, Clinton's 1996 State of the Union, Gingrich Papers (GP), West Georgia State University (WGSU), Box 1889.

10. Bruce Reed interview.

11. John Hilley interview.

12. Hilley interview.

13. Richard Lacayo, "The Big Funk," *Time,* May 6, 1996.

14. Bruce Reed to President, December 13, 1994, Domestic Policy Council, Bruce Reed Papers, Box 21, Clinton Presidential Library, "Memos to the President."

15. Bruce Reed to President, "Welfare Reform Conference," July 23, 1996, Domestic Policy Council, Bruce Reed Papers, Box 19, Clinton Presidential Library, "Legislative Strategy #2."

16. John F. Harris, *The Survivor: Bill Clinton in the White House* (New York: Random House, 2005), 231–32.

17. David Brooks, "What Happened to Newt Gingrich?" *Weekly Standard,* October 21, 1996.

18. Peter T. Kilborn and Sam Howe Verhovek, "Clinton's Welfare Shift Ends Tortuous Journey," *New York Times,* August 2, 1996, A1.

19. Marlon Manuel, "Coles Increases Investment in Race," *Atlanta Journal-Constitution,* October 17, 1996, F2.

20. John E. Yang, "Millionaire Democrat Hopes to Challenge Gingrich in Fall," *Washington Post,* April 10, 1996, A4.

21. Sandy Hume, *The Hill,* October 30, 1996.

22. E. J. Dionne Jr., "The Burdens of Overkill," *Washington Post,* August 18, 1996, C7; Joe Klein, "Saxophone vs. Sacrifice," *Newsweek,* March 18, 1996.

23. Karen Ball, "Newt's Latest Twet at the Prez," *Daily News* (New York), July 25, 1996.

24. Leslie Wayne, "Gingrich, Politically Weakened, Remains Top GOP Fundraiser," *New York Times,* March 23, 1997.

25. Bill Clinton, *My Life* (New York: Alfred A. Knopf, 2004), 144.

26. Cragg Hines, "Democrats Head Back to the Future," *Houston Chronicle,* August 25, 1996, A1.

27. David Maraniss, "An Enemy for Everybody," *Washington Post,* August 28, 1996, A27.

28. "A Modest Proposal for Getting the Truth Back into the 1996 Campaign," April 15, 1996, GP-WGSU, Box 2582, "Newt Handouts."

29. Gingrich to Dole et al. October 10, 1996, GP-WGSU, Box 2550, Folder: "Dole/Kemp '96."

30. Ruth Marcus and R.H. Melton, "DNC Donor Controversy Widens," *Washington Post,* October 18, 1996, A1.

31. Hume, *The Hill.*
32. Newt Gingrich interview.
33. Harris, *The Survivor,* 252–53.
34. Nicol C. Rae, *Conservative Reformers: The Republican Freshmen and the Lessons of the 104th Congress* (Armonk, NY: M.E. Sharp, 1998), 195.
35. Paul Begala interview.
36. Clinton, *My Life,* 734.
37. E. Michael Myers, "Gingrich Doesn't Trust Clinton, but He Says That Won't Hurt Teamwork," *Washington Times,* November 8, 1996, A1.
38. Erskine Bowles interview.

Chapter Twelve

1. Paul Begala interview.
2. John F. Harris and Peter Baker, "Clinton Urges an End to Divisions," *Washington Post,* January 21, 1997, A1.
3. Michael Waldman interview.
4. "In the Matter of Representative Newt Gingrich," Report of the Select Committee on Ethics, 105th Congress, 1st Session (Washington, D.C.: Government Printing Office, 1997), 91.
5. Richard E. Cohen and Eliza Newlin, "Gingrich's Trials," *National Journal,* January 11, 1997.
6. Jeanne Cummings, "For Gingrich, It's Discipline Day," *Atlanta Journal-Constitution,* January 21, 1997, A4.
7. Mel Steely, *The Gentleman from Georgia: The Biography of Newt Gingrich* (Macon, GA: Mercer University Press, 2000), 342.
8. *Congressional Record*—House, January 7, 1997.
9. "No title, no date," Gingrich Papers (GP), West Georgia State University (WGSU), Box 2602, Folder: "Newt Memos."
10. Bill Clinton, *My Life* (New York: Alfred A. Knopf, 2004), 742.
11. Newt to Staff, GP-WGSU, Box 2608, Folder: "Memos from Newt, March 1997."
12. Special Election Edition, "Kid Gloves," *Newsweek,* November 18, 1996.
13. John E. Yang, "Speaker Accuses Media of Aiding Clinton," *Washington Post,* May 8, 1996, A10.
14. Joe Gaylord interview.
15. Richard Lacayo, "Bringing Down the House G.P.P. Guerrilla," *Time,* November 7, 1994.
16. Waldman interview.
17. John F. Harris, *The Survivor: Bill Clinton in the White House* (New York: Random House, 2005), 261.
18. Waldman interview.
19. Gene Sperling interview.

20. Sidney Blumenthal, *The Clinton Wars* (New York: Farrar Straus, 2003), 237.
21. Todd Purdum, "Facets of Clinton," *New York Times Magazine,* May 19, 1996, 36.
22. Erskine Bowles interview.
23. Newt Gingrich interview.
24. Gaylord interview.
25. Bill Archer interview.
26. Gingrich interview.
27. Bowles interview.
28. Steve Elmendorf interview.
29. Begala interview.
30. Bowles interview.
31. Vic Fazio interview.
32. Begala interview.
33. Begala interview.
34. Bowles interview.
35. David Obey interview.
36. Jerry Gray, "Gingrich Offers an Agenda, but the Christian Coalition Attacks Sharply," *New York Times,* March 7, 1997, A20.
37. Helen Dewar and John E. Yang, "To Democrats' Relief, Republicans Courted Disaster," *Washington Post,* June 14, 1997, A6.
38. Lou Dubose and Jan Reid, *The Hammer Comes Down* (New York: Public Affairs, 2006), 136.
39. Dubose and Reid, *The Hammer,* 137.
40. Tom DeLay, *No Retreat, No Surrender* (New York: Sentinel, 2007), 108.
41. DeLay, *No Retreat, No Surrender,* 108.
42. Kevin Sàck, "Gingrich Reminds Rebels He's Head Coach," *New York Times,* July 22, 1997, A1.
43. "Gingrich Reminds Rebels."
44. Majority Leader Armey later denied any role in the attempt, saying his actions had been misunderstood. He claimed that he had warned the Speaker as soon as he heard of the plot. "At this point, I couldn't care less whether I'll be Speaker, Majority Leader, or dogcatcher," but I'll be damned if I'll let my name and honor be destroyed," he wrote colleagues. See Armey memo, July 21, 1997, Armey Papers, Carl Albert Center, Legislative Files (unprocessed collection).
45. Steely, *Gentleman from Georgia,* 352–53, 358.
46. Nancy Gibbs, "A Conspiracy of Celebration," *Time,* August 11, 1997.
47. Clinton, *My Life,* 754.
48. Waldman interview.
49. Clinton, *My Life,* 761.
50. Gibbs, "A Conspiracy of Celebration."
51. Ceci Connolly, "Disappointment on the Right over Budget Deal," *Washington Post,* August 13, 1997, A4.

52. Connolly, "Disappointment on the Right over Budget Deal."

53. Joe Klein, *The Natural: The Misunderstood Presidency of Bill Clinton* (New York: Doubleday, 2002), 160–61.

54. Linda Divall interview.

55. "A New, Improved Newt," *Atlanta Journal-Constitution,* August 29, 1997, A18.

56. Michael Waldman, *POTUS Speaks: Finding the Words that Defined the Clinton Presidency* (New York: Simon & Schuster, 2000), 182.

57. James A. Barnes and Richard E. Cohen, "Divided Democrats," *The National Journal,* November 15, 1997, 2304.

58. Bruce Reed interview.

59. Wesley Pruden, "Gephardt Gets Lunch, Gore Gets Indigestion," *Washington Times,* November 11, 1997, A4.

60. Waldman interview.

61. "Mr. Gephardt's Manifesto," *Washington Post,* December 5, 1997, A26.

Chapter Thirteen

1. Erskine Bowles interview.

2. John Hilley interview.

3. Michael Waldman, *POTUS Speaks: Finding the Words that Defined the Clinton Presidency* (New York: Simon & Schuster, 2000), 180.

4. John F. Harris, *The Survivor: Bill Clinton in the White House* (New York: Random House, 2005), 263.

5. Waldman, *POTUS Speaks,* 188.

6. Waldman, *POTUS Speaks,* 191, 196.

7. Waldman, *POTUS Speaks,* 189.

8. Bowles interview.

9. Berkowitz, *America's Welfare State: From Roosevelt to Reagan* (Baltimore, MD: Johns Hopkins, 1991), 37; "Social Security Bill Is Signed," *The New York Times,* August 15, 1935, 1.

10. Berkowitz, *America's Welfare State,* 41.

11. John Aloysius Farrell, "Can Social Security Be Fixed," *Boston Globe Magazine,* September 7, 1997, 23.

12. William Goldschlag, "Pols Bullish on Wall St.," *Daily News* (New York), January 7, 1997.

13. Spencer Rich, "Panel Suggests Bold Changes for Social Security," *Washington Post,* January 7, 1997, A1.

14. Jonathan Rauch and Carl M. Cannon, "Clinton's Last Chance," *The National Journal,* June 27, 1998, 1492.

15. David Broder, "Social Security: Clinton's State of Union Opener," *Washington Post,* January 27, 1998, A1.

16. Bowles interview.

17. Charles Stenholm interview.

18. Bill Archer interview.

19. Archer interview.

20. Bowles interview.

21. Arne Christenson interview.

22. Paul Taylor, "Social Security Overhaul Finds Advocates in GOP," *Washington Post,* November 26, 1986, A4.

23. Michael Waldman interview.

24. Newt Gingrich interview.

25. Bruce Reed interview.

26. Gingrich interview.

27. Larry Stein interview.

28. Stenholm interview.

29. Christenson interview.

30. Bruce Reed interview.

31. Waldman interview.

32. Gingrich interview.

33. Gingrich interview.

34. Christenson interview.

35. Gingrich interview.

36. Paul Begala interview.

37. Bruce Reed interview.

38. Bowles interview.

39. John Harris, *The Survivor,* 298–99.

40. Bill Clinton, *My Life* (New York: Alfred A. Knopf, 2004), 770.

41. Mike McNamee, "Social Security Reform: Ready for Prime Time?" *Business Week,* January 19, 1998.

42. Mel Steely, *The Gentleman from Georgia: The Biography of Newt Gingrich* (Macon, GA: Mercer University Press, 2000), 361–62.

43. E. J. Dionne Jr., "Gingrich Plays It Safe," *Washington Post,* January 9, 1998, A21.

Chapter Fourteen

1. Susan Schmidt, Peter Baker, and Toni Locy, "Clinton Accused of Urging Aide to Lie," *Washington Post,* January 21, 1998, A1.

2. Peter Baker, *The Breach: Inside the Impeachment and Trial of William Jefferson Clinton* (New York: Scribner, 2000), 39.

3. Erskine Bowles interview.

4. John Hilley interview.

5. Blumenthal, *The Clinton Wars* (New York: Farrar Straus, 2003), 324.

6. Newt Gingrich interview.

7. Mark Jurkowitz and Don Aucoin, "Questions Still Shadow Scandal's Impact," *Boston Globe,* February 14, 1999, A27.

8. Michael Gartner, "How the Monica Story Played in Mid-America," *Columbia Journalism Review,* May 1999/June 1999, 34.

9. Bill Clinton, *My Life* (New York: Alfred A. Knopf, 2004), 775.

10. Waldman, *POTUS Speaks: Finding the Words that Defined the Clinton Presidency* (New York: Simon & Schuster, 2000), 219.

11. Jurkowitz and Aucoin, "Questions Still Shadow Scandal's Impact."

12. John F. Harris, *The Survivor: Bill Clinton in the White House* (New York: Random House, 2005), 314.

13. Paul Begala interview.

14. "'This Is Not a Time to Rest. It Is a Time to Build,'" *Washington Post,* January 28, 1998, A24.

15. Alessandra Stanley, "If Only for an Hour, Playing by the Time-Honored Rules," *New York Times,* January 28, 1998, A1.

16. Charles Stenholm interview.

17. Arne Christenson interview.

18. Harris, *The Survivor,* 313.

19. David Bonior interview.

20. Begala interview.

21. Larry Stein interview.

22. Vic Fazio interview.

23. David Obey interview.

24. Peter Baker interview.

25. Peter Baker, *The Breach: Inside the Impeachment and Trial of William Jefferson Clinton* (New York: Scribner, 2000), 101.

26. Don Van Natta Jr., "White House's All-Out Attack on Starr Is Paying Off," *New York Times,* March 2, 1998, A12.

27. Kerry to Arne, October 22, 1997, Armey Papers (AP), Carl Albert Center, Legislative Files (unprocessed collection).

28. Armey to Republican Members, January 16, 1998, (AP), Legislative Files, (unprocessed collection).

29. Mark Sherman, "Gingrich Reins in House Actions," *Atlanta Journal-Constitution,* April 5, 1998, A17.

30. "Ill-Prepared for Battle," *Financial Times* (London), March 17, 1998, 1.

31. Baker interview.

32. Sherman, "Gingrich Reins in House Actions."

33. Hillary Clinton, *Living History* (New York: Scribners, 2004), 450.

34. Jean to Newt, March 3, 1998, Gingrich Papers (GP), West Georgia State University (WGSU), Box 2605, "Newt Memos."

35. Alison Mitchell, "On Impeachment Process, House GOP Leaders Consider Timing and Bipartisanship," *New York Times,* March 30, 1998, A14.

36. "Recent Newt Speeches," April 27, 1998, GP-WGSU, Box 2138.

37. Sandy Grady, "Nuclear Newt Is Back," *Arkansas Democrat-Gazette,* May 2, 1998, B8.

38. James Traub, "Newt at Rest," *New York Times Magazine,* October 29, 2000.

39. Jane Fullerton and Terry Lemons, "Clinton Dismisses Jabs by Gingrich over Starr," *Arkansas Democratic-Gazette,* April 29, 1998, A1.

40. John Aloysius Farrell, "If Impeachment Looms, Henry Hyde Would Head Panel," *Boston Globe,* February 22, 1998, A12.

41. Baker, *The Breach,* 77–78.

42. "Judiciary Panel Members Miffed at Gingrich," *Washington Post,* March 18, 1998, A4.

43. Harris, *The Survivor,* 340–41.

44. James Bennet, "Testing of a President," *New York Times,* August 18, 1998, A1.

45. Dan Balz, "Gingrich Raises Bar for Impeachment," *Washington Post,* August 24, 1998, A1.

46. Balz, "Gingrich Raises Bar for Impeachment."

47. Baker, *The Breach,* 42.

48. Baker, *The Breach,* 48.

49. George Stephanopoulos, "The Betrayal," *Newsweek,* August 31, 1998, 44.

50. Richard Berke, "Senate Democrat Rebukes Clinton," *New York Times,* September 4, 1998, A1.

51. Carl A. Cannon, "The Survival Strategy," *National Journal,* September 14, 1998, 6.

52. Mel Steely, *The Gentleman from Georgia: The Biography of Newt Gingrich* (Macon, GA: Mercer University Press, 2000), 382.

53. Jonathan Broder and Harry Jaffe, "Clinton's Sexual Scorched-Earth Plan," *Salon Magazine,* August 5, 1998.

54. Bowles to Mr. Speaker, September 2, 1998, GP-WGSU, Box 2553, Folder: "White House Office."

55. Michael Kelly, "Clinton and Gingrich Go Belly to Belly—and Both Fall Down," *National Journal,* May 30, 1998.

Chapter Fifteen

1. Bob Dart, "Very Special Delivery Arrives," *Atlanta Journal-Constitution,* September 10, 1998, A8.

2. Peter Baker interview.

3. Peter Baker, *The Breach: Inside the Impeachment and Trial of William Jefferson Clinton* (New York: Scribner, 2000), 68.

4. "The House Plan for Handling the Clinton Inquiry," *Washington Post,* September 11, 1998, A36.

5. Jeffrey Toobin, *A Vast Conspiracy* (New York: Random House, 1999), 332.

6. Baker, *The Breach,* 81–82.

7. Howard Fineman, "I Have Sinned," *Newsweek,* September 21, 1998.

8. Mark Sherman, "The Clinton Crisis," *Atlanta Journal-Constitution,* September 20, 1998, A21.

9. Baker, *The Breach,* 108.

10. Baker, *The Breach,* 102.

11. Joe Klein, *The Natural: The Misunderstood Presidency of Bill Clinton* (New York: Doubleday, 2002), 177.

12. Carl M. Cannon, "No Easy Way Out," *National Journal,* September 19, 1998.

13. Greg McDonald, "House Panel Votes to Release Clinton Video," *Houston Chronicle,* September 19, 1998, 1.

14. "President Clinton," *Arkansas Democrat-Gazette,* September 22, 1998, A1.

15. William Glaberson, "The Testing of a President: The Lawyers," *New York Times,* September 25, 1998, A22.

16. Ed Vulliamy, "Focus: Clinton under Siege," *Observer,* September 20, 1998, 18.

17. Alison Mitchell, "The Testing of a President: Political Memo," *New York Times,* September 25, 1998, A28.

18. Jon Sawyer, "Gephardt Accuses GOP of Breaking Fairness Vow," *St. Louis Post-Dispatch,* September 23, 1998, A1.

19. Vincent Morris, "Ragin' Cajun Wagin' War vs. Newt," *New York Post,* September 28, 1998, 5.

20. "Seeking a Way Out," *Maclean's,* October 5, 1998.

21. "Gingrich Spurns Pleas for Quick Inquiry," *St. Louis Post-Dispatch,* September 24, 1998, A1.

22. Bennett Roth, "Gingrich Sees No Speedy Deal," *Houston Chronicle,* September 24, 1998, 1.

23. Dan Balz, "On Defense," *Washington Post,* September 29, 1998, A8.

24. Baker, *The Breach,* 124–26.

25. Jim VandeHei, "Gingrich Forecasts Trouble over China: But Democrats Plan Hearing This Week to Attack 40 Investigations of Clinton," *Roll Call,* May 18, 1998.

26. "Inquiry Launched House Votes 258–176," *Pittsburgh Post-Gazette,* October 9, 1998, A1.

27. Howard Fineman and Matthew Cooper, "The New Impeachment War," *Newsweek,* October 19, 1998, 29.

28. Nancy Gibbs and Michael Duffy, "Down in History," *Time,* October 19, 1998.

29. Bill Clinton, *My Life* (New York: Alfred A. Knopf, 2004), 813.

30. Newt Gingrich interview.

31. Karen Tumulty, "On the Fast Track to Impeach," *Time,* October 12, 1998.

32. Mel Steely interview.

33. Clinton, *My Life,* 836.

34. David Maraniss, *The Clinton Enigma* (New York: Simon and Schuster, 1998), 10–11.

35. Gail Sheehy, "The Inner Quest of Newt Gingrich," *Vanity Fair,* September 1995.

36. David Corn, "The 'Big' One That Got Away," *Salon.com,* August 12, 1999.

37. Dale Russakoff and Dan Balz, "After Political Victory," *Washington Post,* December 19, 1994, A1.

38. Ed Pilkington, "Gingrich Admits Having Affair at Time of Clinton Scandal," *Guardian* (London), March 10, 2007, 17.

39. Chip Kahn interview.

40. "Bill Clinton's Uncertain Journey," *New York Times,* March 8, 1992.

41. Erskine Bowles interview.

42. Bowles to Gingrich, August 3, 1998, Richard Armey papers, Carl Albert Center, Legislative-Budget/Economy, Correspondence, (unprocessed collection)

43. Debra Rosenberg and Lynette Clemetson, "A Quiet Brawl over Billions: The Clinton-Gingrich Budget Showdown," *Newsweek,* October 26, 1998.

44. Michael Waldman, *POTUS Speaks: Finding the Words That Defined the Clinton Presidency* (New York: Simon & Schuster, 2000), 241.

45. Rosenberg and Clemetson, "A Quiet Brawl"; Major Garrett, "Impeachment Politics: Clinton vs. Gingrich," *U.S. News & World Report,* October 5, 1998, 20.

46. John M. Broder, "The Budget Deal," *New York Times,* October 16, 1998, A1.

47. Bob Barr interview.

48. Richard Berke, " 'That 'Woman' Has Turned Politics Upside Down," *New York Times,* August 23, 1998, section 4, 1.

49. Garrett, "Impeachment Politics."

50. Juliet Eilperin, "On Touchy Subject, Speaker Stays Quiet," *Washington Post,* October 24, 1998, A6.

51. Clinton, *My Life,* 814.

52. Richard Berke, "Clinton and Gingrich Press Cases," *New York Times,* November 2, 1998, A1.

53. Baker, *The Breach,* 145.

54. Linda Divall interview.

55. Michael Janofsky, "Democrats Fault Gingrich for His Role in Attack Ads," *New York Times,* October 31, 1998, A9.

56. Margaret Carlson, "Alas, Poor Gingrich, I Knew Him Well," *Time,* November 16, 1998.

57. Dan Balz, "Ready, or Not?" *The Washington Post Magazine,* October 25, 1998.

58. "House Endorsements," *Atlanta Journal,* October 27, 1998, A8.

59. James Rogan interview.

60. Francine Kiefer, "New Hope for a Clinton Legacy," *Christian Science Monitor,* November 6, 1998; Eric Schmitt, "Judiciary Chariman Asks Clinton to Admit or Deny 81 Findings," *New York Times,* November 6, 1998, A1.

61. Bill Archer interview.

62. Joe Gaylord interview.

63. Mel Steely interview.

64. Jay Bookman, "The Gingrich Legacy," *Atlanta Journal-Constitution,* August 29, 1999.

65. "Statement by the President," November 6, 1998, Clinton Presidential Records, Press Office, Box 62, Clinton Presidential Library.

66. Arne Christenson interview.

67. Clinton, *My Life,* 826.

Chapter Sixteen

1. Jane Fullerton and Susan Roth, "Impeachment Mill Grinding Again," *Arkansas Democrat-Gazette,* December 18, 1998, A1.

2. Alison Mitchell, "Impeachment: The Overview," *New York Times,* December 20, 1998, A1.

3. Carl M. Cannon, "Downfall and Defiance," *National Journal,* December 19, 1998, 2978.

4. Cannon, "Downfall and Defiance."

5. Peter Baker, *The Breach: Inside the Impeachment and Trial of William Jefferson Clinton* (New York: Scribner, 2000), 163.

6. "White House Urges Gingrich, Livingston to Speed up Probe," *Atlanta Journal-Constitution,* December 2, 1998, A1.

7. Evan Thomas and Debra Rosenberg, "How Clinton Lost the Capital," *Newsweek,* December 28, 1998/January 4, 1999.

8. Waldman, *POTUS Speaks: Finding the Words that Defined the Clinton Presidency* (New York: Simon & Schuster, 2000), 245.

9. Peter Baker interview.

10. Arne Christenson interview.

11. Cannon, "Downfall and Defiance."

12. Waldman, *POTUS Speaks,* 245.

13. Peter Baker and Juliet Eilperin, "GOP Blocks Democrats' Bid to Debate Censure in the House," *Washington Post,* December 13, 1998, A1.

14. Waldman, *POTUS Speaks,* 246.

15. "President Clinton," *Arkansas Democrat-Gazette,* December 9, 1998, A11.

16. Ken Keys interview.

17. Douglas Elmendorf, Jeffrey B. Liebman, and David W. Wilcox, "Fiscal and Social Security Policy During the 1990s," A paper presented at a conference on "American Economic Policy in the 1990s," held at the John F. Kennedy School of Government, Harvard University, June 27–30, 2001.

18. John Hilley interview.

19. Jim Kolbe interview.

20. Hilley interview.

21. Richard Stevenson, "Ideology Aside, Tough Choices on Social Security," *New York Times,* December 7, 1998, A22.

22. Bill Archer interview.

23. "Social Security Reform Process Getting Serious," *Pittsburgh Post-Gazette,* December 6, 1998, A8.

24. Archer interview.

25. Carolyn Lochhead, "Social Security Rehab Died First under Clinton-Lewinsky Scandal," *San Francisco Chronicle,* April 11, 2005.

26. Archer interview.

27. Robert Rubin, *In an Uncertain World: Tough Choices from Wall Street to Washington* (New York: Random House, 2004), 273–74.

28. Erskine Bowles interview.

29. Lochhead, "Social Security Rehab Died First under Clinton-Lewinsky Scandal."

30. "Interview of the President by Joe Klein," October 10, 2000, Clinton Presidential Records, Press Office, Box 84, Clinton Presidential Library.

31. Archer interview.

32. James Bennet and John Broder, "The President's Acquittal," *New York Times,* February 13, 1999, A1.

33. Richard Cohen, "The 'Third Tier' Years," *Washington Post,* June 7, 2005, A23.

34. Bruce Reed interview.

35. Megan Twohey, "Promised Unrealized," *National Journal,* December 16, 2000, 3884.

36. Kerry Kantin and Albert Eisele, "Gingrich Blames Self and Clinton for Failure to Take Stronger Measures Against Terrorism," *The Hill,* October 10, 2001, 19.

Chapter Seventeen

1. Blumenthal, *Clinton Wars* (New York: Farrar Straus, 2003), 392–93.

2. David Frum, "A Generation on Trial," *Weekly Standard,* February 16, 1998.

3. Richard A. Posner, *An Affair of State: The Investigation, Impeachment, and Trial of President Clinton* (Cambridge, MA: Harvard University Press, 1999), 204.

4. "Starr's House," *Wall Street Journal,* September 11, 1998.

5. John Kenneth White, *The Values Divide: American Politics and Culture in Transition* (Chatham, NJ: Chatham House, 2002), 31.

6. Alan Wolfe, *One Nation, After All: What Americans Really Think about God, Country, Family, Racism, Welfare, Immigration, Homosexuality, Work, the Right, the Left and Each Other* (New York: Penguin, 1999), 54.

7. Mary Leonard, "American View of Sex Shows Clash of Values," *Boston Globe,* October 3, 1998, A1.

8. Richard Morin and David Broder, "Worries about the Nation's Morals Test a Reluctance to Judge," *Washington Post,* September 11, 1998, A1.

9. David Brooks, "Goof and Plenty: Morality in an Age of Prosperity," *Weekly Standard,* February 1, 1999.

10. Thomas Edsall, "Spirit of the Body Politic Worries Religious Right," *Washington Post,* November 12, 1998, A6.

11. James Traub, "Newt at Rest," *New York Times Magazine,* October 29, 2000.

12. Ronald Brownstein, "Clinton: The Untold Story," *American Prospect,* February 25, 2002, 33.

13. Ramesh Ponnuru, "Public Judgment: Is It Time to Give up on the American People?" *National Review,* March 22, 1999.

14. David Frum, "Newt's Legacy," *Weekly Standard,* September 13, 1999, 14.

15. Thomas Edsall, "Party Hardy," *New Republic,* September 25, 2006.

16. Erskine Bowles interview.

17. Richard Stevenson, David Rosenbaum, and Robin Toner, "Many Hurdles for Bush Plan," *New York Times,* March 2, 2005, A1.

18. David Broder, "Swift Boats and Old Wounds," *Washington Post,* August 24, 2004, A17.

19. Barbara Sinclair, *Party Wars: Polarization and the Politics of National Policy Making* (Norman, OK: University of Oklahoma Press, 2006), 25–28.

20. Ronald Brownstein, "The Internet and Democrats," *National Journal,* July 2, 2005.

21. R. Emmett Tyrrell Jr., "2008: The Battle for a Generation," *American Spectator,* March 2007.

INDEX

Page numbers in italics refer to illustrations.

Starr, Kenneth (*continued*)
  Whitewater investigation and, 120,
    206
statistical sampling, for U.S. census,
  198, 217
Steely, Mel
  on Clinton's approval ratings, 248
  on Clinton's views of Gingrich, 118
  on Gingrich and the press, 34
  as Gingrich campaign aide, 52
  on Gingrich's campaign strategy, 37
  on Gingrich's first White House
    meeting, 110
  on Gingrich's policies, 257
  on Gingrich's sense of mission, 6
  on Gingrich's strategy with Clinton,
    153, 237
  on Gingrich's views of Clinton, 114
  on government shutdown, 148
Steeper, Frederick T., 121
Stein, Larry, 214, 229
Stenholm, Charles, 210–11, 214, 228,
  261, 268
Stephanopoulos, George
  as Clinton advisor, 111, 116
  as Clinton campaign worker, 101,
    104
  as Clinton's communications director,
    141, 143, 149, 157–60
  as Gephardt aide, 89, 96
  as news commentator, 237
Stevenson, Adlai, 7
Stockman, David, 148
stock market, 168, 200, 280
Stonewall bar riot, 46
Student NonViolent Coordinating
  Committee (SNCC), 19
Students for a Democratic Society
  (SDS), 13, 20–21, 27, 30
"subcommittee bill of rights," 50
Sullivan, Andrew, 279
Summers, Lawrence, 264–65
supply side economics, 51

Supreme Court, 279
Sutknecht, Gil, 129
Sweeney, John J., 202, 265

Taking Back Our Streets Act, 124
tax
  credits, 63, 266, 271
  cuts, xv, 38, 51, 54, 114, 121,
    123–25, 132, 140, 144, 147, 149,
    154, 177, 200–201, 211, 215, 280
  evasion, Gingrich and, 188
  increases, 37, 52, 66, 113, 148
  payroll, 208
  reform, 211
  relief, 253
  revenues, 206
  revolt, 38
  on tobacco sales, 270
Taylor, John, 55
teachers' unions, 82
"Team Gingrich," 129
television
  Clinton's ads on, xiv, 75–77, 96,
    154–55, 171, 174, 246
  Gingrich's ads on, 100, 254–55
  House of Representatives and, 50–51,
    59–60
  influence of, 10, 64, 102
  Johnson, Lyndon's ads on, 255
Teresa (Mother), 151
terrorist attacks
  in Oklahoma City, 146
  of September 11, 2001, 280
  on U.S. embassies, 271
Test Ban Treaty, 215
Tet offensive, 23–24
Thatcher, Margaret, 179
"third way," 94, 107, 136
Thomas, Bill, 220
Thomas, Dylan, 15
Thomas, Evan, 261
Tilton, Linda, 16
tobacco sales, legislation on, 270